D1566219

Phenomenal Phenomena

Phenomenal Phenomena

Biblical and Multicultural Accounts of Spirits and Exorcism

Joy L. Vaughan

BAYLOR UNIVERSITY PRESS

Cover design by *the*BookDesigners
Cover art: Tissot, James Jacques Joseph (1836-1902) / French, *The Possessed Man
    in the Synagogue*, illustration from The Life of Our Lord Jesus Christ (w/c over
    graphite on paper), © Brooklyn Museum / Bridgeman Images

Book design by Baylor University Press
Book typeset by Scribe Inc.

Library of Congress Cataloging-in-Publication Data

Names: Vaughan, Joy L., author.
Title: Phenomenal phenomena : biblical and multicultural accounts of
    spirits and exorcism / Joy L. Vaughan.
Description: Waco : Baylor University Press, 2023. | Includes
    bibliographical references and index. | Summary: "Examines New Testament
    accounts of spirit possession and exorcism in light of modern
    anthropological and ethnographic data of these phenomena"-- Provided by
    publisher.
Identifiers: LCCN 2023017765 (print) | LCCN 2023017766 (ebook) | ISBN
    9781481318365 (hardcover) | ISBN 9781481318396 (adobe pdf) | ISBN
    9781481318389 (epub)
Subjects: LCSH: Demonic possession. | Spirit possession--Christianity. |
    Demonic possession--Biblical teaching. | Exorcism.
Classification: LCC BF1555 .V38 2023 (print) | LCC BF1555 (ebook) | DDC
    133.4/26--dc23/eng/20230629
LC record available at https://lccn.loc.gov/2023017765
LC ebook record available at https://lccn.loc.gov/2023017766

Contents

Foreword

Ben Witherington III

I was watching the television and yet another advertisement came on for a new Russell Crowe movie entitled *The Pope's Exorcist* and the ad claimed the movie was based on real incidents and cases not previously made known. Any time the subject of demon or spirit possession comes up, many persons will gravitate in one of two directions—avoidance at all costs out of fear or sheer disbelief that there are such things as demons, much less possession. On the other hand, there have been some, especially in the more charismatic or Pentecostal portions of the Protestant and Catholic Churches, who have found the subject fascinating, indeed perhaps too fascinating, such that the studying of the subject of possession becomes an obsession.

There is, however, a better way to investigate and carefully study this subject, and Dr. Joy Vaughan has taken that route. She compares the New Testament accounts of exorcisms to modern testimonies and other evidence about "spirit" possession in many, many different cultures. The evidence of the latter is not merely widespread, but one could even say it is worldwide, and frankly not all of it can be easily explained; nor can it be explained away.

Vaughan's study asks the right questions, presents the empirical evidence, and allows the reader to draw his or her own conclusions. Not since Graham Twelftree's fine study *Jesus the Exorcist* has there been a monograph that presents the necessary evidence on this subject in so compelling a fashion, and unlike Twelftree, Vaughan does the hard comparative work, examining the modern evidence in many contexts. This evidence shows that dismissing the phenomena of possession as nothing more than mental illness or delusions will not do. I highly recommend Dr. Vaughan's careful study.

Ben Witherington III
Amos Professor of NT for Doctoral Studies
Asbury Theological Seminary

Acknowledgments

First and foremost, I would like to acknowledge key mentors in my educational journey. During my first semester of PhD studies, I met Craig S. Keener, who guided me in choosing the topic of spirit possession for further study. Dr. Keener served on my dissertation committee (this monograph is developed from my dissertation research), along with Sue Russell and Paul Rhodes Eddy. I am grateful for their feedback and for the many ways their mentorship has made this project better. I express special gratitude for Ben Witherington III, who has guided me through the publication process and provided feedback for my work, as well as friendship and encouragement along the way. I express gratitude for Asbury Theological Seminary's PhD in Biblical Studies program, which challenged my academic growth. Further, Asbury University provided space for further study, along with a Small Research Grant from the Faculty Development committee that has helped to make this project possible. Additionally, thanks goes to one of my Asbury University students, Shawn Hamilton, for preparing the indices for this monograph. Lastly, I would like to acknowledge my husband, Tim Vaughan, who has made sacrifices so that I could research and write. His encouragement has kept me on the journey. And to my daughter, Evangelina, thank you for running into my arms every day I returned home from work. I will never forget these days.

Introduction

The topic of spirit possession has had a growing focus within scholarship over the recent decades. This scholarship is not limited to those who write within the field of biblical studies but includes a surge of literature in the fields of anthropology, sociology, missiology, psychiatry, and psychology. Even medical studies have addressed this issue, attempting to grapple with the complicated relationship between the physicality, psychology, and reality of those who explain their experience as possession. Especially in anthropological studies, spirit possession is a widely recognized topic. In fact, denying the experience of spirit possession in anthropological studies has been equated with maintaining flat earth theories![1] In anthropological sources spirit possession is widely attested as occurring in comparable ways in numerous cultures.[2] This

---

[1]   Kenelm Burridge, *New Heaven, New Earth: A Study of Millenarian Activities* (Oxford: Blackwell, 1969), 4, n. 2, as cited in David C. Lewis, *Healing: Fiction, Fantasy, or Fact?* (London: Hodder & Stoughton, 1989), 321–22, n. 15. The recognition of this reality in anthropological studies is flatly contradictory to what has been stated in past biblical scholarship. For example, Rudolf Bultmann wrote, "It is impossible to use electric light and the wireless and to avail ourselves of modern medical and surgical discoveries, and at the same time to believe in the New Testament world of demons and spirits." See Rudolf Bultmann, "New Testament and Mythology," in *Kerygma and Myth: A Theological Debate*, ed. Hans-Werner Bartsch, trans. Reginald H. Fuller (London: SPCK, 1972), 5. For further discussion on Bultmann's view see James D. G. Dunn and Graham H. Twelftree, "Demon-Possession and Exorcism in the New Testament," *Churchman* 94.3 (1980): 210. Further, sociologist Peter Berger famously notes the irony involved in Bultmann's statement. He points out that "the electricity—and radio—users are placed intellectually above the Apostle Paul," as noted in Paul Rhodes Eddy and Gregory A. Boyd, *The Jesus Legend: A Case for the Historical Reliability of the Synoptic Jesus Tradition* (Grand Rapids: Baker, 2007), 73.

[2]   Erika Bourguignon, ed., *Religion, Altered States of Consciousness, and Social Change* (Columbus: Ohio State University Press, 1973), 9–12. Bourguignon states that in a survey of 488 societies worldwide, 437 (90 percent) have provided accounts of altered states of

multicultural bed of research, including many ethnographic studies, has great potential to aid and inform Western readers of the NT who approach the spirit possession and exorcism stories. In other words, global perspectives of spirit possession offer a challenge to some Western readings of the New Testament's spirit possession and exorcism accounts. What if listening to these global voices also provides an opportunity to reconsider the historical plausibility of the accounts found in the Synoptic Gospels and Acts?

A brief parable, crafted by John S. Mbiti, illustrates the reductionistic nature of Westernized viewpoints. The parable tells of a talented and gifted African student who travels Westward to receive a theological education for ministry in his home setting. Mbiti narrates,

> Finally he got what he wanted: a Doctorate in Theology. . . . He was anxious to return home. . . . At home relatives, neighbors, old friends, dancers, musicians, drums, dogs, cats, all gather to welcome him back. . . . Suddenly, there is a shriek. Someone has fallen to the ground. . . . The chief says to him, "You have been studying theology overseas for ten years. Now help your sister. She is troubled by the spirit of her great aunt." He looks around. Slowly he goes to get Bultmann, looks at the index, finds what he wants, reads again about spirit possession in the New Testament. Of course, he gets the answer: Bultmann demythologized it.[3]

While this anecdote may at first seem humorous, it alerts to a larger problem, namely, a chasm in cultural viewpoints related to the phenomena of spirit possession and exorcism. Even clearer comes the realization that Westernized theological training has lacked enough participation in a multicultural reading of biblical spirit possession and exorcism stories. With this anecdote in mind, it is revealing to consider how spirit possession and exorcism stories have been treated throughout the history of biblical interpretation.

In the Western worldview and within Western Christianity, spirit possession remains largely as a metaphor.[4] Robin A. Parry writes, "Exorcism does not appear on the radar of many forms of Western Christianity. . . . It seems that

---

consciousness (ASCs) that are culturally patterned. Two states of cultural classification are widely recognized: (1) states interpreted as possession by spirits or "possession trance" and (2) states not interpreted as possession by spirits or "trance." A more detailed definition will be given in the definition of terms to follow in chapter 2.

[3]   John S. Mbiti, "Theology in Context: Theological Impotence and the Universality of the Church," in *Mission Trends No. 3: Third World Theologies*, ed. Gerald H. Anderson and Thomas F. Stransky (Grand Rapids: Eerdmans, 1976), 7–8.

[4]   William K. Kay and Robin Parry, eds., *Exorcism and Deliverance: Multi-disciplinary Studies* (Eugene, Ore.: Wipf and Stock, 2011), 2.

the devil and his demonic hordes have been largely 'cast out' of many Western Christian worldviews—exorcised through the rite of deliberate amnesia."[5] As a result, a problem occurs when Western readers approach the NT, since a major part of Jesus' ministry in the Synoptic Gospels involves exorcism accounts, and no consensus is maintained on how these texts ought to be interpreted. Various interpretive options have been offered, but, even more seriously, the historical plausibility of the stories has largely remained within question.

The vast amount of literature within anthropological studies offers indispensable research for biblical scholars, because this literature has documented spirit possession as a phenomenon that occurs cross-culturally in a wide variety of social, political, and economic situations.[6] Leaving the interpretation of the phenomenon of spirit possession aside, multicultural evidence brings to light the fact that one can no longer doubt the occurrence of these experiences today, or their existence in antiquity as found in the NT text. Craig Keener identifies a more sensible approach: "We need not dismiss their occurrence in ancient sources as necessarily fictitious or legendary rather than potentially based on eyewitness claims, but we should evaluate those reports on a case-by-case basis (involving a work's genre, source, and similar factors)."[7] Aside from a group of NT scholars who have pointed towards the potential that anthropological research may have for this conversation, and a few who have explored potential parallels, this comparison between New Testament and modern anthropological accounts of spirit possession remains largely undone. Therefore, it is the aim of this monograph to analyze and apply the insights of anthropological research to NT studies, since this body of research has the potential to help recognize the plausibility of the exorcism accounts as eyewitness testimony. A key focus will be placed upon the analogy that exists between cross-cultural characteristics of spirit possession and the characteristics represented in the Gospels and Acts. Illuminating is the evidence

[5] Kay and Parry, *Exorcism and Deliverance*, 1–2.

[6] See Craig S. Keener, "Spirit Possession as a Cross-cultural Experience," *BBR* 20.2 (2010): 215–36, who points to the anthropological literature available on spirit possession taken from various geographical areas. For a response to Keener see Clint Tibbs, "Mediumistic Divine Possession among Early Christians: A Response to Craig S. Keener's 'Spirit Possession as a Cross-cultural Experience,'" *BBR* 26.2 (2016): 17–38. Tibbs expands the application of the anthropological evidence to consider early Christians as experiencing divine possession that resulted in inspired speech forms (prophecy and glossolalia). For a sampling of other related sources with excellent bibliographies see appendix B in Keener, *Miracles: The Credibility of the New Testament Accounts*, 2 vols. (Grand Rapids: Baker, 2011), 2:788–856; see also Janice Boddy, "Spirit Possession Revisited: Beyond Instrumentality," *Annual Review of Anthropology* 23 (1994): 407–34 for a bibliography of 221 sources.

[7] Keener, "Spirit Possession as a Cross-cultural Experience," 215–36.

for a bedrock of comparable characteristics of possession that are found in both ancient and modern possession accounts. In other words, a multicultural reading of spirit possession accounts allows for an eye-opening trend to emerge: spirit possession experiences in global context often contain similar characteristics when compared to biblical accounts.

To begin, we must first unveil the root of the problem and the key influencers of Western scholarship. What effect did the Enlightenment mentality have on interpretation? Secondly, a variety of New Testament scholars have already indicated the potential fruitfulness of an interdisciplinary study that considers global perspectives on spirit possession. These scholars deserve note, and in chapter 1 we will briefly survey their key contributions to this vein of scholarship. Thirdly, the field of anthropology has its own history of interpretation that has led to the vast production of literature about spirit possession. Why is it that in the past fifty to sixty years or so anthropologists have become increasingly interested in the topic of spirit possession and exorcism stories globally? How have anthropological approaches related to spirit possession changed over time? How do the histories of interpretation in NT studies and anthropology compare and contrast? These questions all emerge from considering other questions: How do the biblical accounts of spirit possession and exorcism compare with multicultural perspectives? What characteristics of possession and exorcism are cross-cultural? Further, given an analysis of ancient context and a plethora of modern eyewitness accounts, is it possible to reconsider the historical plausibility of the possession and exorcism accounts in the Synoptics and Acts in view of a multicultural context? In other words, what insights are gained when considering a multicultural perspective?

The monograph will follow in two major parts. Part 1 will address the need to read through multicultural and genre-specific lenses, while part 2 will survey spirit possession characteristics in biblical and modern contexts.

I

Reading through Multicultural and Genre-Specific Lenses

1

Demythologizing the Demythologizers

The Need to Hear Multicultural Voices

If one were to ask what the predominant view is of the historicity of Jesus as exorcist and the historicity of the exorcism accounts in current biblical scholarship, the following chasm of thought would result from a survey of a wide variety of contributors: Jesus is widely recognized in biblical scholarship as a historical exorcist. In fact, the historicity of Jesus as an exorcist is rarely in doubt within the field of biblical studies.[1] For example, E. P. Sanders states,

> Exorcism . . . is the most prominent type of cure in the synoptic gospels. The sheer volume of evidence makes it extremely likely that Jesus actually had a reputation as an exorcist. . . . I think that we may be fairly certain that initially Jesus'

---

[1] See also the sources listed in Craig S. Keener, *Miracles: The Credibility of the New Testament Accounts*, 2 vols. (Grand Rapids: Baker, 2011), 1:23, n. 12. A range of interpretive options is available, including historical "plausibility" or acceptance devoid of supernatural interpretation. Archibald M. Hunter, *The Work and Words of Jesus* (Philadelphia: Westminster; London: SCM Press, 1973), 86, and Kamila Blessing, "Healing in the Gospels: The Essential Credentials," in *Religious and Spiritual Events*, vol. 1 of *Miracles: God, Science, and Psychology in the Paranormal*, ed. J. Harold Ellens (Westport, Conn.: Praeger, 2008), 186, demonstrate Bultmann's acceptance of Jesus as miracle worker and exorcist. Gerd Theissen and Annette Mertz, *The Historical Jesus: A Comprehensive Guide* (Minneapolis: Fortress, 1998), 113, argue a step further, noting that healings and exorcisms are central to Jesus' activity.

fame came as the result of healing, especially exorcism. This is an important corrective to the common view, that Jesus was essentially a teacher.[2]

Even though Jesus acting historically as an exorcist is a well-established position in scholarship, the main purpose of his exorcistic activity is debated among scholars.[3] Further, the interpretations of his exorcisms vary widely. Lastly, the content of the exorcism stories as found in the Gospels is widely debated related to its historical plausibility. So, how is it that in modern scholarship such a chasm exists between Jesus, historically known as an exorcist, and the details of Jesus' exorcistic activity found in the Gospel accounts? How did we get here, and must we stay? Does the field of anthropological study, when considered alongside the biblical accounts, offer any sort of helpful bridge between the historical Jesus as exorcist and what can be viewed as historically plausible related to the exorcism stories found in the Gospel accounts? Before we grapple with these larger questions, it is helpful to consider the interpretive story and to ask how each interpretation unveils or conceals what can be known of the details of Jesus' exorcism stories.

History of Interpretation of Biblical Spirit Possession Accounts

With the dawn of the Enlightenment, a new strain of interpretation was characterized by skepticism related to the historical plausibility of the New

[2]   E. P. Sanders, *The Historical Figure of Jesus* (London: Penguin, 1993), 149–52. Sanders argues that the "authors of the gospels, and probably the early Christian tradition prior to our gospels, expanded on Jesus' reputation as an exorcist." The best examples of this expansion include Matt 9:32–34 and Luke 10:17 (151). Sanders argues that Luke 10:17 is derived from Mark 6:7/Luke 9:1 and that since Luke had no new material, he recycled with some minor alterations Jesus' sending out of the Twelve. Sanders concludes that early Christians at times created exorcism material, even though it is unlikely that they invented the theme of exorcism found in the Gospels.

[3]   Graham H. Twelftree, *In the Name of Jesus: Exorcism among Early Christians* (Grand Rapids: Baker, 2007), 26, argues that in modern interpretation the main view "has been that exorcism played a significant role in the success of early Christianity." For example, see Adolf von Harnack, *The Expansion of Christianity in the First Three Centuries*, vol. 1 (New York: Arno, 1972), 160. Ramsay MacMullen, *Christianizing the Roman Empire (A.D. 100–400)* (New Haven: Yale University Press, 1984), 27, argues, "not only that miracles were the primary engine for producing conversions in the ancient world, but also that exorcism was 'possibly the most highly rated activity of the early Christian church.'" Twelftree, *In the Name of Jesus*, 27, also argues for their role in the expansion of Christianity: "Healing miracles, notably exorcism, were critical for early Christians' success in winning many people to the faith." On the other hand, Kenneth Grayston and Ernest Best argue there was not much interest in exorcism. See Ernest Best, "Exorcism in the New Testament and Today," *Biblical Theology* 27 (1977): 1–9; Kenneth Grayston, "Exorcism in the New Testament," *Epworth Review* 2 (1975): 94.

Testament. Particularly, accounts that seemingly resist the principles of natural law were suspect. This Enlightenment mentality caused analyses and new explanations of miracles and exorcism stories to arrive onto the scene. However, when approaching the field of biblical scholarship, more than one camp of interpreters remains in modern scholarship. The task here is not to prove the correctness or superiority of a specific interpretation related to the experience or interpretation of spirit possession. Rather, an emphasis will be placed on understanding the methodologies employed for interpretation and the related interpretive outcomes.

When we survey interpretive views of spirit possession stories, three major trends of interpretation emerge. These include the interpretation of spirit possession as: (1) a mental condition or physical illness, (2) the result of sociopolitical pressures and environments, and (3) a battle with Satan and the demonic. Below I will survey key interpreters representing each interpretive trend, along with their methodological approach. Due to space limitations, the following survey is not exhaustive but representative of each avenue of the interpretive taxonomy. Although a larger story could be told about the diachronic interpretations of possession and exorcism throughout history, the focus here will be on the more modern story.

Exorcism as Legendary Tales: Rudolf Bultmann, Martin Dibelius

The story begins with two influencers, Rudolf Bultmann and Martin Dibelius. Rudolf Bultmann, who did agree that Jesus was known historically as an exorcist, classified the gospel accounts as "expanded cult legends"[4] or legendary tales. Bultmann serves as our first representative for this viewpoint since his writings are representative of the widest expansion of the demythologizing perspective. As summarized by Esther E. Acolatse,

> Bultmann's primary thesis is that there exists an enormous gap between the modern worldview and the biblical worldview, and the leap of faith it requires to read and believe the testimony of Scripture is inaccessible to modern human beings—with their scientific worldview. . . . Since the purpose of Scripture is that it may be believed and faith may work redemption in the hearer, it is only right that the elements that hinder this hearing and believing be removed so that the kernel of the message . . . be accessed without the myth that bogs it down.[5]

---

[4]   Rudolf Bultmann, *The History of the Synoptic Tradition*, trans. John Marsh (Oxford: Blackwell, 1963), 371.

[5]   Esther E. Acolatse, *Powers, Principalities, and the Spirit: Biblical Realism in Africa and the West* (Grand Rapids: Eerdmans, 2018), 52.

In other words, Bultmann argues for a chasm between the preached Christ and the Christ of faith. His interpretation denies the historical credibility of the gospel material since it is viewed as inseparable from legendary tales. Bultmann writes,

> Further, it is quite natural for legends and historical stories to run into each other in ancient, and especially popular stories of religious interest, even though here the difference is quite clear conceptually. . . . I do not think it is possible to separate historical stories from legends, for although there are admittedly some passages of a purely legendary character, the historical stories are so much more dominated by legends that they can only be treated along with them.[6]

A deeper look into Bultmann's interpretation of exorcisms (and healings) as legendary tales reveals his bias regarding exorcism accounts that precludes their historicity:

> Now that the forces and the laws of nature have been discovered, we can no longer believe in *spirits, whether good or evil.* We know that the stars are physical bodies whose motions are controlled by the laws of the universe, and not daemonic beings which enslave mankind to their service. Any influence they may have over human life must be explicable in terms of the ordinary laws of nature; it cannot in any way be attributed to their malevolence. Sickness and the cure of the disease are likewise attributable to natural causation; they are not the result of daemonic activity or of evil spells.[7]

The key deficit in Bultmann's perspective, related to this monograph, is the lack of reading in light of a wider context of spirit possession stories globally. In light of modern evidence for the belief in demons, Bultmann's assumption may be challenged.[8] Bultmann's skepticism is not new, as skeptics existed even in the first century.[9]

Acolatse helpfully and concisely summarizes the effect of Bultmann's demythologizing:

---

[6]   Bultmann, *History of the Synoptic Tradition*, 245.

[7]   Rudolf Bultmann, "New Testament and Mythology," in *Kerygma and Myth: A Theological Debate*, ed. Hans-Werner Bartsch, trans. Reginald H. Fuller (London: SPCK, 1972), 5 (emphasis added).

[8]   John Meier cites a 1989 Gallup Poll indicating that 82 percent of Americans believe God does miracles. Only 6 percent disagreed.

[9]   See Richard H. Bell, *Deliver Us from Evil: Interpreting the Redemption from the Power of Satan in New Testament Theology*, WUNT 216 (Tübingen: Mohr Siebeck, 2007), 80–81. "Pagan" skeptics include Cicero and Philostratus; Jewish ones include Josephus, Philo, and the Sadducees.

If we have followed the Bultmannian demythologizing route, we have to declare that not only are the devil and the demons nonpersonal spirit beings, but that in reality they do not exist. Jesus did not really cast out demons, since the only world we have and know in which we operate is that of tangible reality. In the final analysis, what we may glean from Bultmann is that the gospel is better served by jettisoning concepts such as the Fall, Satan, demons, miracles, resurrection, eschatology in the biblical sense—in short, the whole realm of otherworldly beings. In doing so, we also deny the Hebrew worldview that gave context and meaning to the proclamation of the gospel.[10]

More helpfully, Bultmann tracks the typical form of an exorcism story, and this may be a helpful element for determining accounts as eyewitness testimony.[11] In summary, Bultmann's main thesis concludes that the exorcism stories are legendary tales serving as "the chief demonstration of the Messiahship of Jesus."[12]

Martin Dibelius, a contemporary to Bultmann, echoes the same interpretive approach concerning the exorcism stories. The miracle stories are tales "meant to show Jesus as the Lord of divine powers . . ."[13] Dibelius argues the origin of the tales likely began in the form of a short paradigm. Then one may presume a process of "free handing down" wherein the original story is augmented by men accustomed to narrating "according to the plan of usual miracle-stories or in the style of current anecdotes."[14] In other words, Dibelius argues that the early church's motives allow them to fill in the details to prove their belief about Jesus or even take over and transform non-Christian stories to support their own aims.[15] As a result, the accounts are considered as lacking historicity since they are expansions of paradigmatic forms.

[10] Acolatse, *Powers, Principalities, and the Spirit*, 66.
[11] See Bultmann, *History of the Synoptic Tradition*, 210. Bultmann argues the Gerasene demoniac story contains the typical order of features: (1) meeting with the demon(s), (2) description of the dangerous character of such sickness, (3) the demon recognizes the exorcist, (4) the exorcism, (5) demonstrative departure of the demon, and (6) the impression on the spectator.
[12] Bultmann, *History of the Synoptic Tradition*, 219.
[13] Martin Dibelius, *From Tradition to Gospel*, ed. William Barclay, trans. Bertram Lee Woolf (Cambridge: James Clarke, 1971), 97.
[14] Dibelius, *From Tradition to Gospel*, 99.
[15] Dibelius, *From Tradition to Gospel*, 100. Dibelius states that this transference was possibly an "unconscious process." Jewish-Christian writers would "make Jesus the hero of well-known legends of prophets or rabbis." Dibelius uses Mark 5:1–17 as an example. However, Dibelius misses the fact that the demoniac's health is restored in his analysis of the odd ending of this account.

Exorcism as a Psychosomatic Cure: John Dominic Crossan and E. P. Sanders

A second trend of interpretation views exorcism as a psychosomatic cure. E. P. Sanders is representative of this viewpoint and contends that modernity produced the requirement for an explanation of Jesus' miracles. In other words, modern people need viable explanations to certain parts of the Bible to trust in the historical and scientific accuracy of the Bible. Sanders summarizes the effort behind the interpretive explanations: "The numerous efforts have a conservative aim: if Jesus' miracles can be explained rationally, it is easier for modern people to continue to believe that the Bible is true. That is, true in the modern sense: historically accurate and scientifically sound."[16] Even though Sanders recognizes the modern agenda, he personally suggests it is plausible to explain exorcism in terms of a psychosomatic cure. John Dominic Crossan[17] echoes Sanders' interpretation, along with James D. G. Dunn,[18] J. Keir Howard,[19] Eric Eve,[20] and Maurice Casey.[21]

Exorcism as Sociopolitical

Thirdly, there are several scholars who interpret exorcism with regard to sociopolitical factors. Paul W. Hollenbach's work is representative of this approach. He writes,

> The evidence in the Gospels indicates prima facie that Jesus was an exorcist, or, if one prefers, that Jesus at least regularly exorcised demons. In modern terms this means that Jesus healed people who had various kinds of mental or psychosomatic illnesses. In past scholarship the historicity and significance of Jesus' exorcising, as well as his other healing activities were most often issues because

[16]   Sanders, *Historical Figure of Jesus*, 158. Even so, Sanders argues, "It is, however, an error to think that rational explanations of the miracles can establish that the gospels are entirely factual. Some of the miracle stories cannot be explained on the basis of today's scientific knowledge."

[17]   John Dominic Crossan, *Jesus: A Revolutionary Biography* (San Francisco: HarperSanFrancisco, 1994), 84–93.

[18]   James D. G. Dunn, *Jesus and the Spirit: A Study of the Religious and Charismatic Experience of Jesus and the First Christians as Reflected in the New Testament* (London: SCM Press, 1975), 71. Dunn argues that there is "no instance of a healing miracle which falls clearly outside the general category of psychosomatic illnesses."

[19]   J. Keir Howard, *Disease and Healing in the New Testament: An Analysis and Interpretation* (Lanham, Md.: University Press of America, 2001). Howard is a physician and Anglican priest.

[20]   Eric Eve, *The Jewish Context of Jesus' Miracles*, JSNTSup 231 (London: Sheffield, 2002). Eve compares the healings of Jesus to the healing activities of shamans living in Korea.

[21]   Maurice Casey, "The Healing of the Paralytic (Mark 2:1–12)," in *The Solution to the "Son of Man" Problem*, LNTS 343 (London: T&T Clark, 2007), 144–67.

they were tied up with the question of the miraculous. But the question of the miraculous need no longer be a serious issue because the phenomena of possession and exorcism are now examined and understood via the social sciences as common world-wide phenomena throughout most of history. This makes it possible to address the question of historicity and significance in new ways.[22]

Hollenbach then argues for the major role that exorcism played in Jesus' career, especially noting Luke 11:20 and the association Jesus realized between exorcism and the Kingdom of God. He employs the social sciences and social-psychological theories of mental illness to argue that oppressive situations (like colonial domination) are the cause of the mental illness that is spirit possession. The reverse argument is then made that mental illness at times serves as a socially acceptable way to assuage or "cure" the feelings of oppression. Anthropologists refer to this as a practice of "oblique aggressive strategy" as the powerless seek to cope under oppression.[23] As a result, Hollenbach interprets the story of the Gerasene demoniac in light of social dominance, a "possession protest," or "salvation by possession."[24] He writes, "His possession was thus at once both the result of oppression and an expression of his resistance to it. He retreated to an inner world where he could symbolically resist Roman domination."[25] In light of Jesus' exorcistic activity, Hollenbach argues that it interrupted social norms. He concludes,

> Because demon possession and exorcism were integral parts of the social structure and manifested in important ways its dominant value of *social stability*, when Jesus disrupted this structure by countering it in his exorcisms with his own dominant value of *social healing*, conflict between Jesus and the public authorities was inevitable. Through his exorcising activity Jesus became a militant exorcist, or in Old Testament terms, an activist prophetic disturber of the peace.[26]

[22]   Paul W. Hollenbach, "Jesus, Demoniacs, and Public Authorities: A Socio-historical Study," *JAAR* 49.4 (1981): 567. See also works like: Ched Myers, *Binding the Strong Man: A Political Reading of Mark's Story of Jesus* (Maryknoll, N.Y.: Orbis, 1994), 31; Santiago Guijarro, "The Politics of Exorcism: Jesus' Reaction to Negative Labels in the Beelzebul Controversy," in *The Social Setting of Jesus and the Gospels*, ed. Wolfgang Stegemann, Bruce Malina, and Gerd Theissen (Minneapolis: Fortress, 2002), 159–74.
[23]   I. M. Lewis, *Ecstatic Religion: A Study of Shamanism and Spirit Possession*, 3rd ed. (London: Routledge, 2003), 34.
[24]   Hollenbach, "Jesus, Demoniacs, and Public Authorities," 577.
[25]   Hollenbach, "Jesus, Demoniacs, and Public Authorities," 581.
[26]   Hollenbach, "Jesus, Demoniacs, and Public Authorities," 584 (emphasis original). See also George Rosen, *Madness in Society: Chapters in the Historical Sociology of Mental Illness* (Chicago: University of Chicago Press, 1968), 59–64.

More recently, Richard Horsley has nuanced this perspective in view of anthropological insights.[27]

In this vein of interpretation fall ideas of possession as sex-war,[28] rite of passage and social construct,[29] therapy,[30] means of conversion,[31] and protest.[32] Both psychological studies and anthropological studies have produced a wide array of interpretations. It is evident that these theories provide possible and plausible explanations for various manifestations of the phenomena of spirit possession, even though the variety of approaches are too reductive to explain a universal understanding of these cross-cultural phenomena. This fact is not denied by psychologists or anthropologists. As David Bradnick notes, "Many psychologists and anthropologists effectively argue that individual theories alone cannot explain all cases of possession, thus we need to use several theories concomitantly to procure a more comprehensive view of possession."[33]

Exorcism as a Battle with Satan

Graham Twelftree notes that there are two major problems that surface in biblical studies in relation to exorcism accounts. He describes the first as the "fundamental problem," namely, "the premise on which exorcism is based: that malevolent spiritual beings exist and that they can invade, control, and observably impair the health of an individual who, in turn, can be cured

---

[27] Richard A. Horsley, *Empowering the People: Jesus, Healing, and Exorcism* (Eugene, Ore.: Cascade, 2022). Horsley's main arguments will follow in the literature review.

[28] See Lewis, *Ecstatic Religion*; I. M. Lewis, "Spirit Possession and Deprivation Cults," *Man* 1.3 (1966): 314; Eli Somer and Meir Saadon, "Stambali Dissociative Possession and Trance in a Tunisian Healing Dance," *Transcultural Psychiatry* 37.4 (2000): 580–600; Nimrod Grisaru, Danny Budowski, and Eliezer Witztum, "Possession by the 'Zar' among Ethiopian Immigrants to Israel: Psychopathology or Culture-Bound Syndrome?" *Psychopathology* 30.4 (1997): 223–33.

[29] See Peter J. Wilson, "Status Ambiguity and Spirit Possession," *Man* 2.3 (1967): 374; R. L. Stirrat, "Demonic Possession in Roman Catholic Sri Lanka," *Journal of Anthropological Research* 33.2 (1977): 134–35.

[30] See Janice Boddy, "Spirit Possession Revisited: Beyond Instrumentality," *Annual Review of Anthropology* 23 (1994): 414; idem, "Spirits and Selves in Northern Sudan: The Cultural Therapeutics of Possession and Trance," *American Ethnologist* 15.1 (1988): 16.

[31] Janet McIntosh, "Reluctant Muslims: Embodied Hegemony and Moral Resistance in a Giriama Spirit Possession Complex," *Journal of the Royal Anthropological Institute* 10.1 (2004): 93.

[32] Aihwa Ong, "The Production of Possession: Spirits and the Multinational Corporation in Malaysia," *American Ethnologist* 15.1 (1988): 28–42.

[33] David Bradnick, *Evil, Spirits, and Possession: An Emergentist Theology of the Demonic,* Global Pentecostal and Charismatic Studies 25 (Leiden: Brill, 2017), 146.

through someone purportedly forcing the spiritual being to leave."[34] Twelftree acknowledges that many biblical scholars and theologians find this premise implausible and equivalent to the belief in elves or dragons. The second problem is that these interpretations, such as exorcism as "crowd psychology," minimize a significant part of the early Christian worldview.[35] Twelftree addresses this problem by suspending judgment concerning the reality of the demonic and placing emphasis upon the cultural milieu in which the text is found. For example, when interpreting the exorcisms of Mark, Twelftree argues against a sociopolitical interpretation. Twelftree does not find an interest in political matters in the effects of exorcism in Mark's Gospel. He states, "Our conclusion on Mark's broad understanding of Jesus' almost uninterrupted battle with Satan and his disfiguring grip on people (cf. Mark 3:27)—not least in the exorcisms (3:22–27)—is bound to be that Mark does not see it as taking place in the socio-political but in the spiritual or cosmic arena, which is expressed in the personal realm."[36] In other words, Twelftree argues, "Jesus and (by implication) the readers of this Gospel were battling Satan, not the Romans. . . . Liberation came not through political freedom but on a personal level through exorcism."[37]

A second example from this perspective comes from Richard Bell, who more directly makes an argument for the reality of Satan and the demonic. For Bell Satan is a "mythical figure."[38] Further, Bell clarifies that myth is not a "total worldview" in antiquity or in modern times.[39] A key point in this discussion

[34] Twelftree, *In the Name of Jesus*, 25.
[35] Twelftree, *In the Name of Jesus*, 27.
[36] Twelftree, *In the Name of Jesus*, 108. Twelftree argues that the term "legion" functions in the same way as "myriads" and does not allude to a military context.
[37] Twelftree, *In the Name of Jesus*, 111. Preceding Twelftree see also Norval Geldenhuys, *The Gospel of Luke*, NICNT (Grand Rapids: Eerdmans, 1951), 174–75, who recognizes the emic perspective of the NT as defining demon possession as "a person dominated by the spirit of a demon."
[38] Bell, *Deliver Us from Evil*, 23. Bell distances his use of the term from the "Entmythologisierung" debate. His use of "myth" is not to argue against the existence of the devil as the biblical text presumes (2). Bell also clarifies his view of myth as separate from that of anthropologist E. B. Tylor, who argues that science replaces myth as cultures mature. In other words, Bell (27) argues that "myth" is not simply "a pre-scientific attempt to understand the world." See also James Barr, "The Meaning of 'Mythology' in Relation to the Old Testament," *VT* 9.1 (1959): 1–10.
[39] Bell, *Deliver Us from Evil*, 28–29. Bell defines "myth" meticulously, arguing that it involves the "narrated world," deals with existential problems, defines its ontology, combines both the idea and the material, relates to the "numinous," and may contain a subject-object relationship.

is the inclusion of the numinous within myth.[40] For Bell the category of myth has more explanatory power than metaphor as myth allows one to "encounter reality."[41] This setup allows Bell to argue that the exorcisms in the Synoptic Gospels and Acts function by "attacking Satan himself; through the exorcisms, Satan's kingdom is being destroyed and God's kingdom is being established."[42] He concludes, "One can say that the devil and his demons 'exist.'"[43] Exorcism in the ministry of Jesus is an attack on Satan himself. Bell's definition of myth opens the door for him to consider the historicity of Jesus' exorcisms. He makes several key arguments: (1) The early church did not likely invent the accounts of Jesus' exorcisms. (2) The opponents of Jesus do not deny Jesus' exorcistic activity. (3) The use of Jesus' name in successive exorcisms implies that Jesus had a reputation as an exorcist. (4) The presence of exorcistic stories and exorcistic sayings strengthens an argument for historicity. (5) Jesus' exorcisms vary from those standard to the Jewish and Greco-Roman world. If the early church simply invented these stories, the stories would likely adhere more closely to contemporary exorcistic trends (such as use of a physical aid, prayer, laying on of hands, use of a powerful name/formula). (6) Jesus linked exorcism with eschatology.

Employing the Nevius Rule, Mark Crooks argues for the explanation of demon possession as "the hypothesis nearest to the data" since other explanations "are necessarily at least one or more steps removed from the primary evidence."[44] Crooks acknowledges the array of evidence involving descriptive testimony and argues, due to the considerable amount of evidence of the phenomenology of spirit possession, that it is no longer acceptable to dismiss the

[40]   Bell, *Deliver Us from Evil*, 45. The numinous indicates: "1. Indication of the (divine) will; 2. Divine power and divinity." Bell makes a distinction between the phenomenal and the noumenal: the noumenal is "the thing-in-itself which is behind the 'veil,'" while the phenomenal is "a world of representation" (143).

[41]   Bell, *Deliver Us from Evil*, 64. Bell argues that metaphors can be exchanged with other metaphors (even absolute ones). As a result, metaphor only depicts reality rather than allowing one to experience it.

[42]   Bell, *Deliver Us from Evil*, 64–65. Bell also draws out the relationship between exorcism and physical healing that is found in the NT.

[43]   Bell, *Deliver Us from Evil*, 341. See also 349–50, where Bell continues his argument for demons as disembodied spirits, stating, "Satan and his demons can only be perceived when we, the subject, are in a receptive state, when we respect the myth as a 'holy narrative.'" Bell also argues for the personality of demons (350). His key goal is to replace the supernatural/natural semantic with a phenomenal/noumenal one (categorizing Satan and his demons as part of the noumenal world, yet still part of this real world).

[44]   Mark Crooks, "On the Psychology of Demon Possession: The Occult Personality," *Journal of Mind and Behavior* 39.4 (2018): 287.

evidence as anecdotal. The uniformity of the phenomenological evidence, for Crooks, is strong enough to cancel out the bias of the interpretive observer.[45]

When reviewing interpretive trends, one will quickly realize that each interpretive strategy employs a different methodology related to modern parallels. Bultmann, Dibelius, and their followers challenge historicity based upon naturalistic standards that disallow the genuine existence of modern experiences of possession and exorcism. Those who consider possession a psychosomatic condition, with exorcism as the psychosomatic cure, continue to employ naturalistic assumptions in their consideration of the exorcism accounts. Providing a modern explanation assuages the modern problem of needing a reasonable explanation to consider the accounts as historically reliable. Hollenbach takes a step in the right direction by considering the phenomenology of possession and exorcism that can be diachronically traced through much of history. For Hollenbach the social sciences offer interpretive strategies for understanding exorcism accounts. The problem with this approach is its reductive nature and the fact that it does not represent indigenous voices (ancient or modern) in their own contexts. Lastly, scholars such as Twelftree suspend belief in the reality of spirits and carefully consider the contextual elements of the Gospels to realize that Jesus' battle was with Satan. As a result, the ancient context is finally considered as a key for understanding. This vein of biblical interpretation has been somewhat more open to considering the ways indigenous voices may illuminate the interpretation of biblical texts, especially since the phenomenology is so widely attested.

To be clear from the start, the task of this monograph is not to untangle the interpretive web of options related to Jesus' exorcism stories. Additionally, the goal is not to prove the reality of spirits. This brief history of interpretation gives clues to how we have arrived at this chasm of thought between Jesus as historical exorcist and what can be considered as historically plausible when considering what Jesus did when he exorcised the possessed. To state it succinctly, the larger goal is to demonstrate that one major premise for demythologizing accounts hinges on a weak assumption that modern occurrences of such events no longer exist. The weakness of this premise is easily seen when we look through the comparative lens of anthropological contributions.

This chapter will conclude with a survey of voices from biblical studies that have pinpointed a need for this type of research. The voices are unanimous in their demonstration of the need for a multicultural reading involving

---

[45]   See also Keener's response to Crooks, which acknowledges the explanatory power of Crooks' thesis yet refines it. Craig S. Keener, "Crooked Spirits and Spiritual Identity Theft: A Keener Response to Crooks?" *Journal of Mind and Behavior* 39.4 (2018): 345–72.

interdisciplinary voices, yet they diversly represent a variety of interpretive perspectives when considering the possession and exorcism accounts in the biblical text. In each of the brief summaries of scholarly contributions below, an emphasis is placed on the recognition of the value of interdisciplinary work between anthropological and biblical studies as a way to see the possession and exorcism accounts of Jesus and the early church in new light.

Scholarly Stewards: Interpreters Suggesting the Need for a Multicultural Approach

A brief review of each contribution is summarized below with the purpose of giving credit to the predecessors of this research. Given the limitations of space, each interpreter's methodology for interdisciplinary work is not discussed. Rather, the literature review traces the hope for interdisciplinary work among biblical scholars.

David Friedrich Strauss (1839)

Surprisingly, David Friedrich Strauss is one of the first to consider modern accounts of possession experiences.[46] Despite Strauss' commonly known skepticism, his work visibly engages with emic perspectives of belief in possession from the German countryside. In his early writings, Strauss sincerely treats the topic of spirit possession and ghost stories in response to his contemporaries Justinus Kerner and Carl August von Eschenmayer.[47] Jean-Marie Paul remarks that these stories shaped his *Life of Jesus*: "One gets the impression in reading the critical treatment of demon possessions that Strauss could speak of demoniacs in familiar terms."[48] As a result, Strauss rejects the Gospels as legendary tales/intentional fictions. However, he analyzes the possession accounts of the NT as demonstrating an "ancient mode of consciousness" that framed

---

[46]   David Friedrich Strauss, "Zur Wissenschaft der Nachtseite der Natur," in *Charakteristiken und Kritiken: Eine Sammlung zerstreuter Aufsätze aus den Gebieten der Theologie, Anthropologie und Aesthetik* (Leipzig: Wigand, 1839), 301–90. See also Thomas Fabisiak, *The "Nocturnal Side of Science" in David Friedrich Strauss's Life of Jesus Critically Examined* (Atlanta: Society of Biblical Literature, 2015), 177–98. See especially Fabisiak's argument considering how Strauss' early encounters with German countryside possession stories impact his view of the resurrection of Jesus, namely, the disciples experience an altered mode of consciousness that produces a collective vision of resurrection.

[47]   Justinus Kerner and Carl August von Eschenmayer, *Geschichten Besessener neuerer Zeit: Beobachtungen aus dem Gebiete kakodämonisch-magnetischer Erscheinungen nebst Reflexionen über Besessenseyn und Zauber* (Stuttgart: Wachendorf, 1834), 20–103. Justinus Kerner's *Die Seherin von Prevorst: Eröffnungen über das innere Leben des Menschen und über das Hereinragen einer Geisterwelt in die Unsere* (Stuttgart: Cotta, 1829) was the most familiar text for the study of spirits in the mid-latter half of the nineteenth century.

[48]   Jean-Marie Paul, *Strauss et son époque* (Paris: Les Belles Lettres, 1982), 144.

the testimony of the eyewitnesses.[49] Strauss opined that if one could remove a colored lens, some historical truth could be asserted regarding possession stories. Notably, as seen by Thomas Fabisiak, Strauss exhibited sympathy for the emic perspectives.

Strauss held, on the contrary, that the events themselves, including their historical frame, were only the expression of the mentality that crafted them. There was no universally accessible objective field underneath their confused reports. Like possessed people speaking of demons or ghosts, the authors of the narratives represented their symbolic world in the terms that were already at hand. Jesus' followers in the first century thought the appearance of a messianic figure could only be accompanied by dramatic, miraculous signs and events. Whether or not eyewitnesses reported events accurately was beside the point; the accounts turned on the religious categories people used to express their ideas.[50]

As Fabisiak argues, Strauss' consideration of these perspectives was groundbreaking. In the fields of history, religion, and psychology, Strauss' approach was ahead of its time as it applied "methodological agnosticism and openness to foreign, unsettling phenomena."[51] Fabisiak concludes,

> It presages a wide field of social and psychological research as well as major aspects of the twentieth- and twenty-first-century study of religion. In particular, Strauss sets the tone for later scholarship by refusing to reject strange beliefs outright; on the contrary, he takes them utterly seriously and struggles to understand them on their own terms. And he does so within a materialist cosmology that he has defined in advance.[52]

As a result, Strauss challenged the interpretations of the day by allowing for a hearing of the emic perspective and noting the undeniable evidence for the experience of the phenomena. Despite modern interpretations, Strauss argued that Kerner, Eschenmayer, and others who were documenting possession stories recorded facts that could not be ignored. Strauss asked for a "sharp, but not already unbelieving testing of the facts."[53] In other words, Strauss asked his readers to stop turning their heads away from stories that were repulsive

[49] See Fabisiak, *Nocturnal Side of Science*, 18.
[50] Fabisiak, *Nocturnal Side of Science*, 18.
[51] Fabisiak, *Nocturnal Side of Science*, 20.
[52] Fabisiak, *Nocturnal Side of Science*, 20.
[53] David Friedrich Strauss, *Charakteristiken und Kritiken: Eine Sammlung zerstreuter Aufsätze aus den Gebieten der Theologie, Anthropologie und Aesthetik* (Leipzig: Wigand, 1839), 307. Translation in Fabisiak, *Nocturnal Side of Science*, 44. As Strauss develops in thought, his approach may be characterized as equivocal. He takes the accounts seriously; however, he demythologizes them in interpretation.

to their modern frameworks. For Strauss, these repulsive elements were the "most essential parts of Christianity."[54]

Marcus J. Borg (1987)

More recently, Marcus J. Borg picks up the conversation and notices the chasm between the Western worldview of possession as an alien phenomenon (especially since exorcism requires a presupposed belief in the reality of the spirit world)[55] and other modern views. More specifically, he detects the value of cross-cultural studies that have pinpointed several "typical traits" common to spirit possession. Characteristics include self-destructive behavior, sweating, seizures, convulsions, and unexplainable knowledge.[56] Realizing the presence of cross-cultural studies characterizing the phenomenon of spirit possession, Borg carefully parses out the difference between a modern explanation of spirit possession (identifying it as a psychosomatic delusion and indicating that certain sociological conditions play a role)[57] and the ancient emic perspective. He summarizes, "In any case, they did not simply *think* of these as cases of possession and exorcism; rather, all of the participants—possessed, exorcist, onlookers—*experienced* the event as exorcism of a spiritual force which had taken possession of the person."[58] In summary, Borg sees the disparity between modern Western interpretations of spirit possession and the ancient emic perspective.

---

[54] David Friedrich Strauss, *The Life of Jesus Critically Examined: Translated from the 4th German Edition*, trans. George Eliot (New York: MacMillan, 1892), 40.

[55] Marcus J. Borg, *Jesus: A New Vision: Spirit, Culture, and the Life of Discipleship* (San Francisco: Harper & Row, 1987), 61.

[56] Borg, *Jesus: A New Vision*, 62. In addition, Paul Rhodes Eddy and Gregory Boyd have outlined a list of parallel characteristics. They note that in anthropological sources demonized people (1) "are sometimes 'seized' by a demon, causing them to fall in seizures or trances"; (2) "frequently engage in uncontrollable and uncharacteristic outbursts of violent behavior, sometimes exhibiting strength seemingly beyond their natural capacities"; (3) "sometimes recite information whose acquisition is difficult to explain by natural means"; (4) "sometimes exhibit a temporary ability to speak in languages they did not learn"; and (5) "on occasion manifest bizarre physical behavior that seems to go beyond anyone's natural capacities—for example, fantastic facial contortions and physically improbable limb rotations"; and that (6) observers "sometimes report objects moving, or even flying, in the vicinity of the demonized person." See Paul Rhodes Eddy and Gregory A. Boyd, *The Jesus Legend: A Case for the Historical Reliability of the Synoptic Jesus Tradition* (Grand Rapids: Baker, 2007).

[57] Borg, *Jesus: A New Vision*, 64, lists political oppression, social deprivation, and rapid social change.

[58] Borg, *Jesus: A New Vision*, 64 (emphasis original).

J. J. Pilch (1991/1998/2001)

Pilch's contribution comes from the perspective of medical anthropology. He aims to employ anthropological perspectives in order to overcome "medical materialism" and "medical ethnocentrism."[59] This approach allows Pilch to interpret Jesus as a folk-healer whose power ought to be understood in political terms. Jesus' use of power may "be identified as political actions performed for the purpose of restoring correct order to society."[60] This conclusion is drawn from the definition of disease in medical anthropology, which defines it as "a sign or emblem that marks what a group values, disvalues, and preoccupies itself with."[61] For Pilch, Jesus' exorcisms are then interpreted as a way of keeping good order in society. Pilch helpfully points out that sickness and healing are often coded by culture. For this reason his underlying thesis is a call for sensitivity to cross-cultural views of sickness and healing. He argues that his approach "serves as a useful check against the ethnocentric bias or theological creativity of an investigator."[62]

John Dominic Crossan (1991/1994)

John Dominic Crossan, who follows in Pilch's footsteps by utilizing concepts from medical anthropology, opines that possession ought to be interpreted in view of sociological factors. Further, Crossan points out that modern anthropological sources provide analogies to compare with ancient Judaism and early Christianity. He cites the work of a German philosopher, Traugott Konstantin Oesterreich, who traced cases of possession from antiquity to modern times. Oesterreich referred to the "striking similarity between the New Testament accounts and cases of possession reported in later time, and . . . suggests that this similarity enhances the credibility of the gospels."[63] Despite his own

---

[59]   John J. Pilch, "Sickness and Healing in Luke-Acts," in *The Social World of Luke-Acts: Models for Interpretation*, ed. Jerome H. Neyrey (Peabody, Mass.: Hendrickson, 1991), 182. Pilch defines this term as "an anthropological term for the tendency to utilize modern, Western, scientific medical concepts and models to interpret apparent health concerns in all cultures of all times without regard for cultural differences."

[60]   Pilch, "Sickness and Healing in Luke-Acts," 198.

[61]   Pilch, "Sickness and Healing in Luke-Acts," 198.

[62]   Pilch, "Sickness and Healing in Luke-Acts," 183.

[63]   Traugott Konstantin Oesterreich, *Possession Demoniacal and Other among Primitive Races, in Antiquity, the Middle Ages, and Modern Times,* trans. D. Ibberson (New Hyde Park, N.Y.: University Books, 1966), as cited in John Dominic Crossan, *The Historical Jesus: The Life of a Mediterranean Jewish Peasant* (San Francisco: HarperSanFrancisco, 1991), 316–17. Oesterreich's work provides a partial explanation, suggesting that this similarity is prevalent because later possessions used earlier cases as models.

interpretive choice of exorcism as psychosomatic cure, he recognizes his own viewpoint belongs to the minority view:

> I myself, for example, do not believe that there are personal supernatural spirits who invade our bodies from outside and, for either good or evil, replace or jostle for place with our own personality. But the vast, vast majority of the world's people have always so believed, and according to one recent cross-cultural survey, about 75 percent still do. So while I may not accept their *explanation*, I tread very carefully in discussing the *phenomenon* that leads them to that diagnosis. . . . To debate an interpretation is not the same as negating a phenomenon.[64]

Crossan's argument carefully dissects the difference between his viewpoint, influenced by Western presuppositions, and the experience of the majority world. His work points to the need for more research to understand the phenomenon of spirit possession cross-culturally and its impact upon readings of biblical accounts of spirit possession.

Crossan also notes the work of Paul Hollenbach, who expressed that "the phenomena of possession and exorcism are now examined and understood via the social sciences as common world-wide phenomena throughout most of history."[65] Further, in his *Jesus: A Revolutionary Biography*, Crossan employs the work of anthropologist Erika Bourguignon to help his readers realize the presence of trance, defined as anything outside the normal range of physical or mental activity, as a human universal.[66] Crossan argues that this universal human experience is culturally defined. As a result, the actualization of the event is culturally trained and controlled by certain expectations. This leads Crossan to two major principles. He states, "The good news is that trance's form, the *that* of trance, is absolutely cross-culturally and trans-temporally

---

[64] Crossan, *Jesus: A Revolutionary Biography*, 85 (emphasis original).

[65] Hollenbach, "Jesus, Demoniacs, and Public Authorities," 567–88. Hollenbach argues that possession "may have functioned as a 'fix' for people who saw no other way to cope with the horrendous social and political conditions in which they found their lot cast" (576–77). From his social-scientific study he concludes that spirit possession compares with mental illness which is viewed as an acceptable form of escape from stressful societal factors. Jesus was viewed as an "unauthorized exorcist." Hollenbach asserts that it was not socially appropriate for Jesus "to make so much over demon possession and demoniacs that he identified their healing with God's saving presence and led a widespread exorcising mission that attracted a large following, thereby challenging the prevailing social system and its underlying value system" (583). As a result of this action, the exorcisms Jesus performed caused conflict with the authorities.

[66] Crossan uses this term as inclusive of ecstasy, dissociation, or altered states of consciousness. Crossan, *Jesus: A Revolutionary Biography*, 87.

universal. The bad news is that the trance's content, the *what* of trance, is absolutely psychosocially conditioned and psychoculturally determined."[67] This leads Crossan to allow for natural and supernatural explanations of this phenomenon to exist side by side as "different interpretations of the same psychosomatic phenomenon."[68]

Stevan L. Davies (1995)

Stevan L. Davies' approach is similar to those of Pilch and Crossan. He argues, "By cross-cultural anthropological studies we can presume that most of Jesus' clients were presently in situations of social, mainly familial, stress and that for them demon-possession was a somewhat effective, but socially unacceptable, coping mechanism."[69] He performs comparative studies to argue that Jesus is a "medium" or "spirit-possessed," and that demon possession may be interpreted as a form of multiple personality disorder.

John Ashton (2000)

John Ashton recognizes Jesus as exorcist: "That Jesus was an exorcist is one of the most secure elements in the whole tradition; but in the majority of the lives of Jesus that have appeared in the last two centuries it is a fact in search of a context."[70] Ashton's study of Jesus' exorcistic ministry leads him to conclude that Jesus ought to be given the title of shaman due to the number of parallel features. Ashton also concludes that Paul was likely a shaman.[71] What is alarming about Ashton's conclusion is that sufficient engagement with anthropological data is missing, even when his conclusion seemingly depends upon it.

Todd Klutz (2004)

Todd Klutz's work has helped to bring the exorcism stories of Luke-Acts back into the scholarly limelight by arguing that they do not fall into a category of peripheral importance in Lukan scholarship. Klutz argues, "Exorcism stands somewhere between the background and the foreground in Luke's writings, between periphery and centre, enjoying an intermediate level of prominence

---

[67] Crossan, *Jesus: A Revolutionary Biography*, 88.

[68] Crossan, *Jesus: A Revolutionary Biography*, 88.

[69] Stevan L. Davies, *Jesus the Healer: Possession, Trance, and the Origins of Christianity* (New York: Continuum, 1995), 89.

[70] John Ashton, *The Religion of Paul the Apostle* (New Haven: Yale University Press, 2000), 63.

[71] Ashton, *Religion of Paul the Apostle*, 72.

that might be best characterized as the narrative's foreground."[72] Relating to the use of anthropology, Klutz addresses the presence of anthropological sources and performs a comparison between the exorcism account in Luke 9:37–43a and accounts of shamanic ecstasy and exorcism rituals.[73] Klutz draws his definition of a shaman from anthropologist Fiona Bowie,[74] and argues that the transfiguration account represents an experience that is comparative to a visionary trance or an altered state of consciousness.[75] Klutz argues that this pattern of a visionary trance or an altered state of consciousness followed by an exorcism, namely, a "vision-healing sequence," is present in both Jesus' exorcistic ministry in Luke 9:28–43[76] and shaman practitioners.[77] Although Klutz probes the comparison, he ultimately concludes that the Lukan exorcism stories "feature an exorcistic-healer who in several respects looks less like a shaman than like the ultimate source of therapeutic power in the entire cosmos."[78]

Louise J. Lawrence (2005)

Louise J. Lawrence, like Klutz and Pilch, probes the comparison between Jesus and shamanic healers and argues that a comparison of traits shared between Jesus and shamanic healers has the potential of illuminating possession accounts in the NT. Before performing her own comparison, Lawrence critiques Pilch for falling into the trap of "parallelomania," since it is necessary for comparative work to discuss both the similarities and the differences that are present. For example, Jesus' teaching ministry, especially his eschatological emphasis, does not fit into a shamanic scheme.[79] As a result, Lawrence aims

---

[72] Todd Klutz, *The Exorcism Stories in Luke-Acts: A Sociostylistic Reading*, SNTSMS 129 (Cambridge: Cambridge University Press, 2004), 13.

[73] Klutz, *Exorcism Stories in Luke-Acts*, 194–97.

[74] Klutz, *Exorcism Stories in Luke-Acts*, 195. Klutz states that a shaman is "someone who (a) demonstrates mastery over the spirits of fortune and misfortune; (b) has access to and makes use of powerful spirit allies; (c) attracts apprentices to whom he transmits the methods and paraphernalia of his role; (d) legitimates his practices and actions in terms of a recognized theoretical or cosmological perspective; and (e) acquires special status and recognition due to the services he provides to his clients and community." See also Fiona Bowie, *The Anthropology of Religion: An Introduction* (Oxford: Oxford University Press, 2000), 198.

[75] See Luke 9:28–36 (Matt 17:1–8; Mark 9:2–8); Klutz, *Exorcism Stories in Luke-Acts*, 198.

[76] Klutz, *Exorcism Stories in Luke-Acts*, 206. Klutz admits that the Marcan parallel fits more neatly with the shamanic parallel. He concludes, "Jesus is more conspicuously divine and less shamanic in Luke 9:38–43a than he is in the Marcan Parallel (9:2–8, 14–29)."

[77] Klutz, *Exorcism Stories in Luke-Acts*, 196–99.

[78] Klutz, *Exorcism Stories in Luke-Acts*, 267.

[79] Louise J. Lawrence, *Reading with Anthropology: Exhibiting Aspects of New Testament Religion* (Waynesboro, Ga.: Paternoster, 2005), 42.

to compare the selection and training process (the baptism of Jesus and his wilderness experiences) and trance (the transfiguration). Lawrence draws a helpful limitation as she does not press the comparison further than it ought to go. She argues against Jesus' identity as a shaman, noting that "'shamanic' or 'Spirit' Christology will never produce an incarnational Christology."[80] However, Lawrence rightly realizes that the comparison allows readers to "reimagine a cosmology entirely different from our own . . . to reclaim the category of experience in the lives of ancestors of faith . . . to inflate the tyre of New Testament studies with the '*pneuma*' it has at times seemed to lack."[81]

William A. Heth (2006)

William A. Heth presented a need for cross-cultural studies related to spirit possession studies in a paper given at the annual meeting of the Evangelical Theological Society. Heth combats a strict naturalistic inquiry related to possession stories and calls for a consideration of how contemporary accounts may aid in the reading of NT accounts.[82] Heth cites the work of missionary John L. Nevius as a catalyst for pursuing this inquiry in a deeper way.[83] Heth frequently assigned the task of tracing parallels between modern day possession reports and biblical reports to his students and includes examples of their work in the appendices of his article.

Paul Rhodes Eddy and Gregory A. Boyd (2007)

In a volume addressing the historical reliability of the synoptic tradition, Eddy and Boyd employ anthropological evidence to demonstrate demonization as a "cross-cultural supernatural phenomenon" that is plausibly comparable to the experience of demonization found in the NT accounts.[84] Eddy and Boyd note the unwillingness of many Western scholars to take seriously cross-cultural reports when arguing from the principle of analogy and charge

---

[80] Lawrence, *Reading with Anthropology*, 54.

[81] Lawrence, *Reading with Anthropology*, 54.

[82] William A. Heth, "Demonization Then and Now: How Contemporary Cases Fill in the Biblical Data" (paper presented at the Annual Meeting of the Evangelical Theological Society, 2006).

[83] Heth, "Demonization Then and Now," 5. See John L. Nevius, *Demon Possession* (Grand Rapids: Kregel, 1968). Nevius altered his position on spirit possession based upon experiences in China. The foreword to the book (p. v) by Merrill F. Unger expresses the congruencies between modern and New Testament characteristics of possession. Unger writes, "One cannot peruse Dr. Nevius' account of his experiences with demonism as a Christian missionary in China, without being struck by the fact that it reads like a page from the Gospels where demon possession and expulsion play so large a part."

[84] Eddy and Boyd, *Jesus Legend*, 67.

Western scholarship with bias when determining which "present human experience" is permitted as evidence in academic study. They state, "The last thing one might expect is for critical scholars striving for objectivity to restrict the pool of 'present human experience' they draw from to understand the past *to a single slice of one culture* (i.e., the academic elite of the modern Western culture)."[85] Since most Westerners a priori reject supernatural elements as a part of the natural world, the argument is made that no present analogy exists that warrants an acceptance of past supernatural incidents. Eddy and Boyd claim that anthropological evidence related to the cross-cultural experience of spirit possession breaks down the argument opining for no present analogy. They demonstrate (1) the presence of the phenomena as diachronically and cross-culturally experienced, (2) a number of typical characteristics that are difficult to explain by naturalism, and (3) that typical features commonly parallel the characteristics presented in New Testament reports.[86] In summary, the focal point of their argument centers around doing historical research that applies the principle of analogy in an objective manner by including reports of "present human experience" from non-Western cultures and not dismissing them as "hearsay, legend, hallucination, psychosomatic hysteria, exaggeration, intentional fabrication, or something of the sort."[87] In other words, Eddy and Boyd argue against circular reasoning that employs the principle of analogy in support of a thesis that a priori rejects a large part of the evidence. In this case, Eddy and Boyd demonstrate the fact that "conclusion . . . drives the principle."[88] They challenge scholars to make room for anthropological studies that establish spirit possession as a cross-cultural phenomenon. Eddy and Boyd do not dismiss the plausibility of natural explanations as possible for interpretation. Rather, their goal is to establish an "epistemological humility" that allows learning from others rather than setting Western culture and naturalism as the benchmark by which cultures are interpreted. For them, "this means we must

[85] Eddy and Boyd, *Jesus Legend*, 67. Italics original.
[86] Eddy and Boyd, *Jesus Legend*, 67–68. The characteristics outlined include: (1) being "seized" resulting in falling, seizures, or trances; (2) exhibiting violent behavior and exceptional strength beyond natural ability; (3) having special knowledge inexplicably obtained by natural measures; (4) speaking in unlearned languages; (5) manifesting in fantastical physical behavior such as facial or limb contortions beyond natural ability; and (6) moving or flying objects during an exorcism of a demonized person. See also James K. Beilby and Paul Rhodes Eddy, eds., *Understanding Spiritual Warfare: Four Views* (Grand Rapids: Baker, 2012), 13, where "spirit beings" are referred to as part of a "wide range of human religious systems."
[87] Eddy and Boyd, *Jesus Legend*, 69.
[88] Eddy and Boyd, *Jesus Legend*, 70. Eddy and Boyd argue that not only is this reasoning circular, it is also ethnocentric, eurocentric, and chronocentric.

remain open to the possibility that . . . the Gospel writers and others living and moving within a first-century Jewish worldview may in some respects be 'one up' on us, epistemologically speaking."[89]

Pieter Craffert (2008)

Pieter Craffert enters the conversation related to cross-cultural considerations of possession belief by critiquing at least one of the predominant assumptions utilized by New Testament scholars in their aim to appropriately apply anthropological insights. Craffert is not positivistic about the helpfulness of the distinction commonly made between illness and disease as a taxonomy for interpreting the New Testament. He argues that an assessment must be made as to whether the taxonomy actually works or if it more generally obfuscates cross-cultural interpretation. Craffert generously credits his predecessors, like Pilch and his followers, with helpfully bringing awareness to the need for a cross-cultural approach. However, he criticizes their application as too dependent on an incorrect and limited understanding of medical anthropology that does not devoid itself of ethnocentrism. Ultimately, he argues that the divide between illness and disease fails to explain any more clearly the healings or exorcisms of Jesus. Instead, he states that the approach involves "a selective poaching of 'insights' or concepts from medical anthropology without really engaging in cross-cultural interpretation. It is difficult to escape the suspicion that the illness-disease distinction functions in Jesus research to serve a theological or ideological agenda."[90]

Craig Keener (2010)

Keener, in his article entitled "Spirit Possession as a Cross-cultural Experience," indicates the need for a transcultural analysis of the phenomenon of spirit possession within the field of biblical studies. In this article Keener leaves matters of interpretation aside and attunes himself to one key question concerning whether the NT exorcism accounts can be classified as eyewitness testimony. His thesis statement asserts that the resemblance between the NT accounts and modern-day claims of spirit possession (that are globally attested within anthropological sources) questions the skeptical view that the NT accounts are not reflective of eyewitness testimony.[91] He concludes, "Nevertheless, it should

[89] Eddy and Boyd, *Jesus Legend*, 73.
[90] Pieter F. Craffert, "Medical Anthropology as an Antidote for Ethnocentrism in Jesus Research? Putting the Illness-Disease Distinction into Perspective," *HTS Teologiese Studies/ Theological Studies* 67.1 (2011): 1–14.
[91] Craig S. Keener, "Spirit Possession as a Cross-cultural Experience," *BBR* 20.2 (2010): 235.

be evident that anthropologists' accounts of this transcultural phenomenon can enrich our reading of the early Christian accounts, illustrating both what they share with other accounts and where they prove distinctive."[92] Further, "nothing in the early Christian descriptions requires us to assume that they could not depend on genuine eyewitness material."[93] While the above authors have pointed towards a need for a comparison with anthropological sources, Keener further denotes that an analysis of the anthropological texts as representative of eyewitness testimony also has the possibility to advance an interpretation of the NT accounts.

Amanda Witmer (2012)

Amanda Witmer, drawing on the work of John Gager, notes that, while ample evidence for the ancient belief in spirit possession exists in the form of curse tablets, binding spells, and incantation bowls, the "aristocratic biases of both ancient writers and modern scholars" have led to a lack of scholarly attention to these sources.[94] Witmer works to move beyond this bias by engaging modern anthropological evidence in her study of Jesus as exorcist. Witmer first notices the lack of scholarly writing that applies conclusions from anthropological research to the topic of spirit possession. She states clearly that this topic lacks treatment in biblical scholarship:

> Because anthropology offers a unique perspective on spirit possession and exorcism and the interdependence between culture and these kinds of expressions within it, it allows us to ask and answer questions that exegetical methods cannot, such as how being religious is embodied in a particular culture, how the phenomena of spirit possession and exorcism could mediate the experience of political and social oppression that existed in first-century Jewish Palestine, and why this evoked opposition from the political and religious authorities.[95]

Witmer correspondingly notes that this type of work is also lacking within historical Jesus scholarship even when anthropological studies "have consistently demonstrated that spirit possession is a widespread phenomenon, virtually

[92] Keener, "Spirit Possession as a Cross-cultural Experience," 235.
[93] Keener, "Spirit Possession as a Cross-cultural Experience," 235.
[94] Amanda Witmer, *Jesus, the Galilean Exorcist: His Exorcisms in Social and Political Context*, LNTS 459 (London: T&T Clark, 2012), 23–24, referencing John Gager, ed., *Curse Tablets and Binding Spells from the Ancient World* (New York: Oxford University Press, 1992), 3–30, 243–45.
[95] Witmer, *Jesus, the Galilean Exorcist*, 15.

universal in human experience, and that it has been linked particularly with agrarian societies and with social and political oppression."[96]

Witmer employs this anthropological evidence by summarizing the implications from anthropological studies that have pinpointed that possession states and ecstatic phenomena "often occur among socially peripheral, dispossessed or deprived groups,"[97] as well as specifically in agrarian societies.[98] Therefore, the aim of Witmer's study is specifically to attempt "a full study which links the phenomenon of spirit possession and exorcism in the early Jesus traditions with the socio-political context."[99] As a result, she tackles one important application of the implications of anthropological research, namely, how oppressive political and taxing sociological environments are relevant factors in possession accounts. Witmer notes points of similarity between the ancient background material and the political and sociological factors that are common backgrounds in modern accounts of possession.[100] Sociological and political factors are in play, as she has argued, but these factors are not fully able to account for the variety of anthropological or NT data.[101] Her study, however, strongly points out the need for a connection between the two fields.

---

[96]   Witmer, *Jesus, the Galilean Exorcist*, 15.

[97]   Witmer, *Jesus, the Galilean Exorcist*, 59.

[98]   Witmer, *Jesus, the Galilean Exorcist*, 57.

[99]   Witmer, *Jesus, the Galilean Exorcist*, 13. Witmer notes that her research was foreshadowed by Gerd Theissen, "The Political Dimension of Jesus' Activities," in Stegemann, Malina, and Theissen, *Social Setting of Jesus and the Gospels*, 225–50; Guijarro, "Politics of Exorcism," 159–74; Douglas E. Oakman, "Rulers' Houses, Thieves, and Usurpers: The Beelzebul Pericope," *Foundations and Facts Forum* 4.3 (1988): 109–23; Crossan, *Historical Jesus*, 313–20.

[100]   Witmer, *Jesus, the Galilean Exorcist*, 17–18. The use of anthropological evidence is one of many tools that Witmer employs. She also does textual work to uncover the "earliest level of tradition (Mark, Q, M, and L)" and applies the five criteria common to historical Jesus studies (embarrassment, multiple attestation, coherence, discontinuity/dissimilarity, rejection, and execution/Semitisms/Palestinian background) in order to attest to the historical plausibility of Jesus as exorcist.

[101]   Keener, "Spirit Possession as a Cross-cultural Experience," 228, questions the scope of this analysis and notes that "sociological factors seem to influence susceptibility but do not by themselves appear adequate to explain all the phenomena." See also Craig S. Keener, *A Commentary on the Gospel of Matthew* (Grand Rapids: Eerdmans, 1999), 285. Further, the anthropological data describes possession as a phenomenon that occurs among the social elite as well. One example from India includes Daniel Côté, "Narrative Reconstruction of Spirit Possession Experience: The Double Hermeneutics of Gaddis Religious Specialties in Western Himalaya (India)," e-paper, University of Sherbrooke, https://www.nomadit.co.uk/easa/easa08/panels.php5?PanelID=333.

David Bradnick (2017)

David Bradnick recently produced a theological volume on spirit possession. Bradnick describes his theology as emergentist, and he maintains an interpretive aim to prove the reality of the demonic. He writes, "In this book I argue that the demonic is real, that it exerts influence within the world, and that beliefs concerning the demonic are plausible within a late modern context."[102] Emergence theory is the tool employed by Bradnick to produce an ontological framework, informed by philosophy and science, for evil, spirits, and possession that explains the causative effects of the demonic on the physical domain.[103] Related to his use of anthropological sources, Bradnick bases his arguments upon the presence of the phenomenon of possession as cross-cultural and evaluates the interpretations provided by anthropologists, including possession as sex-war, rite of passage, social construct, therapy, a means of conversion, and protest.[104] After surveying these interpretations, Bradnick ultimately concludes that anthropological interpretations of spirit possession are reductive and that no one interpretation given by anthropologists is capable of providing an interpretive framework for cross-cultural experiences of spirit possession. However, Bradnick sees these interpretive options as parallel and complementary to his theological approach. He states, "Theologically, I suggest that beliefs in the demonic origin of possession can parallel and even complement explanations from the field of cultural anthropology. . . . Some cases may be 'spiritual' in origin while others have psychological, anthropological, sociological or cultural explanations."[105] Bradnick concludes by asserting the need for discernment when surveying the "levels of analyses and methods" that are available to the interpreter as they are "complementary if not interdependent."[106]

Marius Nel (2019)

Marius Nel argues that the pneumatic culture found in African traditional religion is analogous to the worldview of early Christians.[107] Stated more specifically, Nel argues, "For Africans, what happens on earth is directly interrelated with what happens in the dimension of the spiritual, agreeing with the cosmic principalities and powers that provide the mystical causality of a worldview

---

[102] Bradnick, *Evil, Spirits, and Possession*, 1.

[103] Bradnick, *Evil, Spirits, and Possession*, 1.

[104] Bradnick, *Evil, Spirits, and Possession*, 137–45.

[105] Bradnick, *Evil, Spirits, and Possession*, 145.

[106] Bradnick, *Evil, Spirits, and Possession*, 145–46.

[107] Marius Nel, "The African Background of Pentecostal Theology: A Critical Perspective," *In die Skriflig* 53.4 (2019): 1–8.

found in the New Testament."[108] Nel views the Global South (Africa, Asia, Latin America, and nearby islands) as maintaining a "remarkably similar" worldview when compared with early Christian views because of the beliefs in an "ever-present spirit world" and "constant fear of serious harm caused by spirits with evil intent."[109] Nel contends the data is ripe for comparison with biblical accounts and suggests that the data will raise an "existential challenge" that Western Christianity fails to respond to adequately.[110]

Ian G. Wallis (2020)

In *The Galilean Wonderworker*, Wallis engages with the anthropologist named Arthur Kleinman, known for his work *Patients and Healers in the Context of Culture*, to consider how medicine and culture interconnect. Wallis concludes in agreement with Kleinman that "medicine is a cultural system."[111] If illness and its treatment are interconnected with culture, then the cultural framework for understanding how illness and treatments are perceived is of first most importance. Wallis critiques both Humean approaches and biomedical approaches to illness that make a division between illness (social effect) and disease (physical effect), since this distinction is anachronistic in Jesus' own context. Rather, Wallis' goal is to deeply consider the experience and understanding of illness in the first century, and consider what bearing it has on understanding how Jesus' miracles and exorcisms were perceived within their own cultural milieu. Chapter 4, dealing with spirit-related illness, will offer more interaction with Wallis' thesis and key points.

Giovanni B. Bazzana (2020)

In *Having the Spirit of Christ*, Giovanni B. Bazzana responds to a variety of biblical scholars who have grappled with the topic of spirit possession and the effect of Kleinman's anthropological contributions. Bazzana considers anthropological engagement as offering two "advantages":

> It provides one with the opportunity to defamiliarize readers from some well-known New Testament stories and pericopes. The latter have been otherwise interpreted for centuries in Christian circles in ways that erase or marginalize

---

[108] Nel, "African Background of Pentecostal Theology," 1.

[109] Nel, "African Background of Pentecostal Theology," 1–2.

[110] Nel, "African Background of Pentecostal Theology," 2.

[111] Ian G. Wallis, *The Galilean Wonderworker: Reassessing Jesus' Reputation for Healing and Exorcism* (Eugene, Ore.: Cascade, 2020), 17; Arthur Kleinman, *Patients and Healers in the Context of Culture: An Exploration of the Borderland between Anthropology, Medicine, and Psychiatry* (Berkeley: University of California Press, 1980), 24.

the component of possession that should be instead central for their under-standing. On the other hand, the richness of the ethnographic record enables one to "imagine" the cultural and religious contexts that in all likelihood stood behind the historical events and their transduction into writing.[112]

Even so, Bazanna is modest when considering what historical reconstruction is possible for the ancient context.

Richard Horsley (2022)

Richard Horsley, similarly to Pilch and Bazanna, also distinguishes between illness and disease in an attempt to avoid reductionist interpretations.[113] His most recent book, entitled *Empowering the People: Jesus, Healing, and Exor-cism*, directly engages with the anthropological accounts that connect spirit possession and illness. Considering the political, economic, and social con-text, along with a focus on medical anthropology, Horsley engages by distin-guishing between "disease" and "illness" and "cure" and "healing," reminding readers that the focal point is not deciphering nature but cultural constructs.[114]

Challenging the Chasm with a Multicultural Reading

We have now seen that even though some have pointed out the potential aid found in joining hands with anthropological studies, a larger majority of West-ernized scholarship treats spirit possession accounts without considering the large pool of analogous phenomena present in global stories. In fact, some remain skeptical about the fruitfulness of this type of comparative and cross-cultural study.[115]

Even so, no major work has significantly displayed the varieties of mod-ern cross-cultural characteristics that cohere between ancient and modern accounts. While it is very helpful to consider each cultural framework, the cross-cultural framework also deserves attention. Craig Keener helpfully sum-marizes the need for a broader engagement:

---

[112] Giovanni B. Bazzana, *Having the Spirit of Christ: Spirit Possession and Exorcism in the Early Christ Groups* (New Haven: Yale University Press, 2020), 10.

[113] See Richard A. Horsley, "'My Name Is Legion': Spirit Possession and Exorcism in Roman Palestine," in *Inquiry into Religious Experience in Early Judaism and Christianity*, ed. Frances Flannery, Colleen Shantz, and Rodney A. Werline, vol. 1 of *Experientia* (Atlanta: Society of Biblical Literature, 2008), 43.

[114] Horsley, *Empowering the People*, 82–120.

[115] See, for example, John H. Walton and J. Harvey Walton, *Demons and Spirits in Biblical Theology: Reading the Biblical Text in Its Cultural and Literary Context* (Eugene, Ore.: Cas-cade, 2019), 49–54.

Whereas the availability of concrete ancient sources regarding customs . . . sometimes relativizes the value of more abstract anthropological approaches to the New Testament, beliefs in control by a foreign spirit are so common among unrelated cultures that they appear to reflect a common human experience of some sort more than a mere custom. . . . Their wide occurrence beyond a particular culture warns against assuming that they are generated solely from a particular cultural framework (e.g., early Judaism or Hellenism), although I readily acknowledge that such ancient contexts are the primary ones for understanding New Testament interpretations of the reports.[116]

This larger cross-cultural (or transcultural) framework is a key focus of this monograph. In no way does this dismiss the need for analysis at each cultural level. Rather, an attempt is made to see additionally from a larger, multicultural perspective.

As a result, this study may be eye-opening due to the vast amount of evidence for the phenomenology of spirit possession in multicultural and interreligious settings. However, before we dive much deeper into the main goals of the project, it is now time to peer over into the field of anthropology to consider why so much interest in spirit possession accounts evolved into the presence of a wide contribution of anthropological and ethnographic study. How do anthropologists define spirit possession? How do these two scholarly worlds meet in their histories of interpretation and in their methodologies?

[116] Keener, "Spirit Possession as a Cross-cultural Experience," 217.

2

When Two Worlds Meet

The Hope of a Multicultural Approach

At this point it is illuminating to take a step back to see more specifically how the field of anthropology developed. This history reveals the methodological backbone behind the types of social-scientific interpretations explored above (related to their use in biblical studies). The interpretive framework that follows addresses a broader segment of anthropological studies involving witchcraft and magic, since spirit possession and exorcism are often found as a subcategory of these themes in anthropological studies. This genealogy of anthropological studies is presented to provide a historical and contextual framework for reading anthropological reports. The goal is to help the reader (1) become familiar with the major schools of thought and interpretive trends in anthropological studies, and (2) consider the biases that are present in generalized models of anthropological studies. One will note that the history of interpretation of both disciplines (NT studies and anthropology) track together on the same path, especially with interest in emic perspectives on spirit possession found in multicultural and indigenous reports. In earlier expressions of anthropological reports about spirit possession, experiences of people groups were more often read about and interpreted by armchair anthropologists. This approach eventually lost favor in the progression of anthropological theory, which began to have more concern for the localized perspectives of the people being observed. This shift in methodological focus placed a wide variety of multicultural reports about spirit possession at the fingertips of New Testament scholars. After briefly summarizing this disciplinary story, I introduce anthropological definitions of spirit possession and a proposed methodology for the comparative interdisciplinary work that will follow in chapters 4–6.

History of Anthropological Theory and Interpretive Frameworks

The earliest modern Western ethnographers (1500s–1600s) viewed themes of witchcraft and magic through a Christian lens. Indigenous practices were often interpreted as devil worship. As a result, many of the earliest ethnographers who studied themes of witchcraft and magic aimed to fit these practices into their own established frameworks.[1] Robert J. Wallis summarizes, "Indeed, these accounts tell us more about the western reporters themselves than the practices of magic and witchcraft in these communities."[2] When the Reformation arrived on the scene and transubstantiation was charged as magical, a modern distinction was made to subdivide themes of religion and magic into disparate categories. Following this, the Enlightenment, with intellect and reason leading the way, deepened the divide between what were known as rationalism and irrationalism, the latter often involving the supernatural.

Religious themes such as witchcraft and magic were then studied within the framework of Darwin's theories on evolution. These themes were interpreted as "mistaken beliefs" that would eventually diminish with time due to their primitive nature.[3] As the discipline of anthropology developed, the same religious themes were analyzed with in-vogue theories such as functionalism, structuralism, and postmodernism.[4] Wallis summarizes the lasting effect of the Enlightenment on the West by stating, "Witchcraft and magic are things against which the West has defined itself for 500 years or more. They are labels loaded with baggage, 'discursive constructs' and problematic grounds on which to characterize indigenous ontologies (ways of being) and epistemologies (ways of knowing), or 'lifeways.'"[5] This pejorative tone would remain for quite some time, even as new methodologies for study were employed for analysis.

When anthropology developed as a formal discipline, armchair anthropologists such as Sir Edward Burnett Tylor and Sir James Frazer continued to reproduce evolutionary ideas in their writing. Tylor's definition of religion centered on the soul. He described the soul as the "cause of life and thought." The soul could leave the body and go "from place to place." For Tylor the soul was immortal and existed after the death of the body. After leaving one body,

---

[1]   These terms were not used in a comparative manner, as they are by anthropologists today, but were used to describe "self-evident and real" phenomena. See Robert J. Wallis, "Witchcraft and Magic in the Age of Anthropology," in *The Oxford Illustrated History of Witchcraft and Magic*, ed. Owen Davies (New York: Oxford University Press, 2017), 226–27.

[2]   Wallis, "Witchcraft and Magic in the Age of Anthropology," 226.

[3]   Wallis, "Witchcraft and Magic in the Age of Anthropology," 226.

[4]   Wallis, "Witchcraft and Magic in the Age of Anthropology," 226.

[5]   Wallis, "Witchcraft and Magic in the Age of Anthropology," 226.

the soul was "able to enter into, possess, and act in the bodies of other men, of animals, and even of things."[6]

Tylor's concept of animism was founded on his belief in the soul.[7] He defined animism as belief in both "souls and phantoms." Savages were depicted as believing in phantoms, namely, "figures who visited them during their dreams and trances."[8] Therefore, souls range from low to high grades. Tylor located other spirits that possess the material world in the lower grade. He stated that spirits range "from the tiniest elf that sports in the long grass up to the heavenly Creator and Ruler of the World, the Great Spirit."[9]

In other words, Tylor advocated for a hierarchical arrangement of conceptions of the spirit realm that are associated with the evolutionary ideals of progress from barbarians to civilized thinkers. Tylor's paradigm includes eight stages of development that center on his definition of religion, founded upon the belief in the soul. The stages include: (1) a nonreligious condition, (2) a belief in souls/phantoms, (3) a belief in ghosts/souls, (4) a belief in spirits (spirits "hover about" humans, animals, and other things and are capable of acting out and affecting the things/persons they "hover about"[10]), (5) a belief in individual guardian spirits, (6) a belief in specific deities, (7) polytheistic beliefs, and (8) a belief in a supreme deity (which does not necessarily equate with monotheism for Tylor).[11] This paradigm was interpreted alongside definitions of where the soul could go upon a person's death, and three locations were given. The most primitive belief, according to Tylor, was that souls stayed on the earth. More developed religions, Tylor suggested, thought that souls traveled to Hades. Thirdly, at Tylor's highest level is the belief that souls travel to heaven.

Tylor's definition of animism was founded on progress and the evolutionary models that were prevalent at the time. His work assumed that one ought to progress from a belief in many spirits to the sole belief in one spirit, namely, a supreme deity (the belief in this deity also involved a belief in the hosts of saints and angels that were associated with the Christian God). Anthropologists like James George Frazer, J. J. Bachofen, and Henry Maine continued to base their theories on such evolutionary ideals. Eventually, science was seated at the top of the hierarchy, followed by religion and then magic. The work

[6]   Edward Burnett Tylor, *Primitive Culture: Researches into the Development of Mythology, Philosophy, Religion, Language, Art and Custom* (London: John Murray, 1903), 429.

[7]   Tylor's view of the soul is reflective of the Greek view of the soul as a nonmaterial part of personality.

[8]   L. L. Langness, *The Study of Culture* (Novato, Calif.: Chandler and Sharp, 2004), 24.

[9]   Tylor, *Primitive Culture*, 110.

[10]   Langness, *Study of Culture*, 25.

[11]   Langness, *Study of Culture*, 27.

of this period heavily impacted subsequent generations of anthropological thinkers. Over time the gap between science and religion expanded. In fact, it must be remembered that Tylor's work on the systemization of a definition of animism did not reflect his own personal belief in animistic viewpoints. George Stocking reminds us that Tylor's scientific naturalism did not allow him to believe in spiritual phenomena even when he had been an eyewitness. Tylor stated, "I admit to a prima facie case on evidence, and will not deny that there may be a psychic force causing raps, movements, levitations, etc." However, he concluded even after witnessing these supernatural phenomena that "seeing has not been believing."[12]

Stocking (writing at a much later date in 1987) reinforces this prioritization of rationalism: "It was one thing to find, as some searching Victorians did, traces of more general religious truth in the myths of other peoples; it was quite another to reduce the Christian Bible to the general category of myth."[13] In other words, Stocking supports the anti-supernatural bent that was held by Tylor and finds it equally acceptable to exclude evidence from those who had contradictory experiences. This chasm between natural and supernatural and between dominant approaches in science and theology widened. The field of philosophy had also heavily influenced and reinforced the dichotomy. Wallis succinctly summarizes and critiques the conclusions of Edward Burnett Tylor and Sir James Frazer:

> They both thought that belief in witchcraft and magic in "primitive" societies were "survivals" from prehistoric times, and that these fossils of "superstition" evidenced a ladder of progress by which cultures develop from "savagery" to "civilization," with religions developing from animism through totemism and polytheism to monotheism. "Magic," as superstitious practice, was destined to die out, but remained of interest to science as a relic of primitive practices. . . . This thinking is problematic, however, because: 1) it is ethnocentric, belittling the complex and sophisticated ontologies and epistemologies of indigenous communities, 2) ethnographic and archaeological evidence shows that cultures do not "progress" along evolutionary lines, but do adapt to ongoing internal and external pressures, 3) the mechanism by which one stage succeeds another is not explained. . . . Neither technological determinism . . . nor cultural Darwinism (that certain cultures are unable to progress and so will become extinct—a racist, incorrect . . . notion) offers a corrective.[14]

[12]   George W. Stocking, *Victorian Anthropology* (New York: Free Press, 1987), 191.
[13]   Stocking, *Victorian Anthropology*, 190.
[14]   Wallis, "Witchcraft and Magic in the Age of Anthropology," 229. Archaeological research in Göbeckli Tepe helps to problematize this argument. The evidence demonstrated that humans are inherently religious and that religion is not catalyzed by civilization or the

It would take some time before these trends would begin to dissipate in anthropological studies. A minor pushback began when a functionalist approach to anthropology came to dominate the field.

The Effect of Functionalist Anthropology

The functionalist school of anthropology was led by Émile Durkheim (1858–1917), who classified the divide between magic and religion as between the profane and sacred. Durkheim's student Marcel Mauss (1872–1950) viewed magic, science, and religion as distinct social phenomena but also realized that they do overlap and resemble one another in some ways. At the root of their analysis, magic and religion are both social expressions and reflections of society. Durkheim and Mauss removed magic from the classification and considered it as "outmoded," and "illogical or incorrect." They classified it as "a 'social fact' with its own common sense."[15]

Functionalism brought further change as anthropologists began to perform ethnographic research in indigenous cultures. Anthropologist Bronislaw Malinowski (1884–1942) labeled indigenous fieldwork "participant observation" and regularly interfaced with the local community. Through observation Malinowski saw the interrelated nature of magic, science, and religion and defined magic as reasonable and functional rather than irrational. The function of magic "supplies primitive man with a number of ready-made rituals, acts and beliefs, with a definite mental and practical technique which serves to bridge over the dangerous gaps in every pursuit or critical situation."[16] Therefore, magic has a social and psychological function, as it has an ability to provide explanation where science and religion may fail. As a result, the focal point shifted from the reality of whether magic is effective to the social role that it plays in indigenous communities. Wallis summarizes the functionalist mantra as a way to "enable people to deal with instability" for the purpose of producing social cohesion.[17] Because of this approach, witchcraft and magic were viewed as a part of every society and were analyzed according to their function, even though some functionalists contended that eventually magic would be supplanted by science.[18]

---

development of agriculture. See Ben Witherington III, "The Gobeckli Tepe Temple and the Origins of Religion: Are Humans Inherently Religious?" (paper presented at Bible and Archaeology Fest XIV, 2011).

[15] Wallis, "Witchcraft and Magic in the Age of Anthropology," 231.

[16] As cited in Wallis, "Witchcraft and Magic in the Age of Anthropology," 233.

[17] Wallis, "Witchcraft and Magic in the Age of Anthropology," 234.

[18] See Edward Evans-Pritchard, *Witchcraft, Oracles and Magic among the Azande* (Oxford: Clarendon, 1937).

The Effect of Structuralism

Claude Lévi-Strauss proposed that understanding symbolic communication was fundamental to understanding magic and witchcraft as a universal part of society. He built his theory on the shoulders of Ferdinand de Saussure and Carl Gustav Jung's theory of myth as "an expression of the collective unconscious."[19] As a result, he considered how myth as a "coded language of the unconscious"[20] worked in various cultures. He argued for the significance of the magician in each culture since the mind is capable of producing meaning, noting that "the universe is never charged with sufficient meaning" and "the mind always has more meanings available than there are objects to which relate to them."[21] Wallis summarizes the interpretive approach as one that explains the power of magic as stemming from the human mind. He argues that neither structural functionalism nor this symbolic approach effectively engages social change, inequality, and social agency.[22]

The Effect of the Symbolic/Interpretive Approach

Next, Victor Turner (1920–1983),[23] with his functionalist background, introduced the presence of a liminal state into the conversation. His approach was aimed at understanding social change and the role of ritual throughout. Turner's approach paid attention to how rituals help to bring resolution to conflicts, involving rituals as social dramas that take place in a three-part rite of passage comprising: (1) preliminal, (2) liminal, and (3) postliminal. The process involves separation, transition, and reincorporation. The highlight of Turner's work came in his ability to understand symbols through ritual performance. Each performance was viewed as a social dynamic and could be looked at on its own terms instead of as a piece of social structure. Turner noted the role of witchcraft and healing in society and the psychological benefit for the participants. Pertinent to this conversation is his consideration of rite of passage rituals and shamans as liminal figures. Additionally, Turner considered the

---

[19] Wallis, "Witchcraft and Magic in the Age of Anthropology," 237.

[20] Claude Lévi-Strauss, *Mythologiques*, 4 vols. (Chicago: University of Chicago Press, 1964–1971).

[21] Lévi-Strauss, *Mythologiques*, as cited in Wallis, "Witchcraft and Magic in the Age of Anthropology," 238.

[22] Wallis, "Witchcraft and Magic in the Age of Anthropology," 238.

[23] Victor Turner is classified as belonging to the symbolic/interpretive school of anthropology. I would be remiss not to also mention other important members of this school, especially Mary Douglas and Clifford Geertz. See Mary Douglas, *Purity and Danger: An Analysis of Concepts of Pollution and Taboo* (London: Routledge, 1966), and Clifford Geertz, *The Interpretation of Cultures* (New York: Basic Books, 1973).

relationship between symbols utilized in rituals and how rituals are played out in symbolic performances. Exorcism is considered as one type of symbolic performance.[24] Edith Turner noted that Victor Turner finally concluded with his own interpretation of the Ndembu rituals as "a mixture of moving poetry and undoubted hocus-pocus."[25]

Eventually, a turn to participant observation would challenge the etic interpretation of spirits, witchcraft, and magic that characterized the discipline of anthropology. Up until this point, etic explanations characterized definitions of the "supernatural." Wallis summarizes, "The intellectualists such as Tylor and Frazer dismissed the supernatural as incorrect in the light of rational thinking; the functionalists such as Radcliffe-Brown attributed beliefs in the supernatural to their function in society and reproduction of underlying social structures; and interpretive anthropologists such as Victor and Edith Turner focused on the agency of witchcraft and magic, and the valuable experience of ritual healing."[26] Now I turn to a landmark article by Paul Hiebert, who sought to turn the tide concerning the Western approach to these matters.

Paul Hiebert and the "Excluded Middle": The Situation in the West

In 1982 a critical work by missiologist Paul Hiebert titled *The Flaw of the Excluded Middle* seriously challenged the Western world's presuppositions (especially among missiologists) concerning the Western sociocultural constructions that had not allowed for consideration of the realm of experience included in possession phenomenology, including experiences that fall into the category of animistic belief. Hiebert questioned the over-prioritization of conventional science and challenged Western thinkers who had the tendency to relegate to the irrational those who believed in the reality of any supernatural matter. Hiebert began by questioning his own Western assumptions. He realized that being a part of Western academia affected his reading of the Bible, especially his over-prioritization of reason. In his analysis of Jesus' ministry, he began to recognize that experience played a significant role in interpretation. Hiebert began to find a need for an emic understanding of other worldviews. He began to ask key questions, including:

> Was the problem, at least in part, due to my own world view—to the assumptions I as a Westerner made about the nature of reality and the ways I viewed the world?

---

[24] For more detail see Victor Turner, *The Forest of Symbols: Aspects of Ndembu Ritual* (Ithaca, N.Y.: Cornell University Press, 1967).

[25] Edith Turner, *Experiencing Ritual: A New Interpretation of African Healing* (Philadelphia: University of Pennsylvania Press, 1992), 8.

[26] Wallis, "Witchcraft and Magic in the Age of Anthropology," 240.

But how do I discover these assumptions? They are so taken for granted that I am rarely even aware of them. One way is to look at the world view of another culture and then to contrast it with the way I view the world.[27]

Through his experience with the Indian worldview, Hiebert ultimately concluded that "I had excluded the middle level of the supernatural. . . . I had given little thought to the spirits of this world, to local ancestors and ghosts or to the souls of animals."[28]

Hiebert recognized that his training in the fields of science and theology reinforced the exclusion of the middle. Hiebert defined the middle in terms of the Platonic constructions of reality. As science was influenced by secularism, religion was simultaneously influenced by mysticism. But as science expanded in knowledge, religion took a subordinate position. Religion functioned to explain matters that could not be explained naturally, but as science continued to develop, natural explanations became more available, and these explanations were often preferable as they were based upon empirical proof. Hiebert states, "As a scientist I had been trained to deal with the empirical world in naturalistic terms. As a theologian, I was taught to answer ultimate questions in theistic terms. For me the middle did not really exist."[29] Hiebert concluded that he had consigned spirits of this world—ancestor spirits, ghosts, or animal souls—to the category of "mythical beings." His scientific and theological starting points failed to allow him to answer genuine questions that non-Westerners were asking.

Due to the priority given to science, Hiebert named Western Christian missions as "one of the greatest secularizing forces in history,"[30] and he proposed several questions for which Western theology had no answer:

Because the Western world no longer provides explanations for questions on the middle level, it is not surprising that many Western missionaries have no answers within their Christian world view. What is a Christian theology of ancestors, of animals and plants, of local spirits and spirit possession, and of "principalities, powers and rulers of the darkness of this world" (Ep 6:12)? What does one say when new tribal converts want to know how the Christian God tells them where and when to hunt, whether they should marry this daughter to that young man, or where they can find the lost money? Given no answer, they

---

[27] Paul Hiebert, "The Flaw of the Excluded Middle," *Missiology* 10.1 (1982): 36.
[28] Hiebert, "Flaw of the Excluded Middle," 43.
[29] Hiebert, "Flaw of the Excluded Middle," 43.
[30] Hiebert, "Flaw of the Excluded Middle," 44.

return to the diviner who gave them definite answers, for these are the problems that loom large in their everyday life.[31]

Considering this exclusion of the middle, Hiebert offered a three-part model for "holistic theology" that takes seriously the importance of the "middle" and the realm of experience.[32] In other words, what Hiebert called for was the importance of understanding the "meaning of human experience," which involves "animistic spiritism."[33]

Another important move was the recognition of the interpretive over-simplification that led to reductionism. Susan Rasmussen's remarks warn the interpreter of these pitfalls:

> Early anthropological interpretation of possession trance as an altered state of consciousness that predominately strikes selected categories of "deprived" persons is now widely regarded as an oversimplification. Such a perspective does not pursue the metacommunication surrounding possession among local participants, who may or may not become possessed themselves. Nonepidemiological studies, however, have all too often assumed that the meaning of these rituals is consensual, and have treated them as aberration, paying insufficient attention to the conflicting definitions and viewpoints of persons representing different interest groups.[34]

As a result, a cross-cultural study of spirit possession has widened the interpretive framework and more carefully considered local views and communications

---

[31] Hiebert, "Flaw of the Excluded Middle," 45.
[32] Hiebert, "Flaw of the Excluded Middle." See Hiebert's appendix A to view the paradigm.
[33] Hiebert, "Flaw of the Excluded Middle," 45.
[34] Susan J. Rasmussen, *Spirit Possession and Personhood among the Kel Ewey Tuareg* (New York: Cambridge University Press, 1995), 5–6. Related to this oversimplification see also I. M. Lewis, "Spirit Possession and Deprivation Cults," *Man* 1.3 (1966): 306–29; I. M. Lewis, *Ecstatic Religion: A Study of Shamanism and Spirit Possession*, 3rd ed. (London: Routledge, 2003); John G. Kennedy, "Nubian Zar Ceremonies as Psychotherapy," in *Culture, Disease, and Healing*, ed. David Landy (New York: Macmillan, 1977), 377–85; Fremont Bessmer, *Horses, Musicians, and Gods: The Hausa Cult of Possession Trance* (South Hadley, Mass.: Bergen and Garvey, 1983). Related to the critical discussion of the relationship between viewpoints see Jean Comaroff, "Healing and Cultural Transformation: The Tswana of Southern Africa," *Social Science and Medicine* 15B.3 (1981): 367–78; Jean Comaroff, *Body of Power, Spirit of Resistance: The Culture and History of a South African People* (Chicago: University of Chicago Press, 1985); Janice Boddy, *Wombs and Alien Spirits: Women, Men, and the Zar Cult in Northern Sudan* (Madison: University of Wisconsin Press, 1989); Paul Stoller, *Fusion of the Worlds: An Ethnography of Possession among the Songhay of Niger* (Chicago: University of Chicago Press, 1989).

as the key to understanding the phenomena. This trend continued in postmodern approaches.

Postmodern Approaches

Postmodernity brought a shift beyond participant observation in anthropological studies. The "objective" study of a culture was challenged. The bias was inherently clear since there were too many ethnographic accounts of non-Western societies written by white Westerners. Auto-ethnography and experiential anthropology began to become methodological foci. Their goal was to become immersed in the culture rather than just maintaining neutrality. Wallis writes, "Such insider ethnography and experiential anthropology takes the researcher's experience as valid data and recognizes that her own standpoint is woven into the discourse."[35] He concludes that this type of study treats magic and witchcraft differently as it "offers a sensitive treatment of how witchcraft and magic, when experienced as meaningful and embodied as practice, disrupt the insider/outsider, rational/irrational, superstition/science divides."[36]

Within the field of biblical studies, it has been recognized that the Gospels and Acts provide evidence that the first-century audience maintained a belief in the involvement of genuine spirits in those who exhibited trance-like behavior. Even though one aim of some anthropological research has been to maintain neutrality in interpretation and objectively describe the experiences of those they observe, anthropologists are beginning to record the indigenous interpretations of spirit possession and especially the belief in the involvement of genuine spirits.[37] An example includes the work of Edith Turner, who testified to encountering a "visible 'spirit' substance" in Zambia in 1985.[38] Later she reacted to her own experience, stating, "It was a small experience, but one which demanded a reorganization of the way I did anthropology . . ."[39] Edith

[35] Wallis, "Witchcraft and Magic in the Age of Anthropology," 242.
[36] Wallis, "Witchcraft and Magic in the Age of Anthropology," 246. This comment is made in response to Jenny Blain's work *Nine Worlds of Seid-Magic: Ecstasy and Neo-shamanism in North European Paganism* (London: Routledge, 2001). This methodology led Susan Greenwood, *The Anthropology of Magic* (Oxford: Berg, 2009), to argue that magic is a part of the human consciousness that may be expressed differently in each culture. Therefore, in her opinion, magic is a "process of the mind."
[37] Craig S. Keener, "Spirit Possession as a Cross-cultural Experience," *BBR* 20.2 (2010): 230.
[38] Edith Turner, "The Reality of Spirits," *Re-vision* 15.1 (1992): 28–32. Turner values participation in indigenous practices in "The Anthropology of Experience: The Way to Teach Religion and Healing," in *Teaching Religion and Healing*, ed. Linda L. Barnes and Inés Talamantez (Oxford: Oxford University Press, 2006), 193–205.
[39] Edith Turner, "A Visible Spirit Form in Zambia," in *Readings in Indigenous Religions*, ed. Graham Harvey (New York: Continuum, 2002), 152.

Turner's experience was a clarion call for anthropologists to become more open to indigenous views. She stated, "The ethnographer's own experience of spirits and witches should be treated as anthropological data. Is it correct for our discipline to close off from what is of major concern to its field people?"[40] Because of her experience, Turner challenged anthropologists not to pass by the "realm of spiritual experience."[41]

In this vein, anthropologists continue to recognize the problem caused by the Western mindset and participate in critiquing one another for prioritizing their own presuppositions when interpreting these types of accounts. In a response to documentation in Latin America, Barbara Placido notes that in interpretation anthropologists are likely to demonstrate "their own (anthropological) agenda."[42] In addition, Lewis states, "Possession studies do thus indeed tend to mirror the current fashions of anthropological theory and, if we are not careful, the voices of those we seek to report are in danger of being silenced as we pursue our own ethnocentric preoccupations."[43] Morton Klass argues for resisting the dichotomizing terminology of "natural" and "supernatural" since it "remains invincibly ethnocentric and therefore unsuitable for anthropological analysis."[44]

In summary, the established field of anthropology, defined simply as the study of humanity as is particularly related to society and the customs that are a part of society, is a modern convention that has brought forward numerous insights for understanding the "other." Malinowski defined this task of understanding the "other" as a primary focus for all anthropological work. The previous research has shown how some earlier anthropological theorists tended to focus on the etic viewpoint. Today's sociocultural anthropologists tend to favor focusing on the emic viewpoint.[45] Because in many ways the biblical text is representative of the ancient "other" (due to its ancient subjects and ancient context), anthropology's contribution to the study of the "other" offers tools to study the biblical text.

---

[40] Turner, "Visible Spirit Form in Zambia," 151.

[41] Turner, "Visible Spirit Form in Zambia," 151.

[42] Barbara Placido, "'It's All to Do with Words': An Analysis of Spirit Possession in the Venezuelan Cult of María Lionza," *Journal of the Royal Anthropological Institute* 7.2 (2001): 207–24, as cited in Lewis, *Ecstatic Religion*, xii.

[43] Lewis, *Ecstatic Religion*, xii.

[44] Morton Klass, *Ordered Universes: Approaches to the Anthropology of Religion* (Boulder, Colo.: Routledge, 1995), 32. Klass follows John Beattie, *Other Cultures: Aims, Methods and Achievements in Social Anthropology* (New York: Free Press, 1964), 203.

[45] Typically, the anthropological discipline is divided into four categories, including physical anthropology, archaeological anthropology, linguistic anthropology, and sociocultural anthropology. See Louise J. Lawrence, *Reading with Anthropology: Exhibiting Aspects of New Testament Religion* (Waynesboro, Ga.: Paternoster, 2005), 4; Clinton Bennett, *In Search of the Sacred: Anthropology and the Study of Religions* (London: Cassell, 1996), 50–92.

Comparable Trends in Anthropological and Biblical Studies

When comparing the trends of interpretation in both anthropological and biblical studies, one begins to see (probably not surprisingly) how the trends of interpretation mirror one another. The phenomenon of disciplines mirroring trends from broader movements of thought such as the Enlightenment is not restricted to anthropological studies. It is also a phenomenon among biblical scholars, who a priori exclude the existence of spirits who possess, or more specifically do not recognize that others accept the existence of genuine spirits.

The key problem is that this exclusion is supported by presuppositions that affect methodological factors rather than relevant evidence, whether from anthropological sources or ancient texts. This problem has been addressed in detail in the work of Paul Rhodes Eddy and Gregory A. Boyd, who emphasize that by the use of the "principle of analogy" alone, cross-cultural anthropological data, addressing the widespread experience of the phenomena of spirit possession, directly questions the Western interpretation, which argues that "there is no analogy in the present to warrant accepting supernatural experiences in the past."[46] Eddy and Boyd contend that this reasoning fails in light of the modern day anthropological evidence. In other words, the argument is based upon "ethnocentric," "eurocentric," and "chronocentric" presuppositions. They demonstrate the value of what ethnographers have called a "new democratized epistemology," which includes cross-cultural evidence in its full scope even when it might challenge the Western perspective. Eddy and Boyd summarize the ethnographers' rightful repositioning of the Western viewpoint in what follows.

> While affirming the technological benefits that the naturalistic, scientific, Western worldview has brought us, and while not relinquishing the validity of critical reason so valued by Western academia, these individuals are arguing that this worldview should no longer be used as the comprehensive and ubiquitous measuring stick of the truthfulness of all other perspectives.[47]

Because of these Western presuppositions, the current interpretive paradigms produce a framework that is limited in scope and unable to encompass the vast amount of evidence in anthropological literature.

In essence, there is a great need for a reassessment in light of the chasm that remains between Jesus the exorcist and scholarly assessments of Jesus' exorcistic activities. Both anthropological studies and biblical studies have

---

[46] Paul Rhodes Eddy and Gregory A. Boyd, *The Jesus Legend: A Case for the Historical Reliability of the Synoptic Jesus Tradition* (Grand Rapids: Baker, 2007), 69.

[47] Eddy and Boyd, *Jesus Legend*, 71.

at times misunderstood their objects of study due to prioritizing etic perspectives and also due to bias. A multicultural reading of the possession and exorcism accounts is not only needed; it also offers promise to build a bridge between Jesus as a historical exorcist and what could be considered as historically plausible activities that Jesus participated in when exorcising the possessed. The hope is to lift the focus off proving the correctness of interpretive choices related to Jesus' exorcism stories and rather embrace the strangers of a wide variety of cultures, including the literary and historical milieu of Jesus himself. One need not need believe in the genuine nature of spirits to benefit from this monograph. However, this monograph hopes to consider a comparison between modern and ancient evidence without the burden of an priori assumption that supernatural factors must be excluded. It gives place to a viewpoint that has too often been excluded. The intent is not to in turn remove other naturalistic interpretive options from the table. The intent is to allow global views to have a voice at this table, as they have the potential to help us become better readers of the possession and exorcism accounts found in the Gospels and Acts.

As anthropologists began to shift their methodological approach towards emic perspectives of indigenous people groups, a wide body of literature on spirit possession in localized contexts began to appear fruitful for comparison with the NT accounts of spirit possession and exorcism. The bias that was once present in anthropological studies is no stranger to modern interpretations of spirit possession and exorcism in the field of biblical studies. In fact, the taxonomies of interpretation tend to mirror each other. Even despite the bias that is still present in many modern accounts of spirit possession, the literature includes an array of evidence that documents characteristics of spirit possession cross-culturally. As has been noted in chapter 1, I am not the first to notice this lacuna; nor, I hope, will I be the last.

Defining Spirit Possession in Anthropological Studies

Before we continue, it is imperative to note the many variations concerning the definition of spirit possession to avoid misunderstandings concerning the intended scope of the term. Janice Boddy's definition of spirit possession specifies the types of "eternal forces" that commonly are viewed as possessing agents. She argues that possession

> commonly refers to the hold over a human being by external forces or entities more powerful than she. These forces may be ancestors or divinities, ghosts of foreign origin, or entities both ontologically and ethnically alien. . . . [It] is a broad term referring to an integration of spirit and matter, force or power and

corporeal reality, in a cosmos where the boundaries between an individual and her environment are acknowledged to be permeable, flexibly drawn, or at least negotiable. . . . Taking the givenness of spirits as a matter of salience, three parties of variable inclusiveness are implicated in any possession episode: a self, other humans, and external powers.[48]

Boddy's definition attests to the belief in such external forces/entities and their incorporation by persons, while also considering the influence of external powers.

Bourguignon's work has influenced definitions of spirit possession due to her differentiation between possession and trance. Her work is inclusive of psychological factors and incorporates spirit possession and exorcism within the altered states of consciousness (ASC) theory. An "altered state of consciousness" entails a "deviation in quantity of central nervous system arousal from a central, normal state . . ."[49] The central matter here is a neurophysiological factor that results in an aroused central nervous system. Bourguignon places the terms "dissociation," "fugue states," "hysteria," "hallucinations," "catalepsy," "epilepsy," "hypnosis," and "somnambulism" within the category of ASCs. Bourguignon does not mean for this to be an interpretive move, but views that ACSs, trance, and dissociation represent broad categories that fit into an even larger category of psychobiological states.[50]

Éva Pócs echoes the relationship present between spirit possession and ASCs, but narrows their definition, concluding that "possession is an altered state of consciousness, which is accompanied by an experience or explanation according to which the individual can come under the influence of an alien

[48] Janice Boddy, "Spirit Possession Revisited: Beyond Instrumentality," *Annual Review of Anthropology* 23 (1994): 433.

[49] Erika Bourguignon, ed., *Religion, Altered States of Consciousness, and Social Change* (Columbus: Ohio State University Press, 1973), 6.

[50] Bourguignon, *Religion, Altered States of Consciousness, and Social Change*, 5. Emma Cohen, "What Is Spirit Possession? Defining, Comparing, and Explaining Two Possession Forms," *Ethnos* 73.1 (2008): 103, has noted a need to expound further upon Bourguignon's definitions in order to more clearly characterize the observations made in her research. Cohen proposes the terms "executive possession" and "pathogenic possession." She writes, "Both possession forms entail the direct actions of spirit entities in or on a person's body. . . . Pathogenic possession concepts result from the operation of cognitive tools that deal with the representation of contamination (both positive and negative); the presence of the spirit is typically (but not always) manifested in the form of illness. Executive possession concepts mobilise cognitive tools that deal with the world of intentional agents; the spirit entity is typically represented as taking over the host's executive control, or replacing the host's 'mind' (or intentional agency), thus assuming control of bodily behaviours." As a result, other terms will also be considered as they are helpful in describing the nuancing of the analyzed texts.

spirit or entity. The latter can enter his body and reside in it and change his personality or is 'embodied' by the host whom it controls."[51] Pócs' definition is representative of indigenous views, while still classifying possession under the headline of ASC theory.

Arnaud Halloy and Vlad Naumescu, in formulating an approach to "learning possession," remark that the "lowest common denominator of possession studies" is belief in "a transformation of the individual due to a culturally postulated 'spirit entity.'"[52] This starting point is considered as the first level of a person's transformation. The second level of transformation involves what is described as trance states in ASC theory, including the "transformation . . . at the level of self (which) . . . might affect the physiological and psychological functions of the possessed with different degrees of intensity."[53] Halloy and Naumescu are sensitive to the problem that has surfaced in anthropological studies due to the distinction between cultural views and ASC theory. They aim to overcome this dichotomy by projecting a "unified view of possession where the differentiation between these two central axes of embodiment would be better grasped as a continuum organized around two central axes of embodiment."[54] By considering these axes of embodiment and somatic embodiment, Halloy and Naumescu rightly realize the need for interaction

---

[51]   Éva Pócs, "Possession Phenomena, Possession-Systems: Some East-Central European Examples," in *Communicating with the Spirits*, ed. Éva Pócs and Gábor Klaniczay (Budapest: Central European University Press, 2005), 84–152. See also Bourguignon, *Religion, Altered States of Consciousness, and Social Change*, 7–8; Nils G. Holm, "Ecstasy Research in the Twentieth Century: An Introduction," in *Religious Ecstasy: Based on Papers Read at the Symposium on Religious Ecstasy Held at Åbo, Finland, on the 26th–28th of August 1981*, ed. Nils G. Holm (Stockholm: Almqvist and Wiksell, 1982), 8–15; Anna-Leena Siikala, "The Siberian Shaman's Technique of Ecstasy," in Holm, *Religious Ecstasy*, 103–21. Pócs ("Possession Phenomena, Possession-System," 84) notes the tendency for psychologists and psychiatrists to "emphasize the presence of an alien spirit (psychologically the coming about of multiple personality) and use it to refer to phenomenon as such instead of talking about altered states of consciousness." See Traugott Konstantin Oesterreich, *Die Besessenheit* (Langesnsalza, Germany: Wendt and Klauwell, 1921); Loring M. Danforth, *Firewalking and Religious Healing: The Anastenaria of Greece and the American Firewalking Movement* (Princeton: Princeton University Press, 1985); Ernst Arbman, *Ecstasy or Religious Trance: In the Experience of the Ecstatics and from the Psychological Point of View*, 3 vols. (Stockholm: Bokförlaget, 1963), 3:211, 239; Vincent Crapanzano, "Spirit Possession," in *Encyclopedia of Religion*, ed. Mircea Eliade, vol. 14 (Chicago: Macmillan, 1987), 12–19; Felicitas Goodman, *How about Demons? Possession and Exorcism in the Modern World* (Bloomington: Indiana University Press, 1998).

[52]   Arnaud Halloy and Vlad Naumescu, "Learning Spirit Possession: An Introduction," *Ethnos* 77.2 (2012): 156.

[53]   Halloy and Naumescu, "Learning Spirit Possession," 157.

[54]   Halloy and Naumescu, "Learning Spirit Possession," 157.

between cultural and psychobiological aspects of possession. This way of considering possession provides room for the multifaceted experiences that fall under the category of possession.

This division that possession terminology often creates is further reflected in the distinction often made between "possession belief" and "possession trance." Peter Versteeg points out that "possession belief" refers to a change of behavior due to the "interference of a spirit that is different from that person's self or soul."[55] "Possession trance" is "a belief that attributes 'alterations or discontinuity in consciousness' to the presence of a spirit."[56] Therefore, in some cultures a specified characteristic, such as sterility, is characterized by the presence of a spirit.[57] These terms realize the tension that exists between natural and cultural descriptions of possession states.

Further, this research distinguishes between spirit mediumship and shamanism according to anthropological practice. Lewis believes that the difference is based on geographical usage: spirit medium is the British preference and shaman the American preference in anthropology.[58] However, Firth, representing another stream of thought, argues that the two have distinct definitions, especially related to the presence or absence of trance states. For Firth, shamanism demonstrates a level of mastery and control of spirits, and mediums serve as an intermediary between spirits and others where the goal is communication.[59] This monograph recognizes the distinction made by Firth and carefully surveys testimonies in anthropological reports to confirm that

[55]   Peter Versteeg, "Deliverance and Exorcism in Anthropological Perspective," in *Exorcism and Deliverance: Multi-disciplinary Studies*, ed. William K. Kay and Robin Parry (Milton Keynes, UK: Paternoster, 2011), 124.

[56]   Versteeg, "Deliverance and Exorcism in Anthropological Perspective," 124.

[57]   Boddy, *Wombs and Alien Spirits*, 166–94. See also Elizabeth C. Orchardson-Mazrui, "Jangamizi: Spirit and Sculpture," *African Language and Cultures* 6.2 (1993): 147–60. Erika Bourguignon, *Possession* (San Francisco: Chandler and Sharp, 1976), 7, refers to the fact that in the ancient context sickness was often paralleled with a possession by "unclean spirits."

[58]   I. M. Lewis, *Religion in Context: Cults and Charisma* (Cambridge: Cambridge University Press, 1996), 78–91.

[59]   Raymond Firth, "Problem and Assumption in an Anthropological Study of Religion: Huxley Memorial Lecture 1959," *Journal of the Royal Anthropological Institute of Great Britain and Ireland* 89 (1964): 129–48 [reprinted in Raymond Firth, *Essays on Social Organization and Values*, London School of Economics Monographs on Social Anthropology 28 (London: Athlone Press, 1964), 247–48]. He defines spirit mediumship as "a form of possession in which the person is conceived as serving as an intermediary between spirits and men. . . . The accent here is on communication; the actions and the words of the medium must be translatable, which differentiates them from mere spirit possession or madness." In comparison, shamanism is used in a more limited way (in the North Asiatic sense) to refer

they testify to possessed states, rather than simply control of spirits. This is based on the emic interpretation rather than the etic one.[60]

Providing more detail, Pócs demonstrates that the conversation of spirit possession then rests on three common depictions that define the relationship between human and spirit.[61] These three relationship types—possession by evil spirits, possession by deities, and mediumship—are evident in the analysis of anthropological literature that will follow in chapters 4–6 below. Definitions of all three depictions of possession are important to include here to help the reader better understand the anthropological evidence surveyed in chapters 4–6.

The first relationship is defined by the "combative penetration and aggressive reign of spirits (these are by nature 'evil demons')."[62] Secondly, possession by the divine describes

> when a deity enters the body as if it were a holy vessel, or protects the human being or controls him. This type of possession is often at the same time a mystic union, *unio mystica* (the two are overlapping categories), which is underscored by the representation of the deity by masks, dances, or the "imitation" of the deity in the course of collective rites.[63]

Thirdly, mediumship (or mediumism) is defined as

> when the human being—as if s/he were a mediating vessel—transmits the will or message of the deity or the spirits to another individual or community; in the case of divination this takes place in response to people's questions. For the most part in these cases there is no mention of that otherwise important characteristic of possession: controlling the possessed person.[64]

To accurately describe mediumship, one must recognize that there are both possession and nonpossession forms of mediumship that result in trance and

---

to a "master of spirits." This person is normally a spirit medium but has control of the spirits through rituals. Trance is not a part of shamanistic experience in all societies.

[60] Etic and emic are used in a general sense to refer to outsider or insider perspectives. If persons consider themselves possessed, then the report is included. This is not an ontological claim or empirical evidence that proves possessed states. The task is to collect reports where the phenomenon has been experienced and reported.

[61] Pócs, "Possession Phenomena, Possession-Systems," 85.

[62] Pócs, "Possession Phenomena, Possession-Systems," 85.

[63] Pócs, "Possession Phenomena, Possession-Systems," 85.

[64] Pócs, "Possession Phenomena, Possession-Systems," 85. While Pócs may argue from the normative perspective, there are certainly exceptions to her rule (as found in chapters 4–6).

allow for communication with the spirits.[65] Possession evidence is cited in chapters 4–6 that relates to all three of these categories since each type of possession provides reports that relate possession to illness, violent activity, or extraordinary strength, and demonic speech or oracular activity.

Defining spirit possession is difficult since the phenomenon is multitudinous and has many differing subtleties expressed in various cultures. The definition continues to be critiqued and updated in response to anthropological and ethnographic research. One expression of this comes through the work of George N. Appell and Laura W. R. Appell, who critique I. M. Lewis' definition for its lack of specificity and inability to represent the ethnographic evidence with sufficiency. In particular, they critique his division of possession into trance and non-trance states as oversimplistic, arguing that it "muddies the water and leaves out crucial ethnographic detail that might provide greater specificity to each case."[66] The conflation of so many culturally coded expressions of the phenomena under the category of "possession" indicates the wide range of ways in which cultures describe the phenomena in indigenous terms. Appell and Appell conclude that much confusion can be avoided by being inclusive of indigenous perspectives when interpreting the data for definition.[67]

For this reason, whenever possible, I have described the possession experiences that are presented in chapters 4–6 in the indigenous terms that are reported in the research. I use native terminology (with English translations) to describe the phenomena. When anthropologists and ethnographers interpret the experience in depth, I have not often included their own interpretation, as this research aims to gain the indigenous view rather than focus on the options for interpretation. These interpretive strategies are summarized in the following section. Further, one may consult the cited sources for the interpretive approach taken by each anthropologist or ethnographer.

[65] Bourguignon, *Religion, Altered States of Consciousness, and Social Change*, 340–56.
[66] George N. Appell and Laura W. R. Appell, "To Converse with the Gods: The Rungus *Bobolizan*—Spirit Medium and Priestess," in *The Seen and the Unseen: Shamanism, Mediumship and Possession in Borneo*, ed. Robert L. Winzeler, Borneo Research Council Monograph Series 2 (Williamsburg, Va.: Borneo Research Council, 1993), 4–5.
[67] Appell and Appell, "To Converse with the Gods," 5. Appell and Appell ask an excellent array of probing questions that are important for defining possession according to the indigenous view: "In any specific behavioral environment, what does possession refer to? To possession of the body? The consciousness? Or the soul? Does possession involve intrusion into the body by a spirit? Riding on a body? Or only control from an external position? Does it involve loss of part of the personhood, as when the shaman's soul goes wandering in the classic Siberian case . . . ? When possessing a spirit medium, does the diving spirit exercise minimal control or full domination?"

It is of great importance for the terms discussed above to be understood beyond their use in Christian theology or Western thinking and be taken in light of the way that they are used within each specific context. Secondly, the terminology of ASC is present in anthropological literature and is also employed throughout this study. It is retained as a way that anthropologists talk about possession states. The term represents an acknowledgment that possession states often involve a psycho-biological dimension. However, as Pócs argues, the psycho-biological dimension is "not a sufficient explanation for possession because . . . from a social psychological and cultural point of view possession is a religious/cultural phenomenon which goes beyond the use of trance techniques."[68] It is better to treat the category of ASC as a "partly overlapping category which requires specific cultural interpretations."[69] As Lewis argues, "If someone is, in his own cultural milieu, generally considered to be in a state of spirit possession, then he or she is possessed."[70] Pócs argues, "We have to agree with Lewis whose starting point is neither the trance-state, nor the spirit-human relationship but rather people who believe in Gods, spirits and explain ASC as related to their own spirit world, while also defining its role in their own society."[71] In this vein of interpretation, the indigenous views related to spirit possession states and belief in each culture will be a focus in the research below.

Proposed Research and Methodology

The proposed research makes its contribution by directly comparing two bodies of literature (the Synoptic Gospels and modern anthropological accounts of spirit possession) to attest to the plausibility of the Synoptic Gospel accounts. The two overarching research questions ask: (1) If the same types of accounts of spirit possession and exorcism are widely attested within modern anthropological sources and in the Synoptic Gospels and Acts, why must the credibility of the eyewitness accounts be doubted as a plausible report? and (2) What can be gained from a study of the characteristics of ancient possession and exorcism accounts in comparison with the characteristics of modern accounts? In other words, how do these accounts compare with modern anthropological accounts that have been generated from eyewitness testimony and participant observation? To answer these questions, the principle of analogy will be employed to compare these two sets of data.

---

[68] Pócs, "Possession Phenomena, Possession-Systems," 86.
[69] Pócs, "Possession Phenomena, Possession-Systems," 86.
[70] Lewis, *Ecstatic Religion*, 46.
[71] Pócs, "Possession Phenomena, Possession-Systems," 88. For this reason Pócs prefers to talk about "systems based on possession" rather than phenomena.

Use of the Principle of Analogy

The concept of the "principle of analogy" was made famous by Ernst Troeltsch and follows as an extension of the philosophical argument proposed by Scottish philosopher David Hume.[72] The key idea as summarized by Boyd and Eddy is that "the only way we can understand the past is by drawing analogies with the present."[73] When considering how the use of the principle of analogy has historically been applied to topics such as miracles or spirit possession, a problem occurs, since the foundations of the historical-critical method are built upon naturalism, which excludes a priori any explanation involving supernatural influence. Troeltsch's scientific approach to historiography emphasizes that experiences of miracles and the resurrection are unique to Christian beliefs. Troeltsch then situates the standard approach to historical critical studies as "at all points an absolute contrast" to these beliefs.[74] When employed within principles of naturalistic thinking, the argument related to miraculous events runs as follows: "Since it is assumed that people do not experience supernatural occurrences in the present, it arguably follows that we have no analogical way of assessing reports of supernatural occurrences in the past. As a matter of principle, therefore, they must be dismissed."[75] This assumption and circular argument remains part of historical-critical work, and its use is presupposed rather than proven. This study challenges this assumption and seeks to demonstrate that the principle of analogy may be used positively to demonstrate the historical plausibility of the eyewitness reports of spirit possession in the Gospels and Acts. Adding an important note related to the use of the principle of analogy, this study recognizes that one does not need to demonstrate the reality of the "supernatural world" to make the argument for the historical plausibility of these biblical accounts. While some anthropologists may be more sensitive towards the indigenous belief in the reality of spirits than others, all affirm spirit possession experiences and report them as displaying a variety of characteristics. The analogy is based upon comparing these experiences, which requires setting aside their interpretation.

[72] See Craig S. Keener, *Miracles: The Credibility of the New Testament Accounts*, 2 vols. (Grand Rapids: Baker, 2011), 1:83–210 for a full analysis of Humean logic. Keener argues that Hume's a priori objection to the "possibility of supernatural activity" is inadequate as it presupposes atheism/deism and is a circular argument.

[73] Boyd and Eddy, *Jesus Legend*, 28.

[74] Ernst Troeltsch, "Historiography," in *Encyclopedia of Religion and Ethics*, ed. James Hastings (New York: Scribner's Sons, 1914), 718.

[75] Boyd and Eddy, *Jesus Legend*, 28. Possible explanations include myth, legend, propaganda, emotional hysteria, or hallucinations.

Related to understanding human experience, Wolfhart Pannenberg rightly critiqued the anthropomorphic foundations of Troeltsch's application of the principle of analogy, favoring the positive application of the principle rather than the negative one.[76] The key point as argued by Boyd and Eddy (who also argue for no viable negative application of the principle) is "There is nothing in present human experience that warrants limiting all human experience to our present experience."[77] In other words, past experiences are capable of having analogical relationship with present experiences.

For example, in historical Jesus studies Theissen and Mertz argue for the usefulness of the principle of analogy when applied in historiography. They conclude,

> Miracles only become a problem where one's own experience knows no analogies to miracles. We all judge historical reports on the principle of analogy: We tend to regard the elements in them that contradict our own experience as unhistorical. We cannot imagine anyone walking on the water or multiplying loaves in a miraculous way and are therefore rightly skeptical about these reports. But the same principle of analogy which is the basis of our skepticism obliges us to recognize the possibility of healings and exorcisms. For in many cultures there is an abundance of well-documented analogies to them—and even in the "underground" of our culture, though that may be officially denied.[78]

Theissen and Mertz rightly recognize that there is an abundant witness to a differing experience than their own and recognize the reality of the phenomena in many sources.[79] Keener adds, "Many scholars today observe that the principle of analogy, historically used against the reliability of eyewitness miracle reports in the wake of the radical Enlightenment, now favors their probability."[80]

In his book on miracles, Keener recounts the philosophical dilemma Western readers encounter when reading NT accounts of healings. Keener demonstrates a wide array of analogical evidence that recounts an experience that contrasts the philosophical assumptions often made in the Western environment.

[76] Wolfhart Pannenberg, "Redemptive Event and History," in *Basic Questions in Theology*, trans. George H. Kehm, vol. 1 (Philadelphia: Fortress, 1970), 39–53.

[77] Boyd and Eddy, *Jesus Legend*, 63.

[78] Gerd Theissen and Annette Mertz, *The Historical Jesus: A Comprehensive Guide* (Minneapolis: Fortress, 1998), 310–13.

[79] Theissen and Merz, *Historical Jesus*, 312. They propose that a "supernatural element" is present in nature. The presence of a charisma in people may be used positively or negatively. Religious uses are socially constructed. Interestingly, they apply the analogical principle to deny nature miracles (as they were written post-resurrection).

[80] Keener, *Miracles*, 1:214.

Keener's argument for the plausibility of miracle accounts may also be applied to exorcism accounts. He argues, "What the radical Enlightenment excluded as implausible based on the principle of analogy, much of today's world can accept on the same principle of analogy. . . . Radical Enlightenment antisupernaturalism is far from the majority view in the world and thus henceforth ought to argue rather than presuppose its case."[81] Therefore, while interpretations of phenomena may vary, it is not acceptable to deny that reports of these types of phenomena may belong to eyewitness accounts present in historical sources. As Keener argues, "They are not reckoning with the social reality of a sizeable proportion of the world's population."[82]

The heart of the contention lies in what evidence or experiences are considered as viable when we analyze historical data. If the data is reduced to nothing, the outcome will be altered. Boyd and Eddy succinctly make the argument:

> When nothing is allowed to count as evidence against a presupposition, and when nothing is allowed to call into question one's metaphysical commitments, the commitment to the presupposition is, for all intents and purposes, a religious commitment to dogma. And this hardly seems consistent with a discipline that calls itself critical and that strives to be as objective and unbiased as possible in its assessment of evidence.[83]

The key point is that an "unequivocal commitment to naturalism"[84] (such as Bultmann's) limits what counts as evidence in a phenomenological analysis. In other words, one may not dismiss evidence due to a metaphysical assumption.[85] This approach, entitled an "open historical-critical method,"[86] by Boyd and Eddy, is arguably a more critical approach than the alternative as it requires "epistemological humility." Some Western scholars are required to analyze evidence that challenges the presuppositions of their own worldview by letting go of metaphysical commitments that exclude most majority world evidence on this topic. Boyd and Eddy's key contention is that "if someone is open to the *genuine historical possibility* that the portrait of Jesus in the Synoptics is substantially rooted in history, . . . one will find there are many compelling reasons to accept that this portrait is not only *possibly* rooted in history, but that it is *plausibly*—even probably—rooted in history."[87] In light of an array of

---

[81]   Keener, *Miracles*, 1:263.

[82]   Keener, *Miracles*, 1:213.

[83]   Boyd and Eddy, *Jesus Legend*, 51.

[84]   Boyd and Eddy, *Jesus Legend*, 51.

[85]   Boyd and Eddy, *Jesus Legend*, 52–53.

[86]   Versus a "naturalistic historical-critical method"; Boyd and Eddy, *Jesus Legend*, 55.

[87]   Boyd and Eddy, *Jesus Legend*, 55 (emphasis original).

eyewitness reports of spirit possession worldwide, it is easily possible to step outside a Western worldview for the purpose of better understanding Lukan accounts of spirit possession. The application of the principle of analogy allows for the intersection of a wide variety of analogous accounts that demonstrate the lack of uniqueness present in Lukan accounts. As Boyd and Eddy argue, "There is no justifiable, *a priori* point at which critical historians should shut down their analogical imagination. If we are striving to be truly critical, we must commit to being . . . critical of our narrow, culturally conditioned proclivities vis-à-vis reconstruction of the past."[88] Mark Crooks points out the copious amount of work done on spirit possession in a variety of fields and concludes, "The sheer quantity of evidence as to the phenomenology (descriptive facts) of possession means it transcends any dismissal as anecdotal in kind."[89]

Reinforcing the positive application of the principle of analogy, scholars such as Walter Wink have argued for the necessity of analogy in historical-critical work since "historical research depends upon analogy."[90] Further, he also challenges a reductionist approach that is based upon limited experiences. In the anthropological world, the use of analogy is no stranger. Roy Wagner argues that the use of analogy is a way of gaining perspective beyond the limitations of one's own personal experience. He writes,

> What the fieldworker invents, then, is his own understanding; the analogies he creates are extensions of his own notions and those of his culture, transformed by his experiences of the field situation. He uses the latter as a kind of "lever," the way a pole vaulter uses his pole to catapult his comprehension beyond the limitations imposed by earlier viewpoints . . . a set of impressions is re-created as a set of meanings.[91]

Building on Wagner's analogy, a key aim of this research is to allow the analogy of the experience presented in anthropological literature to serve as the "lever" to allow readers to comprehend the accounts of spirit possession in the Gospels and Acts as potentially historically plausible accounts. The following chapters work to provide a systematic approach to pursue these key research aims.

The main argument that this analogical analysis seeks to demonstrate is that NT accounts of spirit possession are compatible with eyewitness testimony and potentially historically plausible. The accounts are not discordant

---

[88] Boyd and Eddy, *Jesus Legend*, 60–61.

[89] Mark Crooks, "On the Psychology of Demon Possession: The Occult Personality," *Journal of Mind and Behavior* 39.4 (2018): 257.

[90] Walter Wink, "Write What You See: An Odyssey," *The Fourth R* 7.3 (1994): 6.

[91] Roy Wagner, *The Invention of Culture* (Englewood Cliffs, N.J.: Prentice Hall International, 1975), 12.

with eyewitness tradition and do not reflect the nature of legendary tales. By addressing the historical matter, this research does not seek to exclude any interpretation from the variety of interpretations present in scholarship. However, it is not acceptable to a priori exclude the emic perspective from the interpretive table, especially since the consideration of the accounts as plausible eyewitness testimony does not hinge upon the interpretive options. In summary, this research asks how modern spirit possession accounts present in anthropological studies compare with analogous NT accounts.

The above research has sought to demonstrate the following: (1) Bias is present in modern interpretive trends concerning spirit possession in both anthropological and biblical studies (even though it was also demonstrated that some in anthropology now favor an emic presentation of accounts). (2) This interdisciplinary project does not favor the use of models to study the analogous data between anthropological and NT studies; instead, a "thick description" of both the ancient and modern data, attuned to the indigenous perspective, will be used to present the analogical data. (3) A lacuna is present since several biblical scholars have noted the potential contribution of such a project, even though no major systematized attempt has been made to pursue how the biblical characteristics of possession compare with modern accounts. Tracing the trends in both anthropology and biblical studies allows one to consider the number of shifts in viewpoints related to how one may observe possession phenomena. These shifts have produced countless volumes written about spirit possession in anthropology. In biblical studies many scholars have noted the need to peer into these anthropological texts and consider how spirit possession is observed and experienced cross-culturally. Metaphorically, it is as though these disciplinary tides, concurrently blown by new winds, have produced the perfect wave for this research. As a result, this project is in debt to many anthropologists, ethnographers, and biblical scholars who have been willing to surf on the tides and see how multicultural voices speak about spirit possession and exorcism, or at least point out the necessity of hearing their voices.

3

History or Hysteria?

Reading the Gospels and Acts with Genre Criticism

While it has already been established that a chasm exists between the historical Jesus as exorcist and the historical substance of the stories of Jesus' exorcistic activities, the reason for this chasm has not been considered in much detail as it relates to genre criticism. The purpose of this chapter is to dive into the assumptions that often lead to disagreements over what Jesus was like as an exorcist, whom he engaged in exorcism, or even what he said when exorcising. The root of the dispute can be traced back to how scholars evaluate the historical reliability of the Gospel accounts. In other words, one's methodological approach to the Gospels will from the outset impact what can be known about Jesus' exorcistic activity. For this reason this chapter will address what it means to read Matthew and Mark as ancient biographies and Luke-Acts as an example of ancient historiography.[1] While many scholars have walked this well-worn path, creating a consensus that the Gospels are most like ancient biography, a review of the matter here is helpful to consider how the possession and exorcism accounts will be read in view of genre. Situating these accounts within their respective genres, along with their contemporaneous cultural matrix, is a critically important step that must be taken before assessing the implications of a multicultural reading. The questions we ask here are: What implications arise from reading spirit possession and exorcism stories through genre-critical lenses? What assumptions are challenged when we place these accounts within the genre of ancient biography? What arises as historically

---

[1]   Luke-Acts is recognized as a two-part work of ancient historiography. Simultaneously, it is also recognized that Luke has a biographical focus in the first part of his work.

plausible when we consider the substance of the possession and exorcism stories found in the Gospels and Acts?

Back to the Basics: The Genre of the Synoptics and Acts

In biblical scholarship today, there is a pervasive acceptance of the Gospels as ancient biography.[2] Even those who diverge from the consensus view[3] acknowledge that a majority of biblical scholars now recognize this genre classification. Even so, this categorization does not nullify the fact that the genre of ancient biography does overlap with other genres, nor the fact that the Gospels do contain elements distinctive from ancient biography. As Keener concludes, "We cannot use ancient biography to predict or explain everything we find in the Gospels."[4] This study is not unique in its effort to understand how to read the Gospels as biographies. A diachronic survey reveals that for the majority of history, the Gospels have been read as biographies. In fact, this consensus withstood the test of time up until the early twentieth century.[5]

Helen Bond helpfully explains why ancient people did not refer to the Gospels as *bioi*, an element that does not prevent their classification as part of the biographical genre. She proposes that Jesus' followers instead preferred Gospels because of the theological significance tied to the title.[6] Helpful for our purposes here, she reminds us that *euangelia* is not a term for a literary genre. The term referred to the "proclamation of significant news or imperial proclamations—to announce a military victory, the accession of a new emperor, or an emperor's benefactions—and would be the occasion for civil rejoicing."[7] Paul primarily carried forward this usage in his writings in his own

---

[2] Craig S Keener, *Christobiography: Memory, History, and the Reliability of the Gospels* (Grand Rapids: Eerdmans, 2019), 27; Helen K. Bond, *Mark: The First Biography of Jesus* (Grand Rapids: Eerdmans, 2020), 27. This classification has gained acceptance in classical studies as well. See Thomas Hägg, *The Art of Biography in Antiquity* (Cambridge: Cambridge University Press, 2012), 148–86.

[3] A few examples of alternative genre classifications for Mark include: (1) Mark as novel: Mary Ann Tolbert, *Sowing the Gospel: Mark's World in Literary-Historical Perspective* (Minneapolis: Fortress, 1989); and (2) Mark as historical monograph: Adela Yarbro Collins, *Is Mark's Gospel a Life of Jesus? The Question of Genre* (Milwaukee: Marquette University Press, 1990); Eve-Marie Becker, *Das Markus-Evangelium im Rahmen antiker Historiographie* (Tübingen: Mohr Siebeck, 2006).

[4] Keener, *Christobiography*, 28.

[5] Examples include Johannes Weiss, *Das älteste Evangelium* (Göttingen: Vandenhoeck & Ruprecht, 1903), 11, 15; Clyde Weber Votaw, "The Gospels and Contemporary Biographies," *AmJT* 19.1 (1915): 45–73; 19.2 (1915): 217–49; and Bond, *Mark*, 20.

[6] Bond, *Mark*, 21.

[7] Bond, *Mark*, 20.

understanding of the term. Strong evidence for the use of the term "Gospel" as representing books about Jesus does not show up until the mid-second century, even though it is possible to consider that this trajectory began in earlier writings.[8]

As we have already noted in chapter 1, the rise of form criticism began to change the way the Gospels were read. As noted by Adela Yarbro Collins, this view goes back to Johan Gottfried Herder's argument for the Gospels as "unsophisticated folk literature," which heavily influenced other form critics to classify the Gospels as a "new Christian genre."[9] Scholars such as Franz Overbeck, Karl Ludwig Schmidt, and Adolf Deissmann led the way for this perspective, hoping that insights from form criticism would allow new insights to arise in relation to the literary style of the texts. Schmidt's classification of the Gospels as popular literature shifted the texts away from their most analogous and contemporary genres and into the category of a "folk book" or "cult legend."[10] Rudolf Bultmann was a product of this interpretive environment, resulting in further steps away from viewing the Gospels with their most contemporaneous literary analogies. For him the Gospels are *sui generis*, "a unique phenomenon in the history of literature."[11] He argued against classifying the Gospels as biographies, not only citing the lack of literary sophistication in writing style, but also citing the lack of interest in Jesus' origin, appearance, personality, education, character, or character development. In short, the myopic focus on units of text eclipsed the larger genre-critical task that eventually gained traction again in the writings of Charles Talbert, Philip Shuler, Klaus Berger, Dirk Frickenschmidt, Graham Stanton, and Richard Burridge. Furthermore, the form critics neglected to take seriously the differences between modern and ancient biographies and historiographies in terms of their genre features.

While the consensus of the Gospels as biographies has substantial support, a wide variety of approaches are still taken in the treatment of the historical reliability of the Synoptics. Further, skepticism about the historicity of the Gospels is deeply rooted as a priori in some parts of biblical scholarship. What

---

[8]   See Bond, *Mark*, 20, who notes the use of the term in Justin Martyr, Irenaeus, and Clement of Alexandria to refer to books and oral proclamation.
[9]   Adela Yarbro Collins, *Mark: A Commentary* (Minneapolis: Fortress, 2007), 19; Keener, *Christobiography*, 30, n. 19.
[10] Karl Ludwig Schmidt, *The Place of the Gospels in the General History of Literature*, trans. Byron R. McCane (Columbia: University of South Carolina Press, 2002), 27.
[11] Rudolf Bultmann, "The Gospels (Form)," trans. R. A. Wilson, in *Twentieth Century Theology in the Making*, ed. J Pelikan, vol. 1 (London: Fontana, 1969), 86–92. See also Rudolf Bultmann, *The History of the Synoptic Tradition*, trans. John Marsh (Oxford: Blackwell, 1963), 371–74.

is needed is a critical and balanced treatment of texts no matter if it is a biblical text or another historical or classical text. This approach is reflective of the approaches of classical historians who attempt to treat Gospel texts and similar texts in analogous ways. No longer is it fashionable to single out the Synoptics or Acts as more suspect than parallel contemporaneous writings. Equal critical treatment is invited, especially critical treatments that avoid the risk of an a priori suspicion and bias about historical reliability. Where the burden of proof lies in debates about the historical plausibility of texts is a matter that ought to be considered thoughtfully and carefully.

Relating more specifically to the matter of possession and exorcism accounts in the Synoptics and Acts, one of the key errors made in the assessment of the possession accounts in the Gospels or Acts as lacking historical reliability results from not carefully assessing the genre of the texts at hand. Without a careful consideration of a work's genre, it is not possible to make positive or negative claims about the historical plausibility of a text. This basic starting point has been too often overlooked in the claims of those who pitch a wide chasm, rooted in naturalistic presuppositions, between Jesus the historical exorcist and what may be viewed as the plausible historical substance of the possession and exorcism stories. Ever since the landmark work by Richard Burridge on the Gospels as ancient biography, many scholars have added precision to genre-critical studies to better understand what implications result from situating the Gospels in this category. In what follows below, we will consider what it means to read the possession and exorcism stories found within the Synoptics and Acts as ancient biography or ancient historiography. Our looming questions remain: Are the possession and exorcism stories of the Gospels and Acts historically plausible when considered in their own historical context and genre? Is it possible to build any sort of bridge between Jesus the historical exorcist and the historical substance of the possession and exorcism stories of these New Testament texts?

The Relationship between Ancient Biography/Historiography and Memory

When one approaches the Synoptics and Acts critically, a primary starting point for gauging historical reliability is to consider how these texts compare with other contemporaneous and analogous texts. Since the probability of historical reliability is dependent upon what default characteristics are set as a part of the expectations of the genre, this task is unavoidable. As already noted, much scholarly work has been penned to substantiate what we can summarize here about ancient biographies and how the Gospels compare and contrast.

After performing comparative studies of analogous texts, Craig Keener indicates that default expectations provide a promising outlook for biographical texts. He writes, "As a matter of probability, we should expect a significant historical core in the average reports in the first-century Gospels except where evidence specifically points in a different direction."[12] In other words, one key factor in determining historical reliability involves considering both the "substance and variation" of the texts. When this comparative task is done on both substance and variation, the Gospels fit into the parameters of what would be expected when we consider historical persons and events. This starting point, of course, does not firmly establish historicity, but sets the Synoptics on the same playing field, a playing field where critical engagement and expectations of genre are considered hand in hand. A review of some of the primary expectations for ancient biography follows, as it has implications for considering the historical reliability of possession and exorcism accounts, as well as the characteristics of possession that are found within the accounts.

Firstly, a detailed study of ancient biography reveals that ancient biographers gathered information from within living memory and depended heavily on that information in the composition of their biographies. Keener marks the implications of this premise, noting that this principle helpfully counterbalances any a priori assumptions that the texts lack historical reliability. He states, "Claims of texts from within living memory of the subject are *themselves* historical evidence, even though historians must weigh such claims, like other evidence, as carefully as possible."[13] In other words, all of the Synoptics belong to a "genre that generally developed prior information rather than displayed unrestrained creativity."[14] Studies in the Synoptic problem provide viable evidence for a literary relationship between the Gospels. Given Markan priority, Luke and Matthew depend on Mark's document.[15] The fact that Matthew and Luke rely on another rather than inventing their own accounts is feasible proof that Matthew and Luke found Mark's reports to be historically reliable.

---

[12] Keener, *Christobiography*, 14.

[13] Keener, *Christobiography*, 15 (emphasis original). This claim flatly opposes form criticism's assumption that there was a long chain of oral tradition developed over many decades. It also opposes redaction criticism's claim that the texts most reflect the immediate situation of the community to which they were written rather than the situation described from the life of Jesus.

[14] Keener, *Christobiography*, 16. Studies in the way early Jews handle tradition are also relevant in this conversation.

[15] Keener, *Christobiography*, 155. Ancient critique of Mark's rhetorical arrangement of material existed. Despite this critique, Papias accepts Mark's account as providing a legitimate tradition about Jesus.

In other words, sources play an important role in historical construction for ancient writers. They were expected to depend upon research, including both written and oral sources, but were not required to cite each source.[16] It is possible that the Evangelists did not cite their sources since so much of the tradition was shared, did not have wide variation, and was within close enough proximity to the timeline of the events.[17]

Secondly, ancient biographers and historiographers were expected to arrange their material into a coherent work that makes a rhetorical point. It is the case that ancient biographers and historians had biases and wrote with a particular *tendenz*. However, this bias does not preclude their writings from containing historical information. Witherington makes an important distinction between bias and being a "neutral observer" of history. He argues that in ancient historiography the two categories need distinction. In his words, "What the claim of lack of bias did *not* mean is that the other was claiming to be a *neutral* observer of the historical process."[18] In other words, ideological beliefs were not viewed as bias in ancient writings.

Further, Keener aptly reminds us that it is idealistic to require biographers and historiographers to write devoid of any hint of bias. This presence of bias requires the reader to read critically and carefully while also asking what *tendenz* may be in play. However, it does not change the categorization of the genre. In Keener's words,

> One may define bias as a fictionalizing tendency, but it does not make biographies into novels; otherwise there would not *be* ancient biographies, or histories, since in literature unbiased works do not exist. We take bias into account when we read works of ancient biography or history, yet at the same time we depend heavily on these sources to understand the persons about whom they wrote. . . . If this is true for other figures of antiquity, why should it be any less true of Jesus?[19]

The key point is that a bias or literary focus does not normally imply that the author of an ancient history or biographic work falsified historical information. Since ancient writers wrote within living memory and were dependent upon prior information, it would follow that they were more capable of evaluating if their sources (literary or oral) were historical than modern readers

[16] For a detailed treatment of the use of sources in the genre of ancient biography see Keener, *Christobiography*, 212–19.

[17] Keener, *Christobiography*, 214–15.

[18] Ben Witherington III, *The Acts of the Apostles: A Socio-rhetorical Commentary* (Grand Rapids: Eerdmans, 1998), 50 (emphasis original).

[19] Keener, *Christobiography*, 64 (emphasis original).

are due to the length of time between text and listener/reader.[20] It takes critical engagement to lean into the emphases of each writer and learn their literary styles and techniques. However, without the Gospels and Acts, little detail will be found to aid in the historical reconstruction of how Jesus or Paul functioned as exorcists. Without the Gospels we also lose the *tendenz* associated with the possession and exorcism stories, along with what characteristics of possession are familiar in the ancient context.

Thirdly, when considering how the genre of ancient biography developed over time, Keener has recently concluded that the Synoptics were written during the period of greatest sensitivity for historical reliability. Keener argues that "expectations for reliable historical content seem to have been highest in roughly the period from the first century BCE to the early third century CE, perhaps peaking in the early second century."[21] Since the Gospels fall into this timeline, were written within living memory of Jesus (the Gospels fall between forty and sixty-five years after the death of Jesus), employ eyewitness testimonies as part of their sources, and were written at the peak of the period when biographers were known to have a higher level of sensitivity towards historicity, it is plausible to suggest that each account contains a level, and quite plausibly a substantial level, of historical information. This interest in matters of preserving historical information about Jesus is not plausibly uprooted in view of *tendenz*, thematic arrangement, or the literary style of each Evangelist. In summary,

> In contrast to a theoretically objective approach, ancient biographers were also concerned with their subject's character and value as positive, negative, or mixed moral examples. Their own perspectives shaped how they composed their works. At the same time, responsible biographers shaped information or traditions that came to them, rather than freely inventing new stories.[22]

Fourthly, ancient biography involves the passing down of testimony. When testimonies that are a part of collective memory are reported within living memory, it is not uncritical to consider the witness as historically reliable. As Bauckham argues, "Gospels understood as testimony are the entirely appropriate means of access to the historical reality of Jesus. . . . We need to recognize that, historically speaking, testimony is a unique and uniquely valuable means of access to historical reality."[23] A critical question of interest relates to

---

20   Keener, *Christobiography*, 67.
21   Keener, *Christobiography*, 103.
22   Keener, *Christobiography*, 149.
23   Richard J. Bauckham, *Jesus and the Eyewitnesses: The Gospels as Eyewitness Testimony* (Grand Rapids: Eerdmans, 2006), 5.

how historically reliable the eyewitness testimonies were and how this matter can be assessed. Bauckham concludes that this process does not mimic the patterns set forth by form criticism. He concludes, "The kinds of differences we find between Plutarch and his sources are quite comparable to the differences between the Gospels, and *nothing in the least like form criticism is postulated by experts on Plutarch.*"[24]

Memory studies and more recent studies of oral tradition shine light on how to assess the historical reliability of the oral transmission of eyewitness testimony. These recent studies on memory offer a challenge to the arguments against the historicity of the NT's exorcism stories. Keener's work urges the discipline to consider the reliability of the first-generation memories that inform the writers of the texts.[25] Keener argues that memory studies (especially related to accounts in living memory) have confirmed that memories are typically based upon actual experiences and are reliable in reconstructing experiences in approximation.[26] This thesis considers the frailties of the memory,[27] yet still notes that "eyewitnesses are normally able to recount many

[24] Richard J. Bauckham, "In Response to My Respondents: *Jesus and the Eyewitnesses* in Review," *JSHJ* 6.2 (2008): 237 (emphasis original).

[25] Keener and Witherington both argue that the difficulty in the traceability of the sources for Acts is likely because they came from oral reports and eyewitness accounts. See Craig S. Keener, *Acts: An Exegetical Commentary: Introduction and 1:1–2:47* (Grand Rapids: Baker, 2012), 177; Witherington, *Acts*, 165–73.

[26] Keener, *Christobiography*, 371. This excludes cases where amnesia, dementia, or schizophrenia are involved. See Steen F. Larsen, Charles P. Thompson, and Tia Hansen, "Time in Autobiographical Memory," in *Remembering Our Past: Studies in Autobiographical Memory*, ed. David C. Rubin (Cambridge: Cambridge University Press, 1996), 153; Alan D. Baddeley et al., "Schizophrenic Delusions and the Construction of Autobiographical Memory," in Rubin, *Remembering Our Past*, 384, 423–24; Daniel L. Schacter, "Memory, Amnesia, and Frontal Lobe Dysfunction," in *Memory Distortion: How Minds, Brains, and Societies Reconstruct the Past*, ed. Daniel L. Schacter (Cambridge, Mass.: Harvard University Press, 1995), 1–43; Wilma Koutstaal, Mieke Verfaellie, and Daniel L. Schacter, "Recognizing Identical versus Similar Categorically Related Common Objects: Further Evidence for Degraded Gist Representations in Amnesia," *Neuropsychology* 15.2 (2001): 268–89; Jon S. Simons et al., "Failing to Get the Gist: Reduced False Recognition of Semantic Associates in Semantic Dementia," *Neuropsychology* 19.3 (2005): 353–61; Benton H. Pierce et al., "Effects of Distinctive Encoding on Source-Based False Recognition: Further Examination of Recall-to-Reject Processing in Aging and Alzheimer's Disease," *Cognitive and Behavioral Neurology* 21.3 (2008): 179–86; A. E. Budson et. al., "Memory for the September 11, 2001, Terrorist Attacks One Year Later in Patients with Alzheimer's Disease, Patients with Mild Cognitive Impairment, and Healthy Older Adults," *Cortex* 43.7 (2007): 875–88.

[27] Keener, *Christobiography*, 400, notes suggestibility, susceptibility to bias, chronological displacement, and conflation. On p. 377, Keener reminds readers that "omissions are not

significant episodes from the prime of their life decades after their experiences."[28] In summary, Keener makes the key point that fallibility does not reduce memory to nonfunctionality.

Bauckham supports this point by arguing that memory works "more like a painting than a photograph."[29] This means that memories do not generally produce verbatim accounts of eyewitness reports.[30] A substance of the actual event is reported. Robert McIver's work in memory studies additionally supports this fact. He argues, in regard to the amount of detail in the eyewitness memories behind the Gospels, that it is not plausible for more than 20 percent to be considered as mistaken.[31] However, even if errors range in this percentage, McIver argues that the mistaken details "are almost always consistent with the broader picture of what actually happened, even if, strictly speaking, they are errors of detail."[32] What this all boils down to, as Keener argues, is that in the minds of the majority of scholars, "in general and for the purposes at hand, memory is more reliable than unreliable."[33] As a result, memory studies increasingly shift the burden of proof towards those who argue against the historical reliability of the first-generation memories that inform our spirit possession and exorcism accounts. In other words, evidence must be substantiated to disprove that the testimonies handed down are reliable in presenting the gist of events.

Those who compare the transmission of healing and exorcism stories in the Gospel accounts will realize that the accounts have not changed the essence of what they received from their sources. As noted above, the alterations in detail and arrangement stand within the bounds of the genre of ancient historiography. Keener argues, "To claim that Jesus was not deemed a miracle worker in his own day and that miracle stories simply 'grew' begs the question of what

---

actual errors." Concerning bias, see p. 382, where he notes that "bias is more likely to shape earlier tradition than to fabricate it." Concerning the rearrangement of material, see p. 383, noting the use of the practice as not limited to the Gospels.

[28] Keener, *Christobiography*, 366.

[29] Bauckham, *Jesus and the Eyewitnesses*, 325.

[30] Bauckham, *Jesus and the Eyewitnesses*, 330. An exception would be made for aphorisms.

[31] Memory errors typically involve matters of "transience, suggestibility, and bias." See Robert K. McIver, *Memory, Jesus and the Synoptic Gospels* (Atlanta: Society of Biblical Literature, 2011), 21. Transience involves an inability to remember the fullness of the whole event. In other words, one may forget certain parts. Suggestibility involves a level of distortion in memories with the invention of plausible details to fill in the substance of the memory. Bias involves the interpretive element of the memory maker.

[32] Robert K. McIver, "Eyewitnesses as Guarantors of the Accuracy of the Gospel Traditions in the Light of Psychological Research," *JBL* 131.3 (2012): 545.

[33] Keener, *Christobiography*, 392.

they grew from."[34] So, if the depiction of the details surrounding the types of people Jesus exorcised and the characteristics of their possession cohere for the most part, can more be said than just that Jesus was an exorcist? It is possible to consider that insights from memory studies related to the passing on of memories (and later a presentation of global characteristics of possession) offers an opportunity to say yes to this question. In summary, oral transmission does involve the shaping of information in the process of transmission. However, the process of shaping does not generally involve the manufacturing of material.

While these four points consider overarching characteristics of ancient biography and historiography and their relationship to assessing historical plausibility, it is also helpful to review the literary conventions of ancient historiographic works as part of this conversation. Michael Licona classifies seven "compositional devices" and one "universal law" that function as literary devices in the works of Plutarch. Helpfully, classics scholars confirm the use of these devices and claim that they are "practically universal in ancient historiography."[35] These "compositional devices" include transferal, displacement, conflation, compression, simplification, expansion of narrative details, paraphrasing, and the "law of biographical relevance."[36] This set of literary techniques is helpful when considering the redactions found in the accounts we will focus on in the following chapters. While source criticism and redaction criticism might have found some of these characteristics to be evidence for the dismissal of historical reliability, a consideration of genre provides a counterbalance to claims of historical unreliability.

With these points established, it is possible to push a little harder, or perhaps from a different angle, into questions of verifying what details are historically plausible. Furthermore, if we start with the premise that the Gospels and Acts do contain historically plausible information (whether a little or a lot), how can we assess what bridges can be built to connect the historical Jesus

---

[34] Keener, *Christobiography*, 337, countering Bart D. Ehrman, *Jesus before the Gospels: How the Earliest Christians Remembered, Changed, and Invented Their Stories of the Savior* (New York: HarperOne, 2016), 221–22. The fact that Jesus is unique in some of his activities is no argument against the plausibility of the experience of those who were eyewitnesses. Keener writes, "If Jesus's contemporaries experienced him as a healer and exorcist, one would expect this element to feature in biographies of him, just as it does in modern biographies of modern healers. This focus does not count against the biographic character of the Gospels" (Keener, *Christobiography*, 345).

[35] Michael Licona, *Why Are There Differences in the Gospels? What We Can Learn from Ancient Biography* (New York: Oxford University Press, 2017), 19.

[36] Licona, *Why Are There Differences in the Gospels?* 20.

with the Evangelists' reports of exorcisms found in the Synoptic Gospels and Acts? These questions additionally relate to the shape of the exorcism stories as found in our texts. Does the shape of the stories prove the Bultmannian theory that the stories grew exponentially through periods of oral tradition?

Digging Deeper: Ancient Biography and Historiography and the Assessment of Historical Plausibility

Since this monograph treats both the Synoptics and Acts, it will be helpful to briefly consider the relationship between ancient historiography and ancient biography, since many scholars classify Luke-Acts as historiography.[37] The most critical starting point is to understand that the two genres contain a significant amount of overlapping characteristics when compared. In other words, scholarship has established that biographers and historiographers share similar interests,[38] and that both are dependent upon various types of sources.[39] It is possible to view ancient historiography as the overarching category into which biography falls as a subtype.[40] In fact, historiographies often provided the information for biographies.[41] The primary distinctive for comparison boils down to the narrowness or broadness of the topic. Biographies are focused on the treatment of a single person rather than a broader group of people and events. While other minor variances do occur, one cannot deny the significant amount of overlap between the two genres. For matters of historical plausibility, there is little difference in implications for historical reconstruction because of the shared characteristics of both genres.[42]

When considering types of biographies, Collins argues that the "historical biography"[43] has consistent objectives when compared to historiography, namely, "to give an account of an important series of events and to explain the events in terms of their causes."[44] This category of biography, she argues, "is the most similar to the Gospels" and is "very close to the historical

---

[37]   Some scholars classify Mark as ancient historiography. For example, see Collins, *Mark*, 1.

[38]   Richard A. Burridge, *What Are the Gospels? A Comparison with Graeco-Roman Biography*, 2nd ed. (Grand Rapids: Eerdmans, 2005), 63–67. See also Keener, *Christobiography*, 161, nn. 81–82.

[39]   Keener, *Christobiography*, 159.

[40]   George A. Kennedy, "Classical and Christian Source Criticism," in *The Relationships among the Gospels: An Interdisciplinary Dialogue*, ed. William O. Walker Jr. (San Antonio: Trinity University Press, 1978), 136.

[41]   Keener, *Christobiography*, 158.

[42]   Keener, *Christobiography*, 165–68.

[43]   Exemplified by Suetonius' *Caesars*, Plutarch's *Caesar*, and Tacitus' *Agricola*.

[44]   Collins, *Mark*, 32–33.

monograph, which focuses on a single person."[45] Additionally, Dihle, classifying the Gospels into the genre of ancient historiography, argues that the Roman style of biographic writings fall near historiography on the genre continuum.[46] In summary, there is not a firm line that is definable, for historiographic considerations, between ancient historiography and ancient biography. Both historiography and biography have historiographic purposes and aims that are in proximity with one another. This classification is helpful in establishing the use of historical data when writing biographical or historiographical works. It is also important to consider how this data was assessed and used. How was it adapted? Did biographers and historiographers fill in details that were lacking in their inherited sources? If so, are these details historically plausible?

Exorcism Stories as Oral Tradition: The Shaping and Transmitting of Possession and Exorcism Stories

In agreement with Bultmann and his followers, it is possible to conclude that the Gospels do adhere to a form (although with variations) for presenting exorcism stories. Considering a multicultural lens, modern possession stories also typically fit into a very similar form. Bultmann described the typical order of the Synoptic form through the lens of the story of the Gerasene demoniac.[47] The big question here is what is the meaning of a similarity in the form of possession and exorcism stories when comparing Synoptic stories and modern anthropological accounts? Why does this matter to the conversation of historical plausibility?

Bultmann presupposed that the form revealed an element of creativity on the part of the authors. Even though Bultmann rightly and with clarity summarizes the formal elements presented in exorcistic narratives, his underlying methodology and the assumptions involved in his form-critical task have been shown to lead to questionable conclusions (due to an a priori assumption about the "supernatural" nature of the texts) regarding the matter of historical plausibility.[48]

In response, Bauckham determined that two conclusions from form criticism are valuable in oral transmission studies and have not been refuted:

---

[45]   Collins, *Mark*, 32–33.

[46]   Albrecht Dihle, "The Gospels as Greek Biography," in *The Gospel and the Gospels*, ed. Peter Stuhlmacher (Grand Rapids: Eerdmans, 1991), 383–84.

[47]   Bultmann, *History of the Synoptic Tradition*, 209–10. Bultmann places exorcisms within the category of healings.

[48]   Bauckham, *Jesus and the Eyewitnesses*, 242. Bauckham argues that even despite the refutations of form criticism's main arguments, these assumptions still pervade the work of many NT scholars. For a summary of main criticisms, see also 246–48.

(1) "individual units of the Synoptic Gospels are close to the oral forms in which they previously existed," and (2) "they were not necessarily linked together as they are in the Gospels."[49] The problem is that these two insights led form critics to the conclusion that the shaping of oral tradition was done in early Christian communities. Forms were connected to particular *Sitze im Leben* ("settings in life") that served certain situations (preaching, worship, catechesis, or apologetic).[50] In summary, form critics claimed to uncover the function of preserved units for community purpose. This aim created a chasm between the historical Jesus and the original communities, and what could be known of the historical Jesus suffered serious limitations for many decades of NT scholarship, since some Gospel units were considered as only informed by the early church, its purposes, and its creations. One of the most important correctives of these conclusions comes from Dunn, who criticized form critics for imposing a literary model upon the study of oral transmission.[51] On the other hand, if one takes into consideration memory studies, without the trajectory of typical form criticism, there is much to be gleaned from the realization that literary forms do reflect closeness to their orally transmitted counterparts. If these are read as memories, it is not surprising to consider that memory is shaped by form.

Interestingly, when considering the form of biblical and modern anthropological accounts, scholars have noted striking similarity in the way possession and exorcism stories are told. Bultmann analyzed the form of miracle and exorcism stories within the NT and described a typical order. The story of the Gerasene demoniac is used as an exemplar version of the typical form. Bultmann's proposed order is "1) meeting with the demons, 2) description of the dangerous characteristics of the affliction, 3) the demons recognize the exorcist and put up a struggle, 4) the exorcism, 5) the demons demonstrably depart, 6) an impression is made upon the spectators."[52] In classifying exorcism stories, Theissen takes a more nuanced approach and names several characteristics that distinguish exorcisms from other healing miracles.[53] He

49 Bauckham, *Jesus and the Eyewitnesses*, 243.
50 Bauckham, *Jesus and the Eyewitnesses*, 244.
51 James D. G. Dunn, "Altering the Default Setting: Re-envisaging the Early Transmissions of the Jesus Tradition," *NTS* 49 (2003): 144–45; J. D. G. Dunn, *Jesus Remembered* (Grand Rapids: Eerdmans, 2003), 194–95, 248–49.
52 Bultmann, *History of the Synoptic Tradition*, 209–10, as referred to in Eric Sorensen, *Possession and Exorcism in the New Testament and Early Christianity* (Tübingen: Mohr Siebeck, 2002), 123.
53 Gerd Theissen, *The Miracle Stories of the Early Christian Tradition*, trans. Francis McDonah (Philadelphia: Fortress, 1983), 87–90.

demonstrates that exorcism stories in the NT include: (1) a person under the power of a demon (under distress until the demon departs), (2) a conflict that occurs between exorcist and demon, and (3) a demonstration by the demon of destructive behavior.

Witmer, like Bultmann, also analyzes the common factors present within exorcism accounts, except her analysis is of anthropological data. Her list includes eight features and three actions performed by the exorcist. The common parts of exorcism stories include (1) the conditions in which the exorcism takes place, (2) the demon's detection of the exorcist, (3) the exorcists' recognition of the demon, (4) the exorcists' work to cause the demon to give its identity (name, number, character, and possibly the manner by which it may be expelled), (5) the involvement of an incantation or spell, (6) a command to expel the demon, (7) evidence that the demon is gone, and (8) the details of the response of the audience.[54] Three features of the demon's response that parallel the success of the exorcism are: (1) the demon's verbal response, (2) the demon's statement of its name and actions (indicating the problem it causes), and (3) evidence of expulsion.[55]

One can quickly notice the number of similarities between Bultmann's description of the form of an exorcism account in the New Testament and Witmer's modern description gained from anthropological sources. The two bodies of material compare not only in the categories they present to tell an exorcism story, but also in form. What does this form tell us? The Bultmannian lens interprets the form as a challenge to historical plausibility, while the multicultural lens does not. The chart below juxtaposes the two sets of categories. The categories are listed in the order presented by each author. While the two sets of categories do not mirror exactly, they do have overlap in a variety of ways.

[54] Amanda Witmer, *Jesus, the Galilean Exorcist: His Exorcisms in Social and Political Context*, LNTS 459 (London: T&T Clark, 2012), 26.

[55] Campbell Bonner, "The Technique of Exorcism," *HTR* 36.1 (1943): 39–49, cited in Witmer, *Jesus, the Galilean Exorcist*, 27.

BULTMANN'S CATEGORIES (BASED ON SYNOPTICS)	WITMER'S CATEGORIES (BASED ON MODERN ANTHROPOLOGICAL DATA)
Meeting with the demon	Conditions in which exorcism takes place
	Demon's detection of the exorcist
Description or dangerous characteristics or affliction of the demon	
Demon recognizes the exorcist and puts up a struggle	Exorcist's recognition of the demon
	Exorcist gets to know the identity of the demon
	Use of incantation or spell
Demon is exorcised	Use of command to expel
Demon departs	Evidence of demon's absence
An impression is made on the crowd	Crowd's response

When we consider an interreligious and global study of possession, a wide variety of ethnographies and anthropological works attest to characteristics of possession that are familiar to our texts. Additionally, the stories, when compared, do adhere to a general form. In other words, certain categories are typically present (even if with variation) to produce an exorcism account whether in the ancient context or in the modern one. Anthropologists have not questioned the reliability of the ethnographic reports due to the form of their testimony. The form, rather, reveals more about how people summarize memories and transmit them.

Assessing "Supernatural" or Miracle Stories

As noted above, a variety of other proposals, related to the choice of genre, are present in biblical scholarship. For example, some have proposed that the Gospels are best placed into the category of novel or mythography, especially due to the "supernatural" characteristics of some of the stories. One major pushback to this categorization comes from Keener, who indicates that the activities in the analogous events must compare in type. A problem arises when one compares the type of supernatural activity in these two genres. For example,

> Whether one believes in supernatural activity or not, the Gospel's reports of healings and exorcisms differ starkly from the composite creatures and divine rapes that characterize so many myths in the engaging myth collections of Apollodorus or Ovid. They appear comparable only through the lens of a modernist Western conflation of all supernatural claims, from all cultures and eras. The Gospels take for granted a theistic worldview, but this factor no more diminishes their character as ancient biography than the works of ancient polytheistic historians (sometimes replete with scenes understood as divine judgments) exclude them from ancient historiography. Millions of people claim experiences today with what they consider miracles, but this does not make the *genre* of their claims, or even their collected claims, mythography.[56]

In other words, examples of supernatural reports or paranormal experience are not unfamiliar to other biographical or historiographical works. While some claims after testing will be dismissed as historically implausible, it is not acceptable to a priori dismiss every claim to anomaly. While some ancient writers may have avoided binding themselves to supernatural explanations, others did not,[57] a parallel that the Gospels have with Israelite historiography, which freely attributed divine involvement.[58] In other words, one must ask if the exalted view of Jesus expressed in the Gospels is a plausible objection to the Gospels as historiographically plausible. While it is true that the Gospels depict more miraculous stories than any other extant ancient text, it does not also follow that this inclusion requires a different genre choice. Historians will grant that biographies contain differing emphases when compared. In other words, as Keener states, "Excluding literary analogies to the Gospels because Jesus's role is distinctive excludes a sort of evidence that is too relevant on other grounds to dismiss."[59]

In essence, this line of argument does not dismiss the need for deciding carefully whether an experience is genuine. Rather, it urges against a clear-cut a priori dismissal of the historicity of a miraculous event that comes from eyewitness testimony. As Keener summarizes, rejecting miracles accounts "simply because they are miracle accounts, a common recourse

---

[56] Keener, *Christobiography*, 340 (emphasis original).
[57] For examples see Keener, *Christobiography*, 332–33.
[58] Keener, *Christobiography*, 333.
[59] Keener, *Christobiography*, 335.

in the heyday of rationalism, is less universally appealing in a multicultural, twenty-first-century world."[60] While NT scholars may vary on the interpretation of the event, just as anthropologists may, or ethnographers may, this matter in of itself does not rule out that an eyewitness story is historical. As a result, interpretations are not the primary essence of the conversation that follows from this point forward. The taxonomy of interpretation for spirit possession and exorcism experiences has been presented in chapter 1, along with the sentiment that one interpretation cannot possibly explain all the relevant evidence when we consider the many multicultural expressions of possession and exorcism. The goal in this study is to consider these "supernatural" or paranormal stories carefully and ask if they are historically plausible in view of their own cultural milieu and genre and the wide variety of parallel reports that remain in modern and global possession accounts.

Summing Up

When we consider the history of interpretation of texts related to the exorcisms performed by Jesus, various reasons exist in scholarship for challenging their historicity. These challenges often include, but are not limited to, (1) correlation with the author's literary aims and *tendenz*; (2) redactional problems, including the addition or subtraction of minor details when we compare with parallels; and (3) the placement of the accounts in each Gospel for literary purposes. Studies in ancient biography and historiography help to ease the grip of these claims as attempts to disprove historicity since they provide a framework for literary conventions, even for stories that contain material that is implausible in view of some Western interpretive frameworks.

In summary, this chapter provides a very brief prolegomenon for how the exorcism stories will be compared in the following chapters. In the following chapters, a key focus is placed on how the global experience of possession and exorcism compare to the experience found in the biblical texts at hand. What does a multicultural lens tell us about the historical plausibility of the exorcisms performed by Jesus? While a wide variety of differences will surface when we broadly consider possession experience globally and interreligiously, there are familiar characteristics of possession and exorcism experience found in both Jesus' ancient cultural matrix and the modern one. This multicultural lens is revealing since it makes clear a bed of cross-cultural elements of spirit possession that are similar in nature to characteristics in the biblical text. In

[60] Keener, *Christobiography*, 333.

summary, we ask if the general impression about Jesus' exorcism accounts is historically plausible when assessed through the cultural lens, the genre lens, and the multicultural lens. This exegetical and multicultural approach provides a framework by which we can genuinely ask if it is possible to perceive the possession and exorcism stories we find in the Gospels and Acts as historically plausible.

II

Characteristics of Spirit Possession in Biblical and Multicultural Perspectives

4

Spirits Make Me Sick!

Spirit Possession and Illness

While the connection between spirit possession and illness may at first seem implausible, the evidence for such a connection is well attested in a variety of ancient texts, as well as modern anthropological and ethnographic writings. This chapter intends to bring forward evidence showing what is already known in anthropological and cross-cultural conversations: the attribution of illness to spirit possession is a prevalent cross-cultural phenomenon. This proposal rests on the widespread belief in spirits that is also present in cross-cultural studies. Ann M. Nolan clearly states this prevailing view found in cross-cultural studies when she argues, "It is widely accepted by scholars who study spirit possession in different countries and cultures that the concept of possession by both good and evil spirits who are capable of taking control of human beings has existed universally from earliest antiquity across many different cultures."[1]

The main thesis of chapters 4–6 can be simply stated: evidence for spirit possession characteristics, analogous to what is described in the New Testament, is ample in cross-cultural research. This analogous evidence cannot be dismissed on either of the following bases: (1) it is possible to interpret the

---

[1]   Ann M. Nolan, "Spirit Possession and Mental Health in New Zealand Context," in *Spirit Possession, Theology, and Identity: A Pacific Exploration*, ed. Elaine M. Wainwright with Philip Culbertson and Susan Smith (Hindmarsh, Australia: ATF Press, 2010), 63. See also Philip Coons, "The Differential Diagnoses of Possession States," *Dissociation* 6.4 (1993): 213–21; Miriam Azaunce, "Is It Schizophrenia or Spirit Possession?" *Journal of Social Distress and the Homeless* 4.3 (1995): 255–63; S. N. Chiu, "Historical, Religious, and Medical Perspectives of Possession Phenomenon," *Hong Kong Journal of Psychiatry* 10.1 (2000): 14–18.

phenomena in a variety of ways (such as some sort of attention-seeking behavior) or (2) that the testimonies are counterfeit. In other words, the accounts are too plentiful and too cross-cultural for varieties of reductive interpretations. Further, the interreligious nature of the accounts forestalls any argument that the characteristics presented in chapters 4 through 6 are influenced by Christianity and reproduced in modernity because of Christian influence.

Rather, echoing the work of Arthur Kleinman, a medical anthropologist, medicine is a cultural system. In other words, cultural understandings of illness are inherently important and critical for understanding how health care is perceived in both the world of Jesus and the world now. Kleinman's own words are helpful in understanding this interconnectedness:

> In the same sense in which we speak of religion or language or kinship as cultural systems, we can view medicine as a cultural system, a system of symbolic meanings anchored in particular arrangements of social institutions and patterns of interpersonal interactions. In every culture, illness, the response to it, individuals experiencing it and treating it, and the social institutions relating to it are all systematically interconnected. The totality of these systems is the health care system. Put somewhat differently, the health care system, like other cultural systems integrates the health-related components of society. These include patterns of belief about the causes of illness; norms governing choice and evaluation of treatment; socially-legitimated statuses, roles, power relationships, interaction settings, and institutions.[2]

This research is an invitation to participate as an observer of a wide variety of cultures, ancient and modern, that exhibit spirit-possession-related illness in ways that are analogous to NT accounts. Simply stated, in many cultures spirit possession is sometimes an explanation for a person's illness. Some texts also demonstrate that spirits can cause ailment without possession; these accounts are included in the study below since even though possession is absent, the ailment is attributed to a spirit. Intriguingly, this cultural expression, which can be interpreted in various etic perspectives, is cross-cultural. In other words, while Kleinman's approach is helpful and balancing in that it requires a "thick description" of each cultural expression of illness, it does not overtly emphasize how to engage when widespread cultural experience acknowledges similar phenomena.

As a result, the primary focus of this chapter is to explore ancient backgrounds, biblical texts, and anthropological literature that reveal the widely

---

[2] Arthur Kleinman, *Patients and Healers in the Context of Culture: An Exploration of the Borderland between Anthropology, Medicine, and Psychiatry* (Berkeley: University of California Press, 1980), 24.

documented cross-cultural relationship between illness and spirit possession phenomena.[3] As noted above, anthropologists have already established a relationship between spirit possession and illness in a wide variety of cultures that maintain belief in spirit possession. Murdock argues that over 97 percent of the societies he studied associate possession and illness.[4] Richard C. Fiddler claims, "Finding societies where it is believed that 'evil spirits' cause illness and misfortune is easy."[5] To clarify, possession belief is expressed with and without associating trance behavior. For example, belief in invading spirits, which provide an aetiology for illness, does not require possession trance.[6]

[3]   Janice Boddy, "Spirits and Selves in Northern Sudan: The Cultural Therapeutics of Possession and Trance," *American Ethnologist* 15.1 (1988): 4; Boddy, *Wombs and Alien Spirits: Women, Men, and the Zar Cult in Northern Sudan* (Madison: University of Wisconsin Press, 1989), 8, 120; Erika Bourguignon, ed., *Religion, Altered States of Consciousness, and Social Change* (Columbus: Ohio State University Press, 1973); Vincent Crapanzano and Vivian Garrison, eds., *Case Studies in Spirit Possession* (New York: Wiley, 1977); Kaja Finkler, *Spiritualist Healers in Mexico: Successes and Failures of Alternative Therapeutics* (South Hadley, Mass.: Bergin and Garvey, 1985); Lauri Honko, *Krankheitsprojektile: Untersuchung über eine urtümliche Krankheitserklärung*, Folklore Fellow Communications 178 (Helsinki: Academia Scientiarum Fennica, 1959), 31–32, documents the widespread notion of spirits as capable of entering bodies and causing illness; Setha M. Low, "The Medicalization of Healing Cults in Latin America," *American Ethnologist* 15.1 (1988): 136–54; Aihwa Ong, "The Production of Possession: Spirits and the Multinational Corporation in Malaysia," *American Ethnologist* 15.1 (1988): 28–42; Larry G. Peters and Douglass Price-Williams, "Toward an Experiential Analysis of Shamanism," *American Ethnologist* 7.3 (1980): 397–413; Lila Shaara and Andrew Strathern, "Preliminary Analysis of the Relationship between Altered States of Consciousness, Healing, and Social Structure," *American Anthropologist* 94.1 (1992): 145–60; Michael James Winkelman, "Shamans and Other 'Macro-Religious' Healers: A Cross-cultural Study of Their Origins, Nature and Social Transformation," *Ethnos* 18.3 (1990): 308–52; Norbert L. Vecchiato, "Illness, Therapy, and Change in Ethiopian Possession Cults," *Africa* 63.2 (1993): 176–96. These sources are only a select few that document the relationship. The remainder of the chapter will provide a broader array and presentation of further evidence that relates the themes cross-culturally. Additionally, Human Resource Area Files (eHRAF) provide 131 documents that relate spirits as a cause of disease.

[4]   George Murdock, *Theories of Illness: A World Survey* (Pittsburgh: University of Pittsburgh Press, 1980), 72–76. See also Benedicte Laste, "Possession, Exorcism, and Mental Illness: A Multiple Case Study across Worldviews" (PhD diss., California Institute of Integral Studies, 2015).

[5]   Richard C. Fiddler, "Spirit Possession as Exculpation, with Examples from the Sarawak Chinese," in *The Seen and the Unseen: Shamanism, Mediumship and Possession in Borneo*, ed. Robert L. Winzeler, Borneo Research Council Monograph Series 2 (Williamsburg, Va.: Borneo Research Council, 1993), 211, 222. Fiddler indicates that cultures where the interpretation of possession falls into the category of "exculpation" are more difficult to find, even though he argues the exculpation view is more widespread than most have thought.

[6]   Carol R. Ember and Christina Carolus, "Altered States of Consciousness," in *Explaining Human Culture*, ed. Carol R. Ember (eHRAF, 2017), 8, https://hraf.yale.edu/ehc/assets/summaries/pdfs/altered-states-of-consciousness.pdf.

Resisting the conclusions of those who adhere to natural law to discount causation that is suprahuman, the phenomenon is not at risk of extinction; nor does it show signs of diminished experience as a strong tendency. Rather, in many areas experience burgeons despite attempts for Western modernization and other impacts of globalization. For example, Smith documents a global increase in the view that possession is a "central concept in the realm of mental health."[7] This ideology is increasingly popular in Taiwan, Korea, Africa, Micronesia, South America, and the U.S. He concludes that "the practice of embodiment healing is now increasingly accepted in Hinduism, Islam, Christianity, folk Buddhism, Chinese religion, and doubtless elsewhere in other forms of religious practice."[8] Further, many cultures associate illness, afflicted upon the person by a spirit(s), with the call to spirit mediumship or cult initiation.[9]

When considering the NT, Keener proposes that while demonization and illness are often linked in summary accounts (Acts 5:17), the summaries also often distinguish between illnesses and illnesses caused by possession.[10] Likewise, medical anthropology also distinguishes between aetiologies of illness. Keener remarks,

> Medical anthropology distinguishes cultures where sickness is caused only naturally from cultures where it can be caused by personal agents such as deities, spirits, or the use of witchcraft. Although some cultures do not associate spirits with sickness, a vast number of cultures do. (Still, in some cultures where many still attribute sickness to spirits, people nevertheless depend more on medicine than on spiritual remedies.)[11]

Despite widespread belief in the relationship between possession and illness in a global consideration, the most common Western view is a reductionist

[7] Frederick M. Smith, "Possession, Embodiment, and Ritual in Mental Health Care in India," *Journal of Ritual Studies* 24.2 (2010): 22.

[8] Smith, "Possession, Embodiment, and Ritual," 23, 30–31. Smith's makes an analogous argument, noting that the ancient Indian possession experiences (for example from *Susruta* 6.60.13) compare with modern experiences. He argues that the "notion of ritual efficacy" was developed in India's ancient worldview.

[9] I. M. Lewis, *Religion in Context: Cults and Charisma* (Cambridge: Cambridge University Press, 1996), 118; Lewis, *Ecstatic Religion: A Study of Shamanism and Spirit Possession*, 3rd ed. (London: Routledge, 2003), 90–113; George N. Appell and Laura W. R. Appell, "To Converse with the Gods: The Rungus *Bobolizan*—Spirit Medium and Priestess," in Winzeler, *The Seen and the Unseen*, 4, argue that the Bulusu' of Borneo are an exception to this crosscultural tendency as they do not associate illness with the call to mediumship.

[10] Craig S. Keener, *Acts: An Exegetical Commentary: 3:1–14:28* (Grand Rapids: Baker, 2012), 2460, n. 1692. See especially Luke 4:40–41; 6:18; 7:21; 9:1; 13:32; Acts 8:7; 19:12.

[11] Craig S. Keener, *Miracles: The Credibility of the New Testament Accounts*, 2 vols. (Grand Rapids: Baker, 2011), 2:803.

and naturalizing interpretation of the phenomenon. Brian Levack traces this trend of thought diachronically from antiquity through the nineteenth century, summarizing its effect on interpreters of NT texts:

> The claim that demoniacs were "really" suffering from a medical condition that had "natural" causes—from an organic disease or a mental illness—has been the most consistent secular, rationalist analysis of demonic possession since the period of Christian antiquity.[12]

However, it is also imperative to note that the Westernized framework of interpretation did not gain pervasive support until the nineteenth century with the dawn of positivistic views.[13]

Elaine M. Wainright additionally recognizes the disparity present in modern interpretive views and the way possession phenomena are experienced and reported among cultures with differing worldviews.

> For many in the contemporary world, the notion of spirit possession would be seen as anachronistic, belonging to a previous era in which belief in a spirit world helped to explain phenomena which now can be given a more scientific explanation, whether that be medical, psychological, sociological, or anthropological. For others, however, the presence of and possession by spirits remains a significant aspect of their worldview and/or religious belief.[14]

Michael Lambeck adds that spirit possession has the possibility of permeating themes of every part of life, including "illness and therapy, interpersonal relationships, private experience, marriage, the articulation of family boundaries and continuity between the generations, world view, divination, social thought, morality, political process, conflict resolution, myth, fantasy and fun."[15] Even so, this monograph must limit what aspects of possession are possible to

---

[12] Brian P. Levack, *The Devil Within: Possession and Exorcism in the Christian West* (New Haven: Yale University Press, 2013), 113.

[13] Levack, *Devil Within*, 113. Levack notes that the Europeans who held this view before the nineteenth century were Reginald Scot, Thomas Hobbes, Baruch Spinoza, and Balthasar Bekker. Others who resisted making such a blanket interpretation include John Deacon, Samuel Harnett, Benito Feijóo, and Johann Salomo Semler. The view that the devil was "worked *through* nature; that he in fact was the ultimate cause of all illness" made interpreters reluctant to reduce all interpretations to biomedical causes. See Levack, *Devil Within*, 114 (emphasis original).

[14] Elaine M. Wainwright, "Introduction," in Wainwright, with Culbertson and Smith, *Spirit Possession, Theology, and Identity*, v.

[15] Michael Lambeck, "From Disease to Discourse: Remarks on the Conceptualization of Trance and Spirit Possession," in *Altered States of Consciousness and Mental Health: A Cross-cultural Perspective*, ed. Colleen A. Ward (Newbury Park, Calif.: Sage, 1989), 45.

survey due to reasons of space and time.[16] The lack of analysis related to the way possession reports differ from NT reports is not meant to diminish the differences or devalue them in any way. The lack of simplicity reflected in the phenomena is notable along with the need to examine its meaning, reproduction, organization, and structure carefully in view of emic terms.[17]

For example, when considering a list of symptoms provided by Rouget one will quickly realize that there are similarities and differences between global and NT reports of spirit possession characteristics. Rouget's list of symptoms associated with a trance state including "trembling, shuddering, horripilation, swooning, falling to the ground, yawning, lethargy, convulsions, foaming at the mouths, protruding eyes, large extrusion of the tongue, paralysis of a limb, thermal disturbances, insensitivity to pain, tics, noisy breathing, fixed stare."[18] This research aims to consider the analogues while also acknowledging the differences, even though they cannot be surveyed fully here.

Empirical proof for the validity of the following reports and aetiological interpretations are not the focus of this study. The focus is on surveying cross-cultural reports of possession and exorcism experience present in anthropological and ethnographic study to consider how they are analogous to NT reports. A goal exists to avoid reductionist interpretations and allow the reports to represent the observed experiences of the people groups that are surveyed. It is quite likely that the Western reader will be challenged by the content of the reports below; an etic interpretation may come to mind. Lambeck summarizes the way that global possession stories challenge natural assumptions and requests that reports are handled carefully:

> In many of its manifestations possession violates our own cultural distinctions and deeply held assumptions concerning the "natural" differences between such pairs of opposites of self and others, seriousness and comedy, reality and illusion, and perhaps most critically, art and life.[19]

While variations in interpretation do exist, and are not discounted, the goal is to read the accounts as eyewitness reports and personal stories about cross-cultural experiences with possession and exorcism. Lambek emphasizes that these experiences are the "lived reality of a significant portion of the human

[16] This statement applies to chapters 4–6, which survey three categories of characteristics.
[17] Lambek, "From Disease to Discourse," 45. Lambek finds aetiological approaches problematic and at times reductive and suggests "turning away from casual, etiological explanations."
[18] Gilbert Rouget, *Music and Trance: A Theory of the Relations between Music and Possession* (Chicago: University of Chicago Press, 1985), 13.
[19] Lambeck, "From Disease to Discourse," 52–53.

population around the world. The spread and diversity of these states of consciousness also offer one of the most intriguing insights into the human mind and experience."[20]

Stated once more, the argument of this chapter is that spirit possession and illness are widely attested interrelated phenomena in global experience. This argument contributes to the larger discussion of NT accounts of possession and exorcism as historically plausible within a cross-cultural framework. As a result, this chapter seeks to provide a global picture of cultures where possession is an expressed aetiology for illness and where exorcism is viewed as a viable cure for illness. Making an important reminder, the goal is not to prove the validity or superiority of any interpretation of spirit possession experience. The trajectory is to trace reports of the experience of spirit possession that causes illness and exorcism that causes cure throughout a variety of cultures. Reports of evil spirits as a cause for certain physical ailments, as found in the NT, are not without parallel in congruent reports of global spirit possession experience. In summary, a global survey of spirit possession phenomena in a wide variety of cultures and religions provides evidence for a persistent belief that evil spirits, deities, ghosts, etc. may be interpreted as a cause of illness. These claims parallel the eyewitness claims found in New Testament accounts of spirit possession where possession characteristics cause ailments such as being mute (Matt 9:32–33; 12:22–23; Luke 9:17; 11:14), deaf (Mark 9:25), or blind (Matt 12:24–30); having epileptic-like fits (Luke 9:37–43); or being bent over for an extended time (Luke 13:10–17).[21]

To survey this theme globally, what follows will provide examples of cultural views of possession-related illness in both ancient perspectives and global perspectives that represent every major region of the world. Given a larger allotment of space much more evidence could be added; it multiplies quickly. However, since the survey covers a wide variety of regions and cultures, an exhaustive approach is not necessary. The documentation below is at minimum adequate in representing a widespread and global relationship between spirit possession and illness from ancient biblical times until now.

Presented first are ancient perspectives. These are followed by modern anthropological perspectives. In anthropological perspective, evidence is

---

[20] Ronald Fischer and Sivaporn Tasananukorn, "Altered States of Consciousness, Spirit Mediums and Predictive Processing: A Cultural Cognition Model of Spirit Possession," *Journal of Consciousness Studies* 25.11–12 (2018): 180.

[21] When considering mental health, we might also consider the account of the Gerasene demoniac (Matt 8:28–34; Mark 5:1–20; Luke 8:26–39) as both Mark and Luke acknowledge that exorcism restored the man to his "right mind." Even so, to keep this monograph sizable, physical maladies will only be addressed for right now.

arranged geographically by major regions of the world. Regions will be treated in the following order: (1) Africa, (2) Asia, (3) the Middle East, (4) Middle America and the Caribbean, (5) Oceania, (6) South America, (7) North America, and (8) Europe. In each region the relationship between spirits and illness will be tracked along with some of the prevailing symptoms of the varieties of maladies that may result.

Ancient Perspectives

Ancient Near East and Israel

Egyptian, Mesopotamian, Syrian, and Anatolian cultures maintained views on demons and their activities. Varieties of demons are found capable of affecting people in different ways. Related to illness, spirits of the dead were capable of afflicting individuals (especially due to improper burial). Further, Joachim Friedrich Quack records that in Egyptian texts, "illness-inducing higher entities who are mentioned in rituals for protection are often considered to be demons."[22] Mesopotamian incantations were utilized to "avert demons or cure illnesses inflicted by them."[23] Hittite incantation rituals were utilized to expel demons that caused illness.[24] Summarizing ANE perspectives, Schmitt describes demons as "credited with being the sources of the sickness of the body, mental insanity, child death, and other forms of distress."[25]

In Israelite perspectives[26] both the belief in spirit possession and spirit-related illness are present. A few examples can illustrate the presence of the correlation. First, in the story of David and Saul (1 Sam 16:14–23) David plays the lyre, causing the tormenting spirit, believed to be sent by God, to depart. Even though no explanation is given as to how the spirit torments Saul (possession or affliction), the contemporaneous context reveals belief in

[22] Joachim Friedrich Quack, "Demons: Ancient Near East: Egypt," in *Encyclopedia of the Bible and Its Reception*, ed. Hans-Josef Klauck et al., vol. 5 (Berlin: De Gruyter, 2012), 532. Quack also highlights that it is difficult to make an ontological difference between demons and gods since these figures are discussed alongside gods.

[23] Daniel Schwemer, "Demons: Ancient Near East: Mesopotamia, Syria and Anatolia," in Klauck et al., *Encyclopedia of the Bible and Its Reception*, 5:534.

[24] Schwemer, "Demons," 536.

[25] Rüdiger Schmitt, "Demons: Hebrew Bible/Old Testament," in Klauck et al., *Encyclopedia of the Bible and Its Reception*, 5:536.

[26] For more detail on the fuller scope of Israelite perspectives related to spirit possession and exorcism, see Eric Eve, *The Jewish Context of Jesus' Miracles*, JSNTSup 231 (London: Sheffield, 2002), 326–49; Graham H. Twelftree, *Jesus the Exorcist: A Contribution to the Study of the Historical Jesus* (Eugene, Ore.: Wipf and Stock, 2011), 13–52; Amanda Witmer, *Jesus, the Galilean Exorcist: His Exorcisms in Social and Political Context*, LNTS 459 (London: T&T Clark, 2012), 22–60.

demons and their ability to affect humanity in a variety of ways, including with illness.[27] Witmer marks the progression of thought that takes place from the original Saul account to Josephus' retelling. In 1 Samuel Saul was assuaged through David's music which caused the departure of the spirit. Josephus' account reflects a shift from affliction to possession as he describes David as driving out (ἐκβάλλω) the evil spirit.[28]

Further, Solomon, in his unmatched wisdom, is linked with having the knowledge to treat possession-related illness. Josephus recapitulates the link, "And God granted him (Solomon) knowledge of the art used against demons for the benefit and healing of men. He also composed incantations by which illnesses are relieved, and left behind forms of exorcisms with which those possessed by demons drive them out, never to return."[29]

Texts from the Second Temple period broaden the link between demons and illness. In the Enochic tradition evil demons are capable of causing plagues, illness, and infertility. Further, the spirits in Testament of Solomon 18 are the cause of infirmities impacting various body parts. In Jubilees 10:1–2 demons bring destruction upon Noah's children by blinding and killing them, the worst impact of illness. Additionally, in 49:2 the demons seemingly assist Mastema in killing the first-born of Egypt.[30] In Tobit, Sarah's seven engagements end just before consummation due to the demon named Asmodeus who murders her fiancés.[31] Additionally, Qumran sectarian texts

---

[27] Ida Fröhlich, "Demons and Illness in Second Temple Judaism: Theory and Practice," in *Demons and Illness from Antiquity to the Early-Modern Period*, ed. Siam Bhayro and Catherine Rider (Leiden: Brill, 2017), 82. Fröhlich suggests that many interpret Saul's illness as bipolar disorder, considering other demonological literature that reveals a connection between mental illness and demons. See also Markham J. Geller, "Freud and Mesopotamian Magic," in *Mesopotamian Magic: Textual, Historical, and Interpretative Perspectives*, ed. Tzvi Abusch and Karel van der Toorn (Groningen: Styx, 1999), 49–55; Marten Stol, "Psychosomatic Suffering in Ancient Mesopotamia," in Abusch and van der Toorn, *Mesopotamian Magic*, 57–68. Stol remarks, "To a Babylonian, illness was not just a corporeal disorder. It had been inflicted upon him by supernatural forces." Stol, "Psychosomatic Suffering," 57.

[28] Witmer, *Jesus, the Galilean Exorcist*, 43.

[29] Josephus, *Ant.* 8.45–49.

[30] Jacques Van Ruiten, "Angels and Demons in the Book of *Jubilees*," in *Angels: The Concept of Celestial Beings—Origins, Development and Reception*, ed. Friedrich V. Reiterer, Tobias Nicklas, and Karin Schöpflin (New York: De Gruyter, 2007), 600.

[31] The name Asmodeus has Persian influence and is possibly a derivative of Aeshma Daeva, who was the "demon of wrath, rage, and violence" of Persian Zoroastrianism. See William Brandt Bradshaw, "Demonology in Hebrew and Jewish Traditions: A Study in New Testament Origins" (PhD diss., University of St Andrews, 1963), 138. See Tobit 3:8 for Sarah's maid's accusation, which aids in concluding that the demon controls Sarah when each murder takes place.

attest to spirit-related illness, likely exemplifying a type of affliction rather than full-scale possession. In the Genesis Apocryphon, the plague affecting Pharoah has demonic causation, and relief is found through Abram's laying-on of hands which presumably rids him of the demon.[32] Similarly, in the Prayer of Nabonidus (4Q242) a king, aided by a Jewish exorcist, prays prayers to the Jewish God that an evil spirit will be expelled from his household. The demon is expelled, and the person is presumably healed from an "evil ulcer."[33] In agreement with Witmer, both Genesis Apocryphon and the Prayer of Nabonidus are evidence that "evil spirits were thought to cause affliction in the form of illness to persons and households in the ancient world."[34]

In the Dead Sea scrolls, incantation prayers are prayed to protect one from the effects of the demonic. For instance, one prayer for deliverance requests the absence of pain: "Neither let pain nor the evil inclination, Take possession of my bones."[35] Other apotropaic texts include 4Q560[36] (portrays demons harming pregnant women with an "evil madness"/illness)[37] and 11Q11 (evil spirit possesses and causes illness), which according to Fröhlich "may have been used for practical purposes, i.e. to prevent or heal illness, physical harm, and mental disorders. Practical texts thus reflect the everyday ideas of their users

[32] R. J. S. Barrett-Lennard, *Christian Healing after the New Testament: Some Approaches to Illness in the Second, Third and Fourth Centuries* (New York: University Press of America, 1994), 334. See also Howard Clark Kee, *Medicine, Miracle and Magic in the New Testament Times*, SNTSMS 55 (Cambridge: Cambridge University Press, 1986), 24, who notes that the Aramaic term used to rebuke the demon is equivalent to the use of ἐπιτιμάω in the New Testament. Even so, some dismiss this example as one of possession due to the absence of the description of a "direct verbal encounter between a possessing spirit and an exorcist." See Witmer, *Jesus, the Galilean Exorcist*, 41.

[33] Both Qumran texts exhibit connections between healing, exorcism, and granting forgiveness for sin. Graham H. Twelftree, *In the Name of Jesus: Exorcism among Early Christians* (Grand Rapids: Baker, 2007), 17–18, argues that an exorcism is not represented here, since in his view "exorcist" is translated better as "diviner" in context. Witmer, *Jesus, the Galilean Exorcist*, 41, agrees, citing the absence of an encounter between spirit and exorcist.

[34] Witmer, *Jesus, the Galilean Exorcist*, 44.

[35] See Hermann Lichtenberger, "Demonology in the Scrolls and the New Testament," in *Text, Thought, and Practice in Qumran and Early Christianity*, ed. Ruth A. Clements and Daniel R. Schwarz, STDJ 84 (Leiden: Brill, 2009), 274.

[36] Fröhlich, "Demons and Illness," concludes, "In 4Q560 the demon is invisible—it penetrates the body and generates symptoms of fever, the feeling of heat inside and outside the body. In 11Q11 the demon is visible—it is similar to that of the Mesopotamian sheriff-demon who kills either by fear or physical harm . . ."

[37] For more detail, see David Hamidović, "Illness and Healing through Spell and Incantation in the Dead Sea Scrolls," in Bhayro and Rider, *Demons and Illness*, 97–110.

regarding illness and healing."[38] Further, Fagen proposes that the tradition of phylacteries began as a means of protection (amulet) from demons.[39]

As the pages of history turned, the world of Jewish demonology proliferated. Texts like the Babylonian Talmud, rabbinic Jewish texts, Aramaic and Hebrew amulets and incantation bowls, and Jewish magical texts all aid in revealing the progression of Jewish demonological perspectives. Gideon Bohak finds connection between possession and illness in this literature, notably in a sixth century CE amulet that was utilized to drive away a variety of demons. In this amulet is the mention of the demon *kephalargia* (which in Greek means headache) that is adjured from the ears and head.

The first-century Palestinian environment inherited Israelite perspectives familiar with the concept of spirit-related illness. Even so, while possession-related illness and the cure of exorcism are part of Israel's framework, other avenues were also sought to treat illness. In essence, spirit-related illness is situated alongside a variety of other perspectives about illness. The one unifying element is the viewpoint that God is the divine source of all healing. Magicians, physicians, healing shrines, natural medicines, and religious healers such as Rabbi Hanina ben Dosa play a role, but the ultimate source for healing comes from Yahweh himself. Jesus enters a cultural milieu with these elements of care and perceptions of illness as "cultural systems" of health care.[40] In other words, Jesus enters a world where it is culturally appropriate to believe that spirits may potentially cause illness and where exorcism is a possible cure. Twelftree makes this clear in his definition of exorcism that characterizes first century A.D., saying, "Exorcism was a form of healing used when demons or evil spirits were thought to have entered a person and to be responsible for sickness and was the attempt to control and cast out or expel evil spiritual beings or demons from people."[41] In this cultural milieu, one finds Jesus the exorcist.

Greco-Roman Antiquity

In Greco-Roman antiquity, the reality of spirits is part of the ancient milieu. Brenk alludes to the prevalence of thought about the spiritual realm. Further, spirit possession and illness were at times associated. One of the most directly related elements to NT study is the ancient conception of "the sacred disease"

[38]　Fröhlich, "Demons and Illness," 85.

[39]　Ruth S. Fagen, "Phylacteries," *ABD* 5:370. Fagen argues that phylacteries were later reframed as an aid for prayer.

[40]　For an introductory survey of each avenue of health care in Israelite thought, see Ian G. Wallis, *The Galilean Wonderworker: Reassessing Jesus' Reputation for Healing and Exorcism* (Eugene, Ore.: Cascade, 2020), 17–34.

[41]　Twelftree, *Jesus the Exorcist*, 13.

and whether it is caused by a spirit. Luck describes the ancient Greco-Roman world as "populated with all sorts of spirits." Luck attests to the ability of spirits, in ancient Greco-Roman conception, to cause "a wide range of pathological conditions—epilepsy, insanity, even sleepwalking or the delirium of high fever—were interpreted as the work of evil spirits."[42]

New Testament Accounts

In NT accounts a variety of illnesses related to spirit possession appear in the scenes of the exorcisms Jesus performs. As noted above, these spirit-possession-related ailments include being mute (Matt 9:32–33; 12:22–23; Luke 9:17; 11:14), deaf (Mark 9:25), and blind (Matt 12:24–30); having epileptic-like fits (Luke 9:37–43); and being bent over for an extended time (Luke 13:10–17). In each text exorcism is shown as a cure to each person's ailments. The goal of this section is to exegete these possession characteristics that are associated with spirit possession.

Distinguishing between Illness and Disease in NT Studies?

Before turning to a variety of modern stories that share the characteristic of possession-related illness, a brief introductory consideration of medical anthropology's proposed distinction between illness and disease, as has been utilized in New Testament scholarship, is helpful. Kleinman defines the parameters utilized to distinguish between disease and illness. Disease is "biological and/or psychological processes," whereas illness is "the psychological experience and meaning of the perceived disease." In other words, "Illness is the shaping of disease into behavior and experience. It is created by personal, social, and cultural reactions to disease."[43] By utilizing this distinction, John Dominic Crossan is able to conclude that Jesus healed illnesses rather than curing diseases.[44] He states, "I presume that Jesus, who did not and could not cure that disease or any other one, healed the poor man's illness by refusing to accept the disease's ritual."[45] In agreement with Wallis, this perspective is attractive given the framework that Jesus liberates the marginalized and grants entrance into the Kingdom of God. Even so, as Wallis suggests, "it is highly questionable whether the distinction between curing a disease and healing an

---

[42] Georg Luck, *Arcana Mundi: Magic and the Occult in the Greek and Roman Worlds* (Baltimore: Johns Hopkins University Press, 1985), 165.

[43] Kleinman, *Patients and Healers*, 72.

[44] John Dominic Crossan, *Jesus: A Revolutionary Biography* (San Francisco: HarperSanFrancisco, 1994), 82–83. See also Crossan, *The Historical Jesus: The Life of a Mediterranean Jewish Peasant* (San Francisco: HarperSanFrancisco, 1991), 320–26.

[45] Crossan, *Jesus*, 82.

illness would have been recognized in first century Palestine where, as we have seen, there was little understanding of the biomedical basis for illness."[46] Secondly, Wallis adds that since this ancient society is communal in nature, it is extremely difficult to draw a line between disease and illness given all disease impacts the group in a variety of ways (contagion, lost workers, lost income, etc). Thirdly, Wallis summarizes that this approach falls short in really explaining why Jesus gains such popularity as a healer:

> It is difficult to see how encouraging communities to welcome ailing members back into the fold would account for his appeal and popularity. Surely Jesus must have been doing more than that to have attracted so much attention among ordinary people who had next to no access to health provision and for whom illness was, as we have seen, a debilitating curse and one that impacted detrimentally upon family and community members as well–people who, in most cases, appear to have shown little interest in Jesus' message, but who were attracted by rumors of Jesus' healing powers. . . . What is more, Jesus conducted an itinerant ministry, and it is difficult to envisage how an itinerant with no institutionally endorsed authority would have been in a position to persuade villagers and townspeople to risk the survival of their communities by reintegrating members thought to be suffering from threatening conditions who had been quarantined for the purpose of containment. For as much as Jesus earned a reputation for charismatic authority (Mark 1:27; 2:10), there is no explicit evidence of him exercising it in this way, nor does it seem plausible.[47]

Given the above considerations, the distinction between disease and illness as utilized in medical anthropology will not be employed in the following exegesis of NT texts and the symptoms suffered by those who experience demonic ailments. Instead, agreeing again with Wallis, what makes more sense is to consider that Jesus gained a reputation for healing encounters that led to the abatement and cessation of varieties of symptoms of disease. In other words, while Kleinman is right to assert the in-depth and complex relationship between culture and medicine, the bifurcation between illness and disease does not seem to wholly apply in contextual NT study.

The Possessed Boy—Mark 9:14–29 (Luke 9:37–43; Matthew 17:14–21)

All three Synoptics record an account of persons who are demonized and experiencing muteness. In Mark 9:14–29 a man from the crowd brings forward his son, whom he describes as ἔχοντα πνεῦμα ἄλαλον ("having a mute spirit"). At the height of the scene, Jesus rebukes the unclean spirit, "mute and

---

[46] Wallis, *Galilean Wonderworker*, 58.
[47] Wallis, *Galilean Wonderworker*, 59–61.

deaf spirit (τὸ ἄλαλον καὶ κωφὸν πνεῦμα), I command you to come out from him and no longer enter him" (Mark 9:25). Adela Yarbro Collins suggests that Jesus likely addressed the demon as both mute and deaf due to the close association with muteness and deafness.[48] It is possible that the spirit is referred to as mute given that this account lacks the spirit's speech through the possessed person. Rather, as Collins describes, "the possession is manifested in physical symptoms." It is possible that the boy becomes mute and deaf during episodes of the demon's acting out since the demon is unable to respond like in other possession accounts. Collins summarizes, "The point may be that the boy was unable to speak or to hear others during a seizure."[49] In this case, the demon sees Jesus, which inspires the boy's symptoms (Mark 9:20). Even so, this proposal is not certain, and the boy could have experienced a long-term form of muteness that is relieved through exorcism. Whether short-term or long-term symptoms occur, the text reveals exorcism as the cure for the boy's ailment.

While Luke's account condenses the story referring only to a spirit who seizes the boy, Matthew records the boy's father as describing his son as suffering from epilepsy. Epilepsy was a known illness in antiquity, and as Collins suggests, "Mark's attribution of the symptoms of the boy to a spirit is similar to the popular or religious view of the sacred disease" described in Hippocratic literature.[50] Even so, the cure prevents complex deliberations related to the aetiology of the boy's illness. In all three accounts, Jesus exorcises the spirit and the removal of the spirit allows for the boy's cure. While Mark's account gives the most detail (the boy appears to be dead and Jesus took his hand and lifted him), Matthew and Luke summarize the effect more precisely, noting that he was instantly cured (Matt 17:18) and healed and returned to his father (Luke 9:42). In other words, the cure reveals the perspective of Synoptic writers who attest to a belief in spirit-possession-related illness and a cure of exorcism. Each account brings forward Jesus as effective in his ability to perceive the cause and bring the cure. Even though a medical approach will often ascribe the cause as epilepsy, what is most important, as M. Carolina Escobar Vargas argues, is that the text offers "a clear identification of symptoms resembling an epileptic attack with demon possession. Christ cured the boy by expelling the spirit that possessed him."[51] This approach reveals more closely the emic viewpoint.

[48]   Adela Yarbro Collins, *Mark: A Commentary* (Minneapolis: Fortress, 2007), 439.

[49]   Collins, *Mark*, 439. Collins notes that this phenomenon was described in Hippocratic literature, sometimes called "falling sickness."

[50]   Collins, *Mark*, 435.

[51]   M. Carolina Escobar Vargas, "Demons in Lapidaries? The Evidence of the Madrid MS Escorial, h.I.15," in Bhayro and Rider, *Demons and Illness*, 269.

The Mute (Blind) Demoniac—Matthew 9:32–34; 12:22–24; Luke 11:14–15

While the previous account seemingly prioritizes epileptic-like symptoms over muteness, the account of the mute demoniac maintains focus on muteness as a characteristic of demonization. Matthew 9:32–34 describes the mute man as being demonized (ἄνθρωπον κωφὸν[52] δαιμονιζόμενον), attributing more directly the muteness to the man rather than the spirit/demon. Upon having the demon cast out, the mute man speaks. In Matthew 12:22 a parallel account is reported, except that the man is also blind.[53] Upon being healed, he speaks and sees. Further, Luke 11:14 is straightforward about the aetiology of the man's muteness.[54] It is caused by τοῦ δαιμονίου (καὶ αὐτὸ ἦν)[55] κωφόν, indicating that the demon itself was κωφός, a term that may indicate muteness or deafness.[56] Considering Luke's indication that the man speaks after the exorcistic event, it seems clear that the term indicates muteness in this instance. Ancients were not unfamiliar with the potential for demons to inflict these ailments on humans. *Testament of Solomon* 12:2 records the demon's response when asked how it causes these afflictions: "I turn their ears around backward and make them dumb and deaf." The verse also adds, "I blind children . . . and make them dumb and deaf."

Both Matthew and Luke record the man's cure. Matthew 9 and Luke 11 record that the demon was cast out while Matthew 12 refers to Jesus' healing of the man, interpreting the exorcism as a form of healing. Interestingly, the cure is not debated in the controversy that follows. Craig Evans adds, "The proof of the exorcism is seen in the man's ability to speak. . . . The Pharisees, however, are not impressed. They cannot deny the miracle, but they can attribute the power to Satan."[57]

---

[52] The term for muteness, κωφός, sometimes also alludes to deafness.

[53] R. T. France argues when comparing the accounts in Matthew 9 and 12, "it is customary to speak of a Matthean doublet, though it is interesting that the demoniac in 12:22 is blind as well as dumb . . ." R. T. France, *Gospel of Matthew*, NICNT (Grand Rapids: Eerdmans, 2007), 369.

[54] E. Earle Ellis, *The Gospel of Luke* (Grand Rapids: Eerdmans, 1974), 167; Erich Klostermann, *Das Lukasevangelium*, Handbuch zum Neuen Testament 5 (Tübingen: Mohr Siebeck, 1929), 127; Darrell L. Bock, *Luke 9:51–24:53*, BECNT (Grand Rapids: Baker, 1994), 1073.

[55] Bruce Metzger, *A Textual Commentary on the Greek New Testament* (Stuttgart: United Bible Societies, 1994), 133, argues for the weightiness of the shorter reading. Due to the possibility of the text as a Semitism written in Lukan style, the text is included but bracketed.

[56] BDAG, "κωφός," 580.

[57] Craig A. Evans, *Matthew*, New Cambridge Bible Commentary (Cambridge: Cambridge University Press, 2012), 211.

Related to the historical plausibility of this account, scholars vary in their assessment. Redaction critics wonder if the Synoptic parallels refer to one or two events.[58] Even so, ancient biography was free to rearrange material for various reasons. While Bock argues, the account is "deeply embedded in tradition,"[59] Meier struggles with it because of its brevity. He assesses Luke's version as originally connected with the sayings associated with the Beelzebul controversy and not as an account created by the author(s) of Q.[60] He interprets the man's muteness as a possible speech impediment.[61] Because of the controversy that follows this exorcism, Garland employs the criterion of embarrassment to argue that the early church would not have created this account.[62] The Jesus Seminar favors this story more than others and attributes much of it to Jesus since it fits the tendencies found in Jesus' way of dealing with opposition. They also allow as evidence, based on the prominence of exorcism, that the contrast between the kingdom and Satan fits Jesus' style.[63] As Craig A. Evans summarizes, "It was commonly believed that demons were causes of various ailments, such as blindness, deafness (and muteness), and a host of other maladies."[64] This account is no exception.

The Disabled Made Able—Luke 13:10–17

When considering the typical characteristics of an exorcism story, a few key parts are missing here, including the meeting with the demon, the demon's recognition of Jesus, and the demon's departure. While Luke does denote that the healing of the woman is the defeat of Satan and freedom from the "spirit of infirmity," there is no exorcistic command given by Jesus. Rather, Jesus proclaims freedom and lays his hands on the woman. The trouble is, as Momolu Armstrong Massaquoi writes, the tendency for modern writers to "create a division between the 'natural' and the 'supernatural,'" which causes distortion

---

[58] See Bock, *Luke 9:51–24:53*, 1067–68, for a summary of six views related to the relationship between the events. Luke abbreviates the account especially for his purposes, namely, to introduce the debate about the healing and the rejection Jesus experienced.

[59] See Bock, *Luke 9:51–24:53*, 1070.

[60] John P. Meier, *A Marginal Jew: Rethinking the Historical Jesus*, vol. 2 (New York: Doubleday, 1994), 656, arguing against Rudolf Bultmann, *The History of the Synoptic Tradition*, trans. John Marsh (Oxford: Blackwell, 1963), 13–14.

[61] Meier, *Marginal Jew*, 656.

[62] David E. Garland, *Luke*, Zondervan Exegetical Commentary on the New Testament (Grand Rapids: Zondervan, 2011), 481.

[63] Robert W. Funk and Roy W. Hoover, *The Five Gospels: What Did Jesus Really Say? The Search for the Authentic Words of Jesus* (Sonoma, Calif.: Polebridge, 1993), 329–30.

[64] Evans, *Matthew*, 210.

regarding accounts like this one.[65] G. Campbell Morgan summarizes the peri-cope's clear emphasis:

> Here, then, was a case in which an evil spirit had produced a physical malady that lasted eighteen years. There is no suggestion in this story that there was any-thing of immorality in this woman's life. She was the victim of demonic activity, under what circumstances we do not know, producing a physical disability. . . . Here, then, was a case of physical suffering, that was directly produced by the power of Satan. I am not attempting to explain this. There may be many other such cases in the world. There are other things we have not fathomed yet in life, concerning the mystery of suffering and the power of evil. We take the facts as revealed.[66]

As a result, even without some of the formal characteristics of an exorcism story, the modern reader concedes that in Luke's perspective some sort of demonic activity is at play here, likely the possession of the woman. Furthermore, Jesus' method for exorcism is different in this pericope. As we have seen in other Lukan exorcism accounts, Luke blurs the vocabulary for healing illness and exorcism.[67] In essence, Luke interprets exorcism as a possible form of healing.

When considering the identity of the woman in Luke 13, evidence reveals that she is almost certainly Jewish due to her presence in the synagogue and her specific identification as a θυγατέρα Ἀβραάμ (daughter of Abraham). Even though Green argues that the woman has marginal status,[68] Witherington and Levine assert that the woman is not exemplary of any of the marginal groups, especially since there are no details present concerning her economic status or her familial status. Disabled people and women were welcome in the syn-agogue, and they argue that nothing remarkable exists in relation to her pres-ence.[69] Contra Green, Levine argues that the synagogue allows her to be seen by Jesus and receive her healing.[70]

Luke starts this account by describing the woman's condition. The woman is depicted as ἔχουσα πηεῦμα ἀσθενείας. Luke then records her condition as

---

[65] Momlu Armstrong Massaquoi, "Jesus' Healing Miracles in Luke 13:10–17 and Their Significance for Physical Health," *Ogbomoso Journal of Theology* 18.1 (2013): 98–123 (98).

[66] G. Campbell Morgan, *The Gospel according to Luke* (New York: Revell, 1931).

[67] John T. Carroll, *Luke: A Commentary*, NTL (Louisville: Westminster John Knox, 2012), 283.

[68] See Joel B. Green, "Jesus and a Daughter of Abraham (Luke 13:10–17): Test Case for a Lukan Perspective on Jesus' Miracles," *CBQ* 51.4 (1989): 649.

[69] Amy-Jill Levine and Ben Witherington III, *The Gospel of Luke*, New Cambridge Bible Commentary (Cambridge: Cambridge University Press, 2018), 369–70.

[70] Levine and Witherington, *Gospel of Luke*, 371.

fixed in a bent over position. The use of ἔχω is employed in five of the seven pericopes where Luke reports a person's condition related to their affecting spirit.[71] Luke does not match Markan parallels (which use the preposition ἐν to grammatically depict the relationship with the spirit).[72] The problem is that some scholars dismiss this Lukan account as an account of possession because it lacks the more formal characteristics of exorcism. As noted above, Luke does not formally include all the elements of an exorcism story in every event. He is capable of summarizing stories in a briefer way. Even so, the accounts do describe the phenomenology that is reported.[73] Moreover, if one is seriously considering Luke's perspective about the condition of the woman, one must note that the woman is described grammatically in parallel ways to the man in the synagogue (Luke 4:33), the Gerasene demoniac (Luke 8:27), the young girl with the spirit of divination (Acts 16:16) and the ones having evil spirits who retaliate against the Jewish exorcists (Acts 19:13). For this reason, I have not dismissed this account in this study. The account indicates, in Lukan perspective, a way a spirit might affect a person.

Various scholars have hypothesized medical diagnoses for the woman's condition including *spondylitis ankylopoietic* (spinal bones fused together)[74] or *skoliasis hysterica* (a type of hysterical/muscular paralysis).[75] However, these diagnoses miss Luke's narrated perspective; Luke projects the aetiology of the illness as resulting from her having of the πηεῦμα ἀσθενείας, which is an

[71] Luke 4:33, 8:27, 15:13, 19:13. In Luke 9:39 the condition is reported in discourse from the Father. In Luke 11:14 the subject is Jesus and he is casting out the spirit.

[72] See Mark 1:23 and 5:2. Mark 9:17 does utilize the verb ἔχω. It is interesting to note that Luke does not carry over the usage of ἔχω when Mark does use it.

[73] Luke prefers to talk about "having" a demon. Some (especially those who write on the discipline of spiritual warfare) might favor the term "demonization" and want to discuss levels of impact upon a person. The term "possession" is retained because of its usage in anthropological writings and the comparability in views between definitions of possession in anthropological writings and the descriptions of what occurs in Lukan texts. The ontological nature of what happens in each report is not directly stated in Lukan reports. Rather, all testimonies, modern or ancient, include attempts to describe the phenomena that are reported. Luke's preferred wording employs the verb ἔχω. BDAG defines the usage in Luke 13:11 as "to experience something, have." When the verb is used in relation to hostile spirits, the verb can carry the sense of possession. In each reported account, experiences with spirits produce a variety of stories and characteristics of "possessed" states. The terminology depicting a variation between possession and oppression is modern, and Luke does not make this classification. Rather, he reports the events with lexical consistency.

[74] I. Howard Marshall, *The Gospel of Luke* (Grand Rapids: Eerdmans, 1978), 557.

[75] Walter Grundmann, *Das Evangelium nach Lukas*, Theologischer Handkommentar zum Neuen Testament 3 (Berlin: Evangelische Verlagsanstalt, 1963), 279.

Aramaism and can be translated, "a spirit that causes infirmity."[76] Therefore, these diagnoses may describe her ailment, but they do not accurately depict Luke's understanding of the cause. At times, Luke seemingly blurs the line between possession and illness, and here the illness is due in some way to "a spirit that causes infirmity."[77]

The length of the malady surely indicates its seriousness and denotes that the woman had suffered for a long time.[78] More specifically, many suggestions have been made concerning the significance of verse 18 in this account.[79] The most convincing is the link to 13:4 and the likelihood that the number depicts that her illness is of no fault of her own.[80]

Jesus' authoritative words free the woman from her malady even before he lays hands on her. He proclaims her release from her painful condition (ἀπολέλυσαι), and when he lays hands on her, she is immediately made straight (ἀνωρθώθη). The laying on of hands was part of exorcistic technique in the ancient world. Even though Twelftree argues that Luke seems to avoid this method as related to exorcism, this text possibly stands as an outlier to his argument.[81] Twelftree notes the clear relationship between sickness and its demonic dimension (especially regarded as evil) in Luke-Acts and rightly demonstrates that even though this relationship is present, not all cases of illness are regarded as caused by demons. The point for Twelftree is that in every Lukan healing story the devil is restrained.[82] The case of the woman here, however, is more than part of a literary trend. In Luke's depiction the woman is "bound by Satan" and suffering from "a spirit that causes infirmity."

Concerning historicity, speculation has occurred about its origin. Bultmann argues for its later construction for usage with the saying in 13:15.[83] Similarly, the Jesus Seminar abandons the dialogue of the account, noting that

[76] Garland, *Luke*, 546.

[77] This is not the first time that Luke has used the two terms together. Luke 8:2 refers to women who were being healed from πνευμάτων πονηρῶν καὶ ἀσθενειῶν.

[78] John Nolland, *Luke 9:21–18:34*, WBC 35b (Waco, Tex.: Word, 1993), 724, argues that the number depicts the length of her suffering.

[79] Ray Summers, *Commentary on Luke* (Waco, Tex.: Word, 1973), 167. Summers emphasizes the symbolic interpretation, invoking the time of Israel's bondage (Judg 3:13–14; Judg 10:8). Mikeal C. Parsons, *Body and Character in Luke and Acts: The Subversion of Physiognomy in Early Christianity* (Grand Rapids: Baker, 2006), 89–95, argues for the numerical significance of the numbers, which add up to abbreviate Jesus' name.

[80] Garland, *Luke*, 547. See also Heidi Togerson, "The Healing of the Bent Woman: A Narrative Interpretation of Luke 13:10–17," *CurTM* 32.3 (2005): 179–80.

[81] Twelftree, *In the Name of Jesus*, 148.

[82] Twelftree, *In the Name of Jesus*, 133–34.

[83] Bultmann, *History of the Synoptic Tradition*, 12.

the discourse (13:12, 15–16) was created for use with this account.[84] Thirdly, others such as Grundmann, Schweizer, Fitzmyer, Marskal, and Hengel root the account within the ministry of Jesus despite the arguments based upon its Lukan style.[85]

Some have viewed the unit more favorably. For example, Roloff regards the unit as traditional, questioning only 13:14b–15 as possibly secondary.[86] Bock pushes the argument further, noting that the synagogue leader's rebuke is not an "inexact fit" to the movement of the story.[87] Meier argues that two details, which do not have redactional motive, are evidence for the rooting of this story in tradition: (1) the synagogue ruler as the opponent is counter to Luke's tendency towards Pharisaic opposition, and (2) the number eighteen carries no symbolic weight. For him, these two details further the idea that there is no explicitly compelling evidence against the historicity of this account.[88] However, attempts to allegorize or rationalize this account take away from understanding Luke's viewpoint related to the woman's healing by missing Luke's stated perspective.

The Synoptic accounts, when considered in their own ancient milieu, prioritize a belief that spirits are capable of causing illness. Additionally, exorcism is a possible cure, or a method of healing, for those who are ailing. While this perspective seems amiss to modern minds who favor rationalistic and naturalistic interpretations, it is one that is acknowledged widely in cross-cultural anthropological studies. To these accounts we now turn.

Global Perspectives

While the focus of this chapter is on comparing ancient and modern parallels of spirit possession illness, one would be remiss not to at least briefly notice that many parallels exist in the intermediary periods.[89] Even so, space does not allow for a treatment of the various expressions of the relationship between possession and illness in a diachronic study. What is possible to maintain is that a

---

[84] Funk and Hoover, *Five Gospels*, 345–46.

[85] Grundmann, *Evangelium nach Lukas*, 279; Eduard Schweizer, *The Good News according to Luke*, trans. David E. Green (Atlanta: John Knox, 1984), 221; Joseph A. Fitzmyer, *The Gospel according to Luke X–XXIV*, AB 28a (Garden City, N.Y.: Doubleday, 1985), 1011; Marshall, *Gospel of Luke*, 556–57; *TDNT* 8:53.

[86] Jürgen Roloff, *Das Kerygma und der irdische Jesus: Historische Motive in den Jesus-Erzählungen der Evangelien* (Göttingen: Vandenhoeck & Ruprecht, 1970), 67–68.

[87] Bock, *Luke 9:51–24:53*, 1213.

[88] Meier, *Marginal Jew*, 684.

[89] See Bhayro and Rider, *Demons and Illness*, for a collection of articles treating various historical periods.

connection has remained throughout history. What follows are modern expressions of a relationship between spirits, spirit possession, and illness in anthropological expressions. Examples multiply quickly and restrictions of space disallow an exhaustive representation of sources. The hope is that the evidence below will demonstrate that a wide variety of societies report a connection between spirits, spirit possession, and illness. These accounts provide a new lens for NT interpreters, one that hears and observes the perspectives of a wide variety of experiences before interpreting these experiences in etic terms.

Africa

Walter Wink once asserted that "angels, spirits, principalities, powers, gods, satan—these along with all other spiritual realities, are the unmentionables of our culture."[90] While this may be a prevailing Western view, this is not the view of African cultures. Rather, belief in spirits is prevalent. A wide variety of African cultures and religions attest to the experience of spirit possession and view it as a cause for illness.

African Christianity

In African Christianity Nel reports that the Indigenous African Churches (Initiated, Independent, or Instituted) have maintained a constant belief that evil spirits are capable of causing ills.[91] Omenyo considers this as possible since Christianity is interpreted in the vein of African traditional religions and not Western missionary influence.[92] He argues that African Pentecostalism additionally attributes illness to demonic causation and exorcism as cure.[93] In the neo-Pentecostalism of African Christianity, Nel reports that illness and infertility are often due to "spiritual phenomena requiring divine intervention."[94] Prophets, functioning as exorcists, serve in a similar way to the diviners, witch-doctors, and *sangomas* of Africa, and fight

---

[90]   Walter Wink, *Unmasking the Powers: The Invisible Forces That Determine Human Existence*, vol. 2 of *The Powers* (Philadelphia: Fortress, 1986), 1.

[91]   Marius Nel, "The African Background of Pentecostal Theology: A Critical Perspective," *In die Skriflig* 53.4 (2019): 1–2. This contrasts with missionary churches, who have been impacted by Western views. For these churches, Nel argues, "to become a Christian was to become less 'African' and 'more civilized,' in Western terms."

[92]   Cephas N. Omenyo, "African Pentecostalism," in *The Cambridge Companion to Pentecostalism*, ed. Cecil M. Robeck Jr. and Amos Yong (New York: Cambridge University Press, 2014), 144–47.

[93]   Omenyo, "African Pentecostalism," 139. Misfortune, infertility, and a variety of other matters are also attributed to demonic involvement.

[94]   Nel, "African Background of Pentecostal Theology," 4.

off, in Jesus' name, "the devil, demons, evil spirits, spiritual authorities and witches who disturb life, nature, and the normal biological functions of the body."[95] David J. Garrard reports the prolificacy of witchcraft and deliverance ministry and the practice of exorcism as widespread in Central Africa.[96] For example, in West Africa "prayer camps" are organized for the purpose of exorcising people troubled by witchcraft.[97] One example is the healing ministry of Monsignor Emmanuel Milingo, who prayed for the healing of many who suffered from *mashave* spirits.[98] Gerrie ter Haar and Stephen Ellis attest to over 250 letters that were sent to the Archbishop between 1979 and 1980 that document the belief in spirit possession and the desire for healing.[99] Ter Haar and Ellis emphasize how these letters give "a first-hand account of an intimate area of people's lives."[100] In Catholic Christianity, approaches are variegated related to a contested or complementary relationship between deliverance ministry and biomedicine.[101] In Catholic Christianity, Climenhaga summarizes the views of local Catholics in Uganda, who "almost invariably claim to believe that spiritual entities exist and can afflict human beings

---

[95] Nel, "African Background of Pentecostal Theology," 4. See also M. L. Daneel, "Exorcism as a Means of Combating Wizardry: Liberation or Enslavement?" *Missionalia* 18.1 (1990): 220–47.

[96] David J. Garrard, "Witchcraft and Deliverance: An Exaggerated Theme in Pentecostal Churches in Central Africa," *Journal of the European Pentecostal Theological Association* 37.1 (2017): 52–67.

[97] Opoku Onyinah, "Akan Witchcraft and the Concept of Exorcism in the Church of Pentecost" (PhD diss., University of Birmingham, 2002); Allan Anderson, "Exorcism and Conversion to African Pentecostalism," *Exchange* 35.1 (2006): 117, writes of his visit to three "prayer camps" in Ghana.

[98] Gerrie ter Haar and Stephen Ellis, "Spirit Possession and Healing in Modern Zambia: An Analysis of Letters to Archbishop Milingo," *African Affairs* 87.347 (1988): 185–206. See pages 189, 101, and 193 for evidence that letters come from urban men and women, including business people, teachers, and executives. This evidence demonstrates that possession experience ranges beyond the poor or socially deprived. For more on possession experience in Zambia, see also Wim M. J. van Binsbergen, *Religious Change in Zambia: Exploratory Studies* (Boston: Kegan Paul International, 1981).

[99] Ter Haar and Ellis, "Spirit Possession and Healing in Modern Zambia," 187. The letters demonstrate a variety of ailments that are believed to be caused by spirit possession. See 195–98.

[100] Ter Haar and Ellis, "Spirit Possession and Healing in Modern Zambia," 188.

[101] Alison Fitchett Climenhaga, "Pursuing Transformation: Healing, Deliverance, and Discourses of Development among Catholics in Uganda," *Mission Studies* 35.2 (2018): 204–24. See also Paul Gifford, *Christianity, Development and Modernity in Africa* (New York: Oxford University Press, 2016), 13–28, 107–24. Gifford traces the expression of "enchanted Catholicism" throughout Cameroon, Zaire, Uganda, Tanzania, and Kenya.

in a variety of ways—causing everything from physical illness to mental or emotional problems."[102]

East Africa

Sixty-six percent of the Ethiopian population affirms that they have witnessed exorcism.[103] Religious traditions in Ethiopia that contribute to the belief in spirit possession include the *zar*[104] and *ayana* cults, the Ethiopian Orthodox Tewahedo Church, and hybrid practices. In the *zar* cult, the *zar* (male spirit) makes a person ill as a signal that it intends to possess her. Further, the *wuqabi* possession cult relates illness with possession and especially the process of initiation.[105]

In a study tracking patterns of change and continuity related to possession characteristics and healing, Norbert Vecchiato argues for a convergence in Ethiopian possession traditions, especially through "shared beliefs in super-naturally based illness aetiologies and a holistic definition of health."[106] The main spirit is named the *sheiṭane spirit*.[107] Specific criteria are culturally set

---

[102] Climenhaga, "Pursuing Transformation," 214.

[103] Stephen Lloyd, "Ethiopia," in *Spirit Possession around the World: Possession, Communion, and Demon Expulsion across Cultures*, ed. Joseph Laycock (Santa Barbara, Calif.: ABC-CLIO, 2015), 118. Seventy-four percent of Christians and 44 percent of Muslims in Ethiopia attest to seeing the devil driven from a person. Laycock notes that spirit possession belief and experience is more widespread than the statistics demonstrate because of belief in "ambivalent spirits."

[104] Lloyd, "Ethiopia," 119. Women are possessed by the male spirit named *zar*.

[105] Alice Morton, "*Dawit*: Competition and Integration in an Ethiopian Wuqabi Cult Group," in *Case Studies in Spirit Possession*, ed. Vincent Crapanzano and Vivian Garrison (New York: Wiley, 1976), 193–233.

[106] Vecchiato, "Illness, Therapy, and Change in Ethiopian Possession Cults," 177. This study focuses on Sidamoland and Protestant, Coptic, and Islamic traditions. Others have also argued for the central place of healing in African independent religious movements. See Edwards, "Healing and Transculturation in Xhosa Zionist Practice," *Culture, Medicine, and Psychiatry* 7.2 (1983): 177–98; J. K. Olupona, "New Religious Movements in Contemporary Nigeria," *Journal of Religious Thought* 46.1 (1989): 53–68; G. C. Oosthuizen et al., eds., *Afro-Christian Religion and Healing in Southern Africa* (Lewiston, N.Y.: Mellen, 1989); Lamin Sanneh, "Healing and Conversion in New Religious Movements in Africa," in *African Healing Strategies*, ed. Brian M. du Toit and Ismail H. Abdalla (New York: Trado-medic, 1985), 108–34.

[107] H. S. Lewis, "Spirit Possession in Ethiopia," *Proceedings of the Seventh International Conference of Ethiopian Studies* (1984): 420, notes the variants *shaytan, zitana, shetana*. The term has Semitic roots and can refer to one who tests humanity's virtue or, in the Middle East and East Africa (within Islamic writings), it refers to a pantheon of evil spirits who are ambivalent.

to determine possession by the *sheiṭane* spirit.[108] The most common ailments include epilepsy (*hawunnate*) and mental illness (*maçararo*), among a variety of other ailments.[109]

In Kenya the Iru people group believe in the *cwezi* spirits, which cause illness, infertility, and misfortune.[110] Linda Giles demonstrates the Muslim Swahili belief in spirits named *jinni*, *sheitani*, and *pepo*. The presence of these spirit(s) is known by sickness, maladies, infertility, and death.[111] In some cases

---

[108] Vecchiato, "Illness, Therapy, and Change in Ethiopian Possession Cults," 180. Criteria include: (1) symptoms, (2) the circumstances at the ailment's onset, (3) the person's medical and behavior history, and (4) the history of possession experience in the patient's family. Specialists are sought for healing.

[109] Vecchiato, "Illness, Therapy, and Change in Ethiopian Possession Cults," 180, 189. This is also documented in other Ethiopian contexts. See R. Giel, Y. Gezahegn, and J. N. van Luijk, "Faith-Healing and Spirit Possession in Ghion, Ethiopia," *Social Science and Medicine* 2.1 (1967): 63–79; Redda Tekle-Haimanot et al., "Attitudes of Rural People in Central Ethiopia towards Epilepsy," *Social Science and Medicine* 32.2 (1991): 203–9. Other categories of illness are noted, including "unexplained physiological ailments, hereditary and chronic disorders, barrenness, intra-personal problems, joblessness, social tensions, and evil eye and sorcery accusations." Vecchiato notes that the "deprivation model" of interpretation is present in many ethnographic studies of spirit possession in Ethiopia. See John Hamer and Irene Hamer, "Spirit Possession and Its Socio-psychological Implications among the Sidamo of South-West Ethiopia," *Ethnology* 5.4 (1966): 392–408; J. Hamer, "Crisis, Moral Consensus, and the Wando Magano Movement among the Sadama of South-West Ethiopia," *Ethnology* 16.4 (1977): 399–413; Simon D. Messing, "Group Therapy and Social Status in the *Zar* Cult of Ethiopia," *American Anthropologist* 60.6 (1958): 1120–25; Morton, "*Dawit*: Competition and Integration in an Ethiopian Wuqabi Cult Group," 193–233. This approach has downplayed the emic view of involving a holistic approach defined by Vecchiato, "Illness, Therapy, and Change in Ethiopian Possession Cults," 188, as involving "physiological, moral, and spiritual domains . . . as mutually interpenetrating." Vecchiato, "Illness, Therapy, and Change in Ethiopian Possession Cults," 189, argues that the "religious movements are therapeutic rather than political." For others arguing for a therapeutic interpretation, see Thomas J. Csordas, "The Rhetoric of Transformation in Ritual Healing," *Culture, Medicine, and Psychiatry* 7.4 (1983): 333–75; Thomas J. Csordas and Arthur Kleinman, "The Therapeutic Process," in *Medical Anthropology: Contemporary Theory and Method*, ed. Thomas M. Johnson and Carolyn F. Sargent (Westport, Conn.: Praeger, 1990), 11–25; Allan Young, "Why Amhara Get *kureynya*: Sickness and Possession in an Ethiopian *Zar* Cult," *American Ethnologist* 2.3 (1975): 567–84, responds by focusing on the religious dimension of the relationship between medicine and religion.

[110] Stephen Lloyd, "Kenya," in Laycock, *Spirit Possession around the World*, 203. Animal sacrifices are made to placate spirits, or in more severe cases the spirit demands the person's initiation to the cult.

[111] Lloyd, "Kenya," 204. The spirits may be beneficial and produce healing powers. The spirit is enticed for its help through the offering of food, incense, or dancing. See also Linda L. Giles, "Possession Cults on the Swahili Coast: A Re-examination of Theories of Marginality," *Africa* 57.2 (1987): 240. Giles notes that the "oft-quoted Muslim position"

the spirit is exorcised for healing.[112] Further, *utsai*, a word used among the Mijikenda tribes to reference "diagnostic, protective, and curative skills that involve medicines," involves the aid of spirits. A divinatory technique called *aganga a mburuga* (healing of confusion or disorder) allows the diviner to determine the agency of the illness (options include "ancestor spirits, witchcraft, spirit possession, the divine creator, and nonfamiliar spirits").[113] Among the Kenyan Luo people, spirits, especially ancestral spirits, are believed to possess people and cause suffering and illness.[114] Disease is interpreted as a "sanction to force the living to maintain proper relations with the dead," and as a result a diseased person would examine these relationships.[115] Additionally, belief exists in a class of spirits, named *juogi*, who are sent by God and cause disease.[116] Hallucinations, depression, hysteria, and cerebral malaria are examples of spirit-possession illness.[117]

Marja-Liisa Swantz argues that spirit possession cults are a part of "institutional forms of religious experience" in eastern Tanzania.[118] Swantz notes the common connection with illness as the "intervention of spirits" which is "most commonly manifested first in an illness or other physical disorder."[119]

---

allows for the reality of spirits but does not condone relationships with spirits as associating with Allah (*shiriki*). *Waganga* (traditional healers/diviners) fall into two dichotomies: (1) "*waganga* of the book," and (2) *waganga* using spirit possession. Their strategies to provide relief differ; the former use Islamic means for exorcism, and the latter use pagan means and focus on placation and cultivation.

[112] Giles, "Possession Cults on the Swahili Coast," 240, notes that exorcism is used if the spirit is related to Koranic methods, if the spirit is evil/useless, or if the spirit is sent by witchcraft.

[113] Diane M. Ciekawy, "*Utsai* as Ethical Discourse," in *Witchcraft Dialogues: Anthropological and Philosophical Exchanges*, ed. George Clement Bond and Diane M. Ciekawy (Athens: Ohio University Press, 2001), 164–65. *Utsai* requires an agreement with the spirits in order to use their power. An "agreement" or "negotiation" is made to determine the payment/act of devotion for the spirit. See p. 177 for more detail.

[114] Michael G. Whisson, "Some Aspects of Functional Disorders," in *Magic, Faith, and Healing: Studies in Primitive Psychiatry Today*, ed. Ari Kiev (New York: Free Press, 1964), 286.

[115] Whisson, "Some Aspects of Functional Disorders," 285–86.

[116] Whisson, "Some Aspects of Functional Disorders," 287. *Juogi* is also used to depict the "disease of spirit possession."

[117] Whisson, "Some Aspects of Functional Disorders," 289–90. Whisson concludes that even after Western influence traditional practices and beliefs have not dissipated. One missionary doctor concluded, "There are some things which they know we cannot cure."

[118] Marja-Liisa Swantz, "Dynamics of the Spirit Possession Phenomenon in Eastern Tanzania," *Scripta Instituti Donneriani Aboensis* 9 (1976): 90–101.

[119] Swantz, "Dynamics of the Spirit Possession Phenomenon in Eastern Tanzania," 91. Exorcism is not the approach taken for cure in all cases. Rather, Swantz, "Dynamics of the

Among the Kimbu, water spirits are associated with sicknesses involving sleep and plagues.[120] Additionally, they cause problems such as "nervous ailments, depressed and deprived people, epileptics and the mentally ill."[121] Exorcism is employed by Christian African priests for relief for the ailing. It is tempting for those with mediumship belief to equate exorcism and mediumship despite mediumship's focus on listening to and reasoning with the spirits rather than removing them. Shorter concludes, "The exorcisms are very popular and large numbers of Christians are evidently ready to accept a demonic explanation for the misfortunes that befall them."[122]

Michael Lambek's study of spirit possession focuses on the Comoros Islands between the Swahili Coast and Madagascar. He studies two villages and focuses on the Mayotto *patros* spirits. Possession experience in Mayotte affects nearly 25 percent of the adult population.[123] Lambeck argues, "Possession is an integral component of society in Mayotte, not a peripheral and inconsequential one."[124] Further, possession is defined in terms of illness, and illness is a manifestation of the embodiment of spirits.[125] More specifically, Lambek documents the testimony that sorcerers can send spirits to cause afflictions. Tambu, interviewed

---

Spirit Possession Phenomenon in Eastern Tanzania," 92, 98, describes the ritual of *kupunga pepo*, which she interprets as a fanning of the spirits or winds, indicating a "refreshing" or "revitalizing" approaching to taming the spirits and finding cure. Exorcism is practiced among the Zaramo and both men and women can function in the role of an exorcist.

[120] Aylward Shorter, "Spirit Possession and Christian Healing in Tanzania," *African Affairs* 79.314 (1980): 47. Shorter asserts that these spirits are well known among those who speak Nyamwezi in western Tanzania.

[121] Shorter, "Spirit Possession and Christian Healing in Tanzania," 48–51. Roman Catholic missionaries ascribed these ailments to demon possession and disallowed participation in the sacraments for those who were involved in the water-spirit association. The water-spirit association fell apart with Maji-ya-Soda's claim that the spirits had departed (ca. 1970). Shorter documents the rise of healing prayer practices and exorcism in this area following the fall of the water-spirit association (he argues that this is due to outside influence).

[122] Shorter, "Spirit Possession and Christian Healing in Tanzania," 52. For more on the relationship between illness and possession and the charismatic community in Tanzania, see Lotta Gammelin, "Gendered Narratives of Illness and Healing: Experiences of Spirit Possession in a Charismatic Church Community in Tanzania," in *Faith in African Lived Christianity: Bridging Anthropological and Theological Perspectives*, ed. Karen Lauterbach and Mika Vähäkangas (Leiden: Brill, 2020), 314–34. Gammelin names symptoms of spirit involvement including "headaches, dizziness, fainting and being unable to work." Additionally, reports of stomach pain, struggle from personality takeover, suicidal thoughts, and thoughts of murder were included.

[123] Michael Lambek, *Knowledge and Practice in Mayotte: Local Discourses of Islam, Sorcery and Spirit Possession* (Toronto: University of Toronto Press, 1993), 321.

[124] Lambek, *Knowledge and Practice in Mayotte*, 321.

[125] Lambek, *Knowledge and Practice in Mayotte*, 321, 336.

by Lambek, describes the affliction in the following terms: "When the bad spirit called up by the sorcerer enters you, you feel a sudden start."[126] Lambek wrote the rest of the testimony in his field notes:

> The person then becomes sick. . . . He may take to his bed, try aspirin, niva-quine, and so on. If none of this works, he goes to a diviner who may recommend a *fundi* to extract the sorcery. The *fundi* . . . can see precisely when the spirit moves. He waits for it to enter the arm and then pulls it down the limb.[127]

Lambek does not refer to this practice in terms of exorcism but rather in terms of the "extraction of the sorcery."[128]

The Yombe in Nothern Zambia believe in ancestral spirits who can cause a variety of misfortunes, including illness. Bond describes them as powerful and "a force to be reckoned with."[129] The Tonga of Zambia additionally reflect this perspective in one of their types of spirit possession, referred to as "ghost possession." Ghosts (viewed as spirits of "forgotten local dead," spirits controlled by sorcerers, "spirit remnants" created at death) possess with a goal of assassinating, and sudden-onset "violent illnesses" are attributed to this possession type. Spirits are fumigated for removal and are known to speak their name as they exit. Exorcisms produce immediate relief for the individual.[130]

In Zanzibar (Mukunduchi area) there is some inconsistency in the view of spirits, namely, belief in spirits is catalyzed by trouble.[131] Koranic healers are often possessed by the *ruhani*, spirits, who cause illness.[132] Further, Larsen concludes that spirits can cause suffering. The explanation given is that "spirits may actually inflict illness or suffering on humans in order to make their demands clear and acted upon."[133]

---

[126] Lambek, *Knowledge and Practice in Mayotte*, 270–71.

[127] Lambek, *Knowledge and Practice in Mayotte*, 270–71.

[128] Lambek, *Knowledge and Practice in Mayotte*, 270–71.

[129] George Clement Bond, "Ancestors and Witches," in Bond and Ciekawy, *Witchcraft Dialogues*, 139, 147. The introduction of Christianity among the Yombe allowed for a new set of spiritual beings but did not replace the ones already present.

[130] Elizabeth Colson, "Spirit Possession among the Tonga of Zambia," in *Spirit Mediumship and Society in Africa*, ed. John Beattie and John Middleton (London: Routledge and Kegan Paul, 1969), 69–103.

[131] Giles, "Possession Cults on the Swahili Coast," 246. Giles cites a government officer who sought aid from spirit-cults when trouble arrived.

[132] Giles, "Possession Cults on the Swahili Coast," 245. For more detail see Kjersti Larsen, *Where Humans and Spirits Meet: The Politics of Rituals and Identified Spirits in Zanzibar* (New York: Berghahn, 2008).

[133] Larsen, *Where Humans and Spirits Meet*, 14.

North Africa

In Egypt, Sudan, Ethiopia, and the Arabian peninsula the term *zar* is employed to indicate a belief in spirit possession and the ceremonies related to possession experience.[134] Lucie Wood Saunders summarizes the essence of *zar* experience: "The central theory of the *zar* is that spirit possession is manifested by illness which can be alleviated by propitiating the spirits through ceremonies that consistently include dance and trance behaviors."[135] Women are more commonly known to be affected by *zar* possession, and diagnosis is made when a patient does not respond to other cures.[136] This matter is emphasized by Khadiga's testimony:

> If they say someone should be taken to a doctor, he goes to a doctor. If his illness is a doctor's illness, he will know it. If it's an illness of zar, that's it (*khallas*), it's an illness of zar, the doctor won't be able to cure him. They'll have to do the things of zar. . . . Some people say he is mad but he's not. This is zar and once the right spirit is correctly diagnosed, he can be cured straightaway.[137]

Symptoms of possession include "swelling of the legs or stomach, stomach pain, loss of appetite, barrenness and, most commonly, nervousness; some participants who had been to physicians said they had diagnoses of heart trouble, abscesses, and epilepsy."[138] When one is initiated into the possession cult, the person is constantly possessed by the spirit.[139] Some explain the zar are contagious and indicate that the illness may be caught.[140]

---

[134] Lucie Wood Saunders, "Variants in Zar Experience in an Egyptian Village," in Crapanzano and Garrison, *Case Studies in Spirit Possession*, 177–91.

[135] Saunders, "Variants in Zar Experience," 177.

[136] Saunders, "Variants in Zar Experience," 179.

[137] Susan Kenyon, *Spirits and Slaves in Central Sudan: The Red Wind of Sennar* (Basingstoke, UK: Palgrave Macmillan, 2012), 87–88.

[138] Saunders, "Variants in Zar Experience," 179. Saunders illustrates that the belief in spirits is viewed as compatible with Muslim religion; however, many do not publicize their private beliefs.

[139] Connor Wood, "Zar," in Laycock, *Spirit Possession around the World*, 380. This possession does not interfere with daily life but requires regular participation in the cult. See also Ahmed Al-Safi, Sayyid Hurreiz, and I. M. Lewis, *Women's Medicine: The* Zar-Bori *Cult in Africa and Beyond* (Edinburgh: Edinburgh University Press, 1991); Boddy, *Wombs and Alien Spirits*; Susan Kenyon, *Five Women of Sennar: Culture and Change in Central Sudan* (Long Grove, Ill.: Waveland, 2004); Kenyon, *Spirits and Slaves in Central Sudan*; Hager El Hadidi, *Zar: Spirit Possession, Music, and Healing Rituals in Egypt* (Cairo: American University in Cairo Press, 2016).

[140] Kenyon, *Spirits and Slaves in Central Sudan*, 82.

In Moroccan belief, certain illnesses are viewed as the result of *jnun*, who possess a "physical agency" and are capable of having a material effect on those they possess.[141] The *jnun* (genies who are invisible beings but not considered as part of the supernatural world) are compared to microbes since they are capable of impacting the human body in the same way as microbes.[142] In essence, there is a biomedical explanation pinned to possession experience. Koranic healers explain the possession as "the effects of the *jnun* in the embodied soul, in so far as the *jnun* cross the human orifices and penetrate into the body and become attached to substances like blood."[143] An example of illness includes infertility, and it is said that a *jinn* is "physically located at the entrance of the vagina or fallopian tubes and prevents sperm from gaining access . . ."[144] Dieste reports of *jinn* attacking the part of the brain that causes blindness are the explanation in the case of a girl who was struck with blindness during an attempt to diagnose whether or not she was being afflicted.[145] Bernard Greenwood lists multiple illnesses that are associated with "spirits" in Morocco's medical system, which is quite pluralistic in nature, involving a detailed description of what is of natural and supernatural causation.[146]

South Africa

In South Africa, ancestral spirits are heavily associated with health-related problems. If the spirits are not assuaged, they may bring about illness, infertility, and misfortune. *Songomas* (diviners) are sought for diagnosis of their illness. If a cure is not found, it is viewed as a sign of a call to initiation into the

[141] Josep Lluís Mateo Dieste, "'Spirits Are Like Microbes': Islamic Revival and the Definition of Morality in Moroccan Exorcism," *Contemporary Islam* 9.1 (2015): 45.

[142] Dieste, "'Spirits Are Like Microbes,'" 45–46.

[143] Dieste, "'Spirits Are Like Microbes,'" 46.

[144] Dieste, "'Spirits Are Like Microbes,'" 46.

[145] Dieste, "'Spirits Are Like Microbes,'" 53–55. Interestingly, *jnun* are also known to dwell in certain locations ("caves, damp places, slaughterhouses, abandoned houses, etc.") and are capable of afflicting machines (explaining cases of broken cassette players used in exorcism rituals, locked cars, etc.). *Jnun* "are able to enter machines and manipulate them."

[146] Bernard Greenwood, "Cold or Spirits? Choice and Ambiguity in Morocco's Pluralistic Medical System," *Social Science Medicine* 15B (1981): 219–35. Page 226 lists rheumatism, neuralgia, sciatica, migraine, tremor, progressive wasting, paralysis of the face and limbs, stroke, sudden blindness, muteness and deafness, and barrenness as caused by spirits. Moroccans do not view their approach as pluralistic as they are pragmatic in nature and their cures validate their hypothesis. See page 232. See also Vincent Crapanzano, "Mohammed and Dawia: Possession in Morocco," in Crapanzano and Garrison, *Case Studies in Spirit Possession*, 141–76. Crapanzano argues possession manifests in "trance, acute hysterical dissociation, in schizophrenic reactions, in multiple personality, in tantrums, or in love." He interprets possession as symbolic.

cult.[147] The *izizwe, amandiki,* and *amandawu* cults of the Zulu people group reflect the same ideology as the *sangomas.*[148] Upon the influence of Christianity in the late nineteenth and early twentieth centuries, some African Christians interpreted the mainline Christian groups as unable to reach their spiritual needs related to health and possession.[149] In 1925 Engenas Lekganyane established the Zion Christian Church (ZCC), and the Holy Spirit was viewed as functioning in a similar way to the *sangomas.* Exorcisms and healings were performed through revelation from the Holy Spirit.[150]

In southern Zimbabwe (formerly named Rhodesia), illness is largely determined to have spiritual aetiology, and severe mental cases often are interpreted as the punishment of ancestral spirits.[151] Medicine men serve as the middle men between individuals and spirits and may reveal the cause and diagnosis.[152] *Mhondoro* (tribal mediums) typically experience mental disorientation during initiation as mediums.[153] The ideology of the Ndembu tribe of northern Zimbabwe is similar, with all "persistent or severe" illness viewed as punitive activity by ancestral activity, sorcerers, and witches.[154]

West Africa

Among the Mande, spirits are believed to cause illness and calamity.[155] This view is also found among the Mende (a subgroup of the Mande), who believe that *genii* are spirits who fit into two categories, including ancestral spirits and spirits who have not been part of humanity. The latter are termed *dyinanga* and are both good and evil. Evil *dyinango* may cause mental illness but may be driven out by the native doctors.[156]

In Nigeria among the indigenous Yoruba, ancestral spirits and other spirits such as *Orisas* can cause health disturbances. The *Orisa* spirits are

---

[147] Stephen Lloyd, "South Africa," in Laycock, *Spirit Possession around the World*, 321.

[148] Lloyd, "South Africa," 321.

[149] Also related to witches and ancestors. See Lloyd, "South Africa," 322.

[150] Lloyd, "South Africa," 322.

[151] Michael Gelfand, "Psychiatric Disorders as Recognized by the Shona," in Kiev, *Magic, Faith, and Healing*, 168.

[152] Gelfand, "Psychiatric Disorders," 161.

[153] Gelfand, "Psychiatric Disorders," 163.

[154] Victor W. Turner, "A Ndembu Doctor in Practice," in Kiev, *Magic, Faith, and Healing*, 230–31.

[155] Patrick R. McNaughton, *The Mande Blacksmiths: Knowledge, Power, and Art in West Africa* (Bloomington: Indiana University Press, 1993), 42. Additionally, malicious sorcery is employed to cause illness.

[156] John Dawson, "Urbanization and Mental Health in a West African Community," in Kiev, *Magic, Faith, and Healing*, 335.

typically sought when sickness or misfortune arises and worshipers seek to appease them. Neglecting *Orisas* may result in psychiatric problems.[157] Two possession cults are present: (1) *Sopono* (typically female), and (2) *Gelede* (typically male). The Sopono is associated with spirits that cause symptoms associated with smallpox, including fevers that at times cause delirium, skin conditions, and psychosis.[158] In the Gelde possession cult, males dress like women and participate in dances for protection from witchcraft. Men typically participate because of their wife's barrenness or other illnesses. If an initiate refuses to dance (wearing the mask) or fails the cult in some way, mental illness may result.[159]

In Niger, among the Kel Ewey Tuareg, possessing spirits are called *Kel Essuf* ("people of solitude"). Possession is considered a form of illness in which muteness is a main characteristic. It is referred to as "being in the wild" or "in solitude."[160] The Tuareg people indicate that "illnesses and depressions that cause trance are the result of spirits passed from mother to daughter."[161] Curing rites, called *t∂nde n goumaten*, are staged public ceremonies that include musicians (such as a drummer and choir of young ladies) and the patient. The effectiveness of the ritual depends in large part on the level of excellence of the musical performance according to the ritualistic rules.[162]

Carl Sundberg argues that among the Kongo illness is often considered in three aetiological categories: "natural, unnatural, and supernatural."[163] Unnatural illness is viewed as the effect of breaking taboo or as the result of witchcraft or sorcery, while supernatural illness is caused by God.[164] In the Republic of Congo (Congo-Brazzaville), some charismatic healers view illness as the effect

---

[157] Raymond Prince, "Indigenous Yoruba Psychiatry," in Kiev, *Magic, Faith, and Healing*, 84–120. *Orisas* are deified spirits.

[158] Prince, "Indigenous Yoruba Psychiatry," 105. Symptoms are beyond Western designations of smallpox symptoms. The cult was eventually disallowed due to the spread of smallpox. An attack is viewed as an invitation for initiation. Not all are initiated and some would rather make sacrifices for healing. The Sopono possession ceremony is performed for the benefit of the community for protection against misfortune and illness.

[159] Prince, "Indigenous Yoruba Psychiatry," 108. The men who wear the mask are described as "half possessed." The mask produces an immediate behavioral change.

[160] Susan J. Rasmussen, *Spirit Possession and Personhood among the Kel Ewey Tuareg* (New York: Cambridge University Press, 1995), 2.

[161] Rasmussen, *Spirit Possession and Personhood among the Kel Ewey Tuareg*, 3.

[162] Rasmussen, *Spirit Possession and Personhood among the Kel Ewey Tuareg*, 3–4.

[163] Carl Sundberg, "Revealed Medicine as an Expression of an African Christian Lived Spirituality," in Lauterbach and Vähäkangas, *Faith in African Lived Christianity*, 339.

[164] Sundberg, "Revealed Medicine as an Expression of an African Christian Lived Spirituality," 339. Disease caused by God is referred to as *kimbevo kia Nzambi* and refers to a wide variety of incurable diseases.

of evil spirits and cure with prayer and *la pierre noire* (petrified black wood boiled in milk). The purpose of the *la pierre noire* is to pull out evil spirits.[165]

Asia

Spirit possession phenomena in South Asia occur in a variety of contexts such as temples, ritual performances, festivals, and in devotional practice. By no means are the phenomena uniform in style, and a wide range of language is used to refer to the experience.[166] However, many South Asians who maintain belief in possession do also associate possession with illness. For example, in Muslim Asian communities, the *jinn* spirit is believed to possess people and cause mental illness.[167] These Muslims believe that the possession is divine punishment for sin and a person's weakness.[168] As surveyed below, the association is present in the anthropological study of Asian cultures.

A stereotype exists in Chinese thought that shamans and mediums belong to the past or are relegated to ethnic minority groups.[169] Because of this

---

[165] Sundberg, "Revealed Medicine as an Expression of an African Christian Lived Spirituality," 336.

[166] Frederick M. Smith, *The Self Possessed: Deity and Spirit Possession in South Asian Literature and Civilization* (New York: Columbia University Press, 2006), 590. As summarized by Smith, the experience is referred to in various languages as "'riding' (Hindi, Nepali, Simhala, Malyalam), as 'dancing' (Tamil, Malyalam), as an 'attack' (Hindi, Nepali), as a force 'coming into the body (e.g., Hindi, Marathi, Tulu, Irula), as 'play' of the deity (Hindi, Marathi, Nepali), as a kind of 'ecstasy' (Bengali, Marathi, Nepali), as a 'weight' (Bengali), as a marker for intense emotional engagement (Sanskrit, Malyalam, Bengali, and many others), as an idiom for impersonation (Tamil), as an emblem of political oppression (Ladakhi), as a sign of debilitated life force (Ladakhi, Sanskrit), as part of a multicultural dialogic interaction (Ladakhi, Nepali), or as a symptom of a multilayered world visible 'as if in a mirror' (Tibetan, Sanskrit)."

[167] F. Islam and R. A. Campbell, "'Satan Has Afflicted Me!': Jinn-Possession and Mental Illness in the Qur'an," *Journal of Religion and Health* 53.1 (2014): 229–43. See also Yaseen Ally and Sumaya Laher, "South African Muslim Faith Healers Perceptions of Mental Illness: Understanding Aetiology and Treatment," *Journal of Religion and Health* 47.1 (2008): 45–56; Amber Haque, "Religion and Mental Health: The Case of American Muslims," *Journal of Religion and Health* 41.1 (2004): 46–58; Stephen Weatherhead and Anna Daiches, "Muslim Views on Health and Psychotherapy," *Pyschology and Psychotherapy* 83.1 (2010): 75–89; Umar Sulaiman Al-Ashqar, *The World of the Jinn and Devils*, trans. Jamaah al-Din M. Zarabozo (Boulder, Colo.: Al-Basheer, 1998).

[168] Islam and Campbell, "'Satan Has Afflicted Me!'" 230, note that this belief is the minority view and that the majority view the cause of mental illness as biological and psychological. Even if this view is the minority, Rothenberg argues that modern accounts of jinn-possession are widely assessed as true in Islamic communities. See Celia E. Rothenberg, *Spirits of Palestine: Gender, Society, and Stories of the Jinn* (Oxford: Lexington, 2004), 29–52.

[169] Barend J. ter Haar, "China," in Laycock, *Spirit Possession around the World*, 77.

viewpoint among the elite, the significance of the phenomenon has not been well documented in literature, especially related to the Han Chinese, who are the majority.[170] However, where studies have been done, there is standing evidence relating illness with the existence of or possession by demons reaching back to antiquity.[171] Richard Von Glahn attests to the view that plagues, illness, and misfortune are all, at times, attributed to malevolent spirits.[172] This belief system is found in the Wotong cult,[173] Song dynasty,[174] Zhou, and Han eras; Von Glahn traces the conceptions diachronically throughout China's history.[175] Xing Wang's ethnographic work in rural Beijing documents a testimony of ancestral possession that left one woman "physically ill and in a vulnerable condition for a month."[176]

Popular Indian religion is full of belief in possession. Gavin Flood describes the matter with succinct brevity: "Indeed, if anything is characteristic of popular religion in India it is possession."[177] Further, Smith argues that "possession is the most common and . . . most valued form of spiritual expression in India."[178] In Central India, among the Balahis, exorcism is a technique employed to relieve illness caused by the possession of a spirit or deity. During trance the spirit reveals instructions for the cure.[179] The Balahis maintain belief

---

[170] Haar, "China," 77, notes that the topic is better documented among minority groups than among the Han majority. This is likely due to the persecution experienced by the Han under the People's Republic of China (established in 1949).

[171] Xing Wang, "Rethinking the 'Magic State' in China: Political Imagination and Magical Practice in Rural Beijing," *Asian Ethnology* 77.1–2 (2018): 333–34, argues that even though exorcism and shamanistic possession (among other things) are considered as superstition (*mi xin*) among the Communist Party, the phenomena persist under Communist control.

[172] Richard Von Glahn, *The Sinister Way: The Divine and the Demonic in Chinese Religious Culture* (Berkeley: University of California Press, 2004), 98.

[173] Von Glahn, *Sinister Way*, 98. In this cult divine and demonic were conflated into one entity with "underlings." Deities that caused plagues were more often perceived as demonic (but are part of both the plague's cause and cure).

[174] Von Glahn, *Sinister Way*, 98–99. Ancestral curses and spirits of the dead were known to cause illness.

[175] Von Glahn, *Sinister Way*, 99–130. Ghosts of the "wrongfully dead" bring revenge and cause illness. Von Glahn surveys the ancient evidence for the belief in spirits that cause illness and argues that the view was deeply held among the elite in antiquity.

[176] Wang, "Rethinking the 'Magic State' in China," 343.

[177] Gavin Flood, *The Tantric Body: The Secret Tradition of Hindu Religion* (London: I. B. Tauris, 2006), 87.

[178] Smith, *Self Possessed*, xxv.

[179] Stephen Fuchs, "Magic Healing Techniques among the Balahis in Central India," in Kiev, *Magic, Faith, and Healing*, 132–33.

that possession occurs frequently and causes most mental illness and a variety of other illnesses, including epilepsy.[180]

Margaret Lyngdoh notes that in northeastern India possession experiences fall in a wide range of categories, "from quiet sickness to raging convulsions."[181] Illness may result from being chosen as a medium or due to malevolent "disease-causing entities," such as Taro possession or by goddess possession.[182]

Smith argues that in southern India possession is "widely held to be responsible for psychological and social dysfunction in the twenty-first century."[183] Temples in Muthaswamy and Balaji are regularly frequented by people who seek to be cured from possession, viewed as "untoward spirits that take over their bodies, causing undesired dissociation."[184] These temples are given more credibility to give effective cure for possession-related psychological and social dysfunction than modern psychiatry among rural and "large swaths of urban" Indians.[185] Smith argues that both "oracular and disease producing possession, are generally acknowledged in India across widely variant demographic groups."[186] Providing a report of physical illness, Smith gives an example of a possessed woman who bled continually for three years. She went to the "best doctors," and they did not find any medical reason for her condition, which they named "a freak of nature." She received healing through seeing a tantric practitioner, who aided her in release from "bothersome spirits," interpreted as the result of black magic performed against her.[187] The woman's sister also experienced the effects of black magic performed by a family

---

[180] Fuchs, "Magic Healing Techniques," 135.

[181] Margaret Lyngdoh, "An Interview with the Goddess: Possession Rites as Regulators of Justice among the Pnar of Northeastern India," *Religious Studies and Theology* 36.1 (2017): 58.

[182] Lyngdoh, "Interview with the Goddess," 61.

[183] Smith, "Possession, Embodiment, and Ritual," 22. Smith also notes that the educated in India do not reject the possibility of spirit possession.

[184] Smith, "Possession, Embodiment, and Ritual," 21.

[185] Smith, "Possession, Embodiment, and Ritual," 22.

[186] Smith, "Possession, Embodiment, and Ritual," 22–23. Smith affirms the thesis of this chapter by also noting that possession exists as a "central concept in the realm of mental health" and that this "is consistent with findings elsewhere in the world, including Taiwan, Korea, Africa, Micronesia, South America, and the U.S., where embodied healing, which is to say healing enacted through spirit mediumship, and forms of possession in general are becoming increasingly popular." See also Frederick M. Smith, "The Current State of Possession Studies in Cross-Disciplinary Project," *Religious Studies Review* 27.3 (2001): 203–13; Michael E. Brown, *The Channeling Zone: American Spirituality in an Anxious Age* (Cambridge, Mass.: Harvard University Press, 1997).

[187] Smith, "Possession, Embodiment, and Ritual," 22.

member and indicated that her family experienced health problems (even their three dogs).[188]

In southern India, the experience of Marian possession in Hinduism and Roman Catholicism manifests in illness. In fact, Bloomer notes the prolific experience with spirit possession in southern India, noting that "spirit possession in South India is about as common as Starbucks or fantasy football in the United States."[189] Mary is believed to embody women and enable women to assist in healing others.[190] Possession by Mary contrasts with possession by *pēy*, spirits of the "untimely dead" that are believed to "catch" women (especially those who are newly married). This results in illness and is interpreted as causing infertility.[191]

In Borneo, one of Indonesia's largest islands, illness is viewed as a result of a variety of components including soul wandering or, more pertinent here, the capture of one's soul by a spirit.[192] As a result, healing is centralized around retrieving or rescuing souls or exorcizing or "slaying" malevolent spirits.[193] *Rogon*, defined as "spirits both of the natural and social world," are described as "capricious" and "irascible." They may "cause afflictions if they are not properly treated or if their living space is intruded upon."[194] If one does intrude, illness or infertility may result in the intruder's family.[195] The Bulusu' of East Kalimantan reflect a comparable view of illness that involves "soul capture," "torment by capricious spirits," and witchcraft.[196] Spirit mediums negotiate with the spirits during trance states for the purpose of the "return of captured souls to cure illness."[197]

Carmen Blacker surveys the most common "symptoms" of possession in Japanese expression. Symptoms that affect the body include "aches, mysterious pains, lumbago, hacking coughs, fainting fits, loss of appetite, inexplicable

---

[188]   Smith, "Possession, Embodiment, and Ritual," 22.

[189]   Kristin C. Bloomer, *Possessed by the Virgin: Hinduism, Roman Catholicism, and Marian Possession in South India* (New York: Oxford University Press, 2018), 15.

[190]   Bloomer, *Possessed by the Virgin*, 23.

[191]   Bloomer, *Possessed by the Virgin*, 2.

[192]   Robert Winzeler, "Shaman, Priest and Spirit Medium: Religious Specialists, Tradition and Innovation in Borneo," in Winzeler, *The Seen and the Unseen*, xv.

[193]   Winzeler, "Shaman, Priest and Spirit Medium," xvi.

[194]   Appell and Appell, "To Converse with the Gods," 11.

[195]   Appell and Appell, "To Converse with the Gods," 11. Misfortune is also interpreted as a result.

[196]   George N. Appell and Laura W. R. Appell, "To Do Battle with the Spirits: Bulusu' Spirit Mediums," in Winzeler, *The Seen and the Unseen*, 64.

[197]   Appell and Appell, "To Do Battle with the Spirits," 64.

fevers."[198] Further, depression, pregnancy ills, and difficulties in childbirth are often viewed as the result of a malevolent spirit. Mental illness including hallucinations (visual and auditory) and symptoms of altered personality are also depicted as a result of possession.[199] Healing is reported through exorcism. Blacker reports the testimony of a woman who was cured from tuberculosis of the spine through exorcism.[200]

Among the Malays spirit possession is commonly related to or considered as the aetiology of mental illness.[201] Bomohs (Malay traditional healers) firmly hold this viewpoint and aid patients in the healing process.[202] Cure comes through exorcism rituals, and among the Kelantanese Malays, dance is also involved as part of the ritual cure.[203] Firth notes that illnesses that are not effectively treated biomedically are as a result attributed to supernatural causation.[204]

The Iban of the Sarawak state in Malaysia attribute all illness to spiritual agencies.[205] When spirits are sought for knowledge, feasts must be held in return. One man who did not hold the required feasts fell feverishly ill and died.[206] Additionally, the ethnic Chinese of Sarawak, only outnumbered in population by the Iban, hold possession views similar to those of the Iban.

[198] Carmen Blacker, *The Catalpa Bow: A Study in Shamanistic Practices in Japan* (New York: Routledge Curzon, 1999), 300.

[199] Blacker, *Catalpa Bow*, 300.

[200] Blacker, *Catalpa Bow*, 306. The woman visited the temple after four months in the hospital with no improvement. She was diagnosed in the temple with possession by an ancestor. Her treatment was exorcism, and she recovered within one week's time. For more on exorcism, see Winston Davis, *Dojo: Magic and Exorcism in Modern Japan* (Stanford: Stanford University Press, 1980).

[201] S. M. Razali, U. A. Khan, and C. L. Hasanah, "Belief in Supernatural Causes of Mental Illness among Malay Patients: Impact on Treatment," *Acta Psychiatrica Scandinavica* 96.4 (1996): 229–33. See also Clive S. Kessler, "Conflict and Sovereignty in Kelantanese Malay Spirit Seances," in Crapanzano and Garrison, *Case Studies in Spirit Possession*, 295.

[202] Mohammed Razali Salleh, "The Consultation of Traditional Healers by Malay Patients," *Medical Journal of Malaysia* 44.1 (1989): 3–13.

[203] Barbara S. Wright, "Dance Is the Cure: The Arts as Metaphor for Healing in Kelantanese Malay Spirit Exorcisms," *Dance Research Journal* 12.2 (1980): 3–10. *Main Peteri* is a specific séance that reportedly is effective for healing as the result of exorcism. See also Raymond Firth, "Ritual and Drama in Malay Spirit Mediumship," *Comparative Studies in Society and History* 9.2 (1967): 190–207.

[204] Firth, "Ritual and Drama in Malay Spirit Mediumship," 192.

[205] Karl E. Schmidt, "Folk Psychiatry in Sarawak," in Kiev, *Magic, Faith, and Healing*, 143. For more information on possession and shamanistic healers who perform curative rites called *pelian*, see Robert J. Barrett, "Performance, Effectiveness and the Iban *Manang*," in Winzeler, *The Seen and the Unseen*, 235–79.

[206] Schmidt, "Folk Psychiatry in Sarawak," 146.

Spirits may afflict with illness, and an exorcist is required for relief.[207] Similarly, in Penang belief, illness is caused by an encounter with Datuk Kong during a possession trance.[208]

Mongolian shamanism involves shamans who practice in trance states and in non-trance states (not all requiring possession).[209] When a trance state is experienced, the term *ongon orox* ("the spirit enters") is used to describe the possession experience.[210] Seizures and fainting are commonly interpreted as the result of spirits making contact for initiation.[211] Exorcisms are sought to banish spirits that cause illness.[212] Manduhai Buyandelger provides a detailed depiction of the possession experience among the Bayan-Uul people in Mongolia. Her ethnography opens with a witness to the prevalence of shamans in this area. She notes, "Almost every family I know has a member who has been initiated as a shaman in order to appease the sudden influx of *ug garval* (origin spirits) . . ."[213] In one case she describes a family who indicated that modern medicine was of no help to the illnesses and deaths experienced in their family.[214] The most harmful spirit, an *uheer*, is only known because of the presence of illness.[215]

A blending of religious culture in Myanmar mixes the worship of *nats* (spirits) with Theravāda Buddhism.[216] *Nats* are known to disrupt the lives of those they would like to initiate as mediums by making them ill or causing

[207] Fiddler, "Spirit Possession as Exculpation," 208.

[208] Jean DeBernardi, *The Way That Lives in the Heart: Chinese Popular Religion and Spirit Mediums in Penang, Malaysia* (Stanford: Stanford University Press, 2006), 182.

[209] Ágnes Birtalan, "Mongolia," in Laycock, *Spirit Possession around the World*, 238.

[210] Birtalan, "Mongolia," 238. In this state the *süns* (soul) of the shaman is viewed to be withdrawn (however, this is debated among anthropologists).

[211] Birtalan, "Mongolia," 238. This is viewed as "uncontrolled possession."

[212] Birtalan, "Mongolia," 238. For more on Mongolian shamanism and the beliefs of Tibetan Buddhists in Mongolia, see Ágnes Birtalan, János Sipos, and J. Coloo, "'Talking to the *Ongons*': The Invocation Text and Music of a Darkhad Shaman," *Shaman* 12.1–2 (2004): 25–62; Ulla Johansen, "Ecstasy and Possession: A Short Contribution to a Lengthy Discussion," in *Rediscovery of Shamanic Heritage*, ed. Mihály Hoppál and Gábor Kósa, Bibliotheca Shamanistica 11 (Budapest: Akadémiai Kiadó, 2003), 135–52; Dávid Somfai-Kara, "Living Epic Traditions among Inner Asian Nomads," in Hoppál and Gábor, *Rediscovery of Shamanic Heritage*, 179–91.

[213] Manduhai Buyandelger, *Tragic Spirits: Shamanism, Memory, and Gender in Contemporary Mongolia* (Chicago: University of Chicago Press, 2013), 2. Origin spirits are ancestral spirits who seek revenge and may cause illness.

[214] Buyandelger, *Tragic Spirits*, 2.

[215] Buyandelger, *Tragic Spirits*, 20.

[216] Bénédicte Brac de la Perrière and Guillaume Rozenberg, "Burma," in Laycock, *Spirit Possession around the World*, 59. *Nats* are either benevolent or malevolent.

madness.[217] In Burmese views of possession, mental illness is attributed "exclusively to supernatural cause."[218] In certain illnesses caused by a *nat*, exorcism is required as a cure.[219]

In Taiwanese practice *Wangye* is a term to depict "deities of epidemics or demons of disease."[220] A belief exists that these spirits can cause epidemics that threaten their communities in great ways. Katz traces the view to the belief, prevalent in China, that the demons were men who died violent deaths, and the epidemics are "heavenly retribution."[221] When disease is inflicted, Taoist priests are called upon to placate or exorcise the spirits.[222] If a spirit is successful in resisting exorcism, they are often deified and appeased.[223]

Belief in spirits both benevolent and malevolent is documented in Southeast Asia.[224] Malevolent spirits are believed to enter a person's body and cause illness. Exorcism is regarded as the cure for illness. Some spirits roam about to cause trouble, while others react if their "space" is offended.[225] "Bad death" is known as the explanation for ancestral spirits (ghosts) who become malevolent spirits.[226]

Ethnographic research in Vietnam (and among Vietnamese in the United States) attests to the Mother Goddess religion (*Dao Mau*) and its spirit possession ritual (*len dong*).[227] The *len dong* ritual "serves their spirits . . . transform(s) their troubles into blessings, and become(s) the focal point for new

[217] de la Perrière and Rozenberg, "Burma," 59.

[218] Melford E. Spiro, *Burmese Supernaturalism* (New Brunswick, N.J.: Transaction, 1996), 157.

[219] Spiro, *Burmese Supernaturalism*, 159. Spiro gives reports of "witch caused illness" that results in severe stomach pain and mental illness (163–67).

[220] Paul Katz, "Demons or Deities?—The *Wangye* of Taiwan," *Asian Folklore Studies* 46.2 (1987): 199. *Wangye* are both malevolent and benevolent. However, one must not speak the name of the malevolent *wangye* as this is interpreted as a call for the spirit. Kenneth Dean, "Field Notes on Two Taoist *jiao* Observed in Zhangzhou in December 1985," *Cahiers d'Extrême-Asie* 2 (1986): 191–210, argues that the belief system of the *wangye* cult is common in both Taiwan and China.

[221] Katz, "Demons or Deities?" 211.

[222] Katz, "Demons or Deities?" 202.

[223] Katz, "Demons or Deities?" 203.

[224] For examples, see Robert L. Winzeler, *The Peoples of Southeast Asia Today: Ethnography, Ethnology, and Change in a Complex Region* (Lanham, Md.: Altamira, 2011), 153–54.

[225] Winzeler, *Peoples of Southeast Asia Today*, 154.

[226] Winzeler, *Peoples of Southeast Asia Today*, 155, See pp. 156–60 for examples from Burma, Thailand, and Malaysia.

[227] The ritual has widespread acceptance in Vietnam. See Karen Fjelstad and Nguyen Thi Hien, *Spirits without Borders: Vietnamese Spirit Mediums in a Transnational Age* (New York: Palgrave Macmillan, 2011), 71.

friendships."[228] Illness is often viewed as an invitation to become a medium.[229] Madness and hysteria are associated with possession by ghosts.[230] Another type of disease caused by spirits is a "knotted-hair disease," which is caused by a spirit who strikes its victim. If one does not pursue the right curative method and instead shaves his/her head, the person will be struck by the spirit, causing madness or death.[231] The yin disease is a disease caused by spirits that cannot be treated biomedically.[232] The only possible cure is to perform rituals and seek a medium who could learn from the spirits the cause and cure. Other spirits can cause sterility.[233] Folk belief includes the view that debts to the spirits may also cause illness.[234] Praying to the spirits allowed mediums the opportunity to cure patients.[235] Fjelstad and Hien report the testimony of one who indicated that "serving the spirits" aided in her recovery from severe headaches.[236] The spirits may punish through illness.[237]

In spirit cults in northern Vietnam,[238] symptoms of illness may be experienced during rituals performed to become a medium. One example includes a boy who frothed at the mouth, turned pale/blue in the face, and then collapsed

[228] Fjelstad and Hien, *Spirits without Borders*, 3, 6. The ritual began in northern Vietnam and has since spread, via fleeing refugees, to central and southern Vietnam, France, several Eastern European countries in the 1980s–1990s, and the United States.

[229] Fjelstad and Hien, *Spirits without Borders*, 20. Karen views her illness as an invitation.

[230] Hien writes about what she learned in the countryside growing up (Fjelstad and Hien, *Spirits without Borders*, 20).

[231] Fjelstad and Hien, *Spirits without Borders*, 21.

[232] Fjelstad and Hien, *Spirits without Borders*, 79. In this case the doctors could not find diagnoses but the medium diagnosed the yin disease and rituals were performed for healing. See also Nguyen Thi Hien, "Yin Illness: Its Diagnosis and the Healing with Len Dong (Spirit Possession) Rituals of the Viet," *Asian Ethnology* 67.2 (2008): 305–21.

[233] Fjelstad and Hien, *Spirits without Borders*, 52. See the story of Pham Nhan and his spirit who harasses women.

[234] Fjelstad and Hien, *Spirits without Borders*, 82. In this story the girl is unable to feed herself, laughs with a strange laugh, and trembles. Doctors could not find a cure.

[235] Fjelstad and Hien, *Spirits without Borders*, 21. Mrs. Nga, known as a "master medium," told of her ability to cure hundreds of her patients.

[236] Fjelstad and Hien, *Spirits without Borders*, 41–42.

[237] Fjelstad and Hien, *Spirits without Borders*, 55. Disrespecting the spirits in the temples or stealing from the temple could cause madness and illness. Pointing at a statue could cause one's finger to be removed. Spiritual punishment exists for violating sacred space.

[238] Thien Do, *Vietnamese Supernaturalism: Views from the Southern Region* (New York: Routledge Curzon, 2003), 90, notes that as of 2003 only two French studies give ethnographic data for this group. See Maurice Durand, *Technique et Panthéon des Médiums Vietnamiens (Dong)*, vol. 45 (Paris: École Française d'Extrême Orient, 1959); Pierre J. Simon and Ida Simon-Barouh, *Hâu Bóng: Un Culte Viêtnamien de Possession Transplanté en France* (Paris: Mouton, 1973).

into unconsciousness.[239] In Cao Dài practice in southern Vietnam, it is believed that malevolent spirits (*tà*) cause illness.[240] Talismans employ exorcism to cure "skin diseases, swellings and pains that did not have psychological causes."[241]

In a study of the popular religion of Vietnam, Pham Quynh Phuong concludes, "I discovered that spirit possession was a popular religious phenomenon of importance to people from all walks of life."[242] Phuong underscores that the Saint Tran cult, worshipping the thirteenth-century hero Tran Hung Dao, is burgeoning in Vietnam despite trends of industrialization and modernization.[243] Huong argues that mental and physical illness (including "barrenness, post-partum illness, sickness, contagious disease") and emotional problems are often viewed as the result of evil spirits (sometimes due to punishment by the evil spirit).[244] Additionally, the power of Saint Tran is often sought by mediums to perform exorcisms and cast out lesser spirits.[245]

Middle East

Among Yemenite Jews there is a belief in *shedim* (spirits) who cause mental illness. Diseases caused by spirits were grouped by Jozef Ph. Hes into three categories: "madness in which there are too many thoughts," "madness in which the patient is too quiet," and "true madness in which the patient is agitated, talks nonsense, and exhibits bizarre behavior like undressing in public."[246]

Many Palestinians maintain belief in *jinn* spirits, known for causing illness. Celia Rothenberg's ethnographic work focuses on the view of the villagers and their experience of "wearing" or being "worn by" a *jinn*.[247] The jinn are often

---

[239] Do, *Vitnamese Supernaturalism*, 92–93.

[240] Do, *Vietnamese Supernaturalism*, 81. Talismans treat these illnesses by banishing *tà* ("perverted spirits") and exterminating *qui* ("demons").

[241] Do, *Vietnamese Supernaturalism*, 81.

[242] Pham Quynh Phuong, *Hero and Deity: Tran Hung Dao and the Resurgence of Popular Religion in Japan* (Chiang Mai, Thailand: Mekong, 2009), 7.

[243] Phuong, *Hero and Deity*, 8.

[244] Phuong, *Hero and Deity*, 68–72. Illness caused by evil spirits is often called "*yin* illness," and one must appease the spirit or exorcise it for relief. "*Yang* illness" is able to be cured biomedically. For possession views and reports, see pp. 97–125.

[245] Phuong, *Hero and Deity*, 79–81. Several scholars have noted that exorcism is the main ritual of the cult of Saint Tran. See for example Durand, *Technique et Panthéon des Médiums Vietnamiens (Dong)*.

[246] Jozef Ph. Hes, "The Yemenite Mori," in Kiev, *Magic, Faith, and Healing*, 372. See pp. 375–76 for details on how they perform exorcism and what they consider plausible evidence that attests to the exit of the spirit(s).

[247] Rothenberg, *Spirits of Palestine*, 30. See p. 35 for the distinction made between being "haunted" and being possessed by a *jinn*.

responsible for fits of madness, infertility,[248] epilepsy,[249] and other varieties of illness. The *jinn* are not viewed as causing mental retardation or insanity in the West Bank.[250] More specifically, one man well known for his success in treating *jinn* cases noted a list of symptoms that could indicate jinn possession.[251] In some cases the illness is a warning or punishment for immorality.[252] One boy attacked by the *jinn* had his mouth paralyzed.[253] *Jinn* spirits are expelled rather than appeased.[254]

Belief in spirits, *jinn*, ghosts, demons, and evil spirits is well attested in Pakistan. A majority (Gallup reports testify to 89 percent belief among all Pakistanis) of Pakistanis maintain belief in *jinn* spirits.[255]

Illness is associated with possession in Pakistani belief, and Qurat ul ain Khan argues that possession is a societal explanation for severe psychiatric illness. ul ain Khan documents the story of a woman who experienced "delirious mania" with characteristics of "anger, agitation, and anxiety and decreased sleep."[256] In Peshawar, Pakistan women are prone to possession and a breakdown of health and especially mental illness. Fainting, weakness, and periods of shaking uncontrollably are often interpreted as a sign that a woman is possessed. Religious approaches are typically attempted for cure.

---

[248] Rothenberg, *Spirits of Palestine*, 36.

[249] Belief in two types of epilepsy exists. There is a "physical type" that indicates problems with the brain's composition and a second type caused by *jinn* spirits (treated by use of the Qu'ran). Rothenberg, *Spirits of Palestine*, 42.

[250] Rothenberg, *Spirits of Palestine*, 45.

[251] Rothenberg, *Spirits of Palestine*, 37–38. Examples include sleeplessness, night visions, bad dreams, seeing animals in one's bedroom, grinding teeth at night, laughing/crying in sleep, sleepwalking, seeing ghosts, experiencing headaches or weakness, having epilepsy, etc.

[252] Rothenberg, *Spirits of Palestine*, 34.

[253] Rothenberg, *Spirits of Palestine*, 33. Children are susceptible to *jinn* possession. This boy was attacked by a *jinn* spirit as a means of punishing his mother, who smacked him in the face.

[254] Rothenberg, *Spirits of Palestine*, 39.

[255] Maleeha Aslam, "Pakistan," in Laycock, *Spirit Possession around the World*, 272. The number is higher among rural Pakistanis—recorded at 91 percent. See also David Pinault, *Notes from the Fortune-Telling Parrot: Islam and the Struggle for Religious Pluralism in Pakistan* (Oakville, Conn.: Equinox, 2008), 134. Pinault notes the pervasive belief in *jinns*, which he describes as "widespread among all social classes." He was surprised by the anxiety present among educated and uneducated, wealthy and poor, related to the "intrusive presence of malevolent spirit-forces." Pinault discovers the local belief that *jinn* dwell in deserted places (151). See also Amira El-Zein, *Islam, Arabs, and the Intelligent World of the Jinn* (Syracuse, N.Y.: Syracuse University Press, 2009).

[256] Qurat ul ain Khan and Aisha Sanober, "'Jinn Possession' and Delirious Mania in a Pakistani Woman," *American Journal of Psychiatry* 173.3 (2016): 219–20.

If these are not successful, the women are engaged in a *baithak* session to remove the evil spirit.[257]

Among those who adhere to the Muslim religion in Turkey there is the belief in spirits (*jinn*), who are known to be aggressive. Mental illness is often viewed as the result of possession by a *jinn* (also called "mixed-up" by the *jinn*). This possession may happen by accident or because of the violation of a taboo.[258] A "strike," "breeze," or "holding" from *jinn* spirits may also cause a variety of illnesses including "aphonia, aphasia, strokes, epileptic attacks, or certain 'mixed up' states known in psychiatry as schizophrenic reactions, manias, and severe delusional depressions."[259]

Middle America and the Caribbean

Afro-Atlantic religions (referring to various religions such as Candomblé, Santería, Umbanda, and Vodou) found in various parts of North America, South America, and the Caribbean typically maintain possession belief and relationships of reciprocity with spirits or deities.[260] Possession by spirits honors deities and spirits, and dishonoring the spirits may result in illness or misfortune. In emic terms, fulfilling obligations to the spirits/deities serves the purpose of sustaining one's *ashe* (spiritual energy). If one does not sustain *ashe*, Schmidt summaries that "a person lives without harmony and suffers emotional, physical, or even social and economic problems."[261] The sections below will treat these religious themes with more specificity as they play out in each context.

The influence of Santería (also referred to as Orisha religion) is prevalent in Cuban religion and draws upon African and Catholic religiosity. In this context a connection is made between spirit possession and mental illness.[262] Further, Spiritists maintain the belief in the possibility that illness is caused by foreign agents, including spirits.[263]

---

[257] Mumtaz Nasir, "*Baithak*: Exorcism in Peshawar (Pakistan)," *Asian Folklore Studies* 46.2 (1987): 159–78. Nasir argues the mental illness is psychosomatic and that the problem is dying out due to modernization in Pakistan.

[258] Orhan M. Ozturk, "Folk-Treatment in Turkey," in Kiev, *Magic, Faith, and Healing*, 351.

[259] Ozturk, "Folk-Treatment in Turkey," 351. Anxiety may also result. These beliefs remain despite the outlawing of sorcery.

[260] Bettina E. Schmidt, "Afro-Atlantic Religions," in Laycock, *Spirit Possession around the World*, 3.

[261] Schmidt, "Afro-Atlantic Religions," 3.

[262] Leonardo Alonso, "Mental Illness Complicated by the Santeria Belief in Spirit Possession," *Hospital and Community Psychiatry* 39.11 (1988): 1188–91.

[263] Diana Espirito Santo, "'Who Else Is in the Drawer?' Trauma, Personhood and Prophylaxis among Cuban Scientific Spiritists," *Anthropology and Medicine* 17.3 (2010): 258.

In Haiti, where Voudou is the national religion, 95 percent of people attest to belief in spirits.[264] When Carol De Lynch was asked to define the force or strength of Vodou, she replied, "We must heal all that (are) suffering."[265] Diagnosis is often sought through possessed healers, who may offer a variety of treatments.[266] A *gad* (guard) may be applied in the treatment of serious cases to prevent a patient from future harm.[267] In *Lwa* possession, when a spirit possesses a person, it is said that the spirit has mounted his/her horse (*chwal*). The *chwal* are used by the *Lwa* to have communication with participants.[268] Illnesses such as schizophrenia are often attributed to spirit possession.[269]

Jamaicans participating in Rastafarian religion maintain belief that spirits are near and that they are hierarchically arranged.[270] Spirits of the dead, *duppies*, are known for their harm and "roam abroad at night, frightening and terrorizing the living"[271] *Obeahmen* use spirits to bring about harm to others. Interestingly, natural remedies are generally believed to provide relief for all illness, even though treatments are known to combine nature along with magic and ritual.[272]

This is especially in reference to spirits sent by witchcraft and represents only part of their taxonomy of aetiologies for illness.

[264] Claudine Michel, "Of Worlds Seen and Unseen: The Educational Character of Haitian Vodou," in *Haitian Vodou: Spirit, Myth, and Reality*, ed. Patrick Bellegarde-Smith and Claudine Michel (Bloomington: Indiana University Press, 2006), 34. Religion in Haiti is syncretistic, with many practicing Catholicism publicly and Voudou privately. They do not name themselves as adherents to religions but identify as "serving spirits."

[265] Claudine Michel, Patrick Bellegarde-Smith, and Marlène Racine-Toussaint, "From the Horses' Mouths: Women's Words/Women's Worlds," in Bellegarde-Smith and Michel, *Haitian Vodou*, 80.

[266] Max-G. Beauvoir, "Herbs and Energy: The Holistic Medical System of the Haitian People," in Bellegarde-Smith and Michel, *Haitian Vodou*, 131. Sacrifices to the spirits are commonly made.

[267] Beauvoir, "Herbs and Energy," 132.

[268] Michel, Bellegarde-Smith, and Racine-Toussaint, "From the Horses' Mouths," 82. See more on this in chapter 6.

[269] Kiev, "The Study of Folk Psychiatry," in Kiev, *Magic, Faith, and Healing*, 9. Sorcery is another attributed cause.

[270] Jesus is the top spirit, but he is not believed to possess people. See Barry Chevannes, "Rastafari and Other African-Caribbean Worldviews," in *Perspectives on the Caribbean: A Reader in Culture, History and Representation*, ed. Philip W. Scher (Chichester, UK: Wiley-Blackwell, 2010), 214.

[271] Chevannes, "Rastafari and Other African-Caribbean Worldviews," 214.

[272] Chevannes, "Rastafari and Other African-Caribbean Worldviews," 215.

Oceania

Religion in Oceania is heavily characterized by belief in ghosts, described as the spirits of the dead who embody spirits.[273] Douglas Oliver notes that "all Oceanian societies" have belief in other spirits who have embodied humans.[274] Following the belief system in spirits and ghosts, several terms are used among the Māori people to refer to a "spiritual illness."[275] The Māori argue that certain illnesses are incurable by a medical doctor and may have a variety of causes, including ghosts or malevolent spirits.[276] The Māori claim the presence of the *wairua a tētahi tangata kē* ("spirit of another person") in their definition of these illnesses.[277]

Mary Caygill and Philip Culbertson address spirit possession among the Samoan and Tongan people.[278] In this context illness and spirit possession are heavily interconnected. Illness and injury may not be understood as happenstance. Spirits are known to intervene. Drozdow-St Christian defines it in the following terms:

> . . . it involves being tripped or hit and occasionally entered by the *aitu*, each of which can cause injury or illness. It is also not necessarily enacted on the specific offender in a family. As often as not, *aitu* will attack some other, usually weaker, family member, including unborn children.[279]

---

[273] Douglas L. Oliver, *Oceania: The Native Cultures of Australia and the Pacific Islands*, vol. 1 (Honolulu: University of Hawai'i Press, 1989), 133.

[274] Oliver, *Oceania*, 134.

[275] Henare Arekatera Tate, "A Māori Perspective on Spirit Possession," in Wainwright, with Culbertson and Smith, *Spirit Possession, Theology, and Identity*, 13.

[276] Tate, "Māori Perspective," 13. Examples of causes include going to a forbidden place or taking something sacred. They say they "are suffering from the ill-will of another, or of others who are exercising spiritual power to diminish or disempower the afflicted person as a form of punishment or retribution."

[277] Tate, "Māori Perspective," 14.

[278] Mary Caygill and Philip Culbertson, "Constructing Identity and Theology in the World of Samoan and Tongan Spirits," in Wainwright with Culbertson and Smith, *Spirit Possession, Theology, and Identity*, 25. Interestingly, Caygill and Culbertson argue that it is not convincing to pathologize the spirit world of the Tongan and Samoan as some Westerners do. For more detail on Tongan views of spirit possession including the link between possession and location and a Tongan reading of Mark 5:1–20, see Winston Halapua, "A *Moana* Rhythm of Well-Being," in in Wainwright with Culbertson and Smith, *Spirit Possession, Theology, and Identity*, 94–97.

[279] Douglass Drozdow-St Christian, *Elusive Fragments: Making Power, Propriety, and Health in Samoa* (Durham, N.C.: Carolina Academic Press, 2002), 127.

Further, the matter is so serious that an attack by an *aitu* (spirit) is considered as the second most dangerous illness (secondary to diabetes).[280] Spirits are also believed to affect mental health.[281] Western attempts to treat spiritual sicknesses are not viewed as effective by Samoans and Tongans, despite attempts by colonizing forces to reformulate the emic perspective. Soa, a man interviewed, described the two positions on mental illness as a "clash of worldviews."[282] Macpherson adds that the relationship between supernatural agents and illness remains, even despite attempts by Christian missionaries to introduce Western explanations and remedies.[283]

The Bosavis of Papua New Guinea view serious illness as the effect of a *sei* creature. The illness represents damage done by the *sei*, which projects the illness onto the physical body. For example, "If the patient could not stand or walk, it implied that the *sei* had cut off the spirit counterpart of his/her legs. If the *sei* had cut his/her (spirit body's) throat, s/he would not be able to swallow or speak."[284] In a phonological accident, the result of Christianization, the Bosavis, who had been told to forget about *sei* since they were not in the Bible, began to refer to *seis* as *seten* because of their first letters.[285]

---

[280] Drozdow-St Christian, *Elusive Fragments*, 172. See also Laurie K. Gluckman, "Clinical Experience with Samoans in Auckland," *Australian and New Zealand Journal of Psychiatry* 11.2 (1997): 101–7. Gluckman describes their syndromes as culturally defined, due to violating customs or upsetting ancestral spirits.

[281] Mary Keller, *The Hammer and the Flute: Women, Power, and Spirit Possession* (Baltimore: Johns Hopkins University Press, 2002), 58. Contrary to Erika Bourguignon, *A World of Women: Anthropological Studies of Women in Societies of the World* (New York: Praeger, 1980) and Felicitas Goodman, *Speaking in Tongues: A Cross-cultural Study of Glossolalia* (Chicago: University of Chicago Press, 1972), Keller does not equate possession and insanity. She argues that possession fulfills a propensity for an experience with an alternate reality. See also David Lui, "Spiritual Injury: A Samoan Perspective on Spirituality's Impact on Mental Health," in *Penina Uliuli: Contemporary Challenges in Mental Health for Pacific Peoples*, ed. Philip Culbertson, Margaret Nelson Agee, and Cabrini 'Ofa Makasiale (Honolulu: University of Hawai'i Press, 2007), 66–76.

[282] Caygill and Culbertson, "Constructing Identity and Theology in the World of Samoan and Tongan Spirits," 46.

[283] Cluny Macpherson, "Samoan Medicine," in *Healing Practices in the South Pacific*, ed. Claire Parsons (Honolulu: Institute for Polynesian Studies, Brigham Young University, 1985), 3.

[284] Edward L. Schieffelin, "Evil Spirit Sickness, the Christian Disease: The Innovation of a New Syndrome of Mental Derangement and Redemption in Papua New Guinea," *Culture, Medicine, and Psychiatry* 20.1 (1996): 9.

[285] Schieffelin, "Evil Spirit Sickness, the Christian Disease," 13.

In the Caroline Islands of Micronesia, a trifold classification of spirits defines domains of illness and cure. Waloeai and Lamotrek groups maintain belief in both malevolent and benevolent spirits. These spirits represent aetiologies for illness and cure, and divination is employed to diagnose and cure.[286]

South America

In South America, cross-religious perspectives on the relationship between spirit possession and illness and curative exorcistic rites are also found. Witnesses from the Christian, Spiritist, Sainto Dame, Muslim, and Umbanda religions provide analogues that further our conversation. Below is a foray into exemplar belief, testimonies, and experiences in this region.

Modern Brazil has a long-standing history of spirit-possession practices. Dawson categorizes possession experience into five religious contexts.[287] In eighteenth-century religion, *Calundu*[288] was performed in Minas Geiras as a spirit-possession ritual for healing. The ritual was widely performed in Minas Gerias by African healers who cared for sick and enslaved miners.[289] Case studies of African healers and healing communities further attest to healing rituals.[290]

Within the Christian context and rituals, "spirit possession is regarded as a pathological condition that needs rectifying through the exorcism of evil, demonic forces."[291] Exorcism is called "liberation" (*libertaçao*), and exorcisms

---

[286] William H. Alkire, "The Traditional Classification and Treatment of Illness on Woleai and Lamotrek in the Caroline Islands, Micronesia," *Culture* 2.1 (1982): 29–41.

[287] Andrew Dawson, "Brazil," in Laycock, *Spirit Possession around the World*, 49. Religious contexts include indigenous, Christian, Afro-Brazilian, Spiritist, and New Religious. For Candomblé and related Afro-religious traditional experience, see Andrew Dawson, *New Era—New Religions: Religious Transformation in Contemporary Brazil* (Farnham, UK: Ashgate, 2007), 17, who notes that benefits of healing were noted in possession and exorcism rites.

[288] Kalle Kananoja, "Infected by the Devil, Cured by Calundu: African Healers in Eighteenth-Century Minas Gerais, Brazil," *Social History of Medicine* 29.3 (2016): 496, notes that the original term was *quilundo* and described possession by an ancestral spirit. The term developed to include the ceremonial rituals and dances that were associated with possession. Broadly, it could refer to any African healing practice, but it typically implied possession ritual (510).

[289] Kananoja, "Infected by the Devil, Cured by Calundu," 491.

[290] Laura de Mello e Souza, *The Devil and the Land of the Holy Cross: Witchcraft, Slavery, and Popular Religion in Colonial Brazil* (Austin: University of Texas Press, 2003), 233–38. For studies of individual healers, see James H. Sweet, *Domingos Álvares, African Healing, and the Intellectual History of the Atlantic World* (Chapel Hill: University of North Carolina Press, 2011); Joäo José Reis, *Domingos Sodré, um Sacerdote Africano: Escravidào, liberddade e candomblé na Bahia do século XIX* (São Paulo: Companhia das Letras, 2008).

[291] Dawson, "Brazil," 49–50. In the neo-Pentecostal context, "liberation" rituals "are explicitly designed to compete with and rectify the consequences of supposedly demonic traditions such as Candomblé, Spiritism, and Umbanda."

are performed on both individuals and congregations.[292] Involvement with exorcistic practices varies when comparing Catholic and Protestant neo-Pentecostal movements, with neo-Pentecostal groups regularly practicing exorcism on Friday evenings. Dawson argues the neo-Pentecostal movement in Brazil appropriated exorcism, a practice already well known in Brazil's religious environment.[293] Additionally, he situates their practice among religious dialogue, showing that these rituals of "liberation" purpose "to compete with and rectify the consequences of supposedly demonic traditions such as Condomblé, Spiritism, and Umbanda."[294]

Within Spiritism,[295] healing from possession[296] is performed through the process of "disobsession" (*desobsessão*), namely, the removal of a "less evolved or disoriented spirit."[297] Dawson summarizes,

> The intrusion of an errant spirit into the body of another causes physical, emotional, and psychological problems that will continue, if not worsen, until the intrusive spirit is ritually persuaded or coerced into returning to the spiritual plane.[298]

Spiritism also plays a large role in mental health and mental health disturbance. Alexander Moreira-Almeida and Francisco Lotufo Neto document the religious

---

[292] Sidney M. Greenfield, *Spirits with Scalpels: The Cultural Biology of Religious Healing in Brazil* (Walnut Creek, Calif.: Left Coast Press, 2008), 141. See also David Lehmann, *Struggle for the Spirit: Religious Transformation and Popular Culture in Brazil and Latin America* (Cambridge, Mass.: Blackwell, 1996), 139–42.

[293] Dawson, *New Era—New Religions*, 14. For more detail, see Ricardo Mariano, *Neopentecostais: Sociologia do Novo Pentecostalismo no Brasil* (São Paulo: Edições Loyola, 1999), 109–46; Paul Freston, "Breve História do Pentecostalismo Brasileiro," in *Nem Anjos, Nem Demônios: Interpretações Sociologicas Do Pentecostalismo*, by Alberto Antoniazzi et al. (Petrópolis, Brazil: Editora Vozes, 1994), 138–39, 142. One might also want to note that the "Romanization" of Catholic Christianity in Brazil worked to modernize views and get rid of "superstitious excesses" such as possession and exorcism beliefs and practices. Dawson, *New Era—New Religions*, 35–36, notes that this attempt "failed ultimately to expunge these elements from the popular religious consciousness of which they remained a fundamental constituent."

[294] Dawson, "Brazil," 50.

[295] Spiritism originated in France in the middle of the nineteenth century with Hyppolyte-Léon Danizard Rivail (Allan Kardec). He sought to scientifically investigate how spirits manifest. See Alexander Moreira-Almeida and Francisco Lotufo Neto, "Spiritist Views of Mental Disorders in Brazil," *Transcultural Psychiatry* 42.4 (2005): 571.

[296] Healing from other physical ailments is also cured by medium healers. Greenfield, *Spirits with Scalpels*, 23–72, documents several accounts of "spiritual surgeries."

[297] "Obsession" is the term used to refer to spirits who compete for the same body.

[298] Dawson, "Brazil," 51. For a fuller description, see Greenfield, *Spirits with Scalpels*, 73–88.

system's "rational spiritual etiology" for mental disturbances.[299] Spiritism is inclusive in its aetiological description of mental illness, including social and biological causes; however, it furthers the aetiology by including what Kardec describes as "the persistent action that an evil spirit exerts over an individual."[300] Spiritism in Brazil was also impacted by Adolfo Bezerra de Menezes Cavalcanti, a physician, who argued for the involvement of spirits in mental illness. He recounts the testimony of a patient who renounces a "persecutor spirit" and his "timely resumption of mental faculties."[301] Inácio Ferreira continued Spiritist treatments from 1934 to 1988 and headed up the institution named Senatório Espírita de Uberaba. Ferreira's views on developing as a medium and reconciling with superior spirits is the predominant view in current Spiritist belief.[302] Spiritists argue that the spiritual cause of mental illness is complementary to other causes.[303]

The new religion of Santo Daime continues to classify spirits into categories. "Suffering spirits," or third-class spirits, cause physical harm to those they inhabit.[304] Spirits can possess involuntarily (Brazilian terminology exists to depict involuntary possession, namely *atuação* ["activation"] and *obsessão* ["obsession"]) and cause "spirit assault" upon victims.[305] These possessions are viewed pejoratively by *daimistas* (spirit mediums) and require resolution by ritual engagement. Dawson records the testimony of a trained medium who states, "What it shows is sickness, bad feelings and bad things."[306] Cases of

---

[299] Moreira-Almeida and Neto, "Spiritist Views," 572. These views are widely embraced in contemporary Brazil (even by health care professionals) and led to the building of approximately fifty Spiritist hospitals from 1930 to 1970.

[300] Allan Kardec, *A gênese, os milagres e as predições Segundo o espiritismo* (Rio de Janeiro: FEB, 1992 [1868]), 45. Translation by Moreira-Almeida and Lotufo Neto, "Spiritist Views," 572. Kardec made three classifications, characterized by severity: (1) simple obsession, which deals with influencing thoughts; (2) fascination, which deals with paralysis of judgment; and (3) subjugation or possession, which deals with paralysis of the will and causes involuntary acts. See Allan Kardec, *The Mediums' Book*, trans. Anna Blackwell (Rio de Janeiro: FEB, 1986 [1861]), 237–40.

[301] Adolfo Bezerra de Menezes Cavalcanti, *A loucura sob novo prisma* (Rio de Janeiro: FEB, 1988 [1897]), 141–43. Bezerra tracked the patient for three years and the patient had no relapse and completed medical school.

[302] Moreira-Almeida and Lotufo Neto, "Spiritist Views," 584.

[303] See Vivian Garrison, "The 'Puerto Rican Syndrome' in Psychiatry and *Espiritismo*," in Crapanzano and Garrison, *Case Studies in Spirit Possession*, 392, for statistics related to the belief in "spiritual causation" of their ailments.

[304] Andrew Dawson, *Santo Daime: A New World Religion* (London: Bloomsbury, 2013), 124, 127. These engagements with spirits are "graded by degrees." A distinction is made between an attachment to the "vibrational field" ("aura," "energy field," "matrix") and the entrance into the person's body. The latter is believed to cause a more severe condition.

[305] Dawson, *Santo Daime*, 127.

[306] Dawson, *Santo Daime*, 128.

possession (especially the most severe ones) are treated through rituals that act therapeutically upon the victim.[307] The "Cross Ritual" (*Trabalho de Cruzes*) is a "work of exorcism and disobsession" for relief.[308]

In the Peruvian Andes, there exists a belief in "mountain spirits," described by Marieka Sax as "named, individualized, and autochthonous powers embodied in specific landforms (i.e. mountains or outcrops), and . . . referred to in various communities as 'lord' (*apu*), 'condor' (*maliku*), and 'hawk' (*wamani*)."[309] Mountain spirits are largely associated with matters of health and offerings are specifically made for matters of prosperity and fertility.[310] The relationship between the mountain spirits and the Peruvians is one of reciprocity, and if offerings are not made, then angry spirits will react by causing illness or misfortune.[311]

Umbanda religiosity includes a hierarchy of spirits. It is believed that spirits of the underworld cause illness (though natural causes are not excluded). They "cause mischief and suffering wherever they can."[312] A medium seeks counsel from higher spirits to provide remedies, which include exorcism or placations.[313]

In the religion of Candomblé, Umbanda spirits (*orixás*) possess mediums to heal. Dawson summarizes,

> Most commonly, illness and misfortune are attributed to the work of "low" spirits attracted by bad thoughts and deeds or summoned by third parties' intent on doing harm.[314]

"Spirit consultants" are often sought for healing from illness. Clients describe their illness, and the "spirit consultant" will diagnose the cause. It is common for the cause to be attributed to "ignorant, backward, suffering or evil spirits." These spirits are exorcised through ritual healing.[315] Diana DeGroat Brown surveyed 403 Umbanda participants and noted that 70 percent believed spirits

---

[307] Dawson, *Santo Daime*, 128, notes that Padrinho Sebastião is known for his rituals (e.g., "the rituals of Cure and Saint Michael").

[308] Dawson, *Santo Daime*, 128. See also https://www.santodaime.org.

[309] Marieka Sax, *An Ethnography of Feeding, Perception, and Place in the Peruvian Andes: Where Hungry Spirits Bring Illness and Wellbeing* (Lampeter, UK: Mellen, 2011), 37.

[310] Sax, *Ethnography of Feeding*, 37.

[311] Sax, *Ethnography of Feeding*, 37. Illness and misfortune may fall on households and livestock.

[312] Dawon, *New Era—New Religions*, 26.

[313] Dawson, *New Era—New Religions*, 26.

[314] Dawson, "Brazil," 49–50.

[315] See also Diana DeGroat Brown, *Umbanda Religion and Politics in Urban Brazil* (Ann Arbor, Mich.: UMI Research Press, 1986), 97.

do cause illness and suffering.[316] Curative measures involve ritual cleansings and exorcisms, among others measures.[317]

Western Experiences

While it is true that much skepticism related to possession accounts has been produced in Western literature, it is not possible to demonstrate that skepticism provides an explanation for the experience of all global societies. Levack notes that scholars tend to cite other skeptical literature as evidence that educated Europeans have banished beliefs in spirits and possession from their "mental landscape."[318] He writes, "They use this literature to document the 'disenchantment' of the world and celebrate the inexorable triumph of rationalism and secularism in European intellectual life."[319] Levack counters this skepticism by acknowledging the slow growth of secular and rationalized thought about possession throughout history. He adds that clergy, those who most commonly deal with instances of possession, "have never adopted an unqualified skepticism regarding demonic possession."[320] Additionally, Stafford Betty reports that in the United States there is an increase in the belief in demonic involvement and the number of exorcisms performed.[321]

Further, June Macklin notes that social scientists have regarded spirit-possession experience as part of a normal range of behavior, except

[316] Brown, *Umbanda Religion and Politics in Urban Brazil*, 98.

[317] Brown, *Umbanda Religion and Politics in Urban Brazil*, 98. Prophylactic measures (such as lighting candles to ward off evil spirits and attract good ones), homeopathic remedies, and practical advice are also utilized in Umbanda religion. Dawson, "Brazil," 49–50, notes the wide range of remedies: "from spiritual cleansing and ritual exorcism, through placatory offerings and counter alliances with 'high' spirits, to visiting a doctor or adopting a more positive mental attitude."

[318] Levack, *Devil Within*, 230.

[319] Levack, *Devil Within*, 230.

[320] Levack, *Devil Within*, 230–31. Levack especially cites the mid-eighteenth-century case in Germany of Friedrich Hoffman, who "tenaciously clung" to his possession beliefs. See Levack, *Devil Within*, 230–34, for documentation of Westerners who held on to their belief despite pressure from skeptics and Enlightenment reason. Levack, *Devil Within*, 239, argues that the history of the "progressive secularization of healing" and the "triumph of secularism" are at times overstated in Western history, especially when one considers examples such as spiritual healing among Russian Orthodox communities during the imperial period. See also Christine D. Worobec, *Possessed: Women, Witches and Demons in Imperial Russia* (DeKalb: Northern Illinois University Press, 2001), 28–30.

[321] Stafford Betty, "The Growing Evidence for 'Demonic Possession': What Should Psychiatry's Response Be?" *Journal of Religion and Health* 44.1 (2005): 13–30.

when it appears in Western culture.[322] She indicates that the phenomena are reported with "anthropological solemnity and interest" when they are reported from other locales.[323] When they are reported in the West, they are considered as part of "deviant" behavior.[324] Even so, possession accounts are reported in Western areas, though maybe not as prolifically as in other locations. However, one might wonder what additional reports could be added if anthropologists and social scientists gave the same attention to Western environments in anthropological and ethnographic studies. Below are some Western examples related to reports of possession experiences that explain the reason for illness.

The Siberian, also known as Asiatic, Eskimos are described as having experienced "exotic forms of mental illness."[325] Possession and seizures are also associated with mental illness and the practice of shamanism.[326] Spirit intrusion is believed to cause and aid in the cure of illness.[327] In the first sense, it accounts for "insanity and episodic hysteria."[328] In the second, spirits aid shamans in the diagnosis for cure.[329]

Adam Blai, a leading exorcist in the Catholic Church[330] in the United States, argues that the Catholic Church has always maintained belief in the reality of spirits and has responded with the practice of exorcism.[331] Blai maintains that

---

[322] June Macklin, "A Connecticut Yankee in Summer Land," in Crapanzano and Garrison, *Case Studies in Spirit Possession*, 41.

[323] Macklin, "Connecticut Yankee in Summer Land," 41.

[324] Macklin, "Connecticut Yankee in Summer Land," 41.

[325] Jane M. Murphy, "Psychotherapeutic Aspects of Shamanism," in Kiev, *Magic, Faith, and Healing*, 55. Some have labeled the syndromes as "arctic hysteria."

[326] Murphy, "Psychotherapeutic Aspects of Shamanism," 56, 81. Seizures are the evidence of possession by a spirit-familiar.

[327] The term "intrusion" in this culture specifically relates to the belief that spirits cause illness that is not diagnosable. "Possession" does not necessarily relate to illness. For example, St. Lawrence shamans are not considered as "insane" during possession. See Murphy, "Psychotherapeutic Aspects of Shamanism," 69.

[328] Murphy, "Psychotherapeutic Aspects of Shamanism," 68.

[329] Murphy, "Psychotherapeutic Aspects of Shamanism," 68–69.

[330] For a history of the views related to exorcism in Catholicism, see Francis Young, *A History of Exorcism in Catholic Christianity* (Cambridge: Palgrave, 2016); Marco Innamorati, Ruggero Taradel, and Renato Foschi, "Between Sacred and Profane: Possession, Psychotherapy, and the Catholic Church," *History of Psychology* 22.1 (2018): 1–16; Renato Foschi, Marco Innamorati, and Ruggero Taradel, "'A Disease of Our Time': The Catholic Church's Condemnation and Absolution of Psychoanalysis (1924–1975)," *Journal of the History of Behavioral Sciences* 54.2 (2018): 85–100.

[331] Adam C. Blai, "Exorcism and the Church: Through Priests, the Church Has the Power to Battle Demons," *The Priest* 73.8 (2017): 16–19. See also Adam C. Blai, *Hauntings, Possessions, and Exorcisms* (Steubenville, Ohio: Emmaus Road, 2017).

cases of demonic possession are on the rise, which has produced a need for trained exorcists. In 1990 the International Association of Exorcists was established by Father Gabriele Amorth and a group of priests. In 2016, 450 members were present for the group's conference.[332] Blai affirms that spirits may afflict the body with mental and physical problems. Related to mental health, he affirms that "it is normal to be frustrated and possibly depressed after being harassed by spirits for some time."[333] Related to physical health, he affirms that "it is not uncommon for spirits to cause physical health problems if they are inside a person."[334] He affirms that there is also a relationship between exorcism and healing by noting that "it is not uncommon for people with spirits in them to have untreatable medical conditions that stop as soon as the spirit is cast out."[335] Blai's approach does not deny the value in medical and psychological evaluations and expertise, and the church requires that all "mundane" explanations and treatment options must be ruled out before exorcism is considered as an option.[336]

The Cochiti Indians in New Mexico maintain belief that demons are responsible for attacks that cause illness. Some doctors have claimed to experience a "terrible battle in the darkness" because witches get "inside them." Witchcraft, resulting in "witch illness," accounts for many Cochiti interpretations of illness. The Medicine Man is turned to for cure.[337]

Mormons do maintain belief in the devil and evil spirits. However, if one seeks an official statement from church officials on the matter, one will look in vain. Stephen Taysom summarizes, "Despite official silence on the subject, Mormons have a long, and continuing, history of casting out evil spirits."[338] Taysom, highlights the founder Joseph Smith's view that spirits seek to embody through possession, a way of mimicking the incarnation.[339] Joseph Smith inherited and absorbed Catholic depictions of possession characteristics and

---

[332] Blai, "Exorcism and the Church," 16. Innamorati, Taradel, and Foschi, "Between Sacred and Profane," 8, note that the most recent figures show 404 members and 124 auxiliaries. A majority are located in Italy (268 members and 62 auxiliaries).

[333] Adam C. Blai, "Basic Information," *Religious Demonology*, accessed May 22, 2023, https://religiousdemonology.com/basics.

[334] Blai, "Basic Information."

[335] Blai, "Basic Information."

[336] Blai, "Exorcism and the Church," 19. See also Alan Bernard McGill, "Diagnosing Demons and Healing Humans: The Pastoral Implications of a Holistic View of Evil," *New Theology Review* 27.2 (2015): 70–80.

[337] J. Robin Fox, "Witchcraft and Clanship," in Kiev, *Magic, Faith, and Healing*, 186, 195.

[338] Stephen Taysom, "'Satan Mourns Naked upon the Earth': Locating Mormon Possession and Exorcism Rituals in the American Religious Landscape, 1830–1977," *Religion and American Culture* 27.1 (2017): 57–94.

[339] Taysom, "'Satan Mourns Naked upon the Earth,'" 61.

had his own experience with satanic attack. As summarized by Taysom, Smith "flatly rejected the belief that the Devil lacked the power to physically afflict, much less possess, human beings."[340] Smith's views are found in the views of his followers, and Taysom documents this in his diachronic study of Mormon belief related to evil spirits and exorcism.

The Navahos reference "foreign powers that can affect a person," and possession by these powers is largely related to mental illness.[341] The Navahos are known for saying, "It is not me who is acting this way but the spirit that is possessing me."[342] One of the main types of mental illness among Navahos has symptoms of epilepsy. The Navaho believe that during these "fits" the person is "not himself."[343]

Considering European expression, a variety of forms of possession cause illness in Hungarian belief. Pócs argues that in Southeastern Europe there is a widespread belief in a form of possession by the dead that is expressed as possession by fairies.[344] Possession by a fairy or illness demons may produce a wide variety of illnesses, including headache, epileptic symptoms, aching limbs, paralysis, a stroke, muteness, a misconfigured face, loss of the mind, and more.[345] Eastern and southern Slavic groups maintain belief in illness demons. Examples include "Russian fever demons" and "Romanian, Serbian cholera demons."[346] These demons are exorcised with specific formulae that result in relief from illness.[347] Taysom attests to exorcism as a continuing practice in response to possession.

Pócs underscores the similarities between the Christian devil and Eastern European "unclean ones" or "evil ones." This merging of or similarity

[340] Taysom, "'Satan Mourns Naked upon the Earth,'" 69. For four case studies of possession, see Taysom, "'Satan Mourns Naked upon the Earth,'" 70–85.

[341] Bert Kaplan and Dale Johnson, "Navaho Psychopathology," in Kiev, *Magic, Faith, and Healing*, 206.

[342] Kaplan and Johnson, "Navaho Psychopathology," 207.

[343] Kaplan and Johnson, "Navaho Psychopathology," 210.

[344] Éva Pócs, "Possession Phenomena, Possession-Systems: Some East-Central European Examples," in *Communicating with the Spirits*, ed. Éva Pócs and Gábor Klaniczay (Budapest: Central European University Press, 2005), 100. Pócs differentiates the belief of the non-Slavic people, indicating that their belief in fairies only has a sort of "dead-like" characteristic.

[345] Pócs, "Possession Phenomena, Possession-Systems," 99–101.

[346] Pócs, "Possession Phenomena, Possession-Systems," 105.

[347] Pócs, "Possession Phenomena, Possession-Systems," 122. Pócs highlights how Christian exorcism "had a serious unifying influence on folk conceptions of demonic possession, because it offered priests, wizards, healers, and ordinary people alike an effective remedy against all the demons and witches discussed here."

of characteristics is found in Hungarian, Estonian, Russian, and Romanian views. She writes, "The influence of Christian notions of the devil and of possession was, however, so significant that by the modern era it has become impossible to describe folk demons and possession concepts independently of Christian notions and church exorcism practices."[348] Reports reflect this Christian influence and substantiate parallel symptoms of illness as characteristic of possession. Characteristics include physical and mental forms of illness: "general malaise, headache, . . . symptoms of depression, such as deep lethargy, the feeling of 'darkness,' death wish, suicidal tendencies . . ."[349]

In Italian Catholicism, Marco Innamorati, Ruggero Taradel, and Renato Foschi attest to the burgeoning need for exorcists in Italy, which is experiencing a "significant revival of the practice of exorcism."[350] Tonino Cantelmi reports that "thousands" of people in Italy are requesting exorcisms.[351] In 2000 the *Associazione Italiana Psicologi e Psichiatri Cattolici* (AIPPC) met to determine how to differentiate between authentic and nonauthentic cases of possession. A wide variety of symptoms were determined as inconclusive. However, three conditions were considered as nearly infallible characteristics of possession including (1) "double personality," (2) "paranormal phenomena," and (3) "phenomena that manifest as different from or contrary to scientific laws."[352] One will quickly note the wide range of characteristics that could fall into the second and third categories. Innamorati, Taradel, and Foschi conclude that the "obvious intent was to endorse the inclusion of the action of demons among possible causes of disease."[353]

Summary and Conclusions

A global survey of spiritual aetiologies for illness produces many parallels to consider when interpreting Synoptic accounts of possession-related illness. Western philosophical systems and methods of health care have understood these curative measures as mostly coping mechanisms for illness.[354] However, this interpretive measure stems from a Eurocentric and ethnocentric bias

[348] Pócs, "Possession Phenomena, Possession-Systems," 111.

[349] Pócs, "Possession Phenomena, Possession-Systems," 114.

[350] Innamorati, Taradel, and Foschi, "Between Sacred and Profane," 1, who attribute the revival to the views of Pope John Paul II's papacy, which also impacted views in Africa and Poland. See also Young, *History of Exorcism*.

[351] Tonino Cantelmi, ed., *Gli dei morti sono diventati malattie* (Cassino, Italy: EDT, 2002).

[352] Innamorati, Taradel, and Foschi, "Between Sacred and Profane," 11.

[353] Innamorati, Taradel, and Foschi, "Between Sacred and Profane," 11.

[354] See Nan Greenwood et al., "Asian In-Patient and Carer Views of Mental Health Care," *Journal of Mental Health* 9.4 (2000): 397–408.

that does not account for the widely documented views and experiences in global witness. Nhlanhla Mkhize summarizes the dichotomy between Western philosophies of health care and traditional healing techniques. He argues that it is not sensible to singularly explain the experience of non-Westerners with only Western philosophical systems, especially since he reports that 80 to 90 percent of persons from developing societies do depend on health care based on traditional methods.[355]

Likewise, it is not sensible to interpret Synoptic accounts of spirit possession and exorcism without a global consideration of spirit-possession phenomena. Synoptic viewpoints, considered by many Westerners as representative of a radical "other," find a home among global aetiologies for illness. At this point it is pertinent to remind the reader that the denial of the historicity of the exorcism stories of the New Testament and their classification as legendary tales was based on Bultmann's assumption that beliefs in spirits and their connection to illness is not an allowable premise, since spiritual aetiologies for illness break the conditions of natural law. However, in view of the global witness to the belief in spirits and the belief in spirits as an aetiology for illness, Bultmann's argument is not possible to defend. The knowledge he values is only Western and severely reductive.

As a result, Western interpretations of the historicity of Synoptic accounts of spirit possession need to incorporate the global evidence for possession views and consider them carefully. Since chapters 4–6 provide parallel arguments, a more detailed analysis of implications for historicity will be saved for the conclusions in chapter 7.

Functionally, this chapter has demonstrated a cross-cultural belief in spirit possession as an aetiology for illness and for the use of exorcism as a curative measure. Ashy summarizes the value of including a cross-cultural expression of evidence: "Knowledge about the human self and behaviour is not a product of a single culture but the result of all human experiences in every human culture. Truth is born in open dialogue, not in isolation."[356] As a result, the evidence above, unveiling a cross-cultural viewpoint on the relationship between spirit possession and illness, allows for a reconsideration of the Synoptic stories as remembered events in the life of Jesus that fit well in their own ancient context, where a belief in spirits and spirit-related illness was assumed, just as it is in many modern cultures today. Even though a variety of etic interpretations

---

[355] Nhlanhla Mkhize, "Psychology: An African Perspective," in *Critical Psychology*, ed. Derek Hook (Landsdowne, R.S.A.: University of Cape Town Press, 2004), 24–52.
[356] Majed A. Ashy, "Health and Illness from an Islamic Perspective," *Journal of Religion and Health* 38.3 (1999): 257.

are not dismissed, it seems most important first to realize that an emic perspective allows us to hear the explanation for illness given by the Synoptic writers, which is that Jesus meets persons who are suffering from spirit-related illnesses (whether through affliction or possession). In each of these cases, when the demon is expelled, the illness is cured. Additionally, this proposal clarifies the response of the crowds, who are in awe of Jesus' ability to cure each person.

In summary, this chapter provides ample cross-cultural evidence for spirit possession as an ancient and modern aetiology for illness. With the consideration of this evidence, an opportunity is provided for the reconsideration of the nature of these accounts as historically plausible eyewitness testimony. This engagement will follow in chapters 5 and 6, two more chapters that consider anthropological evidence of spirit possession as parallel to the accounts in the Synoptics and Acts. Chapter 5 follows with a discussion of spirit possession and violent acts. Chapter 6 discusses spirit possession and vocalic activity/ alterations involving demonic speech and oracular activity.

5

Spirits Make Me Violent and Strong!

Spirit Possession, Violent Acts, and Extraordinary Strength

Spirit possession is characterized by a variety of violent acts in the Synoptic Gospels, including acts of convulsing, being thrown down, being injured bodily, or acquiring extraordinary strength. Global reports of possession contain many parallels of these characteristics. For example, common cross-cultural characteristics of spirit possession include shaking, convulsing, bodily contortions, death, the possession of extraordinary strength, and more. In his classic work on the anthropological study of religion, James G. Frazer defined spirit possession cross-culturally, concluding, "The spirit is revealed by convulsive shiverings and shakings of the man's whole body, by wild gestures and exited looks, all of which are referred, not to the man himself, but to the spirit which has entered into him."[1] His classic work illustrates that these types of observations have been present in anthropological study for a long time. His definition mimics Alfred Métraux's depiction of possession:

> People possessed start by giving an impression of having lost control of their
> motor system. Shaken by spasmodic convulsions, they pitch forward, as though
> projected by a spring, turn frantically round and round, stiffen and stay still

---

[1] James George Frazer, *The Golden Bough: A Study in Magic and Religion* (New York: MacMillan., 1922), 108. He adds characteristics expounded on in chapter 6, namely that "in this abnormal state all his utterances are accepted as the voice of the god or spirit dwelling in him or speaking through him." One will want to remember that Frazer interpreted these experiences as fake. However, he accurately described the cross-cultural experience and its prevalent characteristics.

with the body bent forward, sway, stagger, save themselves, again lose balance, only to fall finally in a state of semi-consciousness.[2]

Mikel Burley, while recognizing that possession experience is not a "unitary phenomenon,"[3] argues that the phenomenon is, as Cohen indicates, "a complex series of patterns of thinking and behavior."[4] Burley indicates that when a spirit enters a person, the "complex patterns of behaviour often include exuberant, sometimes wild and chaotic, bodily movements."[5]

Further, Melville J. Herskovits, after studying possession experience in Haiti, the Caribbean, and Africa, notes that possessed persons' strength levels are vastly different than when they are not possessed.[6] In many instances anthropologists have noted that possession experience is characterized by extraordinary strength that requires (if possible) the restraint of the person.[7]

These cross-cultural definitions of spirit-possession experience suggest that spirit possession can be characterized by violent acts or extraordinary strength. This chapter will first consider how these violent acts are characterized in the Synoptic Gospels. A global survey of parallel accounts will follow. As with the content in the previous chapter, the survey below is not exhaustive;

[2]   Alfred Métraux, *Vodoo in Haiti*, trans. Hugo Charteris (New York: Schocken, 1972), 120–21.

[3]   Kalpana Ram, *Fertile Disorder: Spirit Possession and Its Provocation of the Modern* (Honolulu: University of Hawai'i Press, 2013), 273.

[4]   Mikel Burley, "Dance of the *Deodhās*: Divine Possession, Blood Sacrifice and the Grotesque Body in the Assamese Goddess Worship," *Religions of South Asia* 12.2 (2018): 208. Burley is using the language of Emma Cohen, "What Is Spirit Possession? Defining, Comparing, and Explaining Two Possession Forms," *Ethnos* 73.1 (2008): 105.

[5]   Burley, "Dance of the *Deodhās*," 208.

[6]   Melville J. Herskovits, *Man and His Works: The Science of Cultural Anthropology* (New York: A. A. Knopf, 1948), 66–67.

[7]   Jane M. Murphy, "Psychotherapeutic Aspects of Shamanism," in *Magic, Faith, and Healing: Studies in Primitive Psychiatry Today*, ed. Ari Kiev (New York: Free Press, 1964), 58; Margaret J. Field, "Spirit Possession in Ghana," in *Spirit Mediumship and Society in Africa*, ed. John Beattie and John Middleton (New York: Africana, 1969), 5; Traugott Konstantin Oesterreich, "The Genesis and Extinction of Possession," in *Exorcism through the Ages*, ed. St. Elmo Nauman (New York: Philosophical Library, 1974), 122–23; Stafford Betty, "The Growing Evidence for 'Demonic Possession': What Should Psychiatry's Response Be?" *Journal of Religion and Health* 44.1 (2005): 16, 20; Kurt E. Koch, *God among the Zulus*, trans. Justin Michell and Waldenmar Engelbrecht (Natal, R.S.A.: Mission Kwa Sizabanu, 1981), 45, 191; Felicity S. Edwards, "Amafufunyana Spirit Possession: Treatment and Interpretation," in *Afro-Christian Religion and Healing in Southern Africa*, ed. G. C. Oosthuizen et al., African Studies 8 (Lewiston, N.Y.: Mellen, 1989), 210.

nor is it able to treat the varieties of experiences that are different than what is found in the biblical text. The hope is to provide a survey of the cross-cultural characteristics of violent acts and extraordinary strength through the relevant time periods.

Ancient Perspectives

Israel

In ancient Israelite perspective, some strands of evidence point to violent sorts of activities in association with spirits/demons. Beginning with the LXX, Psalm 91:6 LXX refers to demons that cause terror night and day.[8] Enochic literature refers to evil spirits who "afflict, oppress, destroy, attack, do battle, and work destruction on earth, and cause trouble . . ." (1 En. 15:8–12). In Jubilees demons cause bloodshed on earth (7:27; 11:5) and seek to destroy Noah's children to blind and kill them (10:1–2). They are meant for destruction (10:8). In 49:2 demons seem to assist Mastema in killing all the first-born in Egypt.[9] Tobit further realizes the extent of violence possible through its depiction of the demon Asmodeus who kills Sarah's seven fiancées.[10]

Greco-Roman Antiquity

In Greco-Roman perspectives demons could cause delusion or insanity.[11] The numinous might cause fear or may even potentially throw one out with "sudden mysterious force" so that one might be found "half-dead before the door."[12] Johnston adds that demons could cause physical actions,[13] and they

---

[8]   Everett Ferguson, *Demonology of the Early Christian World* (New York: Mellen, 1984), 73. The LXX names all Gentile gods as demons (Ps 96:5).

[9]   Jacques Van Ruiten, "Angels and Demons in the Book of *Jubilees*," in *Angels: The Concept of Celestial Beings—Origins, Development and Reception*, ed. Friedrich V. Reiterer, Tobias Nicklas, and Karin Schöpflin (New York: De Gruyter, 2007), 600.

[10]   The name Asmodeus has Persian influence and is most likely a derivative of Aeshma Daeva, who was the "demon of wrath, rage, and violence" in Persian Zoroastrianism. See William Brandt Bradshaw, "Demonology in Hebrew and Jewish Traditions: A Study in New Testament Origins" (PhD diss., University of St Andrews, 1963), 138. Debate exists on whether or not Sarah is possessed but it does not seem likely.

[11]   Sarah Iles Johnston, "Demons," in *Brill's New Pauly: Encyclopedia of the Ancient World*, ed. Hubert Cancik and Helmuth Schneider, English ed., ed. Christine F. Salazar (Leiden: Brill, 2010), 4:283. See also Homer, *Od.* 14.488, 12.295.

[12]   Suetonius, *Aug.* 5–6.

[13]   Johnston, "Demons," 283. See also Homer, *Il.* 15.468; Homer, *Od.* 12.169, possibly *Od.* 5.396.

assist in the punishment of evil-doers.[14] They could avenge wrongs[15] and even cause misfortune and death.[16] Luck describes the potential harm acutely:

> Even if they did not take over a human body in order to express themselves or to work some mischief, contacts and communications could be established with them. But on the whole, the ancients believed that only the "unquiet dead"—that is those who had died before their time, met with a violent death (being murdered or killed in battle), or been deprived of proper burial—were earthbound and readily available. Those were the spirits the magicians used, because they were thought to be angry about their fate and therefore ruthless and violent.[17]

Even in this concise summary of Jewish and Greco-Roman perspectives, one realizes that what is found in the NT accounts related to violence and extraordinary strength has had seeds sown in the background data.

New Testament Accounts

In New Testament accounts of possession and exorcism, characteristics of violence and extraordinary strength are particularly exhibited in the story of the boy seized by an unclean spirit and the Gerasene/Gadarene demonic. Following, two accounts are explored exegetically to observe how possession is displayed.[18]

The Boy Seized by the Unclean Spirit—Mark 9:14–29; Matthew 17:14–21; Luke 9:37–43

In this story a possessed boy is brought to Jesus by his Father. The boy's condition is described in various ways in each Synoptic account. In Mark the boy is described as having a dumb spirit that seizes him and throws him down; the boy grinds his teeth and is rigid (Mark 9:17). In Matthew the son is described as a severely suffering epileptic who falls into fire and water (Matt 17:15). In Luke the spirit seizes the boy and convulses with foam from his mouth. He is severely mistreated by the spirit, who convulses him and throws him to the ground. What is interesting is that in all three cases, each Gospel writer does

---

[14] Johnston, "Demons," 283. See also Hesiod, *Op.* 122–26; Aeschylus, *Pers.* 601; Euripides, *Alc.* 1003; Euripides, *Rhes.* 971; Plato, *Resp.* 469b, 540c.

[15] Johnston, "Demons," 283. See also Hesiod, *Op.* 5.396.

[16] Johnston, "Demons," 283. See Aeschylus, *Ag.* 1175; Aeschylus, *Sept.* 812l; Sophocles, *Oed. col.* 76, *Antiphon* 3.3.4.

[17] Georg Luck, *Acana Mundi: Magic and the Occult in the Greek and Roman Worlds* (Baltimore: Johns Hopkins University Press, 1985), 165.

[18] One will note that other passages exhibit similar characteristics. The story of Acts 19:11–20 exhibits violence on the exorcists. For reasons of space, only two accounts are treated here. Both accounts are found in all three Synoptics.

not disregard the father's interpretation of the aetiology of the boy's condition; nor do they dismiss that the disciples were not successful in healing/casting out the boy.[19] Jesus responds by rebuking the unclean spirit, healing the boy, and presenting him back to his father.

Varieties of interpreters have diagnosed the boy's condition throughout interpretive history. Meier labels Luke 9:37–43 "a strange story" and concludes that the boy's illness is psychosomatic. Meier is right to recognize the distance between his interpretation and Luke's emic perspective and diagnosis when he states, "When the patient is some 20 centuries away, diagnosis is nigh impossible."[20] This distance poses a direct challenge to Meier's own view, especially considering Luke's intent to record historiography. Luke gives his own view of the "diagnosis," which is surprisingly different from Matthew's, who describes the boy as epileptic.[21] A deeper analysis of this text is helpful in understanding the boy's condition and what is at play in this exorcism account.

First, Luke adds a significant detail in describing the son as μονογενής ("only"). Considering ancient family values, this boy is important to his family's heritage and family line. The father faces social exclusion due to the condition of his son. Since his son is not in a position to marry, the father's lineage

[19] Bock, however, points out that the criticism of the disciples adds credibility to the story based upon the criterion of embarrassment. See Darrell L. Bock, *Luke 9:51–24:53*, BECNT (Grand Rapids: Baker, 1994), 879. Bock challenges the view of the Jesus Seminar, who rejects that the dialogue in this account can be traced to Jesus. See Robert W. Funk and Roy W. Hoover, *The Five Gospels: What Did Jesus Really Say? The Search for the Authentic Words of Jesus* (Sonoma, Calif.: Polebridge, 1993), 314. Further, Sterling and Achtemeier corroborate the basic historicity of the account. See Gregory E. Sterling, "Jesus as Exorcist: An Analysis of Matthew 17:14–20; Mark 9:14–29; Luke 9:37–43a," *CBQ* 55.3 (1993): 467–93; Paul J. Achtemeier, "Miracles and the Historical Jesus: A Study of Mark 9:14–29," *CBQ* 37.4 (1975): 471–91. Achtemeier concludes that the account has basis in an event in the life of Jesus. G. Petzke, "Die historische Frage nach den Wundertaten Jesu," *NTS* 22.2 (1976): 180–204, made the opposite conclusion that the event was created by the early church as missionary propaganda.

[20] John P. Meier, *A Marginal Jew: Rethinking the Historical Jesus*, vol. 2 (New York: Doubleday, 1994), 656.

[21] Amy-Jill Levine and Ben Witherington III (*The Gospel of Luke*, New Cambridge Bible Commentary [Cambridge: Cambridge University Press, 2018], 264) recognize that a wide range of speculation exists about the boy's condition, including epilepsy, autism, etc. Levine and Witherington rightly point out, "For Luke, the cause of the ailment is 'a spirit.' The Holy Spirit had 'overshadowed' Mary, but the spirit is destroying a child; the face of Jesus had been transfigured into glory; the face of this child is foaming at the mouth."

is at risk due to the lack of an heir to inherit his possessions.[22] Further, the spirit illness is troublesome as it might reflect the presence of sin (by the boy or his surrogate) as a possible reason for the illness.[23] The boy's status is elevated from the beginning of the account to the end as the language used to reference him shifts from υἱος to παῖς. Despite the low place of honor given to children in Gentile practice,[24] Jesus allows the child to come. Allowing the boy to receive hospitality overturns the way Gentile society perceived children by establishing a contrasting social ethic (vv. 47–48).[25] In summary, this boy socially moves from worst-case scenario to best-case scenario upon his exorcism. His restoration potentially saves his family's heritage.

As noted above, the descriptive detail about the condition of the boy varies in the Synoptic Gospel accounts. Even so, all three paint the picture of a boy who is suffering and is seized or falling down. Both Mark and Luke choose to emphasize the spirit's seizing of the boy and his convulsions with foam at the mouth. Luke adds the shattering of the boy and that the demon will scarcely leave the boy, and Mark indicates the boy's grinding teeth and his rigidness. The following exegesis will pay close attention to the features of demonic enterprise that arise in these accounts, including: the use of λαμβάνω as a descriptive for the boy's possession, foaming at the mouth, convulsions (σπαράσσω), being thrown down and shaken, Luke's indication that the demon barely leaves the boy alone, and Matthew's depiction of the boy's grinding teeth and rigidness.

First, the verb employed by Luke for the boy's convulsions, σπαράσσω, is narrated by the boy's father to indicate the continuous impact the demon has on the boy. Klutz notes that this term is entirely absent from Hippocrates' *De morbo sacro* in relation to epileptic symptoms.[26] The term and its cognate only appear five times in the NT,[27] and in all five instances the actor is a demonic

---

[22] Bruce Malina and Richard Rohrbaugh, *Social Science Commentary on the Synoptic Gospels* (Minneapolis: Fortress, 2002), 344. See also David E. Garland, *Luke*, Zondervan Exegetical Commentary on the New Testament (Grand Rapids: Zondervan, 2011), 402. Todd Klutz, *The Exorcism Stories in Luke-Acts: A Sociostylistic Reading*, SNTSMS 129 (Cambridge: Cambridge University Press, 2004), 162, argues that this term marks a theme in this passage, making it as much about "the horizontal dynamics of ancient Mediterranean structures of kinship" as Jesus' "vertical combat" with the unclean spirit.

[23] Klutz, *Exorcism Stories in Luke-Acts*, 187.

[24] Beryl Rawson, ed., *Family in Ancient Rome* (New York: Cornell University Press, 1986); Peter Garnsey and Richard Saller, *The Roman Empire: Economy, Society and Culture* (Berkeley: University of California Press, 1987), 136–41.

[25] See also Joel B. Green, *The Gospel of Luke*, NICNT (Grand Rapids: Baker, 1997), 391–92.

[26] Klutz, *Exorcism Stories in Luke-Acts*, 165.

[27] Mark 1:26; 9:20, 26; Luke 9:39, 42.

figure. The sense of the term is to "shake to and fro" or "handle roughly."[28] Klutz argues that since this term does not fall in the semantic range of descriptors for epilepsy in antiquity, interpreters should hesitate to include it as evidence for an epileptic diagnosis.[29] Further, both Mark and Luke describe that the spirit throws the boy down (Mark 9:10; Luke 9:42).

The boy's foaming of the mouth is unique to this exorcism account and the use of ἀφρός is an *hapax legomenon* in the NT. In other ancient texts, the term is used to describe a characteristic of epilepsy.[30] Even if the diagnosis of epilepsy is made, the Gospel accounts accept and do not alter the father's diagnosis of the boy's condition as caused by a spirit/demon, later regarded as a τὸ δαιμόνιαν and τῷ πνεύματι τῷ ἀκαθάρτῳ (v. 42). Some scholars have argued that Luke, even though a physician, was unfamiliar with the proper diagnosis of epilepsy. However, this argument is one from silence. It was not uncommon for ancients to conjecture about the cause of epilepsy; Hippocrates wrote an entire tractate attempting to understand the "Sacred Disease."[31] It is not impossible that Luke was familiar, but such conjectures go beyond what Luke presents. Pilch points out the bias in assigning epilepsy in place of Luke's emic perspective by arguing that it is a hermeneutical "mediocentrism," meaning that medical categories are mapped onto the text and given more interpretive control than Luke's own perspective.[32]

Even Matthew's depiction of the boy as suffering terribly from epilepsy/ or being epileptic does not remove the fact that there is potentially a spiritual ailment in Matthew's view. Matthew only uses σεληνιάζεται here and in 4:24. As Hagner has shown, the use in 4:24 "occurs in a list of those healed by Jesus and follows the word δαιμονιζομένους, 'demon possessed,' to indicate the boy's condition." Further, Hagner adds, "The fact that the curing of the boy in v. 18b is by means of an exorcism indicates that Matthew also understood the

---

[28]   BDAG, 936.

[29]   Klutz, *Exorcism Stories in Luke-Acts*, 165. Klutz suggests caution in accepting the views of James D. G. Dunn and Graham H. Twelftree, "Demon-Possession and Exorcism in the New Testament," *Churchman* 94.3 (1980): 222, who consider it possible to demythologize the account and view the boy's condition as epilepsy.

[30]   William Kirk Hobart, *The Medical Language of St. Luke* (Eugene, Ore.: Wipf and Stock, 2004 [1882]), 17–18; Hippocrates, *Morb. sacr.* 303, 305, *Epid.* 1222, *Aph.* 1246; Aretaeus, *Sign. acut.* 4, *Do.* 29.

[31]   See François Bovon, *Luke 1: A Commentary on the Gospel of Luke 1:1–9:50*, trans. Christine M. Thomas, ed. Helmut Koester (Minneapolis: Fortress, 2002), 386, 388. See also H. van der Loos, *The Miracles of Jesus*, NovTSup 9 (Leiden: Brill, 1965), 403–5.

[32]   John J. Pilch, "Insights and Models for Understanding the Healing Activity of the Historical Jesus," in *Society of Biblical Literature 1993 Seminar Papers*, SBLSP 32 (Atlanta: Society of Biblical Literature, 1993), 154.

disease of the boy to be caused by a demon . . ."[33] As a result, even though Matthew varies in his description, a spiritual problem is still in view. In summary, σεληνιάζομαι must be taken in light of its ancient context, which involved seizures associated with the "transcendent power of the moon."[34] While the condition presents itself in a similar way to the modern diagnosis of epilepsy, the modern reader must still listen carefully for the aetiology presented in these culturally situated texts.

It is also curious to note Luke's use of ἰάομαι to describe the boy's exorcism. Bock argues that the usage likely indicates the demon's exploitation of the boy's illness, adding to the seriousness of the effect upon the boy.[35] Others suggest that a twofold miracle occurs here, both exorcism and healing.[36] Agreeing with Pilch, Green argues that the assigning of the boy's condition to epilepsy manifests elements of Western bias in interpretation, especially transforming "the illness into a report susceptible in an unmediated way to the categories of Western biomedicine."[37] Green also suggests that this bifold classification (1) dismisses the report of a manifestation of a spirit as "primitive"; and (2) does not take seriously Luke's report about how the healing took place, namely, the spirit was rebuked and the boy was restored to health and family.[38]

Klutz is helpful in recognizing that Luke does not contrast or assert an opposing view to the "folk" diagnoses given in the account by the boy's father, namely, he has a spirit (v. 39). Klutz summarizes, "Neither in the present story nor elsewhere in Luke's Gospel does Jesus or the narrator ever reject the participants' folk diagnosis and its cosmological assumptions."[39] Bovon asserts that the desire to interpret according to modern medical knowledge projects cultural conceptions on the first-century text.[40] Fitzmyer notes the continual

---

[33] Donald A. Hagner, *Matthew 14–28*, WBC 33b (Grand Rapids: Thomas Nelson, 1995), 503.

[34] BDAG, "σεληνιάζομαι," 919.

[35] See also the usage in Acts 10:38. Darrell L. Bock, BECNT (Grand Rapids: Baker, 1994), *Luke 1:1–9:50*, 884.

[36] Norval Geldenhuys, *The Gospel of Luke*, NICNT (Grand Rapids: Eerdmans, 1951), 286; John T. Carroll, *Luke: A Commentary*, NTL (Louisville: Westminster John Knox, 2012), 221.

[37] Green, *Gospel of Luke*, 387.

[38] Green, *Gospel of Luke*, 388.

[39] Klutz, *Exorcism Stories in Luke-Acts*, 165. Cf. John J. Pilch, "Sickness and Healing in Luke-Acts," in *The Social World of Luke-Acts: Models for Interpretation*, ed. Jerome H. Neyrey (Peabody, Mass.: Hendrickson, 1991), 199.

[40] James R. Edwards, *The Gospel according to Luke*, Pillar New Testament Commentary (Grand Rapids: Eerdmans, 2015), 388. Even though Edwards recognizes the element of possible bias in interpretation, he still precludes this story from carrying forward "historical truth" about the boy's healing.

blurring motif, blurring sickness and demonization, in Luke's presentation of the "demon-sickness."[41]

In addition to the foaming at the mouth, Mark portrays the boy as grinding his teeth and becoming rigid. These characteristics likely further reflect the boy's condition as "moonstruck." Even so, as Marcus argues, "Our passage unambiguously attributes this illness to a demon, a fact that may disturb Christians who want to reconcile the biblical worldview with the modern scientific one."[42] Further, Witherington remarks that the fact that the evil spirit intends for the child to fall into the water or fire indicates an intent for the boy's destruction.[43]

Furthermore, the boy experiences severe mistreatment as possession phenomena. The use of the present participle συντρῖβον in Luke reveals the continual torment caused by the demon. Additionally, the term adds vivid imagery to the boy's condition. Bock notes the term indicates that the demon causes the boy to bruise himself.[44] The term indicates the boy's severe mistreatment, which involves severe beatings.[45] Further, the demon will hardly ever leave him alone. The case is severe.

In both Mark and Luke, the approach of Jesus causes the demon to act out, causing convulsions. Two grammatical options exist concerning Luke's aorist usage of ἔρρηξεν since the aorist of ῥήσσω ("cast down to the ground in convulsions"[46]) and ῥήγνθμι ("tear to pieces"[47]) are exact in form. Both options demonstrate that the boy is suffering from violent activity. Jesus' rebuke of the demon ends the account of the violent force displayed upon the boy. Luke narrates that the boy is returned to his father.

In summary, characteristics of this possessed boy include symptoms like epilepsy, even though a biomedical diagnosis is not given in the text. Violence is enacted on the boy through the spirit's seizing of the boy, convulsing with foam at the mouth, severe mistreatment causing bodily harm, and the demon's ability to throw the boy down to the ground. The episodes of demonic attacks hardly pause, and the boy and his family are in a state of despair. Resolution is found through Jesus' rebuke of the spirit and his healing of the boy in all

---

[41] Joseph A. Fitzmyer, *The Gospel according to Luke I–IX: A New Translation with Introduction and Commentary*, AB 28 (New York: Doubleday, 1964), 810.

[42] Joel Marcus, *Mark 8–16*, AB 27A (New Haven: Yale University Press, 2009), 658.

[43] Ben Witherington III, *The Gospel of Mark: A Socio-rhetorical Commentary* (Grand Rapids: Eerdmans, 2001), 267.

[44] Bock, *Luke 1:1–9:50*, 882.

[45] BDAG, "συντρίβω," 976.

[46] BDAG, "ῥήσσω," 905.

[47] Fitzmyer, *Gospel according to Luke I–IX*, 810.

three accounts, revealing that for each Synoptic writer the cause of the boy's condition is spiritual.

The Gerasene/Gadarene Demoniac—Matthew 8:28–34; Mark 5:1–20; Luke 8:26–39

The story of the Gerasene/Gadarene demoniac, one of the most detailed NT accounts, takes readers to the region of the Gerasenes, mainly occupied by Gentiles. The story depicts a man[48] in a severe condition. Mark's account contains the most detail and records that the man with an unclean spirit lives among the tombs, cannot be bound, breaks the bonds utilized in attempts to bind him, and bruises himself with stones. The man is described as extraordinarily strong; no one has the strength it takes to subdue him (Mark 5:1–5).

In all three accounts the man's condition is first described as due to demonization. Matthew refers to two demonized men, Luke describes one man as having demons and Mark describe the demoniac as a man with an unclean spirit. Post-exorcism, each Synoptic writer records that the man is freed from his condition. Mark and Luke describe him as returned to his right mind and directed by Jesus to go and tell what Jesus had done for him.

The historicity of this exorcism account has often been disputed. Some interpreters categorize the story as myth due to embarrassment over the presence of the demonic, and even more so because of the uniqueness of the transfer of the demons into the swine. For example, because of the tale of the "secondary swine," seen as a secondary accretion, Meier argues that despite the lengthy account, the historical residue is small.[49] Jostein Ådna additionally concludes that the swine account is secondary based on the textual critical problem surrounding the geographical designation. He works to prove that the story remains coherent without the swine account.[50]

Marshall grapples with the account as having "legendary features" employed by the church to purport Jesus' power while also considering that Jesus could have deliberately chosen to send the demons into the pigs to demonstrate to the audience proof of the man's exorcism.[51] Bultmann and Dibelius also represent these two streams of thought. Bultmann argues that a

---

[48] Matthew's account refers to two demoniacs.

[49] Meier, *Marginal Jew*, 651–53. Others, such as Franz Annen, *Heil für die Heiden: Zur Bedeutung und Geschichte der Tradition vom besessenen Gerasener*, FTS 20 (Frankfurt am Main: Joseph Knecht, 1976), 653, argue the account was created.

[50] Jostein Ådna, "The Encounter of Jesus with the Gerasene Demoniac," in *Authenticating the Activities of Jesus*, ed. Bruce Chilton and Craig A. Evans (Leiden: Brill, 2002), 279–301.

[51] I. Howard Marshall, *The Gospel of Luke* (Grand Rapids: Eerdmans, 1978), 335–36.

legend about deceiving the devil stands behind the transfer account.[52] Dibelius favors regarding the matter as the narrative's confirmation that the exorcism was successful.[53] Twelftree argues for the appropriateness of viewing the swine account as curative rather than proof of the success of the exorcism.[54]

While Bock rightly indicates that it is not the text's burden to answer why the demons are transferred, some have noted that such an activity would not be disparate from its context. The swine account may be compared with other ancient exorcism stories like those found in Josephus (*Ant.* 8.2.5)[55] and Philostratus (*Vit. Ap.* 4.20),[56] which both include proof of a successful exorcism.[57] In addition, the background evidence does include stories that situate the banishment of demons to a new dwelling place as part of the cure. Further, concession requests by a demon are not uncommon in antiquity.[58] The demons want to avoid their eschatological fate since the ἄβυσσος is a place of punishment.[59] Garland summarizes the weight of the matter and the eschatological dynamic the exorcism represents: "The demons do not ask to be allowed to stay in the same region as in Mark 5:10, but to avoid the eschatological torment (Isa 24:21–22). Even demons hate hell."[60] The demons desire to inhabit something, but despite Jesus' permission to enter the swine, the demons, by the drowning of the swine, ultimately end up in the place of punishment they worked to avoid.

Secondly, the historicity of this episode has been disputed due to the text-critical matter relating to the location of the event. The story of this demoniac is clearly connected with a Gentile locale, namely, a pagan city of the Decapolis (due to the presence of swine).[61] The variance in manuscript tradition (Gadara, Gergesa, Gerasa) is likely due to the attempt to situate the story in a region

---

[52] Rudolf Bultmann, *The History of the Synoptic Tradition*, trans. John Marsh (Oxford: Blackwell, 1963), 210, n. 3. Who deceives whom is a matter of debate. Bultmann argues that Jesus was deceived by the demons since the destruction caused him to leave the area.

[53] Martin Dibelius, *From Tradition to Gospel*, ed. William Barclay, trans. Bertram Lee Woolf (Cambridge: James Clarke, 1971), 88–89.

[54] Graham H. Twelftree, *Jesus the Exorcist: A Contribution to the Study of the Historical Jesus* (Eugene, Ore.: Wipf and Stock, 2011), 75, cf. 155.

[55] The demon overturned a cup of water as proof.

[56] The demon threw down a statue.

[57] Rudolf Pesch, "The Markan Version of the Healing of the Gerasene Demoniac," *Ecumenical Review* 23.4 (1971): 365–67.

[58] A similar concession request is found in T. Sol. 1.6.

[59] See 2 Bar. 59:5; 1 En. 10:4; 18:11; 54:5; 88:1; 90:24–27; Jub. 5:6; Rev 9:1–2, 11; 11:7; 17:8; 20:1. See also "Tartarus" in 2 Pet 2:4.

[60] Garland, *Luke*, 358. See also Twelftree, *Jesus the Exorcist*, 86.

[61] See Lev 11:7 and Deut 14:8.

closer to the lake. Bock points towards the possibility of a general geographical reference which supports Metzger's consideration to prefer the reading "region of the Gerasenes."[62] Bock summarizes the main point when he argues that the "geographical reference . . . is a general one, since a region (χώραν) is referred to. Thus, speaking of an error in either reference is inappropriate."[63] In summary, the main goal is to situate this account on Gentile turf.

A third argument challenging historicity involves the number of possessed people. In view of the parallels in Matthew 8:28, 33 (where two demoniacs are presented) and Mark 5:2 (where one demoniac is presented), some challenge Luke's credibility. Luke's choice to present one possessed man's account is sufficient for his purpose, and as Bock argues, "that is all that is needed to make the essential point."[64] Fourthly, the argument that concerns the placement of the account in each Gospel[65] is easily dismissed considering the conventions of ancient historiography related to chronology.

In summary, the transfer of the demons into the swine, as noted above, is one of the largest challenges for Western interpreters to understand this story as historically plausible. Pesch stresses how typical it is for one's presuppositions concerning the nature of the demonic to be read in and out of this story.[66] Additionally, Bock summarizes the complex nature of the discussion and the tendency to categorize the story as myth due to the difficulty of understanding not only the demonic but also the swine incident.[67] Bock summarizes:

> Obviously, how one approaches the entire area of the demonic, in terms of worldview, will determine how one judges the account. . . . If the demonic is explained naturally . . . then much of the story will be explained on natural terms, though it is difficult to do this with the detail about swine (for which one must then appeal to either legendary accretion or an act of Jesus). Those who

---

[62] Bock, *Luke 1:1–9:50*, 768. For a full text-critical discussion, see p. 783. Other possibilities include: (1) The man was from a different locale than the event took place, (2) The text was corrupted, and (3) More understanding is needed for how ancients refer to regions. See also Bruce Metzger, *A Textual Commentary on the Greek New Testament* (Stuttgart: United Bible Societies, 1994), 84.

[63] Bock, *Luke 1:1–9:50*, 768 (following Alfred Plummer, *A Critical and Exegetical Commentary on the Gospel according to Luke*, ICC [New York: Scribner, 1896], 227).

[64] Bock, *Luke 1:1–9:50*, 768 (following F. Godet, *A Commentary on the Gospel of St. Luke*, vol. 1, trans. E. W. Shalders and M. D. Cusin [Edinburgh: T&T Clark, 1875], 381).

[65] As summarized in Bock, *Luke 1:1–9:50*, 768.

[66] Pesch, "Markan Version of the Healing of the Gerasene Demoniac," 349–50. Possible views include: (1) A belief in the reality of demons leads one to conclude the account emphasizes Jesus' authority and is historical and (2) For the rationalist, its historicity is challenged and it is regarded as a tale of folklore.

[67] Bock, *Luke 1:1–9:50*, 767.

accept the realm of the supernatural and the existence of spirits will have fewer problems with the account and will not try to reformulate its rational.[68]

From even this brief survey on the historicity of this account, it is troubling to consider how bias impacts interpretation. Even so, as Bock argues, the story's point is precisely clear: "Jesus exercises authority over the destructive forces of evil, and he does so visibly by using the swine, so that expulsion is clear to all."[69] The purpose of the exegesis below is to draw forward the perspectives of the Synoptics in context, in order to observe the characteristics of possession present in the exorcism story.

A few specifics are named about the condition of this man, namely that he has multiple demons,[70] has not clothed himself for some time (Luke's account), and lives among the tombs. Additionally, the man was seized by the unclean spirit, producing convulsive fits, and he was exhibiting extraordinary strength in his ability to break the bonds that attempted to hold him. Eventually, the demon would drive him into the desert. Some have argued that it is unclear whether this man is a Jew or a Gentile. Chilton argues that the proximity to pigs does not disqualify categorizing him as a Jew since the parable of Luke 15:11–32 presents a Jewish man as a keeper of swine. This argument is not persuasive, since the Lucan parable depicts the man's swine-herding as a sign of the destitution to which his situation has reduced him, an image that would cause readers to recoil. Even so, Chilton does favor the Gentile descent of the man, due to his reference to Jesus as "the son of God Most High," a classification mostly used by non-Israelites.[71] This usage, along with the location of the event, might suggest that the man is a Gentile. In any case, not too much needs to be made of this matter.

The nakedness of the man has often been argued to signal the man's shameful existence and social isolation. Green summarizes that the man has lost

---

[68]   Bock, *Luke 1:1–9:50*, 767.

[69]   Bock, *Luke 1:1–9:50*, 767.

[70]   Mark 5:2 describes the man as having an unclean spirit; however, the name of the spirits is "Legion," indicating a plural number of spirits. Luke also shifts between the use of "unclean spirit" and "demons." Green, *Gospel of Luke*, 338, argues that the repetition of "demon," "demons," and "unclean spirit" develops this account as one having "cosmic proportions" and emphasizes Jesus' power to save. Additionally, this is not Luke's first presentation of one with multiple demons. See also the account of Mary Magdalene, which is not analyzed here.

[71]   Bruce Chilton, "An Exorcism of History: Mark 1:21–28," in Chilton and Evans, *Authenticating the Activities of Jesus*, 215–45 (234). See Gen 14:19; Num 24:16; Acts 16:17. Israelites also used the title. But the location and this title (cf. Acts 16:18) do suggest that he is a Gentile.

"claim to status. . . . He was scarcely even human."[72] However, Hamel argues that the lack of clothing does not demonstrate this man's social status, but his mental status, especially because nakedness was also associated with madness. In other words, Luke uses his lack of clothing not just to indicate nakedness, but also as a cipher for his mental instability, caused by the unclean spirit/demons.[73] This is supported by the fact that the man is found both clothed and in his right mind after the exorcism. Therefore, it is likely that his clothing refers synonymously to his return to his right mind. Adding to the matter, Witherington and Levine argue that the mention of the man's home in v. 39 is suggestive that the man did have property and even possibly a family in his town. Seemingly, the man is not only restored to his right mind, but also to his place in his own village. Release from the demonization has changed his life.

The man's presence among the tombs is not surprising since tombs were known as demonic dwelling places.[74] Further, one would be remiss to look past the many elements of impurity present in this pericope.[75] In this case, the demons are many. Some interpreters interpret the name Legion as a numeric designation since the term is utilized to depict a military unit of approximately 5,600 men.[76] Twelftree resists this interpretation and its sociopolitical implications, arguing that contemporaneous writers utilized the term in a way that one would use "myriads." Twelftree states, "Although the word may have had military origin, it had lost its exclusively military ties to take on a metaphorical meaning that was no longer determined by its origin. This can be seen in Pliny the Elder (23/24–79 CE) writing about a legion of crime (*Nat.* 33.26). Even in Latin, well before the time Mark was writing, the playwright Plautus (ca. 254–184 BCE) was using the word figuratively for a 'legion of supporters' (*Cas.* 5)." In other words, it is unlikely that the word realizes sociopolitical oppression in this case. Rather, the account depicts the profound power the "myriads" of demons have over the man.

More specifically related to the characteristics of possession found in the Synoptics, the man is described as "fierce," unable to be bound, not able to be subdued, and he is bruising himself with stones. When meeting Jesus, he

---

[72] Green, *Gospel of Luke*, 338. See also Gildas Hamel, *Poverty and Charity in Roman Palestine, First Three Centuries C.E.*, Near Eastern Studies 23 (Berkeley: University of California Press, 1990), 73.

[73] Hamel, *Poverty and Charity in Roman Palestine*, 74.

[74] For example: Ber. 3b; Sabb. 67a; Git. 70a; Sanh. 65b.

[75] Especially on corpse impurity, see Green, *Gospel of Luke*, 292.

[76] For example, Green, *Gospel of Luke*, 339. Edwards, *Gospel according to Luke*, 250, adds that the name is analogical for Roman domination. He states, "The best analogy of the demoniac's oppression is Palestine's subjugation by Rome."

falls[77] before Jesus and begs not to be tormented[78] or thrown into the abyss. What is intriguing and most relevant to this chapter is the man's extraordinary strength, especially considering its ancient background.

Luke 8:29 makes clear that attempts were made to restrain this man with bindings on both the hands and the feet. The noun πέδη is used of a shackle or fetter for the feet.[79] The term δεσμός functions as a more general term for a "means of restraint by tying or fastening."[80] Plummer argues that a mixture of chains and ropes were used in attempts to shackle the man since the term ἁλύεσιν typically refers to chains used to bind the hands.[81] Bock argues that in view of the "shattering" of the bond in Mark 5:4, it is possible to conclude that chains were used for at least part of the restraint.[82] The two terms συναρπάζω and ἐλαύνω additionally draw forward the superhuman power that the demonization enacts on this man, as these two terms in ancient consideration were used in reference to supernatural powers and natural powers, such as the power of a storm to capsize a boat.[83] Like a boat driven by the power of the storm, this man is driven into the desert. Witherington summarizes, "It is the demons who cast the man out, not society."[84] The image sets forth a notion of the loss of control, even the loss of the ability to determine one's choice of locale. More evidence of the power of the demons is expressed through the ability of the demons to destroy the swine, something that would be difficult to do with human force. The power demonstrated by the man having demons is clearly paralleled with the powerlessness of those who attempted to restrain him. He is stronger than any normal human, and Luke attributes this strength to his ἔχων δαιμόνια, while Mark ascribes it to his status as ἐν πνεύματι ἀκαθάρτῳ. Luke additionally indicates that witnesses testify to the man's demonization. He is referred to as ὁ δαιμονισθείς, a term that

---

[77] Green, *Gospel of Luke*, 338, notes that falling down represents reverence or perhaps submission. See Luke 7:38, 44–46; 8:41; 10:39; 17:16; Acts 4:35; 10:25; 22:3; cf. Josh 10:24; 1 Sam 25:24, 41; 2 Sam 22:39; Pss 8:7; 17:10; 46:4.

[78] As compared to the request not to be destroyed in the Capernaum story.

[79] BDAG, "πέδη," 638.

[80] BDAG, "δεσμός," 219.

[81] Plummer, *Gospel according to St. Luke*, 230.

[82] Bock, *Luke 1:1–9:50*, 773. Mark's account also gives more descriptive details to the destructive nature of the man's possession, namely, the man cries out at night and bruises himself with stones. More emphasis is placed on the strength of the man in the Lukan perspective.

[83] Bovon, *Luke 1*, 328. See also BDAG, 314, 966.

[84] Levine and Witherington, *Gospel of Luke*, 239.

semantically can designate a state of possession in its ancient usage.[85] In Matthew's account the two demoniacs are described as preventing anyone from passing by due to their fierce nature, which coheres with both Mark's and Luke's depiction of the man as empowered by unclean spirits/demons. Wilkins summarizes, "The danger is heightened by noting that these two men are 'so violent that no one could pass that way.' Apparently, they are well known among the populace and feared."[86]

Beyond the man's extraordinary strength and reputation, Mark adds another element of violence involving the man's bruising of himself (Mark 5:5). Witherington considers this further evidence of the man's total loss of control and argues, "We may even be meant to think that he was impelled to be involved in satanic rituals (slashing oneself with rocks?). . . . He was so little in control of himself that he could not keep from injuring himself."[87] Bock asserts that the cutting with stones further speaks to the intent of the demonic, namely, destruction. Bock writes,

> Besides stressing the magnitude of the power that possesses the man, 5:3–5 also emphasizes its malevolent destructiveness. This is most obvious from the description of the demoniac shrieking and cutting himself with stones, but is also aided by the depiction of his alienation from other human beings, whose only response to his plight is to try to chain him up; of his sleeplessness; and of his forced inhabitation in terrifying desolate places where no sane person would choose to live. His dwelling among tombs, moreover, suggests that his demons are impelling him toward death, as will become clear when they enter the pigs and drive them over a cliff; as is typical of sadistic tormentors, however, they prefer to keep the man alive for further torture rather than kill him outright.[88]

Luke highlights the man's status changes, indicating that now he is ὁ ἀνὴρ ἀφ' οὗ ἐξεληλύθει τὰ δαιμόνια ("the man from whom the demons had come out"). In other words, he goes from the man having demons to the one possessed by demons to the man from whom the demons had gone out. Summing up, the unique characteristic of possession in this account is the man's superhuman strength and the violence he exhibits towards himself. The legion of demons caused his social isolation, convulsive fits, madness, self-harm, and

---

[85] It is possible for the term to semantically represent a possessed state. See BDAG, "δαιμονίζομαι," 209.

[86] Michael J. Wilkins, *Matthew*, NIV Application Commentary (Grand Rapids: Zondervan, 2004), 353.

[87] Witherington, *Gospel of Mark*, 181.

[88] Bock, *Luke 1:1–9:50*, 350.

extreme strength. Upon exorcism, the man is relieved from these ailments. He is not destroyed.

Global Perspectives

As noted at the outset of the chapter, extraordinary strength and violent sorts of action are often associated with possession behavior. Below, varieties of analogous characteristics are surveyed, including the ability to perform extraordinary feats like firewalking or glass eating. As in chapter 4, spirit possession behavior is surveyed globally and arranged by major regions of the world.

Africa

In interreligious experience in Africa, possession experiences are characterized by their psychophysical impact. Characteristics include convulsions, bodily injury or harm, the presence of extraordinary strength, and more. In some cases the spirits inspire violence in a variety of ways.

African Christianity

One might argue that Christian experiences are influenced by the biblical text. While this is possibly true in some cases, the experiences are one variety of interreligious experience presented in modern literature. By way of reminder, most of the experiences surveyed in this project come from secular sources. In African Christianity evil spirits are known to manifest during prayer in a variety of ways. A. H. Anderson describes these characteristics as sometimes violent, including screaming, the body contorting wildly, jumping, running, or falling.[89] One report from a Catholic parish in Uganda describes Father Tim's experience. He was praying with a woman who violently shook as he prayed. Another possessed man was brought to Father Tim. This man, Peter, was "bound at his wrists and ankles. . . . He lay on the ground writing violently and crying out loudly . . ."[90] He was considered as fully possessed by "unwanted spirits," possibly *iraaro* ("spirit of confusion" or "madness") and a "cannibal spirit."[91]

Soshanguve church members testified about a case where a man, possessed by an ancestral spirit, entered the church. The man was extraordinarily strong and could not be restrained by ten men. He screamed and ripped his clothing.

---

[89] Allan Heaton Anderson, *An Introduction to Pentecostalism*, 2nd ed. (Cambridge: Cambridge University Press, 2013), 108.

[90] Alison Fitchett Climenhaga, "Pursuing Transformation: Healing, Deliverance, and Discourses of Development among Catholics in Uganda," *Mission Studies* 35.2 (2018): 205, 213.

[91] Climenhaga, "Pursuing Transformation," 205.

The members made the man drink "blessed water" and tied him up. After three days of incessant prayer the man was delivered.[92] In another case Petros Shallamo, a student at a Catholic seminary, was described as participating in violent behavior, namely, beating up fellow seminarians. After medical treatment, his condition did not improve, and his father diagnosed him as possessed by the *sheiṭanna* spirits.[93]

In Tanzania, during services at a charismatic church named Gospel Miracle Church for All People (GMCL), a pattern of violent behavior among possessed women often commences with the healing session offered after the preaching. The pattern begins with women who fall into trance. Lotta Gammelin describes what follows: "Usually they scream, resist and try to escape, and several people are required to hold them down. . . . The patients roll around on the mud floor."[94] The congregation joins in prayer and views themselves as "entering a war on behalf of their sisters who are forced to live with malicious spirits and long for redemption."[95]

East Africa

In East African religious experience, convulsions signal the incorporation of spirits. This witness to the possession signals the medium's readiness to participate in the rituals. In Ethiopia, Vecchiato reports the experience of "convulsive body movements" among traditional animistic spirit-possession ceremonies. Both the medium and the participants convulse in the ritual. The convulsions occur after long periods of drumming and indicate a readiness to communicate with spirits.[96] Further, Kjersti Larsen shares her own experience with spirits in Zanzibar, which ultimately led her to believe in the reality of spirits. She experienced her leg trembling as a spirit passed through her during the *ngoma ya kabuki* ritual.[97] In another ritual she fell to the floor. She was told by those performing the ritual that "the reason I fell to the floor when the ritual called

[92] Allan Anderson, "Exorcism and Conversion to African Pentecostalism," *Exchange* 35.1 (2006): 117. Anderson includes more examples, but space limits their inclusion above.

[93] Norbert L. Vecchiato, "Illness, Therapy, and Change in Ethiopian Possession Cults," *Africa* 63.2 (1993): 186. Exorcism in the Protestant church did not avail. He was later treated by a healer-medium and his violent behavior subsided.

[94] Lotta Gammelin, "Gendered Narratives of Illness and Healing: Experiences of Spirit Possession in a Charismatic Church Community in Tanzania," in *Faith in African Lived Christianity: Bridging Anthropological and Theological Perspectives*, ed. Karen Lauterbach and Mika Vähäkangas (Leiden: Brill, 2020), 314.

[95] Gammelin, "Gendered Narratives of Illness and Healing," 314.

[96] Vecchiato, "Illness, Therapy, and Change in Ethiopian Possession Cults," 180.

[97] Kjersti Larsen, *Where Humans and Spirits Meet: The Politics of Rituals and Identified Spirits in Zanzibar* (New York: Berghahn, 2008), 12.

upon my spirit was that the spirit had risen to my head and then left again."[98] Therefore, the local interpretation was that the spirit caused Larsen to fall.

Larsen concludes from her experience that one may perceive when a spirit is about to possess them. Other testimonies corroborated Larsen's view. Rukia testified to her experience: "It says boom when my *sheitani ya kibuki* arrives, not swing as when my *shitani ya ruhani* arrives. But both spirits make me lose control over my actions as soon as they have come to my head."[99] Possession is also characterized by the experience of Zakia, Nariman, and Safia, who regularly inhabit spirits. Initially, they were quiet and appeared to be gazing into the distance. Then they appeared sad, like perhaps they would cry. Larsen describes the remainder of the experience as follows: "Suddenly, when a spirit rose to their heads, they screamed out, rose to their feet and started to dance with great force until their spirit decided to leave. As the spirit left their bodies, they fell down to the floor where they lay as if unconscious."[100]

However, Safia's spirit refused to exit, due to its "chance to participate in the human world."[101] As a result, the spirit spoke out, "I shall beat her, really beat her today."[102] Larsen reported the difference between the way the possessed person and an observer would perceive the event. She stated, "To the outside observer it would appear as if Safia was beating herself. However, to the insider the event meant that the spirit inhabiting Safia's body was punishing Safia by beating her body."[103] Even after greetings to calm the spirit, the spirit continued to beat Safia. Safia's older brother was sent for and eventually the realization came that this spirit was to blame for Safia's suffering over the past year, as a result of Safia's arrogance towards this spirit.[104] Rituals were performed to restore the relationship between Safia and her spirit. The spirit exited and Safia fell to the floor in exhaustion.[105] Larsen testifies to the pain and exhaustion that

---

[98] Larsen, *Where Humans and Spirits Meet*, 13. There was a debate between Larsen and those performing the ritual about the influence of brandy upon Safia's falling. Those performing the ritual argued that "it was because of the spirit that you fell to the floor. Other times when you have been drinking during these rituals you have not reacted like this, nor have you become drunk, or the drunkenness has disappeared when *dawa* (medication in this context referring to the special water) has been poured on your head (*kogeshwa*) and the spirit has left. Those times the spirit took the brandy with him or her when leaving and not like this time when the spirit decided to leave the brandy in your head."

[99] Larsen, *Where Humans and Spirits Meet*, 95.

[100] Larsen, *Where Humans and Spirits Meet*, 96.

[101] Larsen, *Where Humans and Spirits Meet*, 96–97.

[102] Larsen, *Where Humans and Spirits Meet*, 97.

[103] Larsen, *Where Humans and Spirits Meet*, 97.

[104] Larsen, *Where Humans and Spirits Meet*, 97.

[105] Larsen, *Where Humans and Spirits Meet*, 97.

characterize the experience of the exit of spirits in Zanzibar.[106] For example, the next day Safia indicated that she could barely talk because of chest pain from the spirit's beating.[107]

North Africa

In *zār* possession in northern and eastern African countries, spirit possession is associated with changes in consciousness and identity that involve violent activities.[108] Fahimeh Mianji and Yousef Semnani describe these acts as inclusive of "periods of shouting, banging of the head against the wall, laughing, singing, or crying."[109] Susan M. Kenyan records the testimony of Najat, who indicated that *zār* spirits cause people "to feel haunted, shaking a lot."[110]

South Africa

While possession is largely related to matters of healing in South African possession cults, this is not always the case. The Pondo believe in spirit familiars called *tokoloshe*, who are described as "grotesque man-like creatures, which do the witches bidding of destroying property and life."[111] In southern Zimbabwe tribal mediums "shake vigorously" and experience "extensive muscular contractions with rapid to-and-fro movements of the head and limbs."[112] During the spirit's exit, the medium shudders and sometimes the activity is "so intense that he falls to the ground in a state of exhaustion."[113] Gelfland adds that an "interesting feature of African mental disease is the large number of mentally disturbed people living alone in the woods or wilds."[114] These

---

[106] Larsen, *Where Humans and Spirits Meet*, 99.

[107] Larsen, *Where Humans and Spirits Meet*, 100.

[108] Fahlmeh Mianji and Yousef Semnani, "Zār Spirit Possession in Iran and African Countries: Group Distress, Culture-Bound Syndrome or Cultural Concept of Distress?" *Iranian Journal of Psychiatry* 10.4 (2015): 225–32.

[109] Mianji and Semnani, "Zār Spirit Possession in Iran and African Countries," 225.

[110] Susan Kenyon, *Spirits and Slaves in Central Sudan: The Red Wind of Sennar* (Basingstoke, UK: Palgrave Macmillan, 2012), 79.

[111] Stephen Lloyd, "South Africa," in *Spirit Possession around the World: Possession, Communion, and Demon Expulsion across Cultures*, ed. Joseph Laycock (Santa Barbara, Calif.: ABC-CLIO, 2015), 321–22.

[112] Michael Gelfand, "Psychiatric Disorders as Recognized by the Shona," in Kiev, *Magic, Faith, and Healing*, 162.

[113] Gelfand, "Psychiatric Disorders as Recognized by the Shona," 162. Gelfand notes that he did not witness the use of any alcoholic substances during possession rituals. Possession experience here is very common and experienced by men and women in ritual ceremonies.

[114] Gelfand, "Psychiatric Disorders as Recognized by the Shona," 165.

gadanga are feared due to their dangerous reputation, including those known for murder. They are typically ostracized by villagers.[115]

West Africa

Among the Mande the spirits that reside among the bush, *jinew*, are known to be powerful and dangerous. The blacksmiths are considered colleagues with the spirits, and they make alliances with them, giving provisions for them to work in the bush. The alliances grant protection since the spirits are known to cause severe trouble, including death.[116]

One woman experiencing possession in the Sopono possession cult, among the indigenous Yoruba, reportedly grabbed at the people within her reach. She was chained and then cut her shoulder by rubbing it in the dirt. She stripped herself naked and smeared the walls with her feces. Upon soothing the Sopono spirit with medicine, the woman experienced relief.[117] Another woman, during her initiation into the cult, collapsed on the floor upon her possession.[118]

In Mende experience one case of possession by a *dyinanga* spirit resulted in the murder of the possessed boy's father with a machete. The seventeen-year-old son of a *mori*-man known for driving out spirits became troubled by an evil *dyinanga*, and his father was not capable of removing the spirit. Consistent urges came from the *dyinanga* to murder his father, and Dawson reports that eventually the boy succumbed to the urges.[119]

Paul Stoller recounts his experience in Niger, where he witnessed a possessed man who "vomited up black liquid" and rolled around on the ground while eating and throwing sand. He spit sand at Stoller and scorned him with his words. He flailed around, seemingly attempting to strike the onlookers. He frothed from the mouth and his eyes bulged.[120]

In the westernmost city of Dakar, in Colobane, illness is a catalyst for restoring alliance with spirits, since illness results from neglecting the spirits.

---

[115] Gelfand, "Psychiatric Disorders as Recognized by the Shona," 165.

[116] Patrick R. McNaughton, *The Mande Blacksmiths: Knowledge, Power, and Art in West Africa* (Bloomington: Indiana University Press, 1993), 18–21.

[117] Raymond Prince, "Indigenous Yoruba Psychiatry," in Kiev, *Magic, Faith, and Healing*, 106–7.

[118] Prince, "Indigenous Yoruba Psychiatry," 108.

[119] John Dawson, "Urbanization and Mental Health in a West African Community," in Kiev, *Magic, Faith, and Healing*, 335–36. The boy reportedly also experienced phases of hallucination and catatonic states that lasted for days. See p. 336 for two other similar reports.

[120] Paul Stoller, "Horrific Comedy: Cultural Resistance and the Hauka Movement in Niger," *Ethos* 12.2 (1984): 165–88 (166).

Possession is characterized by depression, anorexia, mutism, reproductive problems, and seizures that result in falling.[121]

Asia

Reports of superhuman feats tend to be more prevalent in Asia. For example, in Taiwan self-mutilation, employed to demonstrate immunity to pain during mutilation, is practiced during traditional festivals.[122] Indian mediumship involves the practice of firewalking (also demonstrating immunity to pain), beatings with swords, and an ability to move large rocks that typically would require multiple people to carry them.[123]

China

In rural Beijing, Wang noted a trend of harming others or self-harm among possession stories. He describes it in the following manner: "Someone was possessed by a malicious spirit when he or she (in most cases she) was passing by a cemetery or when their house was built on a tomb, and the possessed person started to harm his or her family or self-harm."[124] When passing the city limit marker (Lugou Bridge), possessed people were known to faint.[125]

In Christian exorcism, symptoms noted by missionaries include "contortions of the body, and twistings of the neck."[126] In possession rituals among the *tang-ki*, the possessed beat themselves with weapons and make themselves bleed. They also pierce their cheeks with skewers. One local interpretation of the event is that the immunity to pain proves their possession.[127]

During exorcism rituals in the Baraskisan Myōgyōji temple in China, Blacker witnessed several congregants begin to convulse simultaneously. He

[121] Andras Zempleni, "From Symptom to Sacrifice: The Story of Khady Fall," in *Case Studies in Spirit Possession*, ed. Vincent Crapanzano and Vivian Garrison (New York: Wiley, 1977), 94–95.

[122] Christian Jochim, *Chinese Religions: A Cultural Perspective*, Prentice Hall Series in World Religions (Englewood Cliffs, N.J.: Prentice Hall, 1986), 154; James McClenon, *Wondrous Events: Foundations of Religious Belief* (Philadelphia: University of Pennsylvania Press, 1994), 97–100.

[123] Erika Bourguignon, *Possession* (San Francisco: Chandler and Sharp, 1976), 12, citing Wolfgang M. Pfeiffer, *Transkulturelle Psychiatrie: Ergebnisse und Probleme* (Stuttgart: Georg Thieme Verlag, 1971), 121–22. The above cases involved participants who entered ASCs, but not all of the indigenous interpretations were as possession.

[124] Xing Wang, "Rethinking the 'Magic State' in China: Political Imagination and Magical Practice in Rural Beijing," *Asian Ethnology* 77.1–2 (2018): 343.

[125] Wang, "Rethinking the 'Magic State' in China," 343. Upon waking up in the city, the people were conscious and cured (but warned not to return to the place of their possession).

[126] John L. Nevius, *Demon Possession* (Grand Rapids: Kregel, 1968), 53.

[127] Barend J. ter Haar, "China," in Laycock, *Spirit Possession around the World*, 80.

reported that one woman was writhing and another violently began "to jig up and down on her heels."[128] The abbot called out the jigging woman and adjured the spirit to come out of the woman. After a conversation between the spirit and the abbot, the spirit was removed and the woman shrieked loudly and collapsed on the floor.[129] Related to extraordinary strength, Blacker attests to *yamabushi* (ascetic healers), who are known for their power to exorcise. They are also capable of performing feats such as firewalking, climbing ladders of swords, and dousing themselves with boiling water.[130]

India

In Central India the *pir* spirit (Mohammedan spirit) is known to be powerful. The spirit is believed to punish with death those who do not make yearly sacrifice at Desehra. The possessed *barwa* trembles, and his head rolls during possession by a familiar spirit at the Desehra ceremony.[131] During sacrifices to the demon-god Mahishasur (Maisoba), *barwas* dance, and some stab their cheeks, arms, or thighs with knives. Or they may whip their bare backs with heated iron chains and walk on fire. They claim to have no pain or scarring.[132]

In northeastern India the Pnar of Jaintia practice divine possession (*hiar blai*). Lyngdoh writes about a Pnar Catholic family who experienced divine possession. One main characteristic of possession involves the head turning around 180 degrees and getting stuck in that position.[133] Possession is also characterized by convulsions.[134]

---

[128] Carmen Blacker, *The Catalpa Bow: A Study in Shamanistic Practices in Japan* (New York: Routledge Curzon, 1999), 308.

[129] Blacker, *Catalpa Bow*, 310.

[130] Blacker, *Catalpa Bow*, 248–51. These abilities characterize the healer's/shaman's "divine power" (firewalking/immersion in boiling water), and the ability to ascend to heaven magically (sword-ladder climbing). Blacker gives an example of a man who immerses himself in boiling water. The community attributed his abilities to possession by the *kami* (spirit), who imparted power to the man through his ascetic training. Related to firewalking, local *yamabushi* spells are cast to make the "alarmingly red" and "smoking" path possible to cross. Blacker himself crossed the path and noted he felt "a mild warmth."

[131] Stephen Fuchs, "Magic Healing Techniques among the Balahis in Central India," in Kiev, *Magic, Faith, and Healing*, 128, 130. The possessed person is assisted by attendants of the ceremony so that the convulsions do not throw him to the ground. Female *barwas* exhibit the same type of convulsions during their annual feast (Ganagaur). See p. 131.

[132] Fuchs, "Magic Healing Techniques," 130. When the spirit does not cooperate with the exorcist's demands, whipping is employed during exorcism rituals. See p. 136.

[133] Margaret Lyngdoh, "An Interview with the Goddess: Possession Rites as Regulators of Justice among the Pnar of Northeastern India," *Religious Studies and Theology* 36.1 (2017): 58.

[134] Lyngdoh, "Interview with the Goddess," 58.

Another example from northeastern India involves the *deodhās*, known for dancing because of possession by the goddess. These dancers demonstrate extraordinary ability by standing (some describe it as dancing) on the tips of swords. They are also known for licking the blade of the sword.[135] Burley notes that "non-academic" works frequently refer to the phenomena as "miraculous physical feats."[136]

In eastern Tibet there is a specific term for affliction by demons, *'dre 'dzin*.[137] The characteristics associated with this sort of possession are described by Ekvall as unwelcome seizures, convulsions, and extraordinary strength.[138] Further, *lha-pa* (those possessed by deities) experience similar symptoms. Bellezza describes the experience vividly:

> Under the influence of a deity, the *lha-pa* commonly exhibit profuse perspiration, signs of great physical strain, extraordinary strength, seizures, foaming at the mouth, and disappearance of the irises in the back of the head. . . . The spirit-mediums make calls and cries like animals and imitate their movements and actions . . .[139]

In Rajasthan India shrieking, cramping, vomiting, writing, and moaning are all known as telltale signs of possession and are often experienced during the process of disembodying the person. Smith reports a woman's testimony of a possession experience, which occurred during the *arti* ceremony for worship:

> In the *arti* itself I started to feel strange. I suddenly wanted to scream and could barely manage to keep standing. It took all my will and strength to consciously avoid falling on the floor and writhing like some of the other women were doing. I was surprised at what was happening to me. . . . I began feeling completely disoriented. My ears started buzzing and suddenly I could not see what was happening. I was shaking all over and could not stand. The last thing I remember is that I was sinking to the ground and one of the temple assistants grabbed hold of me and helped me complete the ritual.[140]

---

[135] Burley, "Dance of the *Deodhās*," 223.

[136] See M. C. Goswami, "An Annual Shamanistic Dance (Deodha Nach) at Kamakhya, Assam," *Journal of the University of Gauhati (Science)* 11.2 (1960): 53; Pradyot Kumar Maity, *Historical Studies in the Cult of the Goddess Manasā: A Socio-cultural Study* (Calcutta: Punthi Pustak, 1966), 297.

[137] John Vincent Bellezza, *Spirit-mediums, Sacred Mountains, and Related Bon Textual Traditions in Upper Tibet: Calling Down the Gods* (Leiden: Brill, 2005), 5.

[138] Robert Ekvall, *Religious Observances in Tibet: Patterns and Functions* (Chicago: University of Chicago Press, 1964), 273.

[139] Bellezza, *Spirit-mediums, Sacred Mountains, and Related Bon Textual Traditions in Upper Tibet*, 7.

[140] Frederick M. Smith, "Possession, Embodiment, and Ritual in Mental Health Care in India," *Journal of Ritual Studies* 24.2 (2010): 27.

The woman then experienced a time lapse of about an hour where she did not know what was happening to her. She could not recollect the events of that period. She was told by the tantric that she "was behaving like all the other possessed people there, writing and moaning on the floor."[141] After this experience she was taken to perform a puja ceremony. Smith transcribes the testimony of her experience:

> I suddenly started getting cramps all over my body. It was like each and every muscle in my body was twisting and contracting. The pain was excruciating. I was coughing and then started to vomit. . . . Then I started bleeding from every orifice of my body. . . . My agony increased until I could feel nothing and think nothing. . . . He had to stop only because it was time to go to the evening *arti*. Now again, I felt the same strange desire to scream.[142]

The tantric requested that the woman stay one more day so that she could be fully free. Due to personal circumstances related to her relationship with her husband, she was unable to stay. However, her situation became more severe, and she became suicidal and began to hear "strange sounds." Eight days later she returned to Balaji to visit the temple to finish the cleansing rituals. This woman's possession experience (shrieking, cramping, vomiting, writing, moaning) is typical for those who attend the Balaji temple.[143]

In southern India possession by *pēy* (spirits of the "untimely dead") is known to cause violent attacks. Bloomer tells of Dhanam's experience during the removal of spirits from her body. Dhanam, who recently birthed a stillborn child,[144] went to a chapel in Mātāpuram for help. During the removal of the spirits, Dhanam danced, fell down to the ground, and rolled on the floor. Her head rocked violently, which caused her hair to fall out of its knot and fly about her face.[145] Her struggle was a violent one, and it was noted that several spirits came out of her.[146]

---

[141] Smith, "Possession, Embodiment, and Ritual," 28.

[142] Smith, "Possession, Embodiment, and Ritual," 28.

[143] Smith, "Possession, Embodiment, and Ritual," 29. See also Antti Pakaslahti, "Family-Centered Treatment of Mental Health Problems at the Balaji Temple in Rajasthan," *Orientalia* 84 (2014): 129–66.

[144] Kristin C. Bloomer, *Possessed by the Virgin: Hinduism, Roman Catholicism, and Marian Possession in South India* (New York: Oxford University Press, 2018), 3. Dhanam interpreted the death of her child as due to her passing by the burial graves of men who had been recently murdered. She also waded into a lake known to be guarded by Hindu gods during her pregnancy. Because of her Christian faith she did not perform Hindu rites for protection.

[145] Bloomer, *Possessed by the Virgin*, 4.

[146] Bloomer, *Possessed by the Virgin*, 4. These include five spirits of the dead men who had been murdered, a *muni* (an incarnation of Shiva), and a *pēy* (the ghost of a Hindu neighbor woman who died while pregnant).

Violence is also considered a characteristic of Marian possession. Bloomer tells the story of three women possessed by Mātā, defined as "compassionate and loving." Yet all experienced or participated in violence and threats as part of their possession by Mātā. For example, Rosalind and Dhanam's possession led them to strike those who were possessed by *pēy* as a means to drive out the spirits.[147]

In Sri Lanka, Gananath Obeyesekere shares Somavati's case of possession as characterized by general aggression. He defines this aggression as her "threatening to assault anyone around."[148]

Malaysia

In Sarawak spirits are known to be both benevolent and malevolent. One woman testifies to an *antu* (spirit) who wanted to marry her. Because of her refusal, she testified that the spirit "always wants to make me die."[149] Another man testified to being misled by a spirit into the jungle. Upon returning, the man was locked up. He was irrational in speech and behaved with violence, ripping his clothing and mat.[150] A third testimony tells of a man whose failure to sacrifice properly led to him being admitted to a mental hospital. The man became "aggressive, withdrawn, and mute" during full moons.[151] A fourth example includes a spirit medium who fell into a trance from possession by an angry god. The angry god forced him to "cut his tongue with a spike ball, writing three characters on a large sheet of yellow paper with the blood."[152]

Acts of violence, especially beating the back with a ball of nails or a sword, or taking a bath in "burning joss sticks," or other self-mortifying activities, are considered "the most powerful proof of the spiritual attainments of the spirit

[147] Bloomer, *Possessed by the Virgin*, 23.
[148] Gananath Obeyesekere, "Psychocultural Exegesis of a Case of Spirit Possession in Sri Lanka," in Crapanzano and Garrison, *Case Studies in Spirit Possession*, 251. Obeyesekere interprets her aggression as "abreactions" of "repressed impulses." Somvati believed herself to be possessed by *prētas*, evil spirits (in Buddhism a *prēta* is a person who was attached to the "things of the world" upon his/her death).
[149] Karl E. Schmidt, "Folk Psychiatry in Sarawak," in Kiev, *Magic, Faith, and Healing*, 145.
[150] Schmidt, "Folk Psychiatry in Sarawak," 145.
[151] Schmidt, "Folk Psychiatry in Sarawak," 146. Improper sacrifice can upset spirits and cause them to punish or seek revenge.
[152] Jean DeBernardi, *The Way That Lives in the Heart: Chinese Popular Religion and Spirit Mediums in Penang, Malaysia* (Stanford: Stanford University Press, 2006), 131.

medium and the reality of the trance performance."[153] This view is explicated by a Hakka spirit medium:

> In order to become a spirit medium, your heart must be honest and your body clean. The god protects the spirit medium, the medium is the god himself. So the medium can play with the ball of nails, or the fire ball [red hot iron balls], and not be harmed. It is the same for the Indian god, who enters men who then can walk over coals.[154]

Further, a dangerous *Datuk* spirit reportedly was the cause of the suicide of several European individuals who had intruded upon the territory of the spirits. Locals attempted to persuade the European developers to offer a feast (*kenduri*) for the spirit to avoid an attack by the spirit. Their feast came too late as the spirit had already been provoked.[155]

Myanmar

Spiro reports the case of a young Burmese man, Maung Oun Yi, who experienced "madness" and became violent when possessed. Spiro describes him as "extremely violent, using abusive and obscene language and indiscriminately attacking everyone with a dagger."[156] Additionally, he (interpreted as under the influence of the possessing witch) challenged them to bring the exorcists as "none can defeat me."[157] Exorcistic séances are practiced to relieve those possessed by a "punitive supernatural."[158]

Thailand

Ronald Fischer and Sivaporn Tasananukorn report that in southern Thailand possession rituals involve "tens of thousands of spirit mediums" who experience altered states of consciousness and participate in self-mutilation during annual

[153] DeBernardi, *Way That Lives in the Heart*, 131.
[154] DeBernardi, *Way That Lives in the Heart*, 140.
[155] DeBernardi, *Way That Lives in the Heart*, 179.
[156] Melford E. Spiro, *Burmese Supernaturalism* (New Brunswick, N.J.: Transaction, 1996), 164.
[157] Spiro, *Burmese Supernaturalism*, 164. Previously, the man wandered around in the fields and experienced attacks where he felt like something was choking him. He had multiple "attacks." During an exorcism he had seven days of alternating between catatonic states and initiated violent acts on anyone present.
[158] For examples of descriptions of the ceremonies, see Spiro, *Burmese Supernaturalism*, 174–203. See pp. 230–45 for information related to the role of the *ahtelan hsaya* ("Master of the Upper Path") exorcist within Buddhism.

Vegetarian Festivals.[159] Deities possess spirit mediums, and the *Mah Song* (individuals who become the "horse of the possessing spirit") fall into a trance that causes acts of self-mutilation and mortification.[160] When the spirits enter the mediums, the heads of the mediums shake, and their eyes roll. At times the gestures are violent, and they may scream, shout, and violently convulse or jump.[161] The mutilations take a variety of forms, including "piercings with needles, skewers, knives, saws, or other objects (typically to the face and tongue), flogging with magic snake-shaped whips, fire walking, knife-ladder climbing, cutting of one's tongue, forehead, or back with swords or other sharp objects, as well as inviting people to throw firecrackers at their bare feet, chest, and face."[162] The narrative shared by these communities is that "these high-ordeal acts are performed to convince spectators that spirit mediums are genuine and are possessed by powerful spirits that give them supernatural powers."[163]

Vietnam

In the rituals of Saint Tran (a Vietnamese spiritual father who is considered the most powerful spirit[164]), possession experience is known to be dramatic and violent. His worshippers are often male mediums who heal through exorcism. Their dramatic possessions often involve self-choking and body piercing.[165]

[159] Ronald Fischer and Sivaporn Tasananukorn, "Altered States of Consciousness, Spirit Mediums and Predictive Processing: A Cultural Cognition Model of Spirit Possession," *Journal of Consciousness Studies* 25.11–12 (2018): 179. The authors interpret this phenomenon in view of predictive processing, which considers the brain as a "predictive machine."

[160] Fischer and Tasananukorn, "Altered States of Consciousness," 187. For more detail on the festival and experience, see Margaret Chan, *Ritual Is Theatre, Theatre Is Ritual: Tang-Ki Chinese Spirit Medium Worship* (Singapore: Wee Kim Wee Centre and SNP, 2009); Emma Cohen, *The Chinese Vegetarian Festival in Phuket: Religion, Ethnicity and Tourism on a Southern Island* (Bangkok: White Lotus Press, 2001).

[161] Fischer and Tasananukorn, "Altered States of Consciousness," 188.

[162] Fischer and Tasananukorn, "Altered States of Consciousness," 187.

[163] Fischer and Tasananukorn, "Altered States of Consciousness," 187.

[164] Pham Quynh Phuong, *Hero and Deity: Tran Hung Dao and the Resurgence of Popular Religion in Japan* (Chiang Mai, Thailand: Mekong, 2009), 67, records the words of a Hanoi exorcist and medium, who describes Saint Tran this way: "He manages all three worlds: heaven, the living world, and hell. Don't you know that he's controlling the world of the spirits and death?"

[165] Karen Fjelstad and Nguyen Thi Hien, *Spirits without Borders: Vietnamese Spirit Mediums in a Transnational Age* (New York: Palgrave Macmillan, 2011), 52. See also Maurice Durand, *Technique et Panthéon des Médiums Vietnamiens (Dong)*, vol. 45 (Paris: École Française d'Extrême Orient, 1959), and Phuong, *Hero and Deity*, 9, who shares his experience receiving a phone call from a stranger who considered herself possessed by Tran Hung Dao and needed help. The spirit was strangling her and she could not breathe. Phuong adds that the hero was also known to shake and violently act out on those he possessed.

More generally related to mediumship, punishment is possible if rituals are not performed because of the agreement made with the spirits. Punishments include harm and possible death.[166]

In northern Vietnam a boy reports the story of his mother's possession, which produced bouts of extraordinarily violent activity. The woman "started to smash things around her room," and "it took two strong farmers to hold her."[167] After attempts for other curative means, the boy's father requested an initiation ritual for his wife, and she began to recover.[168]

Central America and the Caribbean

In this region, convulsions, seizures, superhuman feats, and other violent acts are characteristics of possession states. Central American religions commonly exhibit possession states with these features. Examples from the Dominican Republic, Haiti, and Nicaragua follow below.

Afro-Atlantic Religions

Spirit possession during mediumship is often described as a "shocking experience . . . as rough and uncontrolled."[169] Upon the feeling of the spirit's coming a medium will stumble, shake, wave around, and need support from other people (including the removal of any objects that may become dangerous to the person's well-being during the possession experience).[170]

Dominican Republic

Through extensive fieldwork Yvonee Schaffler concludes that violent behavior accompanies spirit possession (emically referred to as *caballo lobo*, "wolf horse," or *chwal gate*, "spoiled horse")[171] in the Dominican Republic. She noted that voodooists who were starting their careers were prone to violent possession forms characterized by flailing, convulsing, falling on the ground, and

[166] Fjelstad and Hien, *Spirits without Borders*, 98.

[167] Thien Do, *Vietnamese Supernaturalism: Views from the Southern Region* (New York: Routledge Curzon, 2003), 93.

[168] Do, *Vietnamese Supernaturalism*, 93. For more details on this account, see below (chapter 6).

[169] Bettina E. Schmidt, "Afro-Atlantic Religions," in Laycock, *Spirit Possession around the World*, 3–4.

[170] Schmidt, "Afro-Atlantic Religions," 4.

[171] Erika Bourguignon, "The Self, the Behavioral Environment and the Theory of Spirit Possession," in *Context and Meaning in Cultural Anthropology*, ed. Melford E. Spiro (New York: Free Press, 1965), 49.

being tossed around.[172] Violent possession is also associated with muteness in the possessed person, and may also resemble epilepsy with seizures.[173]

Haiti

Two possession types are known in Haiti. In *bosal* (rough) possession, the goal is to release built-up energy. This is done through "violent thrashing of the body and generally disorganized, 'wild' behavior . . ."[174] In *lwa* possession the aim is less violent, and the goal is to produce harmony with the self and the universe's forces. The individual identities of the person are replaced by divinity, and at times this results in superhuman feats, typically glass- or fire-eating.[175]

Nicaragua

Among the Mikitu of northeastern Nicaragua, anthropologists report a sort of involuntary possession called *grisi siknis* (crazy sickness).[176] Johan Wedel describes the violent behavior that characterizes this phenomenon.

> During *grisi siknis* attacks the afflicted often rip their own clothes and hair, hurt themselves and try to bite those who hold them down. Behaviours can be quite violent; victims may grab a machete and run around together, threatening and

---

[172] Yvonne Schaffler, "Diagnose 'Wolfspferd,'" in "Spontanbesessenheiten in der Dominikanischen Republik als Anstoß für den Werdegang zum Heiler/zur Heilerin," *Anthropos* 104.2 (2009): 445–56; Yvonne Schaffler, *Vodú? Das ist Sache der anderen! Kreolische Medizin, Spiritualität und Identität im Südwesten der Dominikanischen Republik*, Wiener ethnomedizinische Reihe (Vienna: LIT-Verlag, 2009); Yvonne Schaffler, "Besessenheit in der Dominikanischen Republik im Frühstadium: 'Wilde' Besessenheit (*caballo lobo*) aus psychodynamischer und praxistheoretischer Perspektive," *Curare* 35.1–2 (2012): 72–84; Yvonne Schaffler, "El caballo que se volvió lobo: Análisis del fenómeno de 'posesión espontánea,'" in *Etnografías de América Latina*, ed. Ocho Ensayos et al. (Guadalajara: Universidad de Gudalajara, 2013), 133–64; Yvonne Schaffler, "'Wild' Spirit Possession in the Dominican Republic: From Expression of Distress to Cultural Expertise," in *Dominicanidad/Dominicanity: Perspectivas de un concepto (trans-)nacional / Perspectives on a (Trans-)National Concept*, ed. Christine Felbeck and Andre Klump (Frankfurt am Main: Peter Lang, 2015), 221–37.

[173] Yvonne Schaffler et al., "Traumatic Experience and Somatoform Dissociation among Spirit Possession Practitioners in the Dominican Republic," *Culture, Medicine, and Psychiatry* 40 (2016): 80.

[174] Max-G. Beauvoir, "Herbs and Energy: The Holistic Medical System of the Haitian People," in *Haitian Vodou: Spirit, Myth, and Reality*, ed. Patrick Bellegarde-Smith and Claudine Michel (Bloomington: Indiana University Press, 2006), 129–30.

[175] Beauvoir, "Herbs and Energy," 129–30.

[176] Johan Wedel, "Involuntary Mass Spirit Possession among the Miskitu," *Anthropology and Medicine* 19.3 (2012): 303–14.

frightening other people. They may also run into the bush or throw themselves into a river or the sea.[177]

The phenomenon of *grisi siknis* has become more pervasive in the last decade and now affects males and females of any age (rather than just adolescents).[178] The Mayangna and some *mestizos* are also affected.[179] The phenomena have been locally referred to as epidemics. For example, in 2003, 139 people living in a village named Raiti were affected. Authorities in the Waspam area expressed fear that their soldiers might be possessed and shoot at locals.[180]

Middle East

Possession states exhibit violent characteristics in the Middle East. Spirits are interpreted as behaving in violent ways and causing harm to those they possess. During exorcisms in Peshawar, women are known to dance in a possession state, as part of a *baithak* session for the removal of the spirit. It is believed that women are incapable of sensing what occurs during this possession dance. A woman may pull hard on her earrings, scratch herself with a bracelet, or pull a scarf tightly around her neck. For this reason many of these items are often removed before the ceremony. Additionally, a woman may beat herself with her hands, leaving her body in a bruised state the next morning. A woman may also gnash her teeth, foam at the mouth, or bite her tongue and make it bleed.[181] Nasir writes, "The face of a beautiful and dignified woman who was lying there quietly may suddenly become virtually unrecognizable."[182]

Jinn spirits are often violent to those they possess. One man testified to his experience of being beaten in the face by an invisible spirit because of his

---

[177] Wedel, "Involuntary Mass Spirit Possession among the Miskitu," 304. Wedel notes that the phenomenon of mass possessions is not an isolated one. Examples of mass possession have been reported in other locales such as Malaysia, Zambia, Thailand, Madagascar, Nepal, Colombia, Papua New Guinea, and India. A wide variety of terminology is used for mass possession, including "mass hysteria," "epidemic hysteria," "medically unexplained epidemic illness," and "mass conversion reaction."

[178] Wedel, "Involuntary Mass Spirit Possession among the Miskitu," 307.

[179] See Gerhild Trübswasser, Sandra David, and Sasha Marley, "Algo anda mal: El bla o wakni en el Río Coco: Occasional Paper," IMTRADEC (Puerto Cabezas, Nicaragua: URACCAN, 2005); Johan Wedel, "Bridging the Gap between Western and Indigenous Medicine in Eastern Nicaragua," *Anthropological Notebooks* 15.1 (2009): 57.

[180] Wedel, "Involuntary Mass Spirit Possession among the Miskitu," 307.

[181] Mumtaz Nasir, "*Baithak*: Exorcism in Peshawar (Pakistan)," *Asian Folklore Studies* 46.2 (1987): 164.

[182] Nasir, "*Baithak*: Exorcism in Peshawar (Pakistan)," 164.

immoral behavior.[183] A famous case of violent possession involves a boy who would frequently bang his head against a wall. The boy was cured by a sheikh.[184] Another example includes a woman who experienced "something pushing" on her chest that the doctors could not help. The woman's son saw "a very tall man next to the wall trying to choke" her, and she struggled with the man, pushing him away (leaving pain in her hands for the following month).[185] Another woman experienced extraordinary strength during possession. The woman, possessed by sixty-seven *jinn* spirits, testified that "I needed six or seven men in order to stay sitting in the chair or to prevent me from doing bad things."[186]

Oceania

Henare Tate, who was a Catholic Māori priest for forty years, writes about his experience in 2007, when he was asked to pray with two possessed people. Initially, he requested if they had already seen a *kaumātua* (male elder). The *kaumātua* had been consulted. However, because of the "violent reactions" of the two possessed people, he "prayed from outside the house and then left."[187] Upon his arrival Tate sprinkled holy water and then approached the young man. He described the man's violence as follows:

> He began to shake, writhe, and cry out with anguish. Two other people in the house, including the young woman who had called for help, rushed to restrain the person's flailing arms and legs, all the while praying that the evil spirit would leave him. After fifteen minutes of prayer and physical struggle, he came out of the attack and calmed down. Everyone was exhausted.[188]

Then, they turned to the possessed woman, a teenage girl, who also writhed, needing to be held in restraint.[189] Tate explained the two stories as instances of extraordinary strength. A third instance involved a forty-year-old woman who also had to be restrained since she "put her arms around her ninety kilogram brother and squeezed him until he fell to the floor."[190] Another example

---

[183] Celia E. Rothenberg, *Spirits of Palestine: Gender, Society, and Stories of the Jinn* (Oxford: Lexington, 2004), 33. Rothenberg writes about her work in a Muslim village called Artas.

[184] Rothenberg, *Spirits of Palestine*, 45. This story was told in a debate about whether *jinn* spirits could cause harm/mental illness.

[185] Rothenberg, *Spirits of Palestine*, 70–71.

[186] Rothenberg, *Spirits of Palestine*, 78.

[187] Henare Arekatera Tate, "A Māori Perspective on Spirit Possession," in *Spirit Possession, Theology, and Identity: A Pacific Exploration*, ed. Elaine M. Wainwright with Philip Culbertson, and Susan Smith (Hindmarsh, Australia: ATF Press, 2010), 3–4.

[188] Tate, "Māori Perspective," 3–4.

[189] Tate, "Māori Perspective," 4.

[190] Tate, "Māori Perspective," 10.

includes two young persons who "split apart the arm-rests of the chairs they were sitting on."[191]

During a period of concentrated Christian evangelization, "evil spirit sickness" or "wild-man behavior" (*dafolab*) emerged in Papua New Guinea among Christian converts and Christians in general.[192] Edward L. Schieffelin describes it as "a disruptive but temporary mental and behavioral derangement in which an individual suddenly became inappropriately angry and verbally abusive while physically thrashing around."[193] Bystanders attempted to restrain these individuals and were met with "vigorous resistance."[194] Additional characteristics included public disrobing and "a curious writhing of the stomach."[195] Five people lost their lives from the sickness. Prayer sessions, lasting at most ninety minutes and requiring restraint, and exorcisms were the treatment for the ailment.[196]

South America

Possession in South America at times leads to convulsive behavior, shrieking, self-harm, or other violent acts. Some cases involve loss of control and no recollection of the event. Below are examples from various Brazilian religions including Umbanda, Santo Daime, and Kardecist-Spiritism.

Brazilian mediums practicing Umbanda exhibit convulsive behavior as the *baixam* (spirits) lower themselves to possess the medium (referred to as lowering onto their horses).[197] They are known for spinning rapidly with their chest and head jerking back and forth. Female mediums may have their hair disarrayed.[198] During ritual ceremonies (often for the purpose of diagnosing illness), a spirit may possess an audience member, evidenced by his/her shrieking and violent shaking.[199] Possessed individuals may fall down as the spirit

---

[191] Tate, "Māori Perspective," 10.

[192] Edward L. Schieffelin, "Evil Spirit Sickness, the Christian Disease: The Innovation of a New Syndrome of Mental Derangement and Redemption in Papua New Guinea," *Culture, Medicine, and Psychiatry* 20.1 (1996): 1–3.

[193] Schieffelin, "Evil Spirit Sickness, the Christian Disease," 1. See chapter 6 (below) for how it affected speech.

[194] Schieffelin, "Evil Spirit Sickness, the Christian Disease," 1.

[195] Schieffelin, "Evil Spirit Sickness, the Christian Disease," 1.

[196] Schieffelin, "Evil Spirit Sickness, the Christian Disease," 1, 22–23.

[197] Horses represent the mediums. Esther Pressel, "Negative Spirit Possession in Experienced Brazilian Umbanda Spirit Mediums," in Crapanzano and Garrison, *Case Studies in Spirit Possession*, 343.

[198] Pressel, "Negative Spirit Possession," 343.

[199] Pressel, "Negative Spirit Possession," 344. This is interpreted as indicating the person's need to develop his/her mediumistic capabilities.

leaves.[200] Esther Pressel writes about two cases of "negative possession."[201] The first, Cecília's possession, was characterized as an uncontrolled case which led to Cecília flailing her arms about wildly. The spirit moved her by a wall, "where he severely pounded her head several times."[202] The second includes the case of a thirty-three-year-old man she refers to as João, who had a decade of experience as a medium. Pressel wrote in her notes that João was "suddenly and violently seized by one of his spirits."[203]

Schmidt, interviewing a medium in São Paulo, records a description of what it feels like to be possessed by various deities in Umbanda. The medium stated,

> I feel differences between the deities in Umbanda. When I incorporate some deities, I do not feel anything. And I have other deities that make me feel ecstatic, even though I did not enter them. The feeling is different from my normal waking state. But when I incorporate an *orixá*, I usually have no control of my movements. In most deities, in the Yoruba tradition, I have no control of my movements. Often when I am conscious, I want to stop, but I cannot.[204]

Bettina highlights the "lack of control, loss of memory and an awareness of an extraordinary presence in their body" as characteristic of possession experience.[205]

In Santo Daime experience, mediums are required to manage the psychophysical effects of becoming possessed, including "shaking, gesticulating and expostulation."[206] Dawson records the testimony of a North American medium, at an inchoate stage in mediumship, who stated, "I started noticing shaking in my hands . . . my hands would start doing things that Katherine [third-person reference to herself] was not doing, and each ceremony it would become more advanced."[207] An Australian witness testified to the reductive ability to maintain self-awareness in possession states. He stated, "When I'm in it, I'm in it. . . . My face will screw up and my mouth assume shapes that

[200] Pressel, "Negative Spirit Possession," 344.

[201] This terminology is taken from I. M. Lewis and represents "uncontrolled and unsolicited possessions" (Pressel, "Negative Spirit Possession," 346).

[202] Pressel, "Negative Spirit Possession," 353–54. The violent behavior was explained as the spirit's rage because she did not want him to possess her.

[203] Pressel, "Negative Spirit Possession," 361.

[204] Bettina E. Schmidt, *Spirits and Trance in Brazil: An Anthropology of Religious Experience* (New York: Bloomsbury, 2016), 94.

[205] Schmidt, *Spirits and Trance in Brazil*, 94.

[206] Andrew Dawson, *Santo Daime: A New World Religion* (London: Bloomsbury, 2013), 138.

[207] Dawson, *Santo Daime*, 138–39.

are not mine, and short or long breaths will emerge, sometimes accompanied by sound that has nothing to do with the words [of the hymn being sung]."[208] In therapeutic mediumship, practiced in settings like the "divine hospital" or "spiritual first-aid centre," the incorporation of spirits allows for the sounds and excited gestures rather than the aim to control them.[209]

In Kardecist-Spiritism medium healers are known to shake violently. Greenfield attests to the story of Carlos Ribeiro, a medium healer, who was beginning a spirit surgery (with knives) and began "to shake almost violently."[210] The man revealed to her that he shakes when the spirits possess him.[211] She also noted a change in the tone and accent of his voice after the possession.[212] In a second example, Greenfield describes another medium who prepared himself to perform spirit surgery. She describes the event as follows:

> We entered the building and went into a small alcove where a dozen people sat on a circle of chairs. I was introduced to the officers from Spiritist groups in other states who had come to observe. The president began to read from a Spiritist version of the Gospel. After fifteen minutes Edson entered and quietly took a seat. As the reading continued, he changed visibly. His body quivered, his eyes bulged, his face was fixed in a stern expression—it was the appearance of the persona of Dr. Adolph Fritz. He took over the prayer session, speaking in a higher tone than I'd heard before, with what seemed to be a German-like accent and a strong sense of authority. "All is ready now," he announced. He walked from the alcove. Even his gait had changed. (*Spirits with Scalpels*, 40)

In this case Greenfield attests to a bodily response to possession that characterizes the inception of the possession state. A similar experience is reported about healings in Umbanda. Greenfield attests to mediums who jerk uncontrollably, spin, or shake upon possession.[213]

Western Experiences

Western reports include similar violent characteristics during possession states. Below are reports from Europe and North America. Additionally, Catholic views are discussed.

[208] Dawson, *Santo Daime*, 147.
[209] Dawson, *Santo Daime*, 145–46. Therapeutic and non-illuminatory mediumship decentralizes mediums and those seeking healing out of the "core ritual space."
[210] Sidney M. Greenfield, *Spirits with Scalpels: The Cultural Biology of Religious Healing in Brazil* (Walnut Creek, Calif.: Left Coast Press, 2008), 24.
[211] Greenfield, *Spirits with Scalpels*, 24.
[212] Greenfield, *Spirits with Scalpels*, 25. She describes this as "like a native speaker of Spanish trying to communicate in Portuguese."
[213] Greenfield, *Spirits with Scalpels*, 129.

In Romanian and Hungarian experience, "personal possession (*possession/ obsession*)" is widely documented.[214] Further, some groups maintain belief in possession by the *tisztátalanok* (evil spirit), which causes a variety of symptoms, including extraordinary strength and the tearing off of clothing. The possessed person turns around multiple times and becomes mute. Upon the exit of the spirit, exhaustion and limpness follows, leaving the person unable to stand.[215] Petzhold lists "trembling" as one of the motifs of Central European folk demonology from the Middle Ages to present times.[216]

The Bristol Spirit Lodge in Bristol, UK, is focused on the development of spirit mediumship through séances. Anthropologist Jack Hunter writes of his experiences of bodily convulsions during participant observation in the development of his mediumship. Namely, he experienced the convulsion of his right arm after panicking at the feeling of a presence standing by him. He writes,

> I began to feel myself distancing from my body. I felt as though there was a space in my body which could easily be filled; it was as though I had made room in my physical body by moving myself out of it. I then felt an energy move into my left hand, and my index finger began to rise of its own accord. It felt as though it were being lifted by a cushion of air. My second finger began to move upwards also, and soon my hand was quivering on the arm of the chair. I was aware of the movement, but also of the fact that I was not consciously willing it to happen. I was observing the moment, but not with my eyes. This motion began to become more vigorous and soon my whole arm was vibrating and shaking side to side.[217]

According to Hunter the intensity of the energy eventually decreased, and he regained bodily control. He remarked, "I was quite shocked by this experience, and it took quite a while before I was fully calm afterwards."[218] Hunter classifies his experience of dissociation and the convulsion of his arm as parallel to the cross-cultural experience of a spirit's attempt to use him as a vehicle for communication and as a marker of early trance behavior. This coheres with how his experience was interpreted by his guides for mediumship. They

---

[214] Éva Pócs, "Possession Phenomena, Possession-Systems: Some East-Central European Examples," in *Communicating with the Spirits*, ed. Éva Pócs and Gábor Klaniczay (Budapest: Central European University Press, 2005), 96.

[215] Pócs, "Possession Phenomena, Possession-Systems," 96.

[216] Leander Petzoldt, "Besessenheit in Sage und Volksglauben," *Rheinisches Jahrbuch für Volkskunde* 15–16 (1964–1965): 84–86.

[217] Jack Hunter, *Engaging the Anomalous: Collected Essays on Anthropology, the Paranormal, Mediumship and Extraordinary Experience* (Hove, UK: August Night, 2018), 113.

[218] Hunter, *Engaging the Anomalous*, 113–14.

concluded that his hand's movement was "indicative of the fact that a spirit was attempting to communicate through my body."[219]

North America

A variety of examples from North America exhibit a parallel range of violent characteristics stemming from possession states. Extraordinary strength is also a common feature of possession behavior in North American experience. Below, a range of examples are provided.

In the process of becoming shamans in St. Lawrence Island, Alaska, extreme strength is associated with the period of initiation. During a five-day period, initiates will fast and become strong. Alaskan natives testified to their strength, noting that "ten men cannot hold them."[220] Shamans in training experience seizures, become unconscious, and become possessed with familiar spirits, who aid curing rituals.[221] One shaman was known for her fits of excitement, and this caused her to mutilate herself by pounding her hands with stones. She attacked others and as a result was restrained to the pole of a house. She would eventually return to lucidity and maintain her practice as a shaman.[222]

Related to Catholic experiences in the United States, Blai responds to many commonly asked questions, including "Can demon possession really do the horrible things to the human body seen in movies?"[223] Blai responds affirmatively, noting that "bodies do sometimes contort, bones may dislocate, people have caught fire spontaneously, levitation does really happen, and they have vomited bizarre things."[224] Blai adds that another common sign of possession is "strength beyond their normal condition."[225] This characteristic is one of the few stated directly in the 1999 document titled *De Exorcismis et Supplicationibus Quibusdam* (Of Exorcisms and Certain Supplications), as it is considered one of the "most reliable signs."[226]

[219] Hunter, *Engaging the Anomalous*, 126.
[220] Murphy, "Psychotherapeutic Aspects of Shamanism," 58.
[221] Murphy, "Psychotherapeutic Aspects of Shamanism," 59. See also the testimony of Riley Moore, who witnessed this in a séance.
[222] Murphy, "Psychotherapeutic Aspects of Shamanism," 76.
[223] Adam C. Blai, "Basic Information," *Religious Demonology*, accessed May 22, 2023, https://religiousdemonology.com/basics.
[224] Blai, "Basic Information."
[225] Adam C. Blai, "Exorcism and the Church: Through Priests, the Church Has the Power to Battle Demons," *The Priest* 73.8 (2017): 19. See also X. F. Marquart, "L'exorciste dans le manifestations diaboliques," in *Satan*, ed. E. Carmélitaines (Paris: Desclée de Brouwer, 1948), 328–51, who cites extraordinary strength as characteristic of possession.
[226] Marco Innamorati, Ruggero Taradel, and Renato Foschi, "Between Sacred and Profane: Possession, Psychotherapy, and the Catholic Church," *History of Psychology* 22.1 (2018): 9.

In the famous case of the exorcism of Annelise,[227] violence and bizarre phenomena were characteristic of her possession state. Ultimately, the girl's violent acts, "self-inflicted blows and starvation," led to her death.[228] Her story stopped exorcistic practice in Germany, and her exorcism was likely the final one performed there for some time. However, ironically, it reinforced traditional viewpoints as her possession was interpreted as "true" possession.[229]

In Navaho experience a possession state known as a sort of "moth craziness" (iich'aa) is often believed to cause fits of crazy behavior. The moth is believed to live within a person and has the capacity to affect behavior. The cure involves vomiting out the moth to regain conscious behavior. Seizures and fits are common symptoms of "moth craziness," which is often interpreted as a form of mental illness.[230] In one severe case of iich'aa, a man acted violently on several occasions and was continually dangerous. The man was disturbed, ran into the woods, was not coherent in speech, and threatened further violence.[231] Navaho experience also involves possession states that result in extraordinary strength, making it nearly impossible to restrain the person.[232]

Among the Cochiti Tribe in New Mexico, doctors and patients experience violence during healing ceremonies.[233] Some doctors claim to experience a "terrible battle in the darkness" because witches get "inside them."[234] These doctors "roll in convulsions and lacerate themselves," and claim that the witches make them act in this way.[235]

---

[227] Written about in Felicitas Goodman, *The Exorcism of Anneliese Michel* (Eugene, Ore.: Resource Publications, 1981). See also literature produced as a result: John Duffey, *Lessons Learned: The Anneliese Exorcism: The Implementation of a Safe and Thorough Examination, Determination, and Exorcism of Demonic Possession* (Eugene, Ore.: Wipf and Stock, 2011); Régis Olry and Michel Cyr, "How Neuroscience May Face Up to Anneliese Michel's Alleged Demoniac Possession: A Contribution to Neuropathy?" (paper presented at the Society for Neuroscience Conference, 2010).

[228] Innamorati, Taradel, and Foschi, "Between Sacred and Profane," 6.

[229] Innamorati, Taradel, and Foschi, "Between Sacred and Profane," 6. See also Jose Antonio Fortea and Lawrence E. U. LeBlanc, *Anneliese Michel: A True Story of a Case of Demonic Possession: Germany—1976* (independently published, 2019).

[230] Bert Kaplan and Dale Johnson, "Navaho Psychopathology," in Kiev, *Magic, Faith, and Healing*, 211–12.

[231] Kaplan and Johnson, "Navaho Psychopathology," 226–27. The man was cured in a ceremony involving chanting.

[232] Kaplan and Johnson, "Navaho Psychopathology," 208.

[233] J. Robin Fox, "Witchcraft and Clanship," in Kiev, *Magic, Faith, and Healing*, 185. These ceremonies are known to last eight days and involve prayer, fasting, invoking spirits, etc.

[234] Fox, "Witchcraft and Clanship," 185.

[235] Fox, "Witchcraft and Clanship," 186. Fox interprets all the phenomena as psychosomatic and as a "cultural mechanism" to deal with illness.

In New York a woman named Maria experienced a phenomenon, titled "Puerto Rican Syndrome," that exhibits violent and convulsive activity. The activity is described in the statement below.

> One hot Friday afternoon in July 1968, Maria, an attractive 39-year-old, married Puerto Rican woman, was sitting at her bench in a handbag factory in New York's garment district, where she had worked for four years. Suddenly, to the surprise of those around her, she began to scream and tear her clothes from her chest. She ran to the window, apparently trying to throw herself through it. When restrained, she fell to the floor in an unconscious or semiconscious state, with her whole body twitching.[236]

This activity catalyzed a variety of interpretations, even though the woman believed that she was possessed (*obsesión*).[237] Maria was angered by her hospitalization for psychiatric treatment.[238] Later she attended a *consulta* and several "reunions" for healing, during which the cause was determined as spiritual and as the result of witchcraft against Maria.[239] "Fully developed" mediums were consulted in the removal of the spirits disturbing Maria.[240] A psychiatric consultation also led to her impression about the diagnosis.[241]

Summary and Conclusions

The above cross-cultural study of spirit possession accounts as involving violent acts and extraordinary strength provides pertinent parallels to NT accounts. The above global examples are only a glimpse into cultures that attribute these kinds of characteristics to possession states. Many parallel accounts could be discussed if space permitted.

---

[236] Vivian Garrison, "The 'Puerto Rican Syndrome' in Psychiatry and *Espiritismo*," in Crapanzano and Garrison, *Case Studies in Spirit Possession*, 383.

[237] Those practicing *Espiritisa* interpreted her experience as the result of three malevolent spirits sent to her through witchcraft. The witchcraft was the result of jealousy among others at work. Three *espiritus obsesores*, defined as "spirits of darkness that fill your mind with base, material, ignorant thoughts, and impulses that you can't get rid of," were sent to Maria, making her *loca*.

[238] Garrison, "Puerto Rican Syndrome," 391–92. They interpreted her as *loca*.

[239] Garrison, "Puerto Rican Syndrome," 397.

[240] Garrison, "Puerto Rican Syndrome," 398.

[241] Garrison, "Puerto Rican Syndrome," 407, 416–17. Maria's diagnostic impression was "borderline schizophrenic; hypomanic, recovering from acute psychotic episode." Garrison followed up five years later and Maria was still very nervous, could not work, and was ill and receiving a disability check. She credited some aid to the *Espiritistas*. See pp. 423–37 for a discussion of Garrison's six levels of possession.

Next, chapter 6 will consider cross-cultural characteristics of spirit possession that are related to one more category of characteristics found in NT accounts: vocalic alterations, demonic speech, and oracular activity. While this chapter has surveyed parallels related to violence/extraordinary strength, the next chapter asks how possession affects vocalic activity in the possessed. Does the intonation of the voice change? Do spirits speak through persons in our cross-cultural evidence? Do spirits inspire oracular activity?

6

Spirits Make Me Speak!

Spirit Possession, Vocalic Alterations, Demonic Speech, and Oracular Activity

The final set of possession characteristics under consideration includes vocalic alterations, demonic speech, and oracular activity/prophetic speech. Anthropologists document numerous cross-cultural accounts of possession experience that involve vocalic alteration and demonic speech, especially in studies of spirit mediumship. The witness to these characteristics has been prevalent in anthropological literature for some time. In early anthropological work, Herskovits describes the possessed as exhibiting "a complete transformation in his personality."[1] In one case, he depicts the stark changes that took place in a possessed man, demonstrating that "the character of his utterances are startlingly different from what they were when he is 'himself.'"[2] Bloomer argues, "Cross-culturally, men and women who are 'possessed' (for lack of a better word) by a deity or a spirit move or speak in 'odd' ways—that is to be considered outside the realm of proper daily behavior."[3]

Secondarily, spirits speaking through persons often relay knowledge that is valued by the hearer. Oracular activity, involving numinous power and communicating with spirits, is also characteristic of spirit possession phenomena in modern parallels. Anthropological studies have documented the widespread

[1]   Melville J. Herskovits, *Man and His Works: The Science of Cultural Anthropology* (New York: A. A. Knopf, 1948), 66–67.
[2]   Herskovits, *Man and His Works*, 66–67.
[3]   Kristin C. Bloomer, *Possessed by the Virgin: Hinduism, Roman Catholicism, and Marian Possession in South India* (New York: Oxford University Press, 2018), 9. Bloomer compares this experience to the expressions found among North American charismatics, who participate in similar expressions as a form of the "gifts of the Spirit."

experience of such phenomena. Jack Hunter's conclusions are helpful in realizing that these characteristics are at the core of the cross-cultural experience of spirit possession. He concludes, "Members believe that they are able to make direct contact with the world of spirits, whether through communicating with spiritual entities channeled via entranced mediums, witnessing ostensibly paranormal phenomena in the context of séances, or through falling into trance themselves and experiencing direct communion with the 'numinous.'"[4] In other words, talking with spirits is a documented cross-cultural phenomenon. Human Resource Area files provide a broad array of documentation for spirits as involved in revelation and divination.[5]

This chapter focuses on cases where possession (involuntary or voluntary) is involved and recognizes the difficulties associated with the use of the terminology of spirit possession and spirit mediumship, especially noting the difference between shamanism and spirit mediumship. It is imperative to recognize the difference between these two roles. Eliade highlights this distinction:

> It will be easily seen wherein a shaman differs from a "possessed" person, for example; the shaman controls his "spirits," in the sense that he, a human being, is able to communicate with the dead, "demons," and "nature spirits," without thereby becoming their instrument.[6]

As a result, the discussion below recognizes that communication with spirits is characteristic of both mediumship and shamanism, and one must listen to emic perspectives to understand if a culture associates shamanism with possession.[7]

[4]   Jack Hunter, *Engaging the Anomalous: Collected Essays on Anthropology, the Paranormal, Mediumship and Extraordinary Experience* (Hove, UK: August Night, 2018), 99.

[5]   eHRAF describes the entry for "Spirits (activities in revelation and divination)" as "practices reflecting anxiety about the future and often also a sense of inspiration; quest for visions and guardian spirits; hallucinatory revelations; communication with spirits (e.g., through spirit possession, through inspired oracles, through mediums); prophecy; clairvoyance; acquiring mystic insight through concentration and contemplation; interpretation of dreams; omens and their interpretation; divinatory practices and techniques (e.g., geomancy, haruspicy, hepatoscopy, necromancy, scapulimancy, scrying, sortilege, astrology); etc." eHRAF lists 315 files that document the relationship between spirits and "activities in revelation and divination."

[6]   Mircea Eliade, *Shamanism: Archaic Techniques of Ecstasy* (Princeton: Princeton University Press, 1964), 6.

[7]   In his work among the Siberian Buriyat, Jokic observed possession as characteristic of shamanism. See Zeljko Jokic, "Yanomami Shamanic Initiation: The Meaning of Death and Postmortem Consciousness in Transformation," *Anthropology of Consciousness* 19.1 (2008): 33–59.

Further, this research is not the first to compare ancient analogues of oracular activity related to spirit possession with modern examples of the phenomena. Geoffrey Arnott made an analogous argument, based upon a comparison of the State Oracle of Tibet and the Oracle of Delphi, that cross-cultural data offer "commonalities in human experience and psychology."[8] Arnott contends that the modern reports might shine light on the means by which the Delphic priestesses induce the trance state, and he cites the emotionally charged atmosphere as useful for attracting belief in the numinous power and authority of the oracle.[9] With these arguments Arnott attempts to use modern analogues to aid in a more thorough understanding of the Oracle of Delphi. He notes that modern practitioners might "provide contemporary authenticated evidence of their workings, power, and credibility."[10] While Arnott's approach reaches beyond the scope of this study because of its bent towards interpreting the phenomena, it does parallel this research because it recognizes the modern analogous data as useful for understanding ancient evidence. Arnott rightly states, "Analogy admittedly is not argument, and the individual reader must judge for himself the applicability of the evidence."[11] The task below is to consider how the NT depictions of changes in vocalic expression, demonic speech, and oracular activity as characteristics of spirit possession compare to modern expressions of spirit possession.

Ancient Perspectives

Israel

The Testament of Job[12] is an elaboration (or Haggadic commentary) on the book of Job in the Old Testament. The final days of Job, who is characterized as an Egyptian king, are portrayed. In the story Job questioned if a local idol was the one God. An angel came to him and informed him that the idol was not the one God. Job planned to destroy the "idol of Satan" and was granted

---

[8] Geoffrey Arnott, "Nêchung: A Modern Parallel to the Delphic Oracle?" *Greece and Rome* 26 (1989): 152–57 (152, 156). Another example is John Vincent Bellezza, *Spirit-mediums, Sacred Mountains, and Related Bon Textual Traditions in Upper Tibet: Calling Down the Gods* (Leiden: Brill, 2005), 8–9. Bellezza notes the continuity between pre-Buddhist and Buddhist expressions of spirit mediumship. Bellezza concludes, "Spirit mediumship in Upper Tibet represents a cultural phenomenon that appears to exhibit a great deal of historical continuity" (484).

[9] Arnott, "Nêchung," 156–57.

[10] Arnott, "Nêchung," 152.

[11] Arnott, "Nêchung," 152.

[12] The Testament of Job dates somewhere between the first century BCE and the first century CE.

permission from the archangels. However, the angels warned Job that if he destroyed the idol Satan would attack him. Job persisted and fifty slaves were sent to destroy the idol. Satan responded by bringing destruction to Job, his possessions, and his family. Chapter 10 of the Testament of Job is the major contributor to its demonology. Elihu, who is "imbued with the spirit of Satan," speaks against Job. Chapter 10:7–8 states, "Then, imbued with the spirit of Satan,[13] Elihu spoke hard words which are written down in the records left of Elihu. And after he had ended, God appeared to me in a storm and in clouds and spoke blaming Elihu and showing me that he who had spoken was not a man, but a wild beast."[14] Therefore, as in other literature, evil spirits can inspire communication.

Greco-Roman Antiquity

In Greco-Roman perspective, Plutarch associated demons with oracular activity. This belief is reflected by the belief in fate in antiquity. Demons have foreknowledge of future events because of the fate that brings the future about. Additionally, gods are known to communicate through demons. Luck summarizes the effect of demons on ancient oracles, "When daemons go into exile or emigrate, the oracles lose their power, but when the daemons come back . . . the oracles speak again, like musical instruments when there are players to use them."[15] Plutarch, influenced by Xenocrates, further describes this phenomenon of prophecy or clairvoyance, indicating that demons generate airborne vibrations that enable other spirits and humans to "receive" their communication.[16] Luck summarizes the overarching view of ancient demonology related

[13]   Satan plays a large role in the Testament of Job. William Brandt Bradshaw, "Demonology in Hebrew and Jewish Traditions: A Study in New Testament Origins" (PhD diss., University of St Andrews, 1963), 193–95, states that "he is mentioned five times, four as a symbol for evil times, and once as a synonym for Mastema, the ruler of the evil spirits." Bradshaw also adds that the Testament of Job is the only text that uses ὁ πονηρός as a reference to Satan. Elsewhere it is used about evil spirits or demons.

[14]   Translated by Montague Rhodes James, ed., Apocrypha anecdota: Second Series (Cambridge: Cambridge University Press, 1897). The Lives of the Prophets also makes one reference to actions like those of a beast. In the chapter on Daniel verse 7 states, "It is the manner of tyrants, that in their youth they come under the yoke of Satan (Beliar); in their later years they become wild beasts, snatching, destroying, smiting and slaying" (translated in The Lives of the Prophets: Greek Text and Translation, trans. Charles Torrey [Atlanta: Society of Biblical Literature, 1946]).

[15]   Georg Luck, Arcana Mundi: Magic and the Occult in the Greek and Roman Worlds (Baltimore: Johns Hopkins University Press, 1985), 207. See Plutarch, On the Cessation of Oracles.

[16]   Plutarch, De Genio Socr. 589B. See also Luck, Arcana Mundi, 172.

to communication with demons. He recognizes the wide variety of spirits present in ancient belief systems and argues, "Even if they did not take over a human body in order to express themselves or to work some mischief, contacts and communication could be established with them."[17] Those who died prematurely or violently, or were not given a proper burial ceremony, were known to become earthbound spirits available for communication.[18] Further, a wide variety of "conditions" are considered as the work of evil demons in ancient literature. Relevant here, Luck lists automatic speech and changes in vocalic intonation. He concludes, "Automatic speech . . . made a much deeper impression on the observer than did most other paranormal phenomena: 'a female autonomist will suddenly begin to speak in a deep male voice; her bearing, her gestures, her facial expression are abruptly transformed; she speaks of matters quire outside her normal range of interests, and sometimes in a strange language or in a manner quite foreign to her normal character; and when her normal speech is restored, she frequently has no memory of what she said.' It is as if a power from above had taken over her body."[19] Platonists and Stoics attempted to analyze these beliefs in a "scientific" manner.[20] In addition, *daimones* could speak through humans, as in the case of the Pythian priestess.[21]

New Testament Accounts

Starting with the account of the man from Capernaum (Mark 1:23–28; Luke 4:33–37), the man cries out with a great voice (φωνῇ μεγάλῃ), which is a widespread characteristic of possession behavior in this milieu.[22] Both Mark and

---

[17] Luck, *Arcana Mundi*, 165.

[18] Luck, *Arcana Mundi*, 165–68.

[19] Luck, *Arcana Mundi*, 165. Luck draws from the depictions of ecstasy in Lucan, *Pharsalia* 6.413–830, and Seneca, *Oedipus* 530–626.

[20] Luck, *Arcana Mundi*, 165.

[21] Maximus of Tyre, *Or.* 9.1. See *Maximus of Tyre: The Philosophical Orations*, trans. M. B. Trapp (Oxford: Clarendon, 1997), 77. He states that demons "spoke through human bodies, just as pipe writer Ismenias used his skill to produce notes from hid pipe." Also, a Pythian priestess experienced mad ecstasy when she prophesied. When referencing the priestess, Plutarch (*De defect. Orac.* 9, *Mor.* 414E) employs a term that later was defined as "ventriloquist." Craig S. Keener, *Miracles: The Credibility of the New Testament Accounts*, 2 vols. (Grand Rapids: Baker, 2011), 2:777–78, argues that the term firstly delineated one "pregnant" with a deity, which likely implied speech in a strange voice. See also Keener's presentation of primary literature, which notes the various ancient depictions of the priestess, including sources that describe her as "impregnated" by Apollo, "filled with divine breath," inspired by the "power of the earth," filled with a *daimon* before prophesying, and experiencing frenzy.

[22] Cf. Ernst Lohmeyer, *Das Evangelium des Markus* (Göttingen: Vandenhoeck & Ruprecht, 1957), 36; Grundmann, *TDNT* 3:900. See also O. Betz, *TDNT* 9:294, who notes

Luke record the words spoken through the man: "What have you to do with us, Jesus of Nazareth? Have you come to destroy us? I know who you are, the Holy One of God." Nolland argues that this description accentuates the degree of disturbance the presence of Jesus causes the demon.[23] Interpreters analyze Luke's addition of ἔα in a variety of ways.[24] What is clear is that Luke adds ἔα to express emotion. The demon addresses Jesus by name to oppose and express displeasure with his presence.

The Semitic nature of the following phrase in v. 34, τί ἡμῖν καὶ σοὶ ("What have you to do with us?"), reflects an element of surprise, and the fact that the unclean spirit clearly wants nothing to do with Jesus.[25] The unclean spirit reveals its assumptions about what Jesus intends to do when asking, "Have you come to destroy us?"[26] The plural usage of ἡμᾶς is peculiar and may denote: (1) the synagogue audience,[27] (2) an inclusive reference to Jesus' power over all spirits,[28] (3) a reference to both the demon and the man,[29] or (4) the presence of multiple demons.[30] Bock argues that the third option particularly has explanatory power due to the man who emerges from exorcism unhurt. The demon presumes that Jesus must harm the man in the process, and as a result, the phrase is a challenge to Jesus. Bock argues that the safe exorcism of the man

---

that the terms are used to describe the great cries that occur when demons resist and when demons are driven out. See also the summary account in Acts 8:7, which indicates that unclean spirits cried out with a loud voice.

[23] John Nolland, *Luke 9:21–18:34*, WBC 35b (Waco, Tex.: Word, 1993), 206.

[24] Possible uses include use as interjection or imperative. See Darrell L. Bock, *Luke 1:1–9:50*, BECNT (Grand Rapids: Baker, 1994), 431.

[25] See LXX Jdg 11:12; 2 Sam 16:10; 19:23; 1 Kgs 17:18; 2 Kgs 3:13; 9:18; 2 Chr 16:3; 35:21; and NT usage: Mark 5:7; Matt 27:19; Luke 4:34; John 2:4. James R. Edwards, *The Gospel according to Luke*, Pillar New Testament Commentary (Grand Rapids: Eerdmans, 2015), 144, provides the wooden translation "What (is it) to us and you?" and more fluidly suggests, "What do you want with us?"

[26] Luke 4:34.

[27] See H. van der Loos, *The Miracles of Jesus*, NovTSup 9 (Leiden: Brill, 1965), 379–80.

[28] Alfred Plummer, *A Critical and Exegetical Commentary on the Gospel according to Luke*, ICC (New York: Scribner, 1896), 134; William Hendriksen, *Exposition of the Gospel according to Luke* (Grand Rapids: Baker, 1978), 264; Joseph A. Fitzmyer, *The Gospel according to Luke I–IX: A New Translation with Introduction and Commentary*, AB 28 (New York: Doubleday, 1964), 545–46; Heinz Schürmann, *Das Lukasevangelium, Erster Teil: Kommentar zu Kap. 1,1–9,50*, Herders theologischer Kommentar zum Neuen Testament 3 (Freiburg: Herder, 1969), 247.

[29] Frederick W. Danker, *Jesus and the New Age according to St. Luke: A Commentary on the Third Gospel* (St. Louis: Clayton, 1972), 432.

[30] Amy-Jill Levine and Ben Witherington III, *The Gospel of Luke*, New Cambridge Bible Commentary (Cambridge: Cambridge University Press, 2018), 125.

represents Jesus' "total control over evil."[31] Jesus is capable of sorting things out without the man being harmed in the process, despite the challenge from the unclean spirit. However, it is also likely that the issue is more than just one demon and that the usage is inclusive of the man and his demons.

Secondly, the account of the boy seized by an unclean spirit contains a similar element of possession. Both Mark (9:27) and Luke (9:39) record crying out as a characteristic of this exorcism account.[32] In Mark the spirit exits after crying out and convulsing the boy until he appears as a corpse. In Luke the boy is described as suddenly crying out when the spirit seizes him. Interpretive complications arise as the boy is described as mute, yet the spirit causes him to cry out. In the case of the Lukan account, C. F. Evans argues that the boy's muteness is healed since the demon cries out.[33] Considering the Markan account, the boy's case gets much worse before the removal of the spirit.

Moving on to Acts, two more accounts are marked by demonic speech. Acts 16:16–24, telling the story of Paul and the slave girl with a "spirit of divination," also highlights the oracular element of possession. While demonic speech has revealed Jesus' identity in previous accounts, this account is further developed when considering the oracular nature of the speech. The girl is described as having a πνεῦμα πύθωνα (python spirit), which evokes most clearly for Luke's audiences a Delphic background. Greeks used this terminology without pejorative connotation to indicate the "spirit of a pythoness," which was like the spirit that inspired and possessed the Pythia and the priestess of Apollo, who was known for dependable prophecies.[34] Brenk proposes the possibility that the term was employed by the girl's owners as a means of upping her value, since to be inspired in this way would make her equivalent to the Delphic prophetess.[35] While this conjecture is possible, the cultural background attests to this type of spirit as connected with soothsaying, which Luke connects with the girl's activity.

The account allows for two cultural perspectives to collide due to the various connotations that πνεῦμα πύθωνα carries. If read from the pagan perspective, this exorcism account would be read with surprise since python spirits

---

[31]   Bock, *Luke 1:1–9:50*, 432. See also Joel B. Green, *The Gospel of Luke*, NICNT (Grand Rapids: Baker, 1997), 223.

[32]   Matthew abbreviates the account.

[33]   C. F. Evans, *Saint Luke*, TPINTC (London: SCM Press, 1990), 423.

[34]   For a detailed presentation of the characteristics of the Pythian priestess, see the excursus entitled "Pythoness Spirits" in Craig S. Keener, *Acts: An Exegetical Commentary: 3:1–14:28* (Grand Rapids: Baker, 2012), 2424–26.

[35]   Frederick E. Brenk, "The Exorcism at Philippi in Acts 16:11–40: Divine Possession or Diabolical Inspiration," *Filologia Neotestamentaria* 13.25–26 (2000): 8.

were viewed positively or neutrally.[36] However, because of the presuppositions of Jewish and Christian readers, no surprise is present. There is no doubt in Luke's report or by the apostles that the woman is possessed.[37] Luke clearly sees the woman as being exploited by her owners, and the exorcism allows for her liberation from the spirit, even though disappointingly he does not present what happens to the girl after her exorcism.

Further, the girl's activity is described with the use of μαντευομένη (a *hapax legomenon* in the NT), which typically indicates fortune-telling or soothsaying. It was not unusual for charlatan prophets to make a profit.[38] Considering the contemporaneous usage of μαντευομένη, Klutz concludes that all LXX uses of the term explicitly or implicitly denote an intermediary agent who inspires oracular activity that is considered as pejorative by the author.[39] The pejorative undertone is represented in the context here as well, since the activity of the girl could have been labeled as προφητεύουσα, a term that usually refers to the activity of prophesy in Luke-Acts without the pejorative undertones.[40] Klutz emphasizes a pejorative depiction of the girl's oracular activity, which in the Jewish mindset would have conveyed the use of illicit intermediaries.[41]

It is not unfamiliar in this context for possession to be depicted through oracular activity. In the Jewish context, demons/fallen angels participated in making secrets known.[42] Additionally, crying out characterizes possession in the NT (as noted above) and in other ancient sources.[43] Further, the literary

[36] Craig S. Keener, *Acts: An Exegetical Commentary: 15:1–23:35* (Grand Rapids: Baker, 2014), 2429.

[37] Brenk, "Exorcism at Philippi in Acts 16:11–40," 9.

[38] Ben Witherington III, *The Acts of the Apostles: A Socio-rhetorical Commentary* (Grand Rapids: Eerdmans, 1998), 494. Examples include Lucian, *Alexander the False Prophet*; Apuleius, *Metam.* 8:26–30. The element of commercial gain was criticized in antiquity.

[39] Todd Klutz, *The Exorcism Stories in Luke-Acts: A Sociostylistic Reading*, SNTSMS 129 (Cambridge: Cambridge University Press, 2004), 216. See especially Deut 18:10; 2 Kgs 17:17; 1 Sam 28:9(8).

[40] Klutz, *Exorcism Stories in Luke-Acts*, 216. See Keener, *Acts 15:1–23:35*, 2459–60, who debunks the argument of F. Scott Spencer, *Acts* (Sheffield: Sheffield Academic, 1997), 166, that the girl is the same type of prophetess depicted in Acts 2:18. Keener lists several reasons why this is not possible. Another possibility is that Luke's choice of terminology stems from his knowledge of what happens at the oracle. The priests interpret the utterings of the Pythia to the inquirer.

[41] Klutz, *Exorcism Stories in Luke-Acts*, 217.

[42] 1 En. 9:6–7; 10:7–8; 64:2; 65:6; T. Sol. 5:12; 20.

[43] Seneca (the Younger), *Dial.* 7.26.8; Mark 1:26; T. Sol. 1:12; 3:4. David E. Aune, *Prophecy in Early Christianity and the Ancient Mediterranean World* (Grand Rapids: Eerdmans, 1983), 41, 268, further discusses this behavior as part of possession trance. See also Keener, *Acts 15:1–23:35*, 2457.

connection is obvious, as spirits reveal Jesus' identity in Luke-Acts in ways that are not acceptable.[44]

Beyond the characteristic of oracular activity, as depicted by μαντευομένη, is the consideration that the spirit spoke through the girl via a kind of ventriloquism. Twelftree and Immanuel argue the background of the term alludes to the phenomenon of "belly-talking."[45] In other words, the term was employed in relation to ventriloquists who had this sort of a spirit impregnating their bellies and speaking through their mouths. Bruce argues based on Plutarch that the term depicts oracular utterances, beyond the control of the conscious.[46]

The talk of ventriloquism leads to debate about the nature of the woman's voice, namely, if there was a vocal alteration and if she fell into ecstasy. Brenk argues that shouting would not likely be enough to demonstrate to Paul that the woman was possessed.[47] He stands in favor of the view that the woman may have lowered her voice in imitation of a supernatural being, tipping Paul off to her possession. In other words, for some readers, following Paul and crying out was not enough to depict possession. However, the word κράζω is often associated with possession in Luke-Acts and in the Synoptic Gospels.[48] Further, and seemingly counting against Brenk's hypothesis, Brenk highlights that in a "normal" visit with the Pythia the voice was not typically altered. Rather, the voice was the voice of the woman.[49] This view is further argued by the

---

[44]   Keener, *Acts 15:1–23:35*, 2457.

[45]   Graham H. Twelftree, *In the Name of Jesus: Exorcism among Early Christians* (Grand Rapids: Baker, 2007), 146; Babu Immanuel, *Acts of the Apostles: Exegetical and Contextual Commentary*, Indian Commentary on the New Testament (Minneapolis: Fortress, 2016), 178.

[46]   F. F. Bruce, *The Book of the Acts*, NICNT (Grand Rapids: Eerdmans, 1988), 312, n. 47. See Plutarch, *Def. orac.* 9.414e.

[47]   Brenk, "Exorcism at Philippi in Acts 16:11–40," 11–17. Witherington, *Acts of the Apostles*, 494, reminds us that even the ancients had suspicion of charlatanism with the motive of profit. See especially Lucian, *Alex.*; Apuleius, *Golden Ass* 8.26–30.

[48]   Hans Conzelmann, *Acts of the Apostles*, trans. James Limburg, A. Thomas Kraabel, and Donald H. Juel, ed. Eldon Jay Epp with Christopher R. Matthews (Philadelphia: Fortress, 1987), 131.

[49]   Brenk, "Exorcism at Philippi in Acts 16:11–40," 15. As a result, Brenk critiques Maruizio's comparison between the woman and African diviners, and he considers it as somewhat implausible due its comparison with a bad consultation with Pythia. Brenk ("Exorcism at Philippi in Acts 16:11–40," 17) highlights that "the slave girl's procedure is somewhat between the Pythia's as described by Plutarch, and Maurizio's African diviners." L. Maurizio, "Anthropology and Spirit Possession: A Reconsideration of the Pythia's Role at Delphi," *JHS* 115 (1995): 72, refutes scholarly views that argue that the Pythia did not issue the oracles, stating, "Every ancient source without exception or modification presents the Pythia as issuing oracular responses." What must be remembered is that the priests conveyed the interpretations to the inquirers.

classical scholar Fontenrose, who surveys the reliable evidence for the Oracle at Delphi and concludes, "The Pythia spoke clearly, coherently, and directly to the consultant."[50] Witherington makes the point that while the process may be ecstatic, the product is not.[51] The girl's crying out parallels well with Luke 4:33–35 and 8:28–35, and in my view it is possible that the alteration in her voice was volume rather than pitch. She cried out in a loud voice and her cries were heard and responded to in a surprising way.

Even if it is possible that the girl's voice in some way depicts possession, the clearest and most obvious characteristic presented in the text is her crying out and her oracular activity that is exploited for monetary gains by her owners. In either case Bruce summarizes the essence of the girl's value to her owners: "The girl's involuntary utterances were regarded as the voice of a god, and she was thus much in demand by people who wished to have their fortunes told or to receive information or advice which they believed could be supplied from such a source."[52] This text allows for a comparison with other experiences of oracular activity in anthropological comparisons.

Several views exist relating to the girl's proclamation that Paul and Silas are sent by the most high God to proclaim salvation. Keener argues that the most likely explanation is the spirit's relativizing attempt to situate the God of Paul and Silas within a polytheistic framework. He states, "By placing their preaching in a polytheistic context, the spirit could relativize the evangelistic value of any miracles they performed."[53] Witherington concurs, noting that her words must be situated in this polytheistic and pluralistic setting, indicating that the words are not a "true proclamation from a dubious source."[54] The consideration that God sits at the top of the pantheon of gods is enough to explain why Paul is bothered and deeply disturbed.

In this pericope, two contextual worlds collide, and Luke delegitimizes the use of the πνεῦμα πύθωνα and the exploitation of the girl's oracular activity/soothsaying for monetary gain. In other words, the πνεῦμα πύθωνα syntactically takes the same position as πνεῦμα ἀκαθάρτον or πνεῦμα πονηρόν in previous texts as also evidenced by the means of the demon being expelled in the same way.[55]

---

[50] Joseph E. Fontenrose, *The Delphic Oracle: Its Response and Operations* (Berkeley: University of California Press, 1978), 494.

[51] Witherington, *Acts of the Apostles*, 494.

[52] Bruce, *Book of the Acts*, 312.

[53] For a summary of these propositions, see Keener, *Acts 3:1–14:28*, 2463. See also p. 2457.

[54] Witherington, *Acts of the Apostles*, 495. See also Keener *Acts 15:1–23:35*, 2457.

[55] Klutz, *Exorcism Stories in Luke-Acts*, 245.

Lastly, demonic speech is found in the story of the Jewish exorcists of Acts 19:13–17. Little can be known for sure about the identity of this possessed man in this pericope. Verse 16 describes him as a man who had τό πνεῦμα τό πονηρόν. The story accounts for his extraordinary strength and his ability to overpower the exorcists (whether two of them or seven). More questions than answers remain about his identity (his socioeconomic status, societal position, ethnicity, etc.). What is clear is that the demon speaks through the man, revealing his knowledge of Jesus and Paul, congruent with the other Lukan speech, which also often alludes to the identity of the exorcist. Similar reports are found in modern accounts of possession and exorcism, and to these we now turn.

Global Perspectives

In global reports, analogous phenomena are reported in interreligious environments. Spirits are often viewed as being capable of speaking through persons and the speech is notably different than the typical speech of the possessed person. As has been patterned in previous chapters, the accounts below are arranged by major regions of the world.

Africa

African Christianity

African Christian movements include diverse interpretations of mediumship and oracular activity and widely attest to the phenomenon. One avenue of the discussion centers around views of ancestral possession. While some consider "ancestors" as demonic impersonators and in opposition to the Holy Spirit, others see value in ancestral possession and do not interpret ancestral possession negatively. The latter view is emphasized by a member of the St. Paul Spiritual Church of God, particularly because of the value of the message from the ancestors that is given after recovery. This member gave the following answer when asked, "Have you ever seen someone possessed by demons?"

> Yes, I have seen someone possessed by "spirits"—we don't call them "demons"; we call them "spirits." This person will jump around and fall to the ground. We call this spirit in a person the spirit of the prophet, because when one sees something one is able to speak a message to the people after one has recovered.[56]

Another responded in favor of respecting the message from the ancestors:

> The Bible might call it "demon possession," but we in our culture, in our context in Africa do not call it that. We know that this is the spirit of the ancestors, and

---

[56]   Allan Anderson, "Exorcism and Conversion to African Pentecostalism," *Exchange* 35.1 (2006): 132.

we respect a person with such a spirit because that person is able to communicate on our behalf with the ancestors.[57]

These testimonies witness to a variegated landscape of views on mediumship and spirit possession.

East Africa

Many people in East Africa maintain the belief that spirits can speak through persons and make verbal exchanges with those who are present. Often the spirits speak to make their demands known. Divination is performed for a variety of reasons, but especially to divine diagnoses for illness. Screaming may indicate a spirit that resists exorcism or signify the exit of the spirit.

In Ethiopian experience *zar* spirits speak through possessed individuals to make their demands known.[58] The *zar*-possessed female may demand things like perfume, jewelry, or clothing.[59] Vecchiato argues for a scream as a characteristic feature in an exorcism's success. He writes, "The pan-Ethiopian possession feature consisting in the 'scream' enacted by the entranced patient in traditional *hayyata* performances was considered the ultimate sign of the spirit's willingness to relinquish the possessed." The lack of a scream indicates a spirit that does not want to vacate. For example, Beko, who refused to scream in her exorcism, was interpreted as having a stubborn spirit.[60] Further, in Coptic healing ceremonies in Sidamoland, Vecchiato describes a "verbal exchange" between the healers and the possessing spirit as part of the encounter. In this Coptic context, a "scream" is evidence of the exit of the spirit.[61]

In a case of possession in Kenya (among the Luo people), divination was used to aid a sick woman named Ann, who was experiencing spirit possession. Neither the doctors nor the church members who prayed could assist Ann. After she was prayed for, she began to experience fits of shouting, and she wildly ran about the streets. Divination was performed by spirit experts,

[57] Anderson, "Exorcism and Conversion to African Pentecostalism," 132.

[58] Stephen Lloyd, "Ethiopia," in *Spirit Possession around the World: Possession, Communion, and Demon Expulsion across Cultures*, ed. Joseph Laycock (Santa Barbara, Calif.: ABC-CLIO, 2015), 119.

[59] Lloyd, "Ethiopia," 119.

[60] Norbert L. Vecchiato, "Illness, Therapy, and Change in Ethiopian Possession Cults," *Africa* 63.2 (1993): 182.

[61] Vecchiato, "Illness, Therapy, and Change in Ethiopian Possession Cults," 183. For more on the scream, see Norbert L. Vecchiato, "Health, Culture, and Socialism in Ethiopia" (PhD diss., University of California, Los Angeles, 1985), 463–65.

who used a speaking gourd, shaking the gourd while asking it questions. The gourd replied in a "gruff voice." During consultation with the gourd, Ann also began to dance, shake (this included shoulder spasms), and speak in tongues (interpreted as her possession by the spirits).[62]

Giles, studying the Coastal Swahili region (Kenya, Tanzania, northern Mozambique), confirms the view that spirits can speak through their inhabitants. In Swahili vernacular this is called *sheitani anapanda mtu* ("the spirit climbs or mounts someone"), and mediums serve as vehicles for the spirits to speak.[63] Further, spirits are known to assist through "gifts of divining" (*uganga*). This gift draws a following for the clientele of the medium and allows one to fill the position of head of the cult.[64]

Among the Kimbu in Tanzania, belief in possession by water-spirits in southern Ukimbu began after World War II.[65] For example, one man named Kipakulo gained apprentices to mediumship,[66] and initiation into mediumship involved falling into a trance state. The water-spirits would then make their goals known by speaking through the mouth of the medium.[67]

South Africa

Ritual ancestral divination is practiced in *songoma* mediumship. The *songoma* enters a possession trance, characterized by the contortions of the body, and claims to lose the ability to hear, speak, see, and move by her own volition. Dialogue with the ancestral spirit follows, especially for diagnosing reasons for illness.[68] Zulu members of other cults such as the *izizwe*, *amandiki*, and *amandawu* have similar belief systems related to possession.[69] In some cases spirits of other ethnicities are believed to possess, resulting in the possessed person speaking in different languages.[70] Further, in southern Zimbabwe, possessed

---

[62] Michael G. Whisson, "Some Aspects of Functional Disorders," in *Magic, Faith, and Healing: Studies in Primitive Psychiatry Today*, ed. Ari Kiev (New York: Free Press, 1964), 297–301.

[63] Linda L. Giles, "Possession Cults on the Swahili Coast: A Re-examination of Theories of Marginality," *Africa* 57.2 (1987): 240.

[64] Giles, "Possession Cults on the Swahili Coast," 240.

[65] Aylward Shorter, "Spirit Possession and Christian Healing in Tanzania," *African Affairs* 79.314 (1980): 48.

[66] Shorter, "Spirit Possession and Christian Healing in Tanzania," 47. Kipakulo was influenced by traditions of coastal spirit-mediumship.

[67] Shorter, "Spirit Possession and Christian Healing in Tanzania," 48.

[68] Stephen Lloyd, "South Africa," in Laycock, *Spirit Possession around the World*, 321.

[69] Lloyd, "South Africa," 321.

[70] Lloyd, "South Africa," 321.

mediums have spirits speak through them. The spirits are known to answer the questions asked of them.[71]

West Africa

Among the Mande, experts at fortune-telling are named "persons who know" (*dònni kelaw*). Techniques vary. One involves "masters of spirits," who depend upon a "wilderness spirit" that "haunts" them and allows them to look at their clients and know everything about them.[72]

In Mali, among *jinn* cults, mediumship is part of the experience of possession. Even though L. Berger's statement is interpretive in nature, he highlights the work of the medium, stating, "When mediums speak for local gods they also seek to show that they have lost control of their movements, facial expressions, voice, kinesthetic awareness, sense of balance, and/or emotional expression."[73] Further, there is a sense that *jinn* can read one's mind and predict action, using this knowledge to influence behavior.[74]

In Ghana, exorcism ritual involves a "mouth cleaning" exercise, wherein a human is prepared for the spirit to speak through the mouth as its vehicle.[75] If the spirit is revealed to be of lower status, the spirit is exorcised rather than used for communication.[76] Some may cry out or shout, as demonstrated by a Yoruba woman who, while experiencing *Sopono* possession, shouted and sang.[77]

A detailed description of linguistic alterations during spirit mediumship practices in the Greater Accra (Ga) region of Ghana was produced by Dale K. Fitzgerald.[78] Fitzgerald carefully studied the prophetic speech of Ga spirit mediums during their possession experience and noted several vocalic

[71] Michael Gelfand, "Psychiatric Disorders as Recognized by the Shona," in Kiev, *Magic, Faith, and Healing*, 156.

[72] Patrick R. McNaughton, *The Mande Blacksmiths: Knowledge, Power, and Art in West Africa* (Bloomington: Indiana University Press, 1993), 52. Typically these are Muslim marabouts or smiths.

[73] Laurent Berger, "Learning Possession Trance and Evaluating Oracles' Truthfulness in Jinè Cults of Bèlèdugu (Mali)," *Journal of Cognition and Culture* 12.3 (2012): 177.

[74] Berger, "Learning Possession Trance," 179. Berger demonstrates this type of thinking with an example of a public oracle.

[75] Emmanuel Kwabena Frimpong, "Mark and Spirit Possession in an African Context" (PhD diss., University of Glasgow, 2006), 165.

[76] Gabriel Bannerman-Richter, *The Practice of Witchcraft in Ghana* (Elk Grove, Calif.: Gabari, 1982), 51.

[77] Raymond Prince, "Indigenous Yoruba Psychiatry," in Kiev, *Magic, Faith, and Healing*, 107. See above for a more detailed version of this woman's possession, which was characterized by violent activity.

[78] Dale K. Fitzgerald, "Prophetic Speech in Ga Spirit Mediumship," *Working Papers of the Language Behavior Laboratory* 30 (1970): 1–19.

and linguistic changes during their inspired speech. The Ga believe that all actions and speech of the possessed person are those of the spirit embodying the medium. Attesting to this belief, the medium has no memory of or accountability for the events that occur during possession.[79] The transformation of the medium's speech, occurring in private séances, is described by Fitzgerald as affecting "nearly the entire range of vocal output."[80] This includes a change in language or dialect, even though this is not regarded as the "most dramatic" effect.[81] Fitzgerald classifies the vocalic changes into nine categories: (1) "pitch," (2) "volume," (3) "vowel elongation," (4) "glottalization," (5) "hyperventilation," (6) "repetition," (7) "interjection of non-linguistic sounds," (8) "changes in syntax," and (9) "rhythm."[82] Despite all of these alterations, the prophetic speech is intelligible and is viewed as a message from the spirit(s).[83]

Related to divination, spirit mediums in Mayotte communicate with their *fundis* (spirits) in trance states.[84] Lambek documents the experience of two spirit mediums named Tumbu and Mohedja (husband and wife). He views their activities as more than mere vehicles for the spirits. The relationship is termed "collaboration," and Tumbu and Mohedja participate in practices including divining, diagnosing, advising, and assisting those who seek their help. Their role in possession cure involves making "the spirits speak and arranging ceremonies by means of which the host and spirit come to terms with one another."[85]

Asia

Asian experience includes spirits speaking through humans during possessed states. Demonic speech results in a variety of vocalic alterations as described below. Additionally, mediumship practices are utilized for communication with spirits.

---

[79] Fitzgerald, "Prophetic Speech in Ga Spirit Mediumship," 2.
[80] Fitzgerald, "Prophetic Speech in Ga Spirit Mediumship," 7.
[81] Fitzgerald, "Prophetic Speech in Ga Spirit Mediumship," 7–8.
[82] Fitzgerald, "Prophetic Speech in Ga Spirit Mediumship," 8.
[83] Fitzgerald, "Prophetic Speech in Ga Spirit Mediumship," 9–10.
[84] Michael Lambek, *Knowledge and Practice in Mayotte: Local Discourses of Islam, Sorcery and Spirit Possession* (Toronto: University of Toronto Press, 1993), 93.
[85] Lambek, *Knowledge and Practice in Mayotte*, 93–94. More specifically, certain requirements are set to aid in possession cure. Lambek summarizes, "To manage a possession cure, the curers must have been possessed by spirits of the same species as the client and gone through the full cure themselves. Their spirits must, in turn, have offered to work as *fundis* in cooperation with human mediums."

Among the majority group of the Han Chinese,[86] there is belief in "Five Household Immortals,"[87] who can come into humans and speak through their mouths.[88] Further, among the *tang-ki*, who beat and pierce themselves, blood is viewed as a "life force" that allows them to become "strong vehicles for the divine voice speaking through them."[89] Further, the speech changes are described as "brutal changes of pace, raising of the voice, sharp cries, whispering followed by bellowing, incomprehensible sentences and shifts from direct to indirect speech."[90] Berger concludes that the person does not "appear to be in control of her vocal chords, as if she were moved to speak by some external force."[91]

In one example from rural Beijing, a bride was possessed by the spirit of her dead mother-in-law. She fell into a trance and "was rambling in a spooky voice."[92] The woman's entire demeanor (voice, behavior, facial expressions) changed to that of her mother-in-law, which indicated ghost possession. Respects were paid to the ancestors, the woman passed out, and then she woke up with no recollection of the events.[93]

In Highland Nepal, Lama Suna Yeshe is known to speak through mediums.[94] One medium named Dodrag would cry out with a loud cry "KI-HI-HI-HI" when becoming possessed, and his cry reportedly "echoed off the cliffs around Te and could even be heard in Tshug."[95] Stewards would approach the medium, and questions would be answered related to the village. A Gola is also known to possess mediums and "provide access to communication with the major, higher gods."[96]

In possession among the *barwa*, the Balahis of Central India believe that a spirit speaks through the possessed to reveal "secrets of the other world,"

---

[86]   Barend J. ter Haar, "China," in Laycock, *Spirit Possession around the World*, 79. This view is well attested in the Jilin, Liaoning, Hebei, Henan, and Shandong provinces.

[87]   These include the fox, weasel, hedgehog, snake, and rat.

[88]   Ter Haar, "China," 79.

[89]   Ter Haar, "China," 80.

[90]   Berger, "Learning Possession Trance," 178.

[91]   Berger, "Learning Possession Trance," 178.

[92]   Xing Wang, "Rethinking the 'Magic State' in China: Political Imagination and Magical Practice in Rural Beijing," *Asian Ethnology* 77.1–2 (2018): 339–40.

[93]   Wang, "Rethinking the 'Magic State' in China," 339–40.

[94]   Charles Ramble, *The Navel of the Demoness: Tibetan Buddhism and Civil Religion in Highland Nepal* (Oxford: Oxford University Press, 2008), 205. The spoken words typically admonish and encourage.

[95]   Ramble, *Navel of the Demoness*, 205. Dodrag would also strip naked and bathe in freezing ice water.

[96]   Ramble, *Navel of the Demoness*, 205.

which deities are causing disease, and a method for their appeasement. It is also believed the spirit gives mind-reading capabilities.[97] During sacrificial ceremonies the possessed *barwa* talks in a higher voice, which is a sign of possession by a familiar spirit.[98] Fuchs records, "In the opinion of the people, however, an opinion that is shared quite sincerely by the *barwa* himself, it is a superhuman spirit or power that has taken possession of the *barwa's* body, inactivated his mind, and now acts and speaks through him."[99]

In northeastern India, among the *Pnar*, Lyngdoh recounts her witness of a divine possession experience. The medium who was experiencing possession was humming a tune. After she became possessed, "there was a perceptible change in the ambiance of light, atmosphere, and personality. Her voice altered from a feminine register to a masculine one."[100] Lyngdoh transcribes the conversation that followed, and she describes the woman's body as being used as a vehicle for the conversation.[101] This experience is echoed in southeastern India in Tamil Nadu, where during the *Kotai* ("Offering") festival, the possessed are described as "vehicles of communication between the audience and the deity."[102]

In northwestern India, among the Tibetans of Dharamsala, Homayun Sidky spent seven years studying Tibetan oracular phenomena. In Tibetan views *dharmapālas* (deities) are considered powerful, especially due to their ability to communicate through mediums. René de Nebesky-Wojkowitz summarizes the essence of belief and the importance of the phenomenon, stating that "the possibility of direct contact with these deities is the basis of Tibetan beliefs in spirit possession as well as the conviction in the legitimacy of oracular prognostication."[103] These deities seize men and women and utilize them as mouthpieces to inform of their wishes and answer prophetically questions that are asked to them.[104] Oracular performance plays a key role in all levels

[97] Stephen Fuchs, "Magic Healing Techniques among the Balahis in Central India," in Kiev, *Magic, Faith, and Healing*, 129.

[98] Fuchs, "Magic Healing Techniques," 129.

[99] Fuchs, "Magic Healing Techniques," 128–29.

[100] Margaret Lyngdoh, "An Interview with the Goddess: Possession Rites as Regulators of Justice among the Pnar of Northeastern India," *Religious Studies and Theology* 36.1 (2017): 66.

[101] Lyngdoh, "Interview with the Goddess," 65.

[102] Mikel Burley, "Dance of the *Deodhās*: Divine Possession, Blood Sacrifice and the Grotesque Body in the Assamese Goddess Worship," *Religions of South Asia* 12.2 (2018): 214.

[103] Homayun Sidky, "The State Oracle of Tibet, Spirit Possession, and Shamanism," *Numen* 58.1 (2011): 78.

[104] René de Nebesky-Wojkowitz, *Oracles and Demons of Tibet: The Cult and Iconography of the Tibetan Protective Deities* (The Hague, Netherlands: Mouton, 1956), 409.

of society, even in matters of statecraft and policymaking.[105] *Lha-pa*, described as "mouthpieces of the gods," are sought for healing and divination.[106] Belief is maintained that the personal identity of the *lha-pa* is replaced by the deity; as a result, the speech is that of the deity and not the person.[107] Further, vocalic alterations also exist, including "unusual voice modulations, indistinct enunciation and low aptitude."[108] At times the *lha-pa* speak in foreign languages that are only able to be interpreted by those who have a long-standing association with *lha-pa*.[109]

In southern India, possession reports include spirits speaking through the mouths of those whom they possess. Dhanam's story, referred to above, is pertinent as during her exorcism experience, "something terribly alien" was reported; namely, someone was seemingly speaking through her mouth. When the voice was threatened by Mātā, the voice cried out in response, "*Illai!* (No!)."[110] Another example of this type of activity includes a report of a woman, Alphonso Mary, who experienced Marian possession. Her experience resulted in her ability to give full messages during her possessed state.[111] Bloomer notes that all three women, whom she provides detailed accounts of, believed that during Marian possession they "were no longer themselves" and spoke as a mouthpiece for Mātā (Mary).[112] She also witnessed one woman speaking in tongues during her possession state.[113]

Among the Bulusu' of East Kalimantan in Indonesia, the foremost function of the spirit medium is to communicate with the spirits for the purpose of

[105] Robert Ekvall, *Religious Observances in Tibet: Patterns and Functions* (Chicago: University of Chicago Press, 1964), 274. See also Hanna Havnevik, "A Tibetan Female State Oracle," in *Religion and Secular Culture in Tibet: Tibetan Studies. Proceedings of the 9th Seminary of the International Association for Tibetan Studies*, ed. Henz Blezer (Leiden: Brill, 2002), 259–87.

[106] Bellezza, *Spirit-mediums, Sacred Mountains, and Related Bon Textual Traditions in Upper Tibet*, 5.

[107] Bellezza, *Spirit-mediums, Sacred Mountains, and Related Bon Textual Traditions in Upper Tibet*, 7.

[108] Bellezza, *Spirit-mediums, Sacred Mountains, and Related Bon Textual Traditions in Upper Tibet*, 7.

[109] Bellezza, *Spirit-mediums, Sacred Mountains, and Related Bon Textual Traditions in Upper Tibet*, 7.

[110] Bloomer, *Possessed by the Virgin*, 4.

[111] Bloomer, *Possessed by the Virgin*, 11. Bloomer cites personal communication with Matthias Frenz, who attended a service where this happened in 2000.

[112] Bloomer, *Possessed by the Virgin*, 23.

[113] Bloomer, *Possessed by the Virgin*, 43.

diagnosing illness.[114] Divination is especially utilized to decipher the aetiology of the illness.[115] Jay Bernstein describes women (*tukang sangiang*—"masters/ adept (at summoning) the spirits") "who lend their bodies to supernatural beings to use their powers to cure sick people."[116]

Spirits are known in Japan to inspire the speech of shamans.[117] These shamans are known for their ability to communicate with the dead. When falling in trance states, "they could see the supernatural inhabitants of the other world, speak to them and hold colloquy with them."[118] Some were known to summon the spirits "to come to our world and speak through their mouths."[119] This characteristic involves both trained mediums and untrained persons. For example, in the Abisha ritual, spirits speak through "unblemished children" who "would tell one everything one wished to know of hidden and future things."[120] Further, Blacker describes complaints of voices speaking in a person's ear as symptomatic of possession.[121] As a result, Blacker classifies instances when "another entity, with a different voice and a different personality, speaks through a patient's mouth" as a symptom of possession.[122]

[114] George N. Appell and Laura W. R. Appell, "To Do Battle with the Spirits: Bulusu' Spirit Mediums," in *The Seen and the Unseen: Shamanism, Mediumship and Possession in Borneo*, ed. Robert L. Winzeler, Borneo Research Council Monograph Series 2 (Williamsburg, Va.: Borneo Research Council, 1993), 69. For similar expression in Central Kalimantan, see Sian E. Jay, "Canoes for the Spirits: Two Types of Spirit Mediumship in Central Kalimantan," in Winzeler, *The Seen and the Unseen*, 151.

[115] Appell and Appell, "To Do Battle with the Spirits," 72–73.

[116] For a discussion of this theme in shamanism among the Taman, see Jay Bernstein, "The Shaman's Destiny: Symptoms, Affliction, and the Re-interpretation of Illness among the Taman," in Winzeler, *The Seen and the Unseen*, 171–199. Bernstein concludes that initiation into shamanism is not related to a person's draw towards a healing vocation. Rather, it is viewed as the result of being "targeted by a spirit" (191–92). See p. 182 for a local man's testimony that expresses that medicine is ineffective for those who are called to become a *balien*: "Someone who is destined to become a *balien* can't be treated by other medicine."

[117] Carmen Blacker, *The Catalpa Bow: A Study in Shamanistic Practices in Japan* (New York: Routledge Curzon, 1999), 9. Blacker indicates that in the custom of ethnologists, she titles the people who fall in trance states shamans. This does not appear to be a self-description. Blacker also notes that this cult's existence was dissipating in Japan, and she writes her ethnography as a memorial. See p. 10.

[118] Blacker, *Catalpa Bow*, 9.

[119] Blacker, *Catalpa Bow*, 9.

[120] Blacker, *Catalpa Bow*, 298.

[121] Blacker, *Catalpa Bow*, 300. In these cases Blacker notes that there is no change in the person's personality.

[122] Blacker, *Catalpa Bow*, 300. On p. 303 Blacker tells the story of witnessing a case where "one fox, three snakes, one jealous woman, one frantic man and one cat" spoke through the mouth of a medium. For more detail and specific reports, see pp. 252–78. Especially

The Malays of rural western Malaysia indicated situations of involuntary "spirit possession hysteria" among schoolgirls who had been integrated with men into mass schooling situations. During school, one girl would start screaming, laughing, or crying in an inconsolable way. Other girls would follow in behavior. At times the school would close, and the girls would report spirit activity.[123]

In her study of possession experience in Penang, Malaysia, DeBernardi describes the vocalic changes that occur in trance states. She compares her experience with Sapir's definition of "linguistic individuality," which involves several dynamics of voice/speech, including "intonation, rhythm, relative continuity of speech, and speaking rate—and pronunciation, vocabulary, and style."[124] De Bernardi argues, "In the trance performance, all these change."[125] One spirit medium suggested that each of the deities possessing him spoke in differing languages.[126] Spirit mediums are known to speak in a "glossalalic register" with utterances that are not intelligible. On the other hand, Pengang mediums are also known to consult with the spirits (usually with an interpreter) for advice and to offer remedies.[127] Further, spirit mediums are also sought after for help with predicting lottery numbers, to ask for dreams (another approach to discovering winning lottery numbers), and for curing illness.[128] DeBernardi writes about her own experience with Mr. Ooi, who predicts her future.[129]

---

note p. 253, where Blacker indicates that a *kami* (spirit) "is cajoled to take possession of a medium and through her mouth to deliver to the community useful knowledge of hidden and future things."

[123] Robert L. Winzeler, *The Peoples of Southeast Asia Today: Ethnography, Ethnology, and Change in a Complex Region* (Lanham, Md.: Altamira, 2011), 167. A variety of explanations were given, including love magic or ghosts of Japanese soldiers who died in World War II. The phenomena spread during times of modernization in the country's most modern areas, such as among women factory workers. See also Aihwa Ong, *Spirits of Resistance and Capitalist Discipline: Factory Women in Malaysia* (Albany: State University of New York Press, 1987), who interprets the phenomena sociologically.

[124] Edward Sapir, "Speech as Personality Trait," in *Selected Writings of Edward Sapir in Language, Culture and Personality*, ed. David G. Mandelbaum (Berkeley: University of California Press, 1949 [1927]), 534.

[125] Jean DeBernardi, *The Way That Lives in the Heart: Chinese Popular Religion and Spirit Mediums in Penang, Malaysia* (Stanford: Stanford University Press, 2006), 141.

[126] DeBernardi, *Way That Lives in the Heart*, 142.

[127] DeBernardi, *Way That Lives in the Heart*, 142, 181 (for the report about a specific Malay medium).

[128] DeBernardi, *Way That Lives in the Heart*, 182.

[129] DeBernardi, *Way That Lives in the Heart*, 275.

The Melanau in Sarawak express similar viewpoints and seek shamans for healing through curative ceremonies.[130] If the cure is not received, a *menurun tou* or *beguda* ceremony will be held for the purpose of fetching the spirit that causes trouble, in the hope that it will possess the patient and reveal its wishes.[131] If these ceremonies are ineffective, an *aiyun* ceremony is the last step, and this ceremony involves the initiation into shamanism.[132] Further, people seek spirits (sometimes in dreams) for knowledge.[133] One man became mute after failure to sacrifice properly. Others witnessed irrational speech.[134]

In Mongolian shamanism spirits are known to speak through shamans, even though in this case the personality of the shaman is in control and present.[135] The shaman dialogues with the spirit (typically one at a time), questions, and then dismisses the spirit at the end of the ritual ceremony. The spirits typically speak in Mongolian, but in some cases other languages are spoken (such as neighboring ethnic languages), glossolalia is exhibited, or animal sounds are made.[136] In some areas of Mongolia, Tibetan Buddhism has uprooted traditional shamanistic practice. In these areas possession experience remains. A *gürtem/gürtum(be)* (religious specialist) will invoke Buddhist deities and function as a medium to deliver prophecy and divine diagnosis for illness.[137] Buyandelger dictates some of the conversations had with the spirits during appeasement ceremonies and indicates that she witnessed the shaman's speech as "scratchy," a variation from the normal voice.[138] She adds that the shaman's claim is "to retrieve knowledge from a supernatural domain."[139]

In the *weikza* possession cult in Myanmar, a *weikza* will possess a medium.[140] This possession type is not as violent or dramatic as in other cults.

---

[130] H. S. Morris, "Shamanism among the Oya Melanau," in Winzeler, *The Seen and the Unseen*, 112–14. The Malanau also attribute illness to the "wind" (*angina* or *pangai*), which is viewed as "an evil influence which floats in the air and affects humans." Animals may also seize human spirits.

[131] Morris, "Shamanism among the Oya Melanau," 115.

[132] Morris, "Shamanism among the Oya Melanau," 115–16.

[133] Karl E. Schmidt, "Folk Psychiatry in Sarawak," in Kiev, *Magic, Faith, and Healing*, 145. For example, the spirits may aid in locating charms for protection.

[134] Schmidt, "Folk Psychiatry in Sarawak," 145–46.

[135] Ágnes Birtalan, "Mongolia," in Laycock, *Spirit Possession around the World*, 239.

[136] Birtalan, "Mongolia," 239.

[137] Birtalan, "Mongolia," 239–40.

[138] Manduhai Buyandelger, *Tragic Spirits: Shamanism, Memory, and Gender in Contemporary Mongolia* (Chicago: University of Chicago Press, 2013), 3.

[139] Buyandelger, *Tragic Spirits*, 18.

[140] Bénédicte Brac de la Perrière and Guillaume Rozenberg, "Burma," in Laycock, *Spirit Possession around the World*, 60. *Weikza* are powerful practitioners of Buddhism who "become invisible, superhuman beings" who defend Buddhism.

Rather, the sign of possession is defined as the change in the timbre of the medium's voice.[141] Rozenberg reports of a *weikza* delivering a sermon through a young female medium.[142] The purpose of *weikza* possession is largely for communication, and "the medium, through possession, serves as the vehicle of their speech and their power."[143] As a result, the person is no longer himself/herself, and he/she speaks and acts in first person.[144]

Men possessed by *weikza* often serve as exorcists. If one is possessed by *payawgwa* (described as involuntary possession), an exorcist will be called up for aid. The exorcist depends on power from the *weikza* to oust the possessing spirit and often converses with the possessing spirit during the exorcism.[145] Further, in another type of possession, possession by *nats*, a "generic utterance" may be part of the possession ceremony. This includes the possibility that a spirit will join itself to the medium and predict the future.[146]

Spirit writing ceremonies, performed in Dàn Tiên temples in southern Vietnam, involve mediums who pass along messages from the spirits in written form. Mediums may petition spirits,[147] receive prescriptions for illness,[148] warn of danger,[149] or reveal knowledge.[150] Thien Do emphasizes that spirit writing exists among educated individuals, and the "scientific and rational attitude does not seem to conflict with faith in spirit writing."[151] In essence, the trance writing phenomenon represents "an unorthodox way of knowing" and

---

[141] de la Perrière and Rozenberg, "Burma," 61.

[142] Guillaume Rozenberg, *The Immortals: Faces of the Incredible in Buddhist Burma*, trans. Ward Keller (Honolulu: University of Hawai'i Press, 2015), 160.

[143] Rozenberg, *Immortals*, 160.

[144] Rozenberg, *Immortals*, 162.

[145] de la Perrière and Rozenberg, "Burma," 60. See also Bénédicte Brac de la Perrière, Guillaume Rozenburg, and Alicia Turner, eds., *Champions of Buddhism: Weikza Cults in Contemporary Burma* (Singapore: NUS Press, 2014).

[146] de la Perrière and Rozenberg, "Burma," 60.

[147] Thien Do, *Vietnamese Supernaturalism: Views from the Southern Region* (New York: Routledge Curzon, 2003), 76. Spirit writers take a sealed envelope containing their request to the podium, pray, and then burn the envelope. Do (*Vietnamese Supernaturalism*, 77) notes that the practice once fell under suspicion for proliferating nationalist agendas. After an investigation, spirit writing was considered "genuine religious activity" by the French colonial authorities.

[148] Do, *Vietnamese Supernaturalism*, 79.

[149] Do, *Vietnamese Supernaturalism*, 79.

[150] Do, *Vietnamese Supernaturalism*, 79. In this humorous example, the spirit reproaches a participant for eating an egg during the retreat (against the ritual practice).

[151] Do, *Vietnamese Supernaturalism*, 88.

"affirms, through access to alternate states of consciousness, a viewpoint that pervades popular religion."[152]

In northern Vietnam a boy recounts the story of his mother's trance state. He witnessed vocalic changes and bouts of crying. Later the boy returned to visit his mother, who became a medium in a shrine for the worship of a Vietnamese goddess, and he described the change he witnessed when his mother was in a possession state. He stated that she had a "completely different countenance, her manners were high-spirited and virile like a man's."[153] Do adds that mediums in Vietnam are sought after as seers and soothsayers.[154]

In the *Len dong* rituals, fortune-telling is performed by mediums to aid their patients. Knowledge is sought for cures for illness.[155] Further, "people ask the spirits all manner of questions dealing with issues such as health, family relations, finances, employment, travel, child rearing and romance."[156] In a spirit possession experience, one woman began screeching loudly and speaking unintelligibly with a high-pitched childish voice. A medium commanded the spirit to leave, and the woman returned to her normal composure for the remainder of the ceremony.[157]

Middle America and Caribbean

In Afro-Atlantic religions spirit possession is positively characterized as "a means of communication between the supernatural entities and human beings."[158] Possession is often considered an obligatory religious rite. Especially during initiation one is obligated to accept possession and learn to manage, control, and end the experience. Various approaches are taken for a medium's

---

[152] Do, *Vietnamese Supernaturalism*, 88. For an ethnographic description of spirit writing in rural Beijing, see Wang, "Rethinking the 'Magic State' in China," 336–41.

[153] Do, *Vietnamese Supernaturalism*, 93.

[154] Do, *Vietnamese Supernaturalism*, 95.

[155] Karen Fjelstad and Nguyen Thi Hien, *Spirits without Borders: Vietnamese Spirit Mediums in a Transnational Age* (New York: Palgrave Macmillan, 2011), 21, 31. Numerous instances of fortune-telling were recorded in interviews. Page 39 tells the story of Mr. Thanh, who has a syncretistic approach and blends rituals, allowing him to be a "ritual master, fortune-teller, and sorcerer." See also p. 91.

[156] Fjelstad and Hien, *Spirits without Borders*, 62.

[157] Fjelstad and Hien, *Spirits without Borders*, 58. The language was not able to be interpreted as a spirit language or a language of an ethnic minority. Observers interpreted the experience as possession by a harmful spirit. See p. 77 for another example involving a possessed woman who cries out in a voice that is not hers. See p. 82 for a girl who laughs in a strange laugh while possessed. See p. 120 for the story of Tania and the alteration of Tania's voice and speech during possession.

[158] Bettina E. Schmidt, "Afro-Atlantic Religions," in Laycock, *Spirit Possession around the World*, 3.

training. Some religions require special training, while others make medium-ship more accessible to devotees.[159]

In *lwa* possession, soothsaying is the result of possession by the *lwa*. Healers are often possessed when they seek treatment options for their patients. The spirit speaks through the possessed person, and the patient approves or disapproves of the spirit-inspired diagnosis.[160]

Middle East

In Pakistan exorcism is a process called *hazri*. The possessed person begins to dance, which testifies to the presence of the spirit. During this state the possessed person serves as the spirit's mouthpiece, allowing the exorcist to engage the spirit with questions. The possessed person may ask about the religious affiliation of the spirit so that the right sacred texts can be used for exorcism, or they may ask the reason for possession.[161] Another example comes from northern Pakistan among the Hunzakut of Hunza. *Pari*, described as fairy creatures who appear human with certain physical characteristics, seek to possess humans and utilize them as a "spokesman" (*bitan*). If the possession is refused, the person will become mentally ill (insane).[162] A specific example of a possession experience causing muteness is given by ul ain Khan. He reports on a jinn-possessed woman who was hearing voices, talking in gibberish (with increased volume and in a masculine voice), and experiencing spells of mute-ness.[163] It is believed that spirits have the ability to speak through a person or to impede or mute speech.

In Peshawar, during a *baithak* session to remove spirits, women yell, scream, shout that they are being abused, or curse their family members. Nasir writes, "Her language may be utterly unlike what the woman would use under any normal circumstances."[164] During the "cooling down" period of the exorcism, a singer will begin to interrogate the spirit to discover how to assuage it. Nasir notes that "the patient will answer her as if she (the patient)

---

[159] Schmidt, "Afro-Atlantic Religions," 4.

[160] Max-G. Beauvoir, "Herbs and Energy: The Holistic Medical System of the Haitian People," in *Haitian Vodou: Spirit, Myth, and Reality*, ed. Patrick Bellegarde-Smith and Claudine Michel (Bloomington: Indiana University Press, 2006), 130–31. If disapproval is given, another healer is often sought for a second opinion.

[161] Maleeha Aslam, "Pakistan," in Laycock, *Spirit Possession around the World*, 273.

[162] Aslam, "Pakistan," 274.

[163] Qurat ul ain Khan and Aisha Sanober, "'Jinn Possession' and Delirious Mania in a Pakistani Woman," *American Journal of Psychiatry* 173.3 (2016): 219–20.

[164] Mumtaz Nasir, "*Baithak*: Exorcism in Peshawar (Pakistan)," *Asian Folklore Studies* 46.2 (1987): 164.

were the controlling spirit. . . . Her voice and appearance change during this question-and-answer-session."[165]

In Artas the *jinn* spirits are relied upon for fortune-telling[166] and are known for speaking through those they possess.[167] During treatment, sheikhs will request the spirit to leave the afflicted body. Often the *jinn* agree, and agreement is recognized through the spirit who speaks through the person. At times, long arguments are made with the spirit(s) to persuade the spirit to exit,[168] or the person will speak in Hebrew.[169]

Oceania

Tate remarks that possession among the Māori also produces similar phenomena. The personality change is at times so drastic that the Māori say, "This is not who we have known this person to be."[170] They cry through the night and "rant and rave and growl like a dog."[171] Further, they obtain knowledge that was previously not known. Tate gives examples of "knowledge of *whakapapa* (genealogy) or *te reo* (Māori language)."[172] Oliver adds that possession is also believed to allow for communication with other humans either by the spirit "acting on its own initiative" or at the request of a medium.[173] The communication is performed "through the voices and other actions of the possessed."[174]

[165] Nasir, "Baithak: Exorcism in Peshawar (Pakistan)," 165.

[166] Celia E. Rothenberg, *Spirits of Palestine: Gender, Society, and Stories of the Jinn* (Oxford: Lexington, 2004), 46–51.

[167] Rothenberg, *Spirits of Palestine*, 31.

[168] Rothenberg, *Spirits of Palestine*, 38. For a transcript of this type of argument, see pp. 78–83.

[169] Rothenberg, *Spirits of Palestine*, 91–93. Women do not typically learn Hebrew, partly due to their lack of need. Additionally, women reject learning the language because the language reflects the "foreign ways" of the Israelis. Rothenberg characterizes the view reflected by Zahia and other women, noting that speaking Hebrew is evidence for the possession state. She summarizes, "These words were evidence enough for her friends, relatives, and neighbors to repeatedly tell the story of how Zahia's Jewish jinn 'spoke' Hebrew through her." Speaking Hebrew signals "the moral transgression of the jinn into her body." Zahia used three common Hebrew words when she spoke Hebrew. This was enough to signify possession.

[170] Henare Arekatera Tate, "A Māori Perspective on Spirit Possession," in *Spirit Possession, Theology, and Identity: A Pacific Exploration*, ed. Elaine M. Wainwright with Philip Culbertson and Susan Smith (Hindmarsh, Australia: ATF Press, 2010), 10.

[171] Tate, "Māori Perspective," 10.

[172] Tate, "Māori Perspective," 14.

[173] Douglas L. Oliver, *Oceania: The Native Cultures of Australia and the Pacific Islands*, vol. 1 (Honolulu: University of Hawai'i Press, 1989), 135.

[174] Oliver, *Oceania*, 135. Oliver adds that while most possession cases were temporary, some people were known to be permanently possessed.

In Papua New Guinea, "evil spirit sickness" is characterized by garbled speech that at times also demonstrates an ability to speak in a foreign language.[175]

South America

Sweet outlines the main activities of *calundu* ceremonies in Brazil. Even though variation is present in the approach of each healer, certain activities are typical. In *calundu*, music and dance lead to possession trance. The possessed healer then speaks "in a strange voice" to call out other spirits.[176] Greenfield reports the screams that occurred when a medium healer went into trance during the dis-obsession process. He reported that the medium "began to scream in pain and roll on the floor."[177] In three other cases, Greenfield attests to the change in voice in mediumship experiences.[178]

In Umbanda, incorporating spirit guides is a known practice. The messages from these spirit guides are highly valued. Schmidt records the words of Mãe M., who explains why speech with these guides is so powerful:

> People like to work with the guides in order to help someone. It is very popular for these guides to be incorporated in Umbanda, everybody likes it because it allows people to talk directly with the spirit. It is very different from talking directly with a medium. You can say the same thing that the spiritual guide says but it has a very different weight (when the guide is talking). . . . Five minutes of conversation with a spiritual guide about something personal is like directing a person for an hour and a half about an individual query.[179]

In summary, spirit guides can give spirit-inspired advice during crisis. Rituals of devotion are performed for the spirit entities.[180] Additionally, Spiritists place emphasis on communicating with the spirits.[181] Communication with "evolved spirits," who are the spirits of doctors and intellectuals, may aid in

[175] Edward L. Schieffelin, "Evil Spirit Sickness, the Christian Disease: The Innovation of a New Syndrome of Mental Derangement and Redemption in Papua New Guinea," *Culture, Medicine, and Psychiatry* 20.1 (1996): 1.

[176] James H. Sweet, *Recreating Africa: Culture, Kinship, and Religion in the African-Portuguese World, 1441–1770* (Chapel Hill: University of North Carolina Press, 2003), 148–49.

[177] Sidney M. Greenfield, *Spirits with Scalpels: The Cultural Biology of Religious Healing in Brazil* (Walnut Creek, Calif.: Left Coast Press, 2008), 77–78.

[178] Greenfield, *Spirits with Scalpels*, 82–83, 132.

[179] Bettina E. Schmidt, *Spirits and Trance in Brazil: An Anthropology of Religious Experience* (New York: Bloomsbury, 2016), 119. Schmidt interviewed Mãe M. on March 22, 2010.

[180] Schmidt, *Spirits and Trance in Brazil*, 119.

[181] Schmidt, *Spirits and Trance in Brazil*, 119. Spiritists categorize the communication as secular rather than religious.

healing or education. Ancestral spirits are also received for communication.[182] Spiritists reject mediumship for profit.[183]

In Puerto Rico, in *Espiritismo* practice, family séances are practiced to communicate with spirits. Spirits possess a family member who has established capabilities as a medium, and this person serves as the vehicle of communication, often communicating with late relatives.[184]

Western Experiences

Europe

In Hungarian experience, necromancers are known to become possessed and act as mediums to communicate messages from the dead.[185] A wise woman of Csíkszentdomokos described her experience by indicating that "the spirits entered into her and prevailed upon her to tell what they had told her."[186] Pócs indicates that in eastern Hungarian beliefs, dead relatives are known to possess the living by accident. An example from Csíkkarcfalva indicates that a "spirit of a man's grandfather spoke through him at night and gave directions to the family."[187] In Keralia the phenomenon of Karelian seers is well attested. The seers take their patients to the cemetery and invoke the dead for possession. During the trance state, they receive information to aid the recovery of their patient.[188] Pócs indicates that transmitting the "predictions of the dead as mediums" is a common characteristic among collective possession cults, divine possession, and possession by the dead.[189] In her summary of possession

---

[182] Schmidt, *Spirits and Trance in Brazil*, 120.

[183] Schmidt, *Spirits and Trance in Brazil*, 121. Schmidt argues that Spiritists focus on the control of spirits during mediumship (126). Possession is referred to in the context of "obsession," which requires disobsession to remove the negative impact of the spirit.

[184] Joan D. Koss, "Spirits as Socializing Agents: A Case Study of a Puerto Rican Girl Reared in a Matricentric Family," in *Case Studies in Spirit Possession*, ed. Vincent Crapanzano and Vivian Garrison (New York: Wiley, 1977), 366.

[185] Pócs notes that parallels exist in Romanian, Bulgarian, and Austrian examples. A specialist exists who has functions beyond that of a necromancer, including seer, diviner, and healer. See Éva Pócs, "A Magyar halottlátó és a keresztény Európa," *Népi vallásosság a Kárpátmendencében* 2 (1996): 25–41.

[186] This testimony was recorded by Pócs and written in Éva Pócs, "Possession Phenomena, Possession-Systems: Some East-Central European Examples," in *Communicating with the Spirits*, ed. Éva Pócs and Gábor Klaniczay (Budapest: Central European University Press, 2005), 98.

[187] Pócs, "Possession Phenomena, Possession-Systems," 99.

[188] Pócs "Possession Phenomena, Possession-Systems," 99. See also Matt T. Salo, "The Structure of Finnish Shamanic Therapy" (PhD diss., University of New York at Binghamton, 1974), 141–60.

[189] Pócs "Possession Phenomena, Possession-Systems," 99.

experience and possession systems in Central-Eastern Europe, Pócs concludes that possession "as a trance phenomenon—seen from a psycho-biological point of view—is a very common, one could say omnipresent, channel of supernatural communication."[190]

North America

In Alaskan experience on St. Lawrence Island, during seizures caused by possession, American anthropologist Riley Moore attests to conversation with spirit-familiars. One of the spirits "talked in tongues."[191] In another case a spirit correctly predicted a woman's loss of several children. The spirit said, "Those five stones will not make you well. They mean your wife will get pregnant five times and each time one or two days later after the child is born it will die."[192] The woman's loss validated her experience of sorcery.

Macklin documents the experience of a Connecticut woman who was recognized at that time as the "only medium in Connecticut with the ability to go into trance, be possessed by a spirit, and so communicate with beings in the Summer Land, a term many Spiritualists use interchangeably with Spirit Land."[193] Mrs. Rita M. is an ordained minister in the National Spiritualist Association of Churches of the United States of America. Macklin describes mediumship as the chance to "become an eloquent and authoritative instrument of other voices of other times."[194] Mrs. Rita M. notes her control over the lower spirits and practices exorcism when they attempt to control or confuse participants.[195]

Summarizing Catholic experiences in the United States, Blai indicates that common signs of possession include knowledge that is beyond a person's normal ability to know, including "knowledge of all languages" and "knowledge of hidden things the person could not know."[196] This is one of the few characteristics of possession stated directly in the 1999 document titled *De Exorcismis*

---

[190] Pócs "Possession Phenomena, Possession-Systems," 131.

[191] Jane M. Murphy, "Psychotherapeutic Aspects of Shamanism," in Kiev, *Magic, Faith, and Healing*, 60.

[192] Murphy, "Psychotherapeutic Aspects of Shamanism," 66. In this case the spirit maintained a different interpretation than the shaman whom the spirit spoke through. The Shaman instructed the man to eat the stones for wellness.

[193] June Macklin, "A Connecticut Yankee in Summer Land," in Crapanzano and Garrison, *Case Studies in Spirit Possession*, 43.

[194] Macklin, "Connecticut Yankee in Summer Land," 61.

[195] Macklin, "Connecticut Yankee in Summer Land," 54.

[196] Adam C. Blai, "Exorcism and the Church: Through Priests, the Church Has the Power to Battle Demons," *The Priest* 73.8 (2017): 19. See also X. F. Marquart, "L'exorciste dans le manifestations diaboliques," in *Satan*, ed. E. Carmélitaines (Paris: Desclée de Brouwer, 1948), 328–51, who lists *xenoglossia* (speaking in unknown tongues) as characteristic of possession.

et Supplicationibus Quibusdam (Of Exorcisms and Certain Supplications). It is considered one of the "most reliable signs."[197]

Summary and Conclusions

The sections above surveyed many examples of possession that produce changes in vocalic states, demonic speech, or oracular activity. These anthropological and ethnographic descriptions of possession states attest to belief in phenomena such as spirits speaking through persons and inspiring possessed persons with knowledge. These accounts are familiar to readers of NT accounts of possession and exorcism that depict demonic speech as characteristic of possession states. The biblical accounts explored above provide examples of the belief in the capability of spirits speaking through possessed persons. Anthropological parallels provide more detail on how speech might be altered in possessed persons, such as in pitch, language, or other variations. In many cases the speech of the possessed person includes speech in other languages (xenolalia) or glossolalia. Notably, both the ancient and modern evidence included here attests to spirits speaking through persons. Although it was not surveyed in thorough detail, one will note that in some anthropological analogies, muteness was included as a characteristic of possession. For some cultures, a spirit may open or close the mouth of a person. The story of the mute boy with the mute demon in biblical accounts parallels these accounts.

The above cross-cultural research additionally demonstrates that spirits are often sought for knowledge. The parallel of this activity in Acts 16:16 tells of a young girl who was used as the mouthpiece of a spirit for fortune-telling or soothsaying. As evidenced above, cross-cultural anthropological literature attests to the widespread experience of communication with spirits for fortune-telling, communication with ancestors, a diagnosis for illness, or learning what demands a spirit is making for appeasement.

This chapter concludes the global survey of possession experiences that parallel the characteristics of possession displayed in the NT. In modern anthropological studies and in the NT, possession (1) is an aetiology for illness; (2) may manifest with violence or extraordinary strength; and (3) produces vocalic alterations, demonic speech, or other oracular activity. The following chapter will summarize the key implications of these anthropological analogies and how these pieces of evidence bear on the reconsideration of NT accounts as plausible eyewitness testimony. Further, a brief history of practitioner perspectives will be surveyed along with some implications for the Western church.

---

[197] Marco Innamorati, Ruggero Taradel, and Renato Foschi, "Between Sacred and Profane: Possession, Psychotherapy, and the Catholic Church," *History of Psychology* 22.1 (2018): 9.

7

A Vision of Transcultural Phenomena

Summary, Implications, and Conclusions

A Review of the Argument

This monograph has identified a thread of cohering characteristics in global accounts of possession. This avenue of research has largely been overlooked because the content of these studies represents an "Other" that has been impossible for students of Enlightenment thinking to embrace. Crapanzano and Garrison conclude,

> For the Westerner, the spirit possessed, representative of "another cultural tradition," embodies the Other in its most extreme, most exotic, most alien form. Such an Other must not remain distinct from us, or be reduced to one of us. . . . The dialectical drama between the possessed and his spirit, between (human) self and (spirit) Other, may well provide an allegory for the confrontation between the ethnographer and his people, between modern man and the primitive.[1]

Some readers of the Synoptics and Acts and their exorcism stories will meet this same Other in the biblical text. By positive use of the principle of analogy, a congruent relationship between the Other of the biblical text and the modern Other is unveiled. The cross-cultural phenomenology of spirit possession and exorcism sets a strong challenge for the reader of the Synoptics and Acts, especially challenging arguments against the credibility of NT exorcism stories as plausible eyewitness testimony. Modern accounts contain copious

---

[1] Vincent Crapanzano, "Introduction," in *Case Studies in Spirit Possession*, ed. Vincent Crapanzano and Vivian Garrison (New York: Wiley, 1977), 33–34.

analogies of spirit possession experiences. Chapters 4 through 6 have documented numerous analogies of the phenomenology of spirit possession that compare with NT reports.

Regarding interpretation, this study provides an opportunity for readers of any culture to hear the reports of possession experience through the voices of those who have testified to their experience. No adherence to any one interpretation of spirit possession is required to consider the plausibility of the argument for the analogous relationship between global reports and NT reports. The above global survey of cross-cultural evidence offers the indigenous interpretation a place at the interpretive table. In other words, readers today may no longer doubt that analogous phenomena are experienced today. As a result, it is simply not justifiable to reject the exorcism stories in the NT accounts as legendary or demythologize them due to the nature of their content. Given the vast acceptance of Mark and Matthew as ancient biography and Luke-Acts as ancient historiography, it is possible to consider the possession and exorcism accounts of these texts as plausibly based on eyewitness claims. The argument is not for the explicit historicity of every detail of each account, an approach far too optimistic, but a recognition that the exorcism stories in the Synoptics and Acts plausibly fit in the ancient context in which they are found.

The collection of evidence above demonstrates that there are many reports of possession experience that are characteristically analogous to the stories of Jesus and those who suffered spiritual ailments. These reports, found in ethnographies and anthropological writings, document a wide range of fieldwork in a wide variety of cultures and demonstrate that the modern possession phenomenology is comparable to the Synoptic depiction of ancient spirit possession. The tracking of these parallels does not dismiss the multifaceted and variegated ways in which expression of possession and exorcistic rites differ cross-culturally.[2] These subtleties are acknowledged even though there is no space for a full expression of them in the limitations of this monograph.

This research has included evidence from as many cultures as possible, although one will quickly find that more evidence could be added. Due to limitations of time and space, this monograph is not exhaustive in finding every culture that has parallel characteristics. No culture was left out intentionally. More research is needed, especially in Western areas, to track down how spirit possession manifests in these settings. However, it has been

---

[2]   Space disallows a full-scale presentation of ways that possession experience varies cross-culturally. The claims of this study do not dismiss the wide variety of subtleties expressed in each culture that may or may not be found as congruent.

demonstrated that possession and exorcism experience is not entirely absent in Western spheres, although with less profligacy in reporting than in other global areas. A brief review serves to summarize the key arguments made in each chapter.

Chapter 1 provided the context for this discussion by considering an interpretive taxonomy related to spirit possession and exorcism in biblical scholarship. Secondly, biblical scholars were surveyed who point towards the potential that an interdisciplinary study might have for interpreting biblical accounts of possession and exorcism. These scholars point out that multicultural voices experience similar possession and exorcism phenomena as in the Synoptic Gospels and Acts. Thirdly, the awareness of multicultural perspectives on spirit possession and exorcism provides an opportunity to approach the hermeneutical challenge that has characterized the history of interpretation with fresh perspectives.

Chapter 2 surveyed approaches to spirit possession and exorcism in anthropological studies. A brief survey of various anthropological frameworks, including functional anthropology, structuralism, symbolic/interpretive approaches, and postmodern approaches, reveals that anthropologists gradually shifted from favoring etic to emic perspectives when studying spirit possession in various cultures. This shift led to the production of well-documented and descriptive writings about spirit possession in a wide variety of cultures. Further, spirit possession was defined anthropologically and a methodology involving the principle of analogy was laid out.

Chapter 3 situated the Synoptics and Acts within their most contemporaneous genres of ancient biography and ancient historiography. In essence, the monograph suggests that reading the Synoptic Gospels with genre criticism and from a multicultural perspective helpfully bridges the chasm between Jesus the historical exorcist and the content of the exorcism accounts in the Synoptic Gospels. For example, in view of genre criticism, a bias towards the reality of spirits found in the Synoptics does not correspondingly mean that the content of the possession and exorcism accounts was falsified since ancient writers wrote ancient biography or historiography with associated *tendenz*. If the stories grew, a study of accounts available in triple tradition does not help one decipher what they grew from with much optimism. In this chapter it was realized that Gospel writers did shape their material, but shaping and falsifying are different matters. The Synoptic Gospels and Acts fit plausibly within their own contextual background, where a belief in spirits, spirit possession, and the practice of exorcism can be documented in a diachronic study of ancient literature. Ancients held that spirits could possess and affect humans in a wide variety of capacities. Exorcisms provided relief and were also attested to in ancient literature.

Chapters 4–6 offered an opportunity to consider accounts of possession and exorcism in the Synoptics and Acts alongside modern anthropological accounts. An exegesis of key texts reveals three categories of characteristics of possession phenomenology that are found in biblical literature. These categories include: (1) possession as illness, (2) possession as producing violent acts or extraordinary strength, and (3) and possession as affecting speech (demonic speech, vocal alterations, or other oracular activity). The main body of anthropological evidence was presented in chapters 4 through 6. Before introducing anthropological perspectives, brief exegesis helped familiarize the reader with the analogous content in the Synoptics and Acts. Admittedly, it was at times more instructive than fluid to present the evidence in these categories. In chapter 4 the reader found a survey of more general information describing how possession is experienced and perceived in each culture. At times the chapters shared reports and the characteristics of the report were divided instructively across the three chapters. Chapter 4 considered biblical and global analogues of possession phenomenology related to possession and illness. Chapter 5 documented biblical and global reports of possession as producing violent acts or extraordinary strength. Chapter 6 surveyed how possession experiences impact speech in biblical and global research. I concluded that many modern accounts contain the same characteristics identified in NT accounts of spirit possession.

It is my hope that the above research narrows the gap between Western and non-Western societies, especially as it pertains to their interpretation of biblical accounts of possession and exorcism. Global views provide a new lens for Western interpreters. George Clement Bond and Diane M. Ceikawy refer to the Western dominant paradigm as problematic, producing a need for more inclusivity in academic debate. They state,

> The boundaries between "First-" and "Third-" World scholarship have been thoroughly eroded, decentering dominant paradigms and contributing to the major paradigm shifts taking place in the current production of scholarly knowledge. A more inclusive community is in the making, a community that includes postcolonial scholars who have reinvigorated the well-established academic debate concerning the ability of existing disciplinary concepts to capture or represent the meaning of local knowledge and experience.[3]

[3] George Clement Bond and Diane M. Ciekawy, "Introduction: Contested Domains in the Dialogues of 'Witchcraft,'" in *Witchcraft Dialogues: Anthropological and Philosophical Exchanges*, ed. George Clement Bond and Diane M. Ciekawy (Athens: Ohio University Press, 2001), 1.

This monograph intends to produce a centering argument that is inclusive of interdisciplinary aims and global perspectives. It invites voices that have at times been ignored or suppressed. As a result, some Western academic interpretations of biblical accounts of possession and exorcism need to be deconstructed. Namely, because of the wide variety of modern analogies, it is no longer possible to argue that these accounts are not based on eyewitness testimony because people no longer experience similar phenomena. People in various cultures do experience these phenomena, and they testify to their experiences.

The field of anthropology has recognized a much-needed shift from etic to emic understandings of possession accounts. This shift is similarly necessary in biblical studies since evidence demonstrates that Western bias and reductive readings predominate interpretation. While some may disagree with how biblical writers interpret possession experience and what characterizes them, it is no longer possible to discount that global reports of possession phenomena are analogous to biblical reports.

In summary, this monograph hopefully narrows the gap often depicted between the Jesus of history and the historical Jesus. Jesus is known and accepted as a historical exorcist, but this monograph hopes to relay that the historical Jesus can be known as more than just an exorcist. It is historically plausible given the nature of the cultural milieu that the historical Jesus very likely exorcised ill ones, and exorcism brought about their healing. He very likely exorcised those who were violent and restored them to their right mind; exorcised those who had demons speaking through them and silenced their demons; exorcised persons in the Synagogue, Gentile persons, and children. Paul followed in Jesus' footsteps and performed exorcisms, notably exorcising the girl with the "python spirit." These stories may challenge some Western thinking, and scholars may choose to interpret them differently. Even so, they are not surprising in contexts that have familiarity with the phenomena. When one considers ancient background and the many modern voices that have echoed similar experiences, it becomes clear that both ancients and moderns testify to analogous phenomena related to spirit possession.

A Few Implications and Guidelines for Praxis
and the Western Church's Response

Taking this research a step further, one may wonder what implications this research bears for either those who reject the reality of spirits or those who are practitioners of spiritual warfare or exorcism ministry. A singular response is difficult to maintain since where one sits on the interpretive spectrum will vary. This section ought to be read as a postscript that considers a brief review of historical approaches to the topic in various Christian expressions. Below a brief survey of prevalent streams of modern practices of exorcism in the West is included. After the brief survey of prevalent streams comes analysis and potential trajectories of response. Each stream has positive and negative characteristics, and these will be briefly exposed in the analysis.

A Survey of Exorcism in Modern Western Christianity

Following the lead of James M. Collins, three historical streams of exorcism ministry are traced to survey a historical approach to exorcism in modern Western Christianity. These include charismatic, Evangelical Fundamentalist (EF), and Catholic approaches to exorcism. Special attention will be given to the characteristics of exorcism that have been surveyed above to see how they have been treated in Western praxis. One will be reminded that early expressions of these ministries grew alongside a more predominant Enlightenment mentality that eschewed their praxis.

To begin, in charismatic tradition[4] demonology is a vivid part of the ministry of the movement. Smith helpfully prompts us towards appropriate terminology for the use of exorcism in this stream: "It is inappropriate to think of any of these groups practicing 'exorcism' since their approach was usually in no way sacramental."[5] Rather, the term "deliverance ministry" is utilized, and gained vernacular in the 1970s. Hence, this terminology will be utilized even though it embraces a theological approach rather than a phenomenological one.

Roots of deliverance ministry in the charismatic tradition can be traced back to John Alexander Dowie. While his focus was predominantly on divine healing, his views on the relationship between demons and illness led to the development of a demonology that would impact his followers. Smith asserts that for Dowie, "sickness was *always* to be considered of diabolic origin."[6] Even so, at the earliest roots, there was no obsession with demonology, and it was practiced as a support to evangelistic goals.

---

[4]   Collins utilizes the term "Charismatic" as a "catch-all" category for early Pentecostals, mid-century itinerant ministries, the charismatic renewal groups, and varieties of post-Pentecostals. See James M. Collins, *Exorcism and Deliverance Ministry in the Twentieth Century* (Eugene, Ore.: Wipf and Stock, 2009), 15.

[5]   Collins, *Exorcism and Deliverance Ministry in the Twentieth Century*, 15. Collins notes that charismatic praxis prefers "spontaneity" and "straightforward expression" rather than the use of liturgy in the practice of exorcism.

[6]   Collins, *Exorcism and Deliverance Ministry in the Twentieth Century*, 47 (emphasis original).

As the Pentecostal movement matured, certain theological perspectives placed limits on deliverance ministry. For example, deliverance ministries were not allowed to be performed on those who were a part of the "Pentecostal community" since demons could not possess Spirit-filled Christians.[7] Even so, itinerant charismatics in the 1940s and 1950s carried on the practice of deliverance ministry, and did not always adhere to the prohibition against ministering to those inside their own community. Key leaders include William Branham, Oral Roberts, and A. A. Allen.

Branham's ministry was characterized by two signs, granted to him by an angel, that aided in convincing others of his success, namely, a vibration in the hand and words of knowledge. Branham believed in a personal devil and personal demons, believing that he had had "face to face" conversations with them. Further, human experience was categorized in dualistic spheres belonging to the work of either God or the devil. As a result, "uncontrollable sin, insanity, and even 'temper tantrums' were attributed to demon-possession."[8] Following Dowie, all sickness was attributed to demonic causation. In other words, exorcism belonged to the realm of healing.

In this vein of thinking, Oral Roberts further popularized this perspective in his healing revivals. Roberts claimed to have heard God's voice calling him to healing ministry: "From this hour your ministry of healing will begin. You will have my power to pray for the sick and to cast out devils."[9] Harrel summarizes the relationship between the demonic and illness that Robert's ministry depicted.

> In his earliest years of his healing ministry, Oral, and his audiences, seemed spellbound by demons about their relation to human sickness. He thought his sermon on demon possession usually turned "the tide of the meeting"; his audiences marveled at Oral's command over the evil spirits.[10]

Roberts expressed belief in demonic transference, often sought to discern the names and numbers of demons as a means of facilitating removal, and did participate in delivering Christians. Relating to a demon's ability to enact violence, Oral records the experience of a man to whom demons transferred: "They (the demons) struck this irreverent man a blow and knocked him completely out of his chair onto the ground. The ushers found him writhing and twisting and

---

[7]   Collins, *Exorcism and Deliverance Ministry in the Twentieth Century*, 23–24.

[8]   Collins, *Exorcism and Deliverance Ministry in the Twentieth Century*, 23–24.

[9]   David Edwin Harrell Jr., *Oral Roberts: An American Life* (Bloomington: Indiana University Press, 1985), 67.

[10]   Harrell, *Oral Roberts*, 123.

biting his own tongue and trying to scream out his misery." Roberts adds, "It took me five minutes to get him delivered by the power of God."[11] His influence is felt on those who came after him.

Allen's approach is characterized by Smith as illustrating "extreme sensationalism." Many spiritual, physical, and mental (including mental illness) ailments were attributed to the demonic. Those searching for cures were encouraged to "name the kind of demon from which you desire to be set free, (if known)."[12] This led innumerable and seemingly limitless problems to be attributed to demonic causation.

Following these predecessors Derek Prince gained prominence. Smith characterizes Prince as "the ablest and clearest exponent of the Pentecostal/ charismatic approach to deliverance ministry."[13] Prince interpreted his own experience with depression as an evil spirit, "a spirit of heaviness" (Isaiah 61:3), leading him to interpret mental illness as demonic, even for the Christian. Further, demons were associated with particular ailments, including "arthritis, cancer, sinusitis adultery, disappointment, masturbation, witchcraft and even tooth decay."[14] Even so, the gift of discernment could aid a person in determining if the cause was demonic or natural.[15] Considering the exorcism stories of Jesus, Prince argued for a scriptural mandate for participation in deliverance ministry.[16] Collins records that there was great demand for this ministry even though hysteria surrounded it, prioritizing freedom from spirits over human dignity.[17] Prince records the phenomena that may take place upon a demon's exit, including coughing, screaming, roaring, or groaning.[18] Like Prince, Francis MacNutt, attributing his involvement with deliverance ministry to personal experience, also prioritizes a "gift of discernment" when deciphering the potential cause of ailments.

Admittedly, MacNutt indicates that his involvement in exorcism ministry was not driven by theoretical perspectives but by experience.[19] Through hands-on experience, the charismatic stream found a deep connection

[11]   Oral Roberts, *Voice of Healing*, November 1951, 8f.
[12]   David Edwin Harrell Jr., *All Things Are Possible: The Healing and Charismatic Revivals in Modern America* (Bloomington: Indiana University Press, 1975), 88.
[13]   Collins, *Exorcism and Deliverance Ministry in the Twentieth Century*, 44.
[14]   Collins, *Exorcism and Deliverance Ministry in the Twentieth Century*, 48.
[15]   Derek Prince, *They Shall Expel Demons: What You Need to Know about Demons—Your Invisible Enemy* (Grand Rapids: Chosen, 1998), 98.
[16]   Prince, *They Shall Expel Demons*, 18–26.
[17]   Collins, *Exorcism and Deliverance Ministry in the Twentieth Century*, 47.
[18]   Prince, *They Shall Expel Demons*, 214.
[19]   Francis MacNutt, *Deliverance from Evil Spirits* (Grand Rapids: Chosen, 2003), 15.

between healing and deliverance and a deep association between sickness and demons. More explicitly, a spectrum of views existed in relation to mental illness. While some earlier proponents thought that all mental illness was demonic, others opted for more nuanced approaches that valued psychological analyses. Instances of vocalic activity and violence are observable in charismatic analysis. For instance, one account depicted a demon asking that "the blood" not be spoken of "because it is so red, because it is so warm, because it is alive, and it covers everything."[20] Further, common manifestations include some of the violent sort of behavior (along with other phenomena) that has been observed cross-culturally, namely, "rapid movement of the tongue in and out of the mouth, a hissing noise via the nostrils, snake-like writhing on the floor, numbing or tingling in the hands, screaming, rhythmic body movements, pain and laughing. Since demons usually leave via the mouth, the moment of deliverance is often accompanied by coughing or even vomiting up blobs of phlegm."[21]

Secondly, Collins introduces the perspectives found in Evangelical Fundamentalist (EF) deliverance ministry. Collins characterizes this group as ones who "often frown on the emotionalism and sensationalism of their charismatic counterparts and assume an air of intellectual superiority; nevertheless, they share many of the same characteristics, most importantly, biblicism, ethical rigorism and, frequently, enthusiasm."[22] Collins adds that even though the EF perspective was influenced by a charismatic stream, sectarianism also played a role in the various positions that were developed. Nevertheless, one finds that the EF deliverance ministry, like charismatic deliverance ministry, prioritizes experience.

The Welsh revival led to further criticism. Figures like Evan Roberts and Jessie Penn-Lewis perceived that the Welsh revival was "very seriously compromised by demonic infiltration."[23] However, Collins suggests that what was really in view was a "classic and literal example of demonizing the opposition,"[24] since aspects of the revival that were not approved of by Roberts and Penn-Lewis were considered as demonic. Even further, those who held such errant views were considered to be demonized. However, as Collins notes, much of what they opposed provided a seedbed for the Pentecostal perspectives.[25]

---

[20] Frank Hammond and Ida Mae Hammond, *Pigs in the Parlor: A Practical Guide to Deliverance* (Kirkwood, Mo.: Impact, 1973), 109.
[21] Hammond and Hammond, *Pigs in the Parlor*, 52.
[22] Collins, *Exorcism and Deliverance Ministry in the Twentieth Century*, 111.
[23] Collins, *Exorcism and Deliverance Ministry in the Twentieth Century*, 119.
[24] Collins, *Exorcism and Deliverance Ministry in the Twentieth Century*, 119.
[25] Collins, *Exorcism and Deliverance Ministry in the Twentieth Century*, 120.

Even though Roberts and Penn-Lewis influenced both charismatic perspectives and EF perspectives, Collins indicates that what definitively showed up in EF perspectives is the "demonisation of Charismatic forms of enthusiasm,"[26] especially considering that many of the phenomena associated with Pentecostalism, such as speaking in tongues, prophecy, healing, and manifestations like falling down or crying, were thought to be associated with spiritism. Even worse, as Collins suggests, the efforts of *The Berlin Declaration* and *War on Saints* to demonize Pentecostalism lacked evidence and were built on forms of "intellectual superiority," and in the end "neither demonstrate much intellectual rigor or clarity or consistency."[27]

As time passed, EF deliverance ministry was birthed in the 1970s through the work of Kurt Koch, who helpfully maintained focus on Christ and his triumph and defeat of Satan. Koch prioritized creating a link between mental illness and possession but also warned that many who believe they are possessed are instead mentally ill. Even so, Koch thought it possible for mental illness and demonic influence to occur simultaneously.[28] Further, Koch warned against participation in the occult, which increasingly became prevalent in this perspective.

Moody Bible Institute and Dallas Theological Seminary reflect the EF approach. Merrill F. Unger wrote to help Christians know how to deal with the demonic but even more so due to the frustrations he had with charismatic streams of deliverance ministry. Unger transitioned away from a purely Evangelical perspective that demons cannot influence or affect "born again Christians" to systematizing an approach to deliverance that names demons according to the vice they cause. In essence, Unger's approach left no Christian behind since sin was always connected to the influence of evil spirits, leaving no room for a consideration of how the Fall impacts human anthropology.[29] He alluded to a variety of characteristics that demons may cause, including personality changes, extraordinary strength, glossolalia, and clairvoyance.[30]

Following in the same vein of thought, Hal Lindsay carried forward the ideology that demons were increasingly invading. They took hold by targeting those who were deeply seeking God, but in turn these ones had opened themselves for varieties of spiritual experiences. Even though not as explicitly, Lindsay seemingly continues the defense against glossolalia (very likely due to the potential of opening oneself to the demonic even though it is not

---

26 Collins, *Exorcism and Deliverance Ministry in the Twentieth Century*, 121.

27 Collins, *Exorcism and Deliverance Ministry in the Twentieth Century*, 124.

28 Kurt E. Koch, *Occult Bondage and Deliverance: Counseling the Occultly Oppressed* (Berghausen, Germany: Evangelization, 1970), 155, 160.

29 Merrill F. Unger, *What Demons Can Do to Saints* (Chicago: Moody, 1991), 132.

30 Unger, *What Demons Can Do to Saints*, 129–40.

stated directly like in other EF writings).[31] Additionally, Lindsay describes typical characteristics of the effects of demons, including increased intelligence or strength, mental illness, and changes in personality so that the demon's personality takes over.[32]

As the 1970s and 1980s unfolded there was an increased interest in both demonology and the occult. Tied to the premillennial persuasion that things were increasingly getting worse, Collins' conclusion is helpful in describing the interwoven nature of these two trending societal factors: "In a secular, agnostic wider culture, enthusiastic Christians seized upon the Occult Revival as evidence of evil supernatural activity. Never mind the need for sober assessment, just feel the apologetic value. In this way the Occult Revival and enthusiastic Christianity enjoyed a perverse symbiotic enmity."[33] In essence, these ideologies led to what we might call a satanic panic in the 1980s and 1990s that led Christians to believe that demons were nearly everywhere and affecting the lives of believers and non-believers alike. Soon after, the phenomenon of satanic ritual abuse came onto the scene after a Christian psychologist suggested that multiple personality disorder was potentially due to the presence of the demonic. Therefore, the patient would undergo exorcism. In reality, these cases of satanic ritual abuse were not as widespread as some had thought, but the story is a painful expression of what may go wrong when demonology is overemphasized. Collins helpfully critiques:

> This is one of the most shameful episodes in the history of the twentieth century enthusiasm. The refusal to approach the issues of Occultism critically and empathetically led to embarrassing gullibility and the development of widespread yet completely unnecessary "Satanic Panic" with tragic consequences. For the many children who were removed from their parents as a result of unfounded fears of SRA the effects have been most serious.[34]

In other words, the overemphasis on demonology eventually led to unhelpful Christian practices that harmed several individuals.

The final stream of thought related to exorcism and deliverance ministry in the West is the "enthusiastic sacramental exorcism."[35] This perspective largely relates to Catholic and Anglican perspectives on demons and exorcism. The

[31]   Hal Lindsay, *Satan Is Alive and Well on Planet Earth* (London: Lakeland, 1973), 133f., cf. 147f.

[32]   Lindsay, *Satan Is Alive and Well on Planet Earth*, 154.

[33]   Collins, *Exorcism and Deliverance Ministry in the Twentieth Century*, 142.

[34]   Collins, *Exorcism and Deliverance Ministry in the Twentieth Century*, 149.

[35]   The title is given by Collins, *Exorcism and Deliverance Ministry in the Twentieth Century*, 151.

rite of exorcism gains pride of place even though its use is more prominent in certain time periods than others. For example, before 1970 the rite had theoretical approval but was practically excluded. Post-1970, several proponents of the rite began to apply it in practice and write about their experiences. These proponents include Malachi Martin, Ed and Lorraine Warren, Malachi Martin, M. Scott Peck, and Gabriele Amorth, to name a few. These proponents all attest to the realities of possession experience and a need for exorcism in their writings. Further, they attest to the same sorts of characteristics of demonic manifestations that have been found as consistent in cross-cultural settings. Different from the charismatic approach and the EF perspective is the requirement that the church evaluate medical records before one was sent for an exorcism. The praxis of orthodox Catholic theology throughout the works of Catholic proponents is somewhat variegated. Some press past the church's comfort zone, while others seem to keep to the boundaries more precisely. For instance, Amorth purports that demons can disguise themselves during the diagnostic procedure, but argues that the one and only clarifying test is to subject the person to an exorcism. In essence, the exorcism attempt itself becomes the true diagnostic.[36] Relating to mental illness, a connection to the demonic is substantiated. M. Scott Peck, a psychologist, initially distinguished between multiple personality disorder and the demonic, but later concluded that both were potentially a diagnosable cause.[37]

From the Anglican perspective, another use of the exorcism ritual surfaces post-1970. Dom Robert Petitpierre, who chaired the Study Group on Exorcism and was a practitioner of exorcism, responded to a letter from Anglican theologians who wanted to end the "dangerous" practice of exorcism in the church of England. Petitpierre attempts to responded to the polarized forces of rationalism and excessive demonologies. In his book *Exorcising Devils*, he criticizes the practices of "certain evangelical groups who, apparently, cannot conceive of ordinary human sin."[38] Even though from a sacramental stream, Petitpierre was warm towards a moderate charismatic approach, and he favors the term "deliverance" rather than "exorcism" due to a wish to avoid any association with magical practices. Collins summarizes Petitpierre as advocating for "a gentle sacramental approach with substantial moderate Charismatic influence in evidence."[39] This is reflected by the later adoption (by some) of the charismatic

---

[36] Gabriele Amorth, *An Exorcist Tells His Story* (San Francisco: Ignatius, 2002), 45.

[37] Michael W. Cuneo, *American Exorcism: Expelling Demons in the Land of Plenty* (London: Bantam, 2001), 72.

[38] Robert Petitpierre, *Exorcising Devils* (London: Robert Hale, 1976), 53. Petitpierre seems to be critiquing charismatics in this case.

[39] Collins, *Exorcism and Deliverance Ministry in the Twentieth Century*, 178.

practice of deliverance as an appropriate means for minor exorcism. Additionally, some charismatics warmed up to the sacramental approach and adopted congruent practices.[40] In essence, boundary lines between streams begin to be blurred in practitioner perspective.

Summing up Catholic and Anglican perspectives, neither grew in practice as wildly as in charismatic or EF traditions. When considering why, Collins asserts,

> The reason is simple. . . . The Roman Catholic Church is institutionalized to a greater degree than any of its Protestant counterparts and sacramental exorcism (in contrast to Charismatic) deliverance may only be practiced by an ordained priest with the permission of his bishop. . . . What this all adds up to is that enthusiastic sacramental exorcism had some fairly powerful institutional hurdles to clear in the Roman Catholic setting. Hence the time lag of 20 years or so. The same forces that led, during the 1970s, to the flowering of Charismatic and EF deliverance ministry and the gentle Anglican version of sacramental exorcism, produced a harvest in the Roman Catholic Church too; it took twenty years or so longer in the latter because the soil was not so easy to work with.[41]

As Anglicanism has progressed into the twenty-first century, psychologist Gerard Leavey characterizes the debates in the Church of England as polarized between "the liberal leadership of the Church of England" and "increasingly muscular evangelicalism" influenced by African Christianity's belief in Satan, possession, and exorcism.[42] Even so, the practice of exorcism has survived. Francis Young summarizes, "The widespread (albeit sometimes reluctant) acceptance from all winds of the Church of England that exorcism forms part of the church's ministry is an indication that the ministry is no longer the preserve of a minority of clergy at the fringe."[43] However, some clergy demonstrated a level of "cognitive strain" towards the reality of spirits. Others felt that medicine and psychiatry were not enough to decipher proper diagnosis. Leavey observed "deep concern that medicine and psychiatry may fail to discern the demonic and may also obstruct legitimate religious intervention."[44] Given the historical opposition to a rightful place for exorcism in the church, Young observes that what is missing is a "meaningful debate on the place of

---

[40] Collins, *Exorcism and Deliverance Ministry in the Twentieth Century*, 189.

[41] Collins, *Exorcism and Deliverance Ministry in the Twentieth Century*, 185.

[42] Gerard Leavey, "The Appreciation of the Spiritual in Mental Illness: A Qualitative Study of Beliefs among Clergy in the UK," *Transcultural Psychiatry* 47.4 (2010): 573–74.

[43] Francis Young, *A History of Anglican Exorcism: Deliverance and Demonology in Church Ritual* (London: I. B. Tauris, 2018), 196.

[44] Leavey, "Appreciation of the Spiritual in Mental Illness," 585.

exorcism in the Church of England."[45] Gardiner asks one of the most difficult questions that some Westerners have failed to ask in academic contributions to ecclesial conversations: "If the church, and particularly the established
church of the land, is unwilling to offer help to those oppressed . . . where can
they go, other than to spiritists and witches?"[46] Some Western academics may
be uncomfortable with the question, but it is an unlikely case that the question simply vanishes from the theological landscape of ecclesiology, given the
plethora of cross-cultural phenomena. Young highlights the role that anthropology plays in this call to more deeply consider an ecclesiastical response,
remarking that both the demand for exorcism remains and "possession phenomena and exorcism are anthropological constants which the church must
negotiate in every age." He summarizes, relaying a message for the Anglican
community, that "'a Christian presence in every community' may also include
being present for those who believe themselves to be demonically possessed."[47]

Analysis of Western Exorcism and Deliverance Ministries

First and foremost, it is interesting to observe that in the experience of the
practitioners and authors that have been surveyed above, the categories of
characteristics are present in all three streams of Western charismatic, Evangelical, Catholic, and Anglican experience. Even though each group takes a
somewhat unique approach to their own demonology, all practitioners and
writers above acknowledge the reality of spirits and the phenomena that are
experienced.

A careful reader will quickly notice that the analysis above largely focuses
on the last thirty years of the twentieth century. While developments have
occurred in the twenty-first century, the main streams of thought have not
substantially changed in their viewpoints. However, in some ways the "Third
Wave" melded together and provided a bridge between various trends in each
perspective. Even so, these three decades of exorcism and deliverance ministry
are a vivid snapshot of the seedbed for further ministries in each stream.[48]

In the charismatic approach, experience takes the lead in systematizing a
wide variety of understanding of what evil spirits can do. As a result, a genuine

---

[45] Young, *History of Anglican Exorcism*, 197.

[46] Ken Gardiner, *The Reluctant Exorcist: A Biblical Approach in an Age of Scepticism*, 2nd
ed. (Watford: Instant Apostle, 2015), 144–45.

[47] Young, *History of Anglican Exorcism*, 192.

[48] Collins argues that the "three major streams of exorcism/deliverance have tended to
converge towards the dominant Charismatic centre ground." The "Third Wave" movement
helped to heal some of the divide between the EF and charismatic perspectives. Collins,
Exorcism and Deliverance Ministry in the Twentieth Century, 187.

risk exists since anything can be attributed to a spiritual problem or demon. In general, there is no explicit procedure to consider other interpretive options, and this weight on experience potentially creates a blind spot towards other interpretive options for such phenomena. Even so, the charismatic perspective does acknowledge the phenomena as genuine experience, even in the West.

In response to trends found in EF deliverance ministry approaches, sectarianism ended up being a major stumbling block, preventing thoughtful reflection, balanced analysis, and deeper biblical and theological reflection. Demonizing other theological perspectives led Evangelical Fundamentalists to define exorcism and deliverance ministry in opposition to charismatic viewpoints. However, a variety of similarities in praxis still developed, including a belief in the reality of spirits, a need for deliverance and exorcism ministry, and overlap, even in the lack of a developed theology, of human fallenness and sin as contrasted with demonic influence.

In the sacramental perspective, the focus on ritual and the Roman rite of exorcism is centralized and a procedure for diagnoses and exorcism is more fully systematized. However, not all practitioners would follow with precision; nor would all Catholic theologians support the actual use of the rite in praxis. In this perspective one feels with more force the effect of the Enlightenment and skepticism about the trustworthiness of the experiences of the practitioners. However, there is seemingly more optimism than there is a way forward for considering a variety of interpretive or diagnostic possibilities when a problem arises.

An analysis of these three streams does not seriously consider Western perspectives that dismiss the reality of a spirit world and the wide variety of cohering experiences of spirit possession and exorcism. After all, what has been surveyed is largely varieties of ministry practitioners from various streams. Those who demythologize the biblical text and dismiss the validity of any sort of spiritual experience must grapple with the potential weight of the evidence that is brought forward in chapters 4–6, not just from practitioners and pastors, but also from the well-developed and thoughtful academic fields of anthropology, ethnography, and sociology. One will recall that these fields birthed a wide variety of literature and have also attempted to decipher if the reality of spirits is permissible or taboo or whether the emic or etic perspective should be favored. These questions helped to catalyze the widespread observation of spirit possession and exorcism experiences that have been surveyed in chapters 4–6.

As the conversation about biblical demonology and spiritual warfare continued, the work of James K. Beilby and Paul Rhodes Eddy defined, for academia, spiritual warfare in four main views. Firstly, the "World Systems Model," largely characterized by the work of Walter Wink, names "principalities and powers" as powerful societal structures that "become oppressive, demonic systems of domination."[49] The church responds nonviolently to expose and engage. Therefore, spiritual warfare is defined as dealing with evil systemic problems in public institutions, including politics. When boiled down, this perspective represents a demythologization of Satan. Secondly, the classical model rather focuses on spiritual warfare as fighting the sinful human nature. Thirdly, the "Deliverance" model of spiritual warfare recognizes the ontological existence of Satan and his demons, which need to be confronted. Strategies for deliverance in this perspective are wide-ranging. While Gregory Boyd focuses on the simplicity of Jesus' dependence on the Holy Spirit, faith, and prayer, others more elaborately seek to systematize the process with guidelines for freedom.[50] Fourthly, the "strategic level deliverance model" builds on the previous model with more systemization and specification. The model relates to the first since it argues that territorial spirits can have authority over regional spaces. Strategies are created to respond to the evil found in such systems and procedures like "spiritual mapping" or "identificational repentance" are utilized to discover systemic ills in the histories of various spaces or institutions. Intercessory prayer is a main focal point of this sort of spiritual warfare.

Considering these various definitions helpfully unveils a variety of presuppositions about what spiritual warfare might mean to a variety of individuals. Even though these viewpoints are often set in opposition to the others, one might holistically envision the reality that each perspective brings forward. In other words, evil systemic problems do exist in our world today and sometimes these are revealed institutionally, politically, and structurally in "principalities and powers" that seek domination. The NT also depicts more than one kingdom, and the Lord's Prayer reminds us that we are to invite the Kingdom of heaven on earth. Secondly, more fruitful biblical and theological discussion is needed to develop a reasoned response to the relationship between the fall of humanity and the impact of original sin alongside the potential effects of demonization. The third and fourth perspectives invite a conversation that engages with an ontological reality of spiritual forces. In other words, a more holistic approach is needed to draw forward the elements of reality that exists in these varieties of spaces. Increasingly, the definitions above allow for a

[49] James K. Beilby and Paul Rhodes Eddy, *Understanding Spiritual Warfare: Four Views* (Grand Rapids: Baker, 2012), 32.
[50] For example, see Neil Anderson, *The Bondage Breaker* (Eugene, Ore.: Harvest House, 2000).

reflection on the varieties of ways that Christians might possibly respond to the evil in the world, whether through evil inspired by the Fall, societal evils, personal spiritual forces, or other unnamed ills of our broken world. All of these represent real wrongs in our world. The larger question remains: how does one sort out what might be considered as demonic influences while also acknowledging that our world is fallen and broken in other ways as well?

Before moving forward, a caveat is necessary: recognizing the belief in spirits and the widespread phenomena of spirit possession containing analogous characteristics does not alone assuage the concerns of every skeptic. That was never the goal of this research. Rather, one primary goal of this research is to hear multicultural voices speak and consider the potential reality of the plethora of experiences along with the voices they represent. When this is done, Westerners have an opportunity to see the NT accounts of possession and exorcism through global eyes and witness that what has been characterized as an ancient Other is a modern reality for many people around the world. Additionally, I suggest that a helpful avenue for each stream would be to grapple with the categories of characteristics of demonization that have been explored in this monograph. While each stream seemingly has its own list of "symptoms" of demonization, a biblically informed list might help to prioritize characteristics that are found cross-culturally.

Imagine yourself sitting at a table and discussing any one of the stories that have been told in this monograph, whether biblical or modern. Next, imagine that each seat at the table represents an interpretive position. The seats could be named sociology, psychology, medicine, and spirituality, just to name a few. For far too long, because of the impact of the Enlightenment and the bent of rationalism, the only seats allowed at the table belonged to scientifically geared disciplines. These disciplines seemingly could disprove the reality of any spirits because they were not observable. This has caused the silencing of the multicultural perspective, which has now been carefully observed and highlighted by anthropologists in a wide variety of cultural expressions. Even if the observed experiences and testimonies of modern anthropological works do not convince one of the reality of spirits, the weight of testimony and the analogy to the NT calls for a seat at the interpretive table. To dismiss the experiences of so many is to relegate their perspectives without careful consideration of widespread, cross-cultural eyewitness testimonies. In essence, the Western academy has much to learn from a multicultural approach to this topic.

Basic Biblical Guidelines for Praxis

As Ben Witherington alluded to in the foreword to this monograph, C. S. Lewis' analysis is still very fitting for the Western Christian perspective. It is worth quoting in full.

> There are two equal and opposite errors into which our race can fall about the devils. One is to disbelieve their existence. The other is to believe, and to feel an excessive and unhealthy interest in them. They themselves are equally pleased by both errors and hail a materialist or a magician with the same delight.[51]

This research, while prioritizing and bringing forward a plethora of experiences, intends to invite Western readers to see through a multicultural lens. This lens optimistically broadens our perspective and may even cause some of us to re-evaluate some biases and starting points.

However, the above research needs to be weighed carefully so as not to overemphasize or overprioritize the demonic in one's theological perspective. A few checkpoints are necessary when considering theological frameworks. First of all, the Synoptics and Acts do not provide a demonological handbook or systematized approach, giving step-by-step guidelines for exorcism. The Synoptics and Acts do not largely explain how persons became demonized and much mystery remains. Rather, the texts we have analyzed have a much larger focus on Christology. The text's priority is to reveal who Jesus is and the force of victory that his Kingdom brings with it. Secondarily, Jesus does not seek out demons or create SWAT teams that hunt for evil and seek to destroy it. Rather, Jesus encounters the demonic while carrying forward his ministry; this is a reminder that Christians are not asked to seek out those who are demonized. In essence, Jesus' ministry is one that reminds us not to overemphasize or build a theology of demonization that is larger than our theologies of Christology, Pneumatology, or the Kingdom of God.

Embedded in the Synoptics and Acts is also the reminder that there is another kingdom at work. For the first Christians, this kingdom is the kingdom of Satan and his evil minions that seek to lead the people of God into deception and have real power to harm. The reality of spirits is a widespread, cross-cultural phenomenon, as we have encountered in the pages above. Further, even in interreligious perspectives, characteristics of possession were analogous. This research is a reminder that many in the world today encounter experiences that allow them to read the possession and exorcism stories in the Synoptics and Acts with lenses that are akin to what the Jewish and earliest

---

[51] C. S. Lewis, *The Screwtape Letters: Letters from a Senior to a Junior Devil* (Glasgow: HarperCollins UK, 2009), 8.

Christians knew, witnessed, and experienced. In summary, grappling with this evidence is not always easy. At times it is genuinely disturbing. However, hearing the multicultural perspectives along with the ancient Jewish and Christian ones is helpful in seeing the texts of the Synoptics and Acts through new lenses. Jesus the historical exorcist is seen with greater contextual clarity as exorcising real spirits from humans who were in desperate need of spiritual help. Both ancient contexts and modern contexts maintain a diachronic presence of such experiences. What used to be thought of as an ancient Other can be found to be a modern reality if multicultural voices are allowed at the interpretive table. Perhaps this is the way forward, with each voice given an opportunity to speak into the complexities that are present in the conversation. Surely—and it is my hope that this is the case—there are many more conversations that will result from this research.

Bibliography

Achtemeier, Paul J. "Miracles and the Historical Jesus: A Study of Mark 9:14–29." *CBQ* 37.4 (1975): 471–91.

Acolatse, Esther E. *Powers, Principalities, and the Spirit: Biblical Realism in Africa and the West*. Grand Rapids: Eerdmans, 2018.

Ådna, Jostein. "The Encounter of Jesus with the Gerasene Demoniac." Pages 279–301 in *Authenticating the Activities of Jesus*. Edited by Bruce Chilton and Craig A. Evans. Leiden: Brill, 2002.

Al-Ashqar, Umar Sulaiman. *The World of the Jinn and Devils*. Translated by Jamaah al-Din M. Zarabozo. Boulder, Colo.: Al-Basheer, 1998.

Alkire, William H. "The Traditional Classification and Treatment of Illness on Woleai and Lamotrek in the Caroline Islands, Micronesia." *Culture* 2.1 (1982): 29–41.

Ally, Yaseen, and Sumaya Laher. "South African Muslim Faith Healers Perceptions of Mental Illness: Understanding Aetiology and Treatment." *Journal of Religion and Health* 47.1 (2008): 45–56.

Alonso, Leonardo, and William D. Jeffrey. "Mental Illness Complicated by the Santeria Belief in Spirit Possession." *Hospital and Community Psychiatry* 39.11 (1988): 1188–91.

Amorth, Gabriele. *An Exorcist Tells His Story*. San Francisco: Ignatius, 2002.

Anderson, Allan. "Exorcism and Conversion to African Pentecostalism." *Exchange* 35.1 (2006): 116–33.

———. *An Introduction to Pentecostalism*. 2nd ed. Cambridge: Cambridge University Press, 2013.

Anderson, Neil. *The Bondage Breaker*. Eugene, Ore.: Harvest House, 2000.

Annen, Franz. *Heil für die Heiden: Zur Bedeutung und Geschichte der Tradition vom besessenen Gerasener*. FTS 20. Frankfurt am Main: Joseph Knecht, 1976.

Appell, George N., and Laura W. R. Appell. "To Converse with the Gods: The Rungus *Bobolizan*—Spirit Medium and Priestess." Pages 3–54 in *The Seen and the Unseen: Shamanism, Mediumship and Possession in Borneo*. Edited by Robert L. Winzeler. Borneo Research Council Monograph Series 2. Williamsburg, Va.: Borneo Research Council, 1993.

———. "To Do Battle with the Spirits: Bulusu' Spirit Mediums." Pages 55–100 in *The Seen and the Unseen: Shamanism, Mediumship and Possession in Borneo*. Edited by Robert L. Winzeler. Borneo Research Council Monograph Series 2. Williamsburg, Va.: Borneo Research Council, 1993.

Arbman, Ernst. *Ecstasy or Religious Trance: In the Experience of the Ecstatics and from the Psychological Point of View*. 3 vols. Stockholm: Bokförlaget, 1963.

Arnott, Geoffrey. "Nêchung: A Modern Parallel to the Delphic Oracle?" *Greece and Rome* 26 (1989): 152–57.

Ashton, John. *The Religion of Paul the Apostle*. New Haven: Yale University Press, 2000.

Ashy, Majed A. "Health and Illness from an Islamic Perspective." *Journal of Religion and Health* 38.3 (1999): 241–57.

Aslam, Maleeha. "Pakistan." Pages 271–75 in *Spirit Possession around the World: Possession, Communion, and Demon Expulsion across Cultures*. Edited by Joseph Laycock. Santa Barbara, Calif.: ABC-CLIO, 2015.

Aune, David E. *Prophecy in Early Christianity and the Ancient Mediterranean World*. Grand Rapids: Eerdmans, 1983.

Azaunce, Miriam. "Is It Schizophrenia or Spirit Possession?" *Journal of Social Distress and the Homeless* 4.3 (1995): 255–63.

Baddeley, Alan D., Andrew Thornton, Siew Eng Chua, and Peter McKenna. "Schizophrenic Delusions and the Construction of Autobiographical Memory." Pages 384–428 in *Remembering Our Past: Studies in Autobiographical Memory*. Edited by David C. Rubin. Cambridge: Cambridge University Press, 1996.

Bannerman-Richter, Gabriel. *The Practice of Witchcraft in Ghana*. Elk Grove, Calif.: Gabari, 1982.

Barr, James. "The Meaning of 'Mythology' in Relation to the Old Testament." *VT* 9.1 (1959): 1–10.

Barrett, Robert J. "Performance, Effectiveness and the Iban *Manang*." Pages 235–79 in *The Seen and the Unseen: Shamanism, Mediumship and Possession in Borneo*. Edited by Robert L. Winzeler. Borneo Research Council Monograph Series 2. Williamsburg, Va.: Borneo Research Council, 1993.

Barrett-Lennard, R. J. S. *Christian Healing after the New Testament: Some Approaches to Illness in the Second, Third and Fourth Centuries*. New York: University Press of America, 1994.

Bauckham, Richard J. "In Response to My Respondents: *Jesus and the Eyewitnesses* in Review." *JSHJ* 6.2 (2008): 225–53.

———. *Jesus and the Eyewitnesses: The Gospels as Eyewitness Testimony*. Grand Rapids: Eerdmans, 2006.

Bazzana, Giovanni B. *Having the Spirit of Christ: Spirit Possession and Exorcism in the Early Christ Groups*. New Haven: Yale University Press, 2020.

Beattie, John. *Other Cultures: Aims, Methods and Achievements in Social Anthropology*. New York: Free Press, 1964.

Beauvoir, Max-G. "Herbs and Energy: The Holistic Medical System of the Haitian People." Pages 112–33 in *Haitian Vodou: Spirit, Myth, and Reality*. Edited by Patrick Bellegarde-Smith and Claudine Michel. Bloomington: Indiana University Press, 2006.

Becker, Eve-Marie. *Das Markus-Evangelium im Rahmen antiker Historiographie*. Tübingen: Mohr Siebeck, 2006.

Beilby, James K., and Paul Rhodes Eddy, eds. *Understanding Spiritual Warfare: Four Views*. Grand Rapids: Baker, 2012.

Bell, Richard H. *Deliver Us from Evil: Interpreting the Redemption from the Power of Satan in New Testament Theology*. WUNT 216. Tübingen: Mohr Siebeck, 2007.

Bellezza, John Vincent. *Spirit-mediums, Sacred Mountains, and Related Bon Textual Traditions in Upper Tibet: Calling Down the Gods*. Leiden: Brill, 2005.

Bennett, Clinton. *In Search of the Sacred: Anthropology and the Study of Religions*. London: Cassell, 1996.

Berger, Laurent. "Learning Possession Trance and Evaluating Oracles' Truthfulness in Jinè Cults of Bèlèdugu (Mali)." *Journal of Cognition and Culture* 12.3 (2012): 163–81.

Bernstein, Jay. "The Shaman's Destiny: Symptoms, Affliction, and the Reinterpretation of Illness among the Taman." Pages 171–206 in *The Seen and the Unseen: Shamanism, Mediumship and Possession in Borneo*. Edited by Robert L. Winzeler. Borneo Research Council Monograph Series 2. Williamsburg, Va.: Borneo Research Council, 1993.

Bessmer, Fremont. *Horses, Musicians, and Gods: The Hausa Cult of Possession Trance*. South Hadley, Mass.: Bergen and Garvey, 1983.

Best, Ernest. "Exorcism in the New Testament and Today." *Biblical Theology* 27 (1977): 1–9.

Betty, Stafford. "The Growing Evidence for 'Demonic Possession': What Should Psychiatry's Response Be?" *Journal of Religion and Health* 44.1 (2005): 13–30.

Bhayro, Siam, and Catherine Rider, eds. *Demons and Illness from Antiquity to the Early-Modern Period*. Leiden: Brill, 2017.

Birtalan, Ágnes. "Mongolia." Pages 237–42 in *Spirit Possession around the World: Possession, Communion, and Demon Expulsion across Cultures*. Edited by Joseph Laycock. Santa Barbara, Calif.: ABC-CLIO, 2015.

Birtalan, Ágnes, János Sipos, and J. Coloo. "'Talking to the *Ongons*': The Invocation Text and Music of a Darkhad Shaman." *Shaman* 12.1–2 (2004): 25–62.

Blacker, Carmen. *The Catalpa Bow: A Study in Shamanistic Practices in Japan*. New York: Routledge Curzon, 1999.

Blai, Adam C. "Exorcism and the Church: Through Priests, the Church Has the Power to Battle Demons." *The Priest* 73.8 (2017): 16–19.

———. *Hauntings, Possessions, and Exorcisms*. Steubenville, Ohio: Emmaus Road, 2017.

Blain, Jenny. *Nine Worlds of Seid-Magic: Ecstasy and Neo-shamanism in North European Paganism*. London: Routledge, 2001.

Blessing, Kamila. "Healing in the Gospels: The Essential Credentials." Pages 186–207 in *Religious and Spiritual Events*. Vol. 1 of *Miracles: God, Science, and Psychology in the Paranormal*. Edited by J. Harold Ellens. Westport, Conn.: Praeger, 2008.

Bloomer, Kristin C. *Possessed by the Virgin: Hinduism, Roman Catholicism, and Marian Possession in South India*. New York: Oxford University Press, 2018.

Bock, Darrell L. *Luke 1:1–9:50*. BECNT. Grand Rapids: Baker, 1994.

———. *Luke 9:51–24:53*. BECNT. Grand Rapids: Baker, 1994.

Boddy, Janice. "Spirit Possession Revisited: Beyond Instrumentality." *Annual Review of Anthropology* 23 (1994): 407–34.

———. "Spirits and Selves in Northern Sudan: The Cultural Therapeutics of Possession and Trance." *American Ethnologist* 15.1 (1988): 4–27.

———. *Wombs and Alien Spirits: Women, Men, and the Zar Cult in Northern Sudan*. Madison: University of Wisconsin Press, 1989.

Bond, George Clement. "Ancestors and Witches." Pages 131–57 in *Witchcraft Dialogues: Anthropological and Philosophical Exchanges*. Edited by George Clement Bond and Diane M. Ciekawy. Athens: Ohio University Press, 2001.

Bond, George Clement, and Diane M. Ciekawy. "Introduction: Contested Domains in the Dialogues of 'Witchcraft.'" Pages 1–38 in *Witchcraft Dialogues: Anthropological and Philosophical Exchanges*. Edited by George Clement Bond and Diane M. Ciekawy. Athens: Ohio University Press, 2001.

Bond, Helen K. *Mark: The First Biography of Jesus*. Grand Rapids: Eerdmans, 2020.

Bonner, Campbell. "The Technique of Exorcism." *HTR* 36.1 (1943): 39–49.

Borg, Marcus J. *Jesus: A New Vision: Spirit, Culture, and the Life of Discipleship*. San Francisco: Harper & Row, 1987.

Bourguignon, Erika, ed. *Possession*. San Francisco: Chandler and Sharp, 1976.

———, ed. *Religion, Altered States of Consciousness, and Social Change*. Columbus: Ohio State University Press, 1973.

———. "The Self, the Behavioral Environment and the Theory of Spirit Possession." Pages 39–60 in *Context and Meaning in Cultural Anthropology*. Edited by Melford E. Spiro. New York: Free Press, 1965.

———. "World Distribution and Patterns of Possession States." Pages 340–56 in *Religion, Altered States of Consciousness, and Social Change*. Edited by Erika Bourguignon. Columbus: Ohio State University Press, 1973.

———. *A World of Women: Anthropological Studies of Women in Societies of the World*. New York: Praeger, 1980.

Bovon, François. *Luke 1: A Commentary on the Gospel of Luke 1:1–9:50*. Translated by Christine M. Thomas. Edited by Helmut Koester. Minneapolis: Fortress, 2002.

Bowie, Fiona. *The Anthropology of Religion: An Introduction*. Oxford: Oxford University Press, 2000.

Bradnick, David. *Evil, Spirits, and Possession: An Emergentist Theology of the Demonic*. Global Pentecostal and Charismatic Studies 25. Leiden: Brill, 2017.

Bradshaw, William Brandt. "Demonology in Hebrew and Jewish Traditions: A Study in New Testament Origins." PhD diss., University of St Andrews, 1963.

Brenk, Frederick E. "The Exorcism at Philippi in Acts 16:11–40: Divine Possession or Diabolical Inspiration." *Filologia Neotestamentaria* 13.25–26 (2000): 3–21.

Brown, Diana DeGroat. *Umbanda Religion and Politics in Urban Brazil*. Ann Arbor, Mich.: UMI Research Press, 1986.

Brown, Michael E. *The Channeling Zone: American Spirituality in an Anxious Age*. Cambridge, Mass.: Harvard University Press, 1997.

Bruce, F. F. *The Book of the Acts*. NICNT. Grand Rapids: Eerdmans, 1988.

Budson, A. E., J. S. Simons, J. D. Waring, A. L. Sullivan, T. Hussoin, and D. L. Schacter. "Memory for the September 11, 2001, Terrorist Attacks One Year Later in Patients with Alzheimer's Disease, Patients with Mild Cognitive Impairment, and Healthy Older Adults." *Cortex* 43.7 (2007): 875–88.

Bultmann, Rudolf. "The Gospels (Form)." Translated by R. A. Wilson. Pages 86–92 in *Twentieth Century Theology in the Making*. Edited by J. Pelikan. Vol. 1. London: Fontana, 1969–1970.

———. *The History of the Synoptic Tradition*. Translated by John Marsh. Oxford: Blackwell, 1963.

———. "New Testament and Mythology." Pages 1–45 in *Kerygma and Myth: A Theological Debate*. Edited by Hans-Werner Bartsch. Translated by Reginald H. Fuller. London: SPCK, 1972.

Burley, Mikel. "Dance of the *Deodhās*: Divine Possession, Blood Sacrifice and the Grotesque Body in the Assamese Goddess Worship." *Religions of South Asia* 12.2 (2018): 207–33.

Burridge, Kenelm. *New Heaven, New Earth: A Study of Millenarian Activities*. Oxford: Blackwell, 1969.

Burridge, Richard A. *What Are the Gospels? A Comparison with Graeco-Roman Biography*. 2nd ed. Grand Rapids: Eerdmans, 2005.

Buyandelger, Manduhai. *Tragic Spirits: Shamanism, Memory, and Gender in Contemporary Mongolia*. Chicago: University of Chicago Press, 2013.

Cadbury, Henry J. *The Book of Acts in History*. London: Adam & Charles Black, 1955.

Cantelmi, Tonino, Silvestro Paluzzi, and Ermes Luparia, eds. *Gli dei morti sono diventati malattie*. Cassino, Italy: EDT, 2002.

Carroll, John T. *Luke: A Commentary*. NTL. Louisville: Westminster John Knox, 2012.

Casey, Maurice. "The Healing of the Paralytic (Mark 2:1–12)." Pages 144–67 in *The Solution to the "Son of Man" Problem*. LNTS 343. London: T&T Clark, 2007.

Caygill, Mary, and Philip Culbertson. "Constructing Identity and Theology in the World of Samoan and Tongan Spirits." Pages 25–60 in *Spirit Possession, Theology, and Identity: A Pacific Exploration*. Edited by Elaine M. Wainwright with Philip Culbertson and Susan Smith. Hindmarsh, Australia: ATF Press, 2010.

Chan, Margaret. *Ritual Is Theatre, Theatre Is Ritual: Tang-Ki Chinese Spirit Medium Worship*. Singapore: Wee Kim Wee Centre and SNP, 2009.

Chevannes, Barry. "Rastafari and Other African-Caribbean Worldviews." Pages 207–26 in *Perspectives on the Caribbean: A Reader in Culture, History and Representation*. Edited by Philip W. Scher. Chichester, UK: Wiley-Blackwell, 2010.

Chilton, Bruce. "An Exorcism of History: Mark 1:21–28." Pages 215–45 in *Authenticating the Activities of Jesus*. Edited by Bruce Chilton and Craig A. Evans. Leiden: Brill, 2002.

Chiu, S. N. "Historical, Religious, and Medical Perspectives of Possession Phenomenon." *Hong Kong Journal of Psychiatry* 10.1 (2000): 14–18.

Ciekawy, Diane M. "*Utsai* as Ethical Discourse." Pages 158–89 in *Witchcraft Dialogues: Anthropological and Philosophical Exchanges*. Edited by George Clement Bond and Diane M. Ciekawy. Athens: Ohio University Press, 2001.

Climenhaga, Alison Fitchett. "Pursuing Transformation: Healing, Deliverance, and Discourses of Development among Catholics in Uganda." *Mission Studies* 35.2 (2018): 204–24.

Cohen, Emma. *The Chinese Vegetarian Festival in Phuket: Religion, Ethnicity and Tourism on a Southern Island*. Bangkok: White Lotus Press, 2001.

———. "What Is Spirit Possession? Defining, Comparing, and Explaining Two Possession Forms." *Ethnos* 73.1 (2008): 101–26.

Collins, Adela Yarbro. *Is Mark's Gospel a Life of Jesus? The Question of Genre*. Milwaukee: Marquette University Press, 1990.

———. *Mark: A Commentary*. Minneapolis: Fortress, 2007.

Collins, James M. *Exorcism and Deliverance Ministry in the Twentieth Century*. Eugene, Ore.: Wipf and Stock, 2009.

Colson, Elizabeth. "Spirit Possession among the Tonga of Zambia." Pages 69–103 in *Spirit Mediumship and Society in Africa*. Edited by John Beattie and John Middleton. London: Routledge and Kegan Paul, 1969.

Comaroff, Jean. *Body of Power, Spirit of Resistance: The Culture and History of a South African People*. Chicago: University of Chicago Press, 1985.

———. "Healing and Cultural Transformation: The Tswana of Southern Africa." *Social Science and Medicine* 15B.3 (1981): 367–78.

Conzelmann, Hans. *Acts of the Apostles*. Translated by James Limburg, A. Thomas Kraabel, and Donald H. Juel. Edited by Eldon Jay Epp with Christopher R. Matthews. Philadelphia: Fortress, 1987.

Coons, Philip. "The Differential Diagnoses of Possession States." *Dissociation* 6.4 (1993): 213–21.

Côté, Daniel. "Narrative Reconstruction of Spirit Possession Experience: The Double Hermeneutics of Gaddis Religious Specialties in Western Himalaya (India)." E-paper, University of Sherbrooke. https://www.nomadit.co.uk/conference/easa08/paper/2447.

Craffert, Pieter F. "Medical Anthropology as an Antidote for Ethnocentrism in Jesus Research? Putting the Illness-Disease Distinction into Perspective." *HTS Teologiese Studies/Theological Studies* 67.1 (2011): 1–14.

Crapanzano, Vincent. "Introduction." Pages 1–40 in *Case Studies in Spirit Possession*. Edited by Vincent Crapanzano and Vivian Garrison. New York: Wiley, 1977.

———. "Mohammed and Dawia: Possession in Morocco." Pages 141–76 in *Case Studies in Spirit Possession*. Edited by Vincent Crapanzano and Vivian Garrison. New York: Wiley, 1977.

———. "Spirit Possession." Pages 12–19 in *Encyclopedia of Religion*. Edited by Mircea Eliade. Vol. 14. Chicago: Macmillan, 1987.

Crapanzano, Vincent, and Vivian Garrison, eds. *Case Studies in Spirit Possession*. New York: Wiley, 1977.

Crooks, Mark. "On the Psychology of Demon Possession: The Occult Personality." *Journal of Mind and Behavior* 39.4 (2018): 257–344.

Crossan, John Dominic. *The Historical Jesus: The Life of a Mediterranean Jewish Peasant*. San Francisco: HarperSanFrancisco, 1991.

———. *Jesus: A Revolutionary Biography*. San Francisco: HarperSanFrancisco, 1994.

Csordas, Thomas J. "The Rhetoric of Transformation in Ritual Healing." *Culture, Medicine, and Psychiatry* 7.4 (1983): 333–75.

Csordas Thomas J., and Arthur Kleinman, "The Therapeutic Process." Pages 11–25 in *Medical Anthropology: Contemporary Theory and Method*. Edited by Thomas M. Johnson and Carolyn F. Sargent. Westport, Conn.: Praeger, 1990.

Cuneo, Michael W. *American Exorcism: Expelling Demons in the Land of Plenty*. London: Bantam, 2001.

Daneel, M. L. "Exorcism as a Means of Combating Wizardry: Liberation or Enslavement?" *Missionalia* 18.1 (1990): 220–47.

Danforth, Loring M. *Firewalking and Religious Healing: The Anastenaria of Greece and the American Firewalking Movement*. Princeton: Princeton University Press, 1985.

Danker, Frederick W. *Jesus and the New Age according to St. Luke: A Commentary on the Third Gospel*. St. Louis: Clayton, 1972.

Davies, Stevan L. *Jesus the Healer: Possession, Trance, and the Origins of Christianity*. New York: Continuum, 1995.

Davis, Winston. *Dojo: Magic and Exorcism in Modern Japan*. Stanford: Stanford University Press, 1980.

Dawson, Andrew. "Brazil." Pages 49–52 in *Spirit Possession around the World: Possession, Communion, and Demon Expulsion across Cultures*. Edited by Joseph Laycock. Santa Barbara, Calif.: ABC-CLIO, 2015.

———. *New Era—New Religions: Religious Transformation in Contemporary Brazil*. Farnham, UK: Ashgate, 2007.

———. *Santo Daime: A New World Religion*. London: Bloomsbury, 2013.

Dawson, John. "Urbanization and Mental Health in a West African Community." Pages 305–42 in *Magic, Faith, and Healing: Studies in Primitive Psychiatry Today*. Edited by Ari Kiev. New York: Free Press, 1964.

Dean, Kenneth. "Field Notes on Two Taoist *jiao* Observed in Zhangzhou in December 1985." *Cahiers d'Extrême-Asie* 2 (1986): 191–210.

DeBernardi, Jean. *The Way That Lives in the Heart: Chinese Popular Religion and Spirit Mediums in Penang, Malaysia*. Stanford: Stanford University Press, 2006.

Dibelius, Martin. *From Tradition to Gospel*. Edited by William Barclay. Translated by Bertram Lee Woolf. Cambridge: James Clarke, 1971.

Dieste, Josep Lluís Mateo. "'Spirits Are Like Microbes': Islamic Revival and the Definition of Morality in Moroccan Exorcism." *Contemporary Islam* 9.1 (2015): 45–63.

Dihle, Albrecht. "The Gospels as Greek Biography." Pages 361–86 in *The Gospel and the Gospels*. Edited by Peter Stuhlmacher. Grand Rapids: Eerdmans, 1991.

Do, Thien. *Vietnamese Supernaturalism: Views from the Southern Region*. New York: Routledge Curzon, 2003.

Douglas, Mary. *Purity and Danger: An Analysis of Concepts of Pollution and Taboo*. London: Routledge, 1966.

Drozdow-St Christian, Douglass. *Elusive Fragments: Making Power, Propriety, and Health in Samoa*. Durham, N.C.: Carolina Academic Press, 2002.

Duffey, John. *Lessons Learned: The Anneliese Exorcism: The Implementation of a Safe and Thorough Examination, Determination, and Exorcism of Demonic Possession*. Eugene, Ore.: Wipf and Stock, 2011.

Dunn, James D. G. "Altering the Default Setting: Re-envisaging the Early Transmissions of the Jesus Tradition." *NTS* 49 (2003): 144–45.

———. *Jesus and the Spirit: A Study of the Religious and Charismatic Experience of Jesus and the First Christians as Reflected in the New Testament*. London: SCM Press, 1975.

———. *Jesus Remembered*. Grand Rapids: Eerdmans, 2003.

Dunn, James D. G., and Graham H. Twelftree. "Demon-Possession and Exorcism in the New Testament." *Churchman* 94.3 (1980): 210–25.

Durand, Maurice. *Technique et Panthéon des Médiums Vietnamiens (Dong)*. Vol. 45. Paris: École Française d'Extrême-Orient, 1959.

Eddy, Paul Rhodes, and Gregory A. Boyd. *The Jesus Legend: A Case for the Historical Reliability of the Synoptic Jesus Tradition*. Grand Rapids: Baker, 2007.

Edwards, Felicity S. "Amafufunyana Spirit Possession: Treatment and Interpretation." Pages 207–25 in *Afro-Christian Religion and Healing in Southern Africa*. Edited by G. C. Oosthuizen, S. D. Edwards, W. H. Wessels, and I. Hexham. African Studies 8. Lewiston, N.Y.: Mellen, 1989.

———. "Healing and Transculturation in Xhosa Zionist Practice." *Culture, Medicine, and Psychiatry* 7.2 (1983): 177–98.

Edwards, James R. *The Gospel according to Luke*. Pillar New Testament Commentary. Grand Rapids: Eerdmans, 2015.

Ehrman, Bart D. *Jesus before the Gospels: How the Earliest Christians Remembered, Changed, and Invented Their Stories of the Savior*. New York: HarperOne, 2016.

Ekvall, Robert. *Religious Observances in Tibet: Patterns and Functions*. Chicago: University of Chicago Press, 1964.

El Hadidi, Hager. *Zar: Spirit Possession, Music, and Healing Rituals in Egypt*. Cairo: American University in Cairo Press, 2016.

Eliade, Mircea. *Shamanism: Archaic Techniques of Ecstasy*. Translated by Willard R. Trask. Bollingen Series LXXVI. Princeton: Princeton University Press, 1964.

Ellis, E. Earle. *The Gospel of Luke*. Grand Rapids: Eerdmans, 1974.

El-Zein, Amira. *Islam, Arabs, and the Intelligent World of the Jinn*. Syracuse, N.Y.: Syracuse University Press, 2009.

Ember, Carol R., and Christina Carolus. "Altered States of Consciousness." In *Explaining Human Culture*. Edited by Carol R. Ember. eHRAF, 2017. https://hraf.yale.edu/ehc/assets/summaries/pdfs/altered-states-of-consciousness.pdf.

Espirito Santo, Diana. "'Who Else Is in the Drawer?' Trauma, Personhood and Prophylaxis among Cuban Scientific Spiritists." *Anthropology and Medicine* 17.3 (2010): 249–59.

Evans, C. F. *Saint Luke*. TPINTC. London: SCM Press, 1990.

Evans, Craig A. *Matthew*. New Cambridge Bible Commentary. Cambridge: Cambridge University Press, 2012.

Evans-Pritchard, Edward. *Witchcraft, Oracles and Magic among the Azande*. Oxford: Clarendon, 1937.

Eve, Eric. *The Jewish Context of Jesus' Miracles*. JSNTSup 231. London: Sheffield, 2002.

Fabisiak, Thomas. *The "Nocturnal Side of Science" in David Friedrich Strauss's Life of Jesus Critically Examined*. Atlanta: Society of Biblical Literature, 2015.

Fagen, Ruth S. "Phylacteries." In *The Anchor Yale Bible Dictionary*. Edited by David Noel Freeman, Gary A. Herrion, David F. Graf, John David Pleins, and Astrid B. Beck. Vol. 5. New York: Doubleday, 1992.

Ferguson, Everett. *Demonology of the Early Christian World*. New York: Mellen, 1984.

Fiddler, Richard C. "Spirit Possession as Exculpation, with Examples from the Sarawak Chinese." Pages 207–34 in *The Seen and the Unseen: Shamanism, Mediumship and Possession in Borneo*. Edited by Robert L. Winzeler. Borneo Research Council Monograph Series 2. Williamsburg, Va.: Borneo Research Council, 1993.

Field, Margaret J. "Spirit Possession in Ghana." Pages 3–13 in *Spirit Mediumship and Society in Africa*. Edited by John Beattie and John Middleton. New York: Africana, 1969.

Finkler, Kaja. *Spiritualist Healers in Mexico: Successes and Failures of Alternative Therapeutics*. South Hadley, Mass.: Bergin and Garvey, 1985.

Firth, Raymond. "Problem and Assumption in an Anthropological Study of Religion: Huxley Memorial Lecture 1959." *Journal of the Royal Anthropological Institute of Great Britain and Ireland* 89 (1964): 129–48. Reprinted in Firth, Raymond, *Essays on Social Organization and Values.* London School of Economics Monographs on Social Anthropology 28. London: Athlone Press, 1964.

———. "Ritual and Drama in Malay Spirit Mediumship." *Comparative Studies in Society and History* 9.2 (1967): 190–207.

Fischer, Ronald, and Sivaporn Tasananukorn. "Altered States of Consciousness, Spirit Mediums and Predictive Processing: A Cultural Cognition Model of Spirit Possession." *Journal of Consciousness Studies* 25.11–12 (2018): 179–203.

Fitzgerald, Dale K. "Prophetic Speech in Ga Spirit Mediumship." *Working Papers of the Language Behavior Laboratory* 30 (1970): 1–19.

Fitzmyer, Joseph A. *The Acts of the Apostles: A New Translation with Introduction and Commentary.* AYB 31. New York: Doubleday, 1998.

———. *The Gospel according to Luke I–IX: A New Translation with Introduction and Commentary.* AB 28. New York: Doubleday, 1964.

———. *The Gospel according to Luke X–XXIV.* AB 28a. Garden City, N.Y.: Doubleday, 1985.

Fjelstad, Karen, and Nguyen Thi Hien. *Spirits without Borders: Vietnamese Spirit Mediums in a Transnational Age.* New York: Palgrave Macmillan, 2011.

Flood, Gavin. *The Tantric Body: The Secret Tradition of Hindu Religion.* London: I. B. Tauris, 2006.

Fontenrose, Joseph E. *The Delphic Oracle: Its Response and Operations.* Berkeley: University of California Press, 1978.

Fortea, Jose Antonio, and Lawrence E. U. LeBlanc. *Anneliese Michel: A True Story of a Case of Demonic Possession: Germany—1976.* Independently published, 2019.

Foschi, Renato, Marco Innamorati, and Ruggero Taradel. "'A Disease of Our Time': The Catholic Church's Condemnation and Absolution of Psychoanalysis (1924–1975)." *Journal of the History of Behavioral Sciences* 54.2 (2018): 85–100.

Fox, J. Robin. "Witchcraft and Clanship." Pages 174–200 in *Magic, Faith, and Healing: Studies in Primitive Psychiatry Today.* Edited by Ari Kiev. New York: Free Press, 1964.

France, R. T. *Gospel of Matthew.* NICNT. Grand Rapids: Eerdmans, 2007.

Frazer, James George. *The Golden Bough: A Study in Magic and Religion.* New York: MacMillan, 1922.

Freston, Paul. "Breve História do Pentecostalismo Brasileiro." Pages 35–162 in *Nem Anjos, Nem Demônios: Interpretações Sociologicas Do Pentecostalismo.* By Alberto Antoniazzi et al. Petrópolis, Brazil: Editora Vozes, 1994.

Frimpong, Emmanuel Kwabena. "Mark and Spirit Possession in an African Context." PhD diss., University of Glasgow, 2006.

Fröhlich, Ida. "Demons and Illness in Second Temple Judaism: Theory and Practice." Pages 81–96 in *Demons and Illness from Antiquity to the Early-Modern Period*. Edited by Siam Bhayro and Catherine Rider. Leiden: Brill, 2017.

Fuchs, Stephen. "Magic Healing Techniques among the Balahis in Central India." Pages 121–38 in *Magic, Faith, and Healing: Studies in Primitive Psychiatry Today*. Edited by Ari Kiev. New York: Free Press, 1964.

Funk, Robert W., and Roy W. Hoover. *The Five Gospels: What Did Jesus Really Say? The Search for the Authentic Words of Jesus*. Sonoma, Calif.: Polebridge, 1993.

Gager, John, ed. *Curse Tablets and Binding Spells from the Ancient World*. New York: Oxford University Press, 1992.

Gammelin, Lotta. "Gendered Narratives of Illness and Healing: Experiences of Spirit Possession in a Charismatic Church Community in Tanzania." Pages 314–34 in *Faith in African Lived Christianity: Bridging Anthropological and Theological Perspectives*. Edited by Karen Lauterbach and Mika Vähäkangas. Leiden: Brill, 2020.

Gardiner, Ken. *The Reluctant Exorcist: A Biblical Approach in an Age of Scepticism*. 2nd ed. Watford: Instant Apostle, 2015.

Garland, David E. *Luke*. Zondervan Exegetical Commentary on the New Testament. Grand Rapids: Zondervan, 2011.

Garnsey, Peter, and Richard Saller. *The Roman Empire: Economy, Society and Culture*. Berkeley: University of California Press, 1987.

Garrard, David J. "Witchcraft and Deliverance: An Exaggerated Theme in Pentecostal Churches in Central Africa." *Journal of the European Pentecostal Theological Association* 37.1 (2017): 52–67.

Garrison, Vivian. "The 'Puerto Rican Syndrome' in Psychiatry and *Espiritismo*." Pages 383–449 in *Case Studies in Spirit Possession*. Edited by Vincent Crapanzano and Vivian Garrison. New York: Wiley, 1977.

Geertz, Clifford. *The Interpretation of Cultures*. New York: Basic Books, 1973.

Geldenhuys, Norval. *The Gospel of Luke*. NICNT. Grand Rapids: Eerdmans, 1951.

Gelfand, Michael. "Psychiatric Disorders as Recognized by the Shona." Pages 156–73 in *Magic, Faith, and Healing: Studies in Primitive Psychiatry Today*. Edited by Ari Kiev. New York: Free Press, 1964.

Geller, Markham J. "Freud and Mesopotamian Magic." Pages 49–55 in *Mesopotamian Magic: Textual, Historical, and Interpretative Perspectives*. Edited by Tzvi Abusch and Karel van der Toorn. Groningen: Styx, 1999.

Giel, R., Y. Gezahegn, and J. N. van Luijk. "Faith-Healing and Spirit Possession in Ghion, Ethiopia." *Social Science and Medicine* 2.1 (1967): 63–79.

Gifford, Paul. *Christianity, Development and Modernity in Africa*. New York: Oxford University Press, 2016.

Giles, Linda L. "Possession Cults on the Swahili Coast: A Re-examination of Theories of Marginality." *Africa* 57.2 (1987): 234–58.

Gluckman, Laurie K. "Clinical Experience with Samoans in Aukland." *Australian and New Zealand Journal of Psychiatry* 11.2 (1997): 101–7.

Godet, F. *A Commentary on the Gospel of St. Luke*. Translated by E. W. Shalders and M. D. Cusin. Vol. 1. Edinburgh: T&T Clark, 1875.

Goodman, Felicitas. *How about Demons? Possession and Exorcism in the Modern World*. Bloomington: Indiana University Press, 1998.

———. *The Exorcism of Anneliese Michel*. Eugene, Ore.: Resource Publications, 1981.

———. *Speaking in Tongues: A Cross-cultural Study of Glossolalia*. Chicago: University of Chicago Press, 1972.

Goswami, M. C. "An Annual Shamanistic Dance (Deodha Nach) at Kamakhya, Assam." *Journal of the University of Gauhati (Science)* 11.2 (1960): 37–58.

Grayston, Kenneth. "Exorcism in the New Testament." *Epworth Review* 2 (1975): 90–94.

Green, Joel B. *The Gospel of Luke*. NICNT. Grand Rapids: Baker, 1997.

———. "Jesus and a Daughter of Abraham (Luke 13:10–17): Test Case for a Lukan Perspective on Jesus' Miracles." *CBQ* 51.4 (1989): 643–54.

Greenfield, Sidney M. *Spirits with Scalpels: The Cultural Biology of Religious Healing in Brazil*. Walnut Creek, Calif.: Left Coast Press, 2008.

Greenwood, Bernard. "Cold or Spirits? Choice and Ambiguity in Morocco's Pluralistic Medical System." *Social Science Medicine* 15B (1981): 219–35.

Greenwood, Nan, Feryad Hussain, Tom Burns, and Frances Raphael. "Asian In-Patient and Carer Views of Mental Health Care." *Journal of Mental Health* 9.4 (2000): 397–408.

Greenwood, Susan. *The Anthropology of Magic*. Oxford: Berg, 2009.

Grisaru, Nimrod, Danny Budowski, and Eliezer Witzum. "Possession by the 'Zar' among Ethiopian Immigrants to Israel: Psychopathology or Culture-Bound Syndrome?" *Psychopathology* 30.4 (1997): 223–33.

Grundmann, Walter. *Das Evangelium nach Lukas*. Theologischer Handkommentar zum Neuen Testament 3. Berlin: Evangelische Verlagsanstalt, 1963.

Guijarro, Santiago. "The Politics of Exorcism: Jesus' Reaction to Negative Labels in the Beelzebul Controversy." Pages 159–74 in *The Social Setting of Jesus and the Gospels*. Edited by Wolfgang Stegemann, Bruce Malina, and Gerd Theissen. Minneapolis: Fortress, 2002.

Hägg, Thomas. *The Art of Biography in Antiquity*. Cambridge: Cambridge University Press, 2012.

Hagner, Donald A. *Matthew 14–28*. WBC 33b. Grand Rapids: Thomas Nelson, 1995.

Halapua, Winston. "A *Moana* Rhythm of Well-Being." Pages 91–112 in *Spirit Possession, Theology, and Identity: A Pacific Exploration*. Edited by Elaine M. Wainwright with Philip Culbertson and Susan Smith. Hindmarsh, Australia: ATF, 2010.

Halloy, Arnaud, and Vlad Naumescu. "Learning Spirit Possession: An Introduction." *Ethnos* 77.2 (2012): 155–76.

Hamel, Gildas. *Poverty and Charity in Roman Palestine, First Three Centuries C.E.* Near Eastern Studies 23. Berkeley: University of California Press, 1990.

Hamer, John. "Crisis, Moral Consensus, and the Wando Magano Movement among the Sadama of South-West Ethiopia." *Ethnology* 16.4 (1977): 399–413.

Hamer, John, and Irene Hamer. "Spirit Possession and Its Socio-psychological Implications among the Sidamo of South-West Ethiopia." *Ethnology* 5.4 (1966): 392–408.

Hamidović, David. "Illness and Healing through Spell and Incantation in the Dead Sea Scrolls." Pages 97–110 in *Demons and Illness from Antiquity to the Early-Modern Period*. Edited by Siam Bhayro and Catherine Rider. Leiden: Brill, 2017.

Hammond, Frank, and Ida Mae Hammond. *Pigs in the Parlor: A Practical Guide to Deliverance*. Kirkwood, Mo.: Impact, 1973.

Haque, Amber. "Religion and Mental Health: The Case of American Muslims." *Journal of Religion and Health* 41.1 (2004): 46–58.

Harrell, David Edwin, Jr. *All Things Are Possible: The Healing and Charismatic Revivals in Modern America*. Bloomington: Indiana University Press, 1975.

———. *Oral Roberts: An American Life*. Bloomington: Indiana University Press, 1985.

Havnevik, Hanna. "A Tibetan Female State Oracle." Pages 259–87 in *Religion and Secular Culture in Tibet: Tibetan Studies. Proceedings of the 9th Seminary of the International Association for Tibetan Studies*. Edited by Henz Blezer. Leiden: Brill, 2002.

Heiser, Michael S. *The Unseen Realm: Recovering the Supernatural Worldview of the Bible*. Bellingham, Wash.: Lexham, 2015.

Hendriksen, William. *Exposition of the Gospel according to Luke*. Grand Rapids: Baker, 1978.

Herskovits, Melville J. *Man and His Works: The Science of Cultural Anthropology*. New York: A. A. Knopf, 1948.

Hes, Jozef Ph. "The Yemenite Mori." Pages 364–83 in *Magic, Faith, and Healing: Studies in Primitive Psychiatry Today*. Edited by Ari Kiev. New York: Free Press, 1964.

Heth, William A. "Demonization Then and Now: How Contemporary Cases Fill in the Biblical Data." Paper presented at the Annual Meeting of the Evangelical Theological Society, 2006.

Hiebert, Paul. "The Flaw of the Excluded Middle." *Missiology* 10.1 (1982): 35–47.

Hobart, William Kirk. *The Medical Language of St. Luke*. Eugene, Ore.: Wipf and Stock, 2004. Original 1882.

Hollenbach, Paul W. "Jesus, Demoniacs, and Public Authorities: A Socio-historical Study." *JAAR* 49.4 (1981): 567–88.

Holm, Nils G. "Ecstasy Research in the Twentieth Century: An Introduction." Pages 7–26 in *Religious Ecstasy: Based on Papers Read at the Symposium on Religious Ecstasy Held at Åbo, Finland, on the 26th–28th of August 1981*. Edited by Nils G. Holm. Stockholm: Almqvist and Wiksell, 1982.

Honko, Lauri. *Krankheitsprojektile: Untersuchung über eine urtümliche Krankheitserklärung.* Folklore Fellow Communications 178. Helsinki: Academia Scientiarum Fennica, 1959.

Horsley, Richard A. *Archaeology, Society, and History in Galilee: The Social Context of Jesus and the Rabbis.* London: T&T Clark, 1996.

———. *Empowering the People: Jesus, Healing, and Exorcism.* Eugene, Ore.: Cascade, 2022.

———. "'My Name Is Legion': Spirit Possession and Exorcism in Roman Palestine." Pages 41–57 in *Inquiry into Religious Experience in Early Judaism and Christianity.* Edited by Frances Flannery, Colleen Shantz, and Rodney A. Werline. Vol. 1 of *Experientia.* Atlanta: Society of Biblical Literature, 2008.

Howard, J. Keir. *Disease and Healing in the New Testament: An Analysis and Interpretation.* Lanham, Md.: University Press of America, 2001.

Hunter, Archibald M. *The Work and Words of Jesus.* Philadelphia: Westminster; London: SCM Press, 1973.

Hunter, Jack. *Engaging the Anomalous: Collected Essays on Anthropology, the Paranormal, Mediumship and Extraordinary Experience.* Hove, UK: August Night, 2018.

Immanuel, Babu. *Acts of the Apostles: Exegetical and Contextual Commentary.* Indian Commentary on the New Testament. Minneapolis: Fortress, 2016.

Innamorati, Marco, Ruggero Taradel, and Renato Foschi. "Between Sacred and Profane: Possession, Psychotherapy, and the Catholic Church." *History of Psychology* 22.1 (2018): 1–16.

Islam, F., and R. A. Campbell. "'Satan Has Afflicted Me!': Jinn-Possession and Mental Illness in the Qur'an." *Journal of Religion and Health* 53.1 (2014): 229–43.

James, Montague Rhodes, ed. *Apocrypha anecdota: Second Series.* Cambridge: Cambridge University Press, 1897.

Jay, Sian E. "Canoes for the Spirits: Two Types of Spirit Mediumship in Central Kalimantan." Pages 151–70 in *The Seen and the Unseen: Shamanism, Mediumship and Possession in Borneo.* Borneo Research Council Monograph Series 2. Edited by Robert L. Winzeler. Williamsburg, Va.: The Borneo Research Council, 1993.

Jochim, Christian. *Chinese Religions: A Cultural Perspective.* Prentice Hall Series in World Religions. Englewood Cliffs, N.J.: Prentice Hall, 1986.

Johansen, Ulla. "Ecstasy and Possession: A Short Contribution to a Lengthy Discussion." Pages 135–52 in *Rediscovery of Shamanic Heritage.* Edited by Mihály Hoppál and Gábor Kósa. Bibliotheca Shamanistica 11. Budapest: Akadémiai Kiadó, 2003.

Johnston, Sarah Iles. "Demons." Pages 279–86 in *Brill's New Pauly: Encyclopedia of the Ancient World.* Vol. 4. Edited by Hubert Cancik and Helmuth Schneider. English edition edited by Christine F. Salazar. Leiden: Brill, 2010.

Jokic, Zeljko. "Yanomami Shamanic Initiation: The Meaning of Death and Postmortem Consciousness in Transformation." *Anthropology of Consciousness* 19.1 (2008): 33–59.

Kananoja, Kalle. "Infected by the Devil, Cured by Calundu: African Healers in Eighteenth-Century Minas Gerais, Brazil." *Social History of Medicine* 29.3 (2016): 490–511.

Kaplan, Bert, and Dale Johnson. "Navaho Psychopathology." Pages 203–29 in *Magic, Faith, and Healing: Studies in Primitive Psychiatry Today*. Edited by Ari Kiev. New York: Free Press, 1964.

Kardec, Allan. *A gênese, os milagres e as predições Segundo o espiritismo*. Rio de Janeiro: FEB, 1992. Original 1868.

———. *The Mediums' Book*. Translated by Anna Blackwell. Rio de Janeiro: FEB, 1986. Original 1861.

Katz, Paul. "Demons or Deities?—The *Wangye* of Taiwan." *Asian Folklore Studies* 46.2 (1987): 197–215.

Kay, William K., and Robin Parry, eds. *Exorcism and Deliverance: Multi-disciplinary Studies*. Eugene, Ore.: Wipf and Stock, 2011.

Kee, Howard Clark. *Medicine, Miracle and Magic in the New Testament Times*. SNTSMS 55. Cambridge: Cambridge University Press, 1986.

Keener, Craig S. *Acts: An Exegetical Commentary: Introduction and 1:1–2:47*. Grand Rapids: Baker, 2012.

———. *Acts: An Exegetical Commentary: 3:1–14:28*. Grand Rapids: Baker, 2012.

———. *Acts: An Exegetical Commentary: 15:1–23:35*. Grand Rapids: Baker, 2014.

———. *Christobiography: Memory, History, and the Reliability of the Gospels*. Grand Rapids: Eerdmans, 2019.

———. *A Commentary on the Gospel of Matthew*. Grand Rapids: Eerdmans, 1999.

———. "Crooked Spirits and Spiritual Identity Theft: A Keener Response to Crooks?" *Journal of Mind and Behavior* 39.4 (2018): 345–72.

———. *The Historical Jesus of the Gospels*. Grand Rapids: Eerdmans, 2009.

———. *Miracles: The Credibility of the New Testament Accounts*. 2 vols. Grand Rapids: Baker, 2011.

———. "Spirit Possession as a Cross-cultural Experience." *BBR* 20.2 (2010): 215–36.

Keller, Mary. *The Hammer and the Flute: Women, Power, and Spirit Possession*. Baltimore: Johns Hopkins University Press, 2002.

Kennedy, George A. "Classical and Christian Source Criticism." Pages 125–55 in *The Relationships among the Gospels: An Interdisciplinary Dialogue*. Edited by William O. Walker Jr. San Antonio: Trinity University Press, 1978.

Kennedy, John G. "Nubian Zar Ceremonies as Psychotherapy." Pages 377–85 in *Culture, Disease, and Healing*. Edited by David Landy. New York: Macmillan, 1977.

Kenyon, Susan. *Five Women of Sennar: Culture and Change in Central Sudan*. Long Grove, Ill.: Waveland, 2004.

———. *Spirits and Slaves in Central Sudan: The Red Wind of Sennar*. Basingstoke, UK: Palgrave Macmillan, 2012.

Kerner, Justinus. *Die Seherin von Prevorst: Eröffnungen über das innere Leben des Menschen und über das Hereinragen einer Gesterwelt in die Unsere*. Stuttgart: Cotta, 1829.

Kerner, Justinus, and Carl August von Eschenmayer. *Geschichten Besessener neuerer Zeit: Beobachtungen aus dem Gebiete kakodämonisch-magnetischer Erscheinungen nebst Reflexionen über Besessenseyn und Zauber*. Stuttgart: Wachendorf, 1834.

Kessler, Clive S. "Conflict and Sovereignty in Kelantanese Malay Spirit Seances." Pages 295–331 in *Case Studies in Spirit Possession*. Edited by Vincent Crapanzano and Vivian Garrison. New York: Wiley, 1976.

Khan, Qurat ul ain, and Aisha Sanober. "'Jinn Possession' and Delirious Mania in a Pakistani Woman." *American Journal of Psychiatry* 173.3 (2016): 219–20.

Kiev, Ari, ed. *Magic, Faith, and Healing: Studies in Primitive Psychiatry Today*. New York: Free Press, 1964.

———. "The Study of Folk Psychiatry." Pages 3–35 in *Magic, Faith, and Healing: Studies in Primitive Psychiatry Today*. Edited by Ari Kiev. New York: Free Press, 1964.

Klass, Morton. *Ordered Universes: Approaches to the Anthropology of Religion*. Boulder, Colo.: Routledge, 1995.

Kleinman, Arthur. *Patients and Healers in the Context of Culture: An Exploration of the Borderland between Anthropology, Medicine, and Psychiatry*. Berkeley: University of California Press, 1980.

Klostermann, Erich. *Das Lukasevangelium*. Handbuch zum Neuen Testament 5. Tübingen: Mohr Siebeck, 1929.

Klutz, Todd. *The Exorcism Stories in Luke-Acts: A Sociostylistic Reading*. SNTSMS 129. Cambridge: Cambridge University Press, 2004.

Koch, Kurt E. *God among the Zulus*. Translated by Justin Michell and Waldenmar Engelbrecht. Natal, R.S.A.: Mission Kwa Sizabanu, 1981.

———. *Occult Bondage and Deliverance: Counseling the Occultly Oppressed*. Berghausen, Germany: Evangelization, 1970.

Koss, Joan D. "Spirits as Socializing Agents: A Case Study of a Puerto Rican Girl Reared in a Matricentric Family." Pages 365–82 in *Case Studies in Spirit Possession*. Edited by Vincent Crapanzano and Vivian Garrison. New York: Wiley, 1977.

Koutstaal, Wilma, Mieke Verfaellie, and Daniel L. Schacter. "Recognizing Identical versus Similar Categorically Related Common Objects: Further Evidence for Degraded Gist Representations in Amnesia." *Neuropsychology* 15.2 (2001): 268–89.

Lambek, Michael. "From Disease to Discourse: Remarks on the Conceptualization of Trance and Spirit Possession." Pages 36–61 in *Altered States of Consciousness and Mental Health: A Cross-cultural Perspective*. Edited by Colleen A. Ward. Newbury Park, Calif.: Sage, 1989.

———. *Knowledge and Practice in Mayotte: Local Discourses of Islam, Sorcery and Spirit Possession*. Toronto: University of Toronto Press, 1993.

Langness, L. L. *The Study of Culture*. Novato, Calif.: Chandler and Sharp, 2004.

Larsen, Kjersti. *Where Humans and Spirits Meet: The Politics of Rituals and Identified Spirits in Zanzibar*. New York: Berghahn, 2008.

Larsen, Steen F., Charles P. Thompson, and Tia Hansen. "Time in Autobiographical Memory." Pages 129–56 in *Remembering Our Past: Studies in Autobiographical Memory*. Edited by David C. Rubin. Cambridge: Cambridge University Press, 1996.

Laste, Benedicte. "Possession, Exorcism, and Mental Illness: A Multiple Case Study across Worldviews." PhD diss., California Institute of Integral Studies, 2015.

Lawrence, Louise J. *Reading with Anthropology: Exhibiting Aspects of New Testament Religion*. Waynesboro, Ga.: Paternoster, 2005.

Laycock, Joseph, ed. *Spirit Possession around the World: Possession, Communion, and Demon Expulsion across Cultures*. Santa Barbara, Calif.: ABC-CLIO, 2015.

Leavey, Gerard. "The Appreciation of the Spiritual in Mental Illness: A Qualitative Study of Beliefs among Clergy in the UK." *Transcultural Psychiatry* 47.4 (2010): 571–90.

Lehmann, David, *Struggle for the Spirit: Religious Transformation and Popular Culture in Brazil and Latin America*. Cambridge, Mass.: Blackwell, 1996.

Levack, Brian P. *The Devil Within: Possession and Exorcism in the Christian West*. New Haven: Yale University Press, 2013.

Levine, Amy-Jill, and Ben Witherington III. *The Gospel of Luke*. New Cambridge Bible Commentary. Cambridge: Cambridge University Press, 2018.

Lévi-Strauss, Claude. *Mythologiques*. 4 vols. Chicago: University of Chicago Press, 1964–1971.

Lewis, C. S. *The Screwtape Letters: Letters from a Senior to a Junior Devil*. Glasgow: HarperCollins UK, 2009.

Lewis, David C. *Healing: Fiction, Fantasy, or Fact?* London: Hodder & Stoughton, 1989.

Lewis, H. S. "Spirit Possession in Ethiopia." Pages 419–27 in *Proceedings of the Seventh International Conference of Ethiopian Studies*. Edited by Sven Rubenson. Addis Ababa: Institute of Ethiopian Studies, 1984.

Lewis, I. M. *Ecstatic Religion: A Study of Shamanism and Spirit Possession*. 3rd ed. London: Routledge, 2003.

———. *Religion in Context: Cults and Charisma*. Cambridge: Cambridge University Press, 1996.

———. "Spirit Possession and Deprivation Cults." *Man* 1.3 (1966): 307–29.

Lewis, I. M., Ahmed Al-Safi, and Sayyid Hurreiz. *Women's Medicine: The Zar-Bori Cult in Africa and Beyond*. Edinburgh: Edinburgh University Press, 1991.

Lichtenberger, Hermann. "Demonology in the Scrolls and the New Testament." Pages 267–80 in *Text, Thought, and Practice in Qumran and Early Christianity*. Edited by Ruth A. Clements and Daniel R. Schwarz. STDJ 84. Leiden: Brill, 2009.

Licona, Michael. *Why Are There Differences in the Gospels? What We Can Learn from Ancient Biography*. New York: Oxford University Press, 2017.

Lindsay, Hal. *Satan Is Alive and Well on Planet Earth*. London: Lakeland, 1973.

Lloyd, Stephen. "Ethiopia." Pages 118–21 in *Spirit Possession around the World: Possession, Communion, and Demon Expulsion across Cultures*. Edited by Joseph Laycock. Santa Barbara, Calif.: ABC-CLIO, 2015.

———. "Kenya." Pages 202–5 in *Spirit Possession around the World: Possession, Communion, and Demon Expulsion across Cultures*. Edited by Joseph Laycock. Santa Barbara, Calif.: ABC-CLIO, 2015.

———. "South Africa." Pages 321–23 in *Spirit Possession around the World: Possession, Communion, and Demon Expulsion across Cultures*. Edited by Joseph Laycock. Santa Barbara, Calif.: ABC-CLIO, 2015.

Lohmeyer, Ernst. *Das Evangelium des Markus*. Göttingen: Vandenhoeck & Ruprecht, 1957.

van der Loos, H. *The Miracles of Jesus*. NovTSup 9. Leiden: Brill, 1965.

Low, Setha M. "The Medicalization of Healing Cults in Latin America." *American Ethnologist* 15.1 (1988): 136–54.

Luck, Georg. *Arcana Mundi: Magic and the Occult in the Greek and Roman Worlds*. Baltimore: Johns Hopkins University Press, 1985.

Lui, David. "Spiritual Injury: A Samoan Perspective on Spirituality's Impact on Mental Health." Pages 66–76 in *Penina Uliuli: Contemporary Challenges in Mental Health for Pacific Peoples*. Edited by Philip Culbertson, Margaret Nelson Agee, and Cabrini 'Ofa Makasiale. Honolulu: University of Hawai'i Press, 2007.

Lyngdoh, Margaret. "An Interview with the Goddess: Possession Rites as Regulators of Justice among the Pnar of Northeastern India." *Religious Studies and Theology* 36.1 (2017): 55–78.

Macklin, June. "A Connecticut Yankee in Summer Land." Pages 41–85 in *Case Studies in Spirit Possession*. Edited by Vincent Crapanzano and Vivian Garrison. New York: Wiley, 1977.

MacMullen, Ramsay. *Christianizing the Roman Empire (A.D. 100–400)*. New Haven: Yale University Press, 1984.

MacNutt, Francis. *Deliverance from Evil Spirits*. Grand Rapids: Chosen, 2003.

Macpherson, Cluny. "Samoan Medicine." Pages 1–15 in *Healing Practices in the South Pacific*. Edited by Claire Parsons. Honolulu: Institute for Polynesian Studies, Brigham Young University, 1985.

Maity, Pradyot Kumar. *Historical Studies in the Cult of the Goddess Manasā: A Socio-cultural Study*. Calcutta: Punthi Pustak, 1966.

Malina, Bruce, and Richard Rohrbaugh. *Social Science Commentary on the Synoptic Gospels*. Minneapolis: Fortress, 2002.

Marcus, Joel. *Mark 8–16*. AYB 27A. New Haven: Yale University Press, 2009.

Mariano, Ricardo. *Neopentecostais: Sociologia do Novo Pentecostalismo no Brasil*. São Paulo: Edições Loyola, 1999.

Marquart, X. F. "L'exorciste dans le manifestations diaboliques." Pages 328–51 in *Satan*. Edited by E. Carmélitaines. Paris: Desclée de Brouwer, 1948.

Marshall, I. Howard. *The Gospel of Luke*. Grand Rapids: Eerdmans, 1978.

Massaquoi, Momlu Armstrong. "Jesus' Healing Miracles in Luke 13:10–17 and Their Significance for Physical Health." *Ogbomoso Journal of Theology* 18.1 (2013): 98–123.

Maurizio, L. "Anthropology and Spirit Possession: A Reconsideration of the Pythia's Role at Delphi." *JHS* 115 (1995): 69–86.

Mbiti, John S. "Theology in Context: Theological Impotence and the Universality of the Church." Pages 6–18 in *Mission Trends No. 3: Third World Theologies*. Edited by Gerald H. Anderson and Thomas F. Stransky. Grand Rapids: Eerdmans, 1976.

McClenon, James. *Wondrous Events: Foundations of Religious Belief*. Philadelphia: University of Pennsylvania Press, 1994.

McGill, Alan Bernard. "Diagnosing Demons and Healing Humans: The Pastoral Implications of a Holistic View of Evil." *New Theology Review* 27.2 (2015): 70–80.

McIntosh, Janet. "Reluctant Muslims: Embodied Hegemony and Moral Resistance in a Giriama Spirit Possession Complex." *Journal of the Royal Anthropological Institute* 10.1 (2004): 91–112.

McIver, Robert K. "Eyewitnesses as Guarantors of the Accuracy of the Gospel Traditions in the Light of Psychological Research." *JBL* 131.3 (2012): 529–46.

———. *Memory, Jesus and the Synoptic Gospels*. Atlanta: Society of Biblical Literature, 2011.

McNaughton, Patrick R. *The Mande Blacksmiths: Knowledge, Power, and Art in West Africa*. Bloomington: Indiana University Press, 1993.

Meier, John P. *A Marginal Jew: Rethinking the Historical Jesus*. Vol. 2. New York: Doubleday, 1994.

de Mello e Souza, Laura. *The Devil and the Land of the Holy Cross: Witchcraft, Slavery, and Popular Religion in Colonial Brazil*. Austin: University of Texas Press, 2003.

de Menezes Cavalcanti, Adolfo Bezerra. *A loucura sob novo prisma*. Rio de Janeiro: FEB, 1988. Original 1897.

Messing, Simon D. "Group Therapy and Social Status in the *Zar* Cult of Ethiopia." *American Anthropologist* 60.6 (1958): 1120–25.

Métraux, Alfred. *Vodoo in Haiti*. Translated by Hugo Charteris. New York: Schocken, 1972.

Metzger, Bruce. *A Textual Commentary on the Greek New Testament*. Stuttgart: United Bible Societies, 1994.

Mianji, Fahimeh, and Yousef Semnani. "Zār Spirit Possession in Iran and African Countries: Group Distress, Culture-Bound Syndrome or Cultural Concept of Distress?" *Iranian Journal of Psychiatry* 10.4 (2015): 225–32.

Michel, Claudine. "Of Worlds Seen and Unseen: The Educational Character of Haitian Vodou." Pages 32–45 in *Haitian Vodou: Spirit, Myth, and Reality*. Edited by Patrick Bellegarde-Smith and Claudine Michel. Bloomington/ Indianapolis: Indiana University Press, 2006.

Michel, Claudine, Patrick Bellegarde-Smith, and Marlène Racine-Toussaint. "From the Horses' Mouths: Women's Words/Women's Worlds." Pages 70–83 in *Haitian Vodou: Spirit, Myth, and Reality*. Edited by Patrick Bellegarde-Smith and Claudine Michel. Bloomington: Indiana University Press, 2006.

Mkhize, Nhlanhla. "Psychology: An African Perspective." Pages 24–52 in *Critical Psychology*. Edited by Derek Hook. Lansdowne, R.S.A.: University of Cape Town Press, 2004.

Moreira-Almeida, Alexander, and Francisco Lotufo Neto. "Spiritist Views of Mental Disorders in Brazil." *Transcultural Psychiatry* 42.4 (2005): 570–95.

Morgan, G. Campbell. *The Gospel according to Luke*. New York: Revell, 1931.

Morris, H. S. "Shamanism among the Oya Melanau." Pages 101–30 in *The Seen and the Unseen: Shamanism, Mediumship and Possession in Borneo*. Borneo Research Council Monograph Series 2. Edited by Robert L. Winzeler. Williamsburg, Va.: Borneo Research Council, 1993.

Morton, Alice. "*Dawit*: Competition and Integration in an Ethiopian Wuqabi Cult Group." Pages 193–233 in *Case Studies in Spirit Possession*. Edited by Vincent Crapanzano and Vivian Garrison. New York: Wiley, 1976.

Murdock, George. *Theories of Illness: A World Survey*. Pittsburgh: University of Pittsburgh Press, 1980.

Murphy, Jane M. "Psychotherapeutic Aspects of Shamanism." Pages 53–83 in *Magic, Faith, and Healing: Studies in Primitive Psychiatry Today*. Edited by Ari Kiev. New York: Free Press, 1964.

Myers, Ched. *Binding the Strong Man: A Political Reading of Mark's Story of Jesus*. Maryknoll, N.Y.: Orbis, 1994.

Nasir, Mumtaz. "*Baithak*: Exorcism in Peshawar (Pakistan)." *Asian Folklore Studies* 46.2 (1987): 159–78.

de Nebesky-Wojkowitz, René. *Oracles and Demons of Tibet: The Cult and Iconography of the Tibetan Protective Deities*. The Hague, Netherlands: Mouton, 1956.

Nel, Marius. "The African Background of Pentecostal Theology: A Critical Perspective." *In die Skriflig* 53.4 (2019): 1–8.

Nevius, John L. *Demon Possession*. Grand Rapids: Kregel, 1968.

Neyrey, Jerome H., ed. *The Social World of Luke-Acts: Models for Interpretation*. Peabody, Mass.: Hendrickson, 1991.

Nguyen, Thi Hien. "Yin Illness: Its Diagnosis and the Healing with Len Dong (Spirit Possession) Rituals of the Viet." *Asian Ethnology* 67.2 (2008): 305–21.

Nolan, Ann M. "Spirit Possession and Mental Health in New Zealand Context." Pages 61–89 in *Spirit Possession, Theology, and Identity: A Pacific Exploration*. Edited by Elaine M. Wainwright with Philip Culbertson and Susan Smith. Hindmarsh, Australia: ATF Press, 2010.

Nolland, John. *Luke 9:21–18:34*. WBC 35b. Waco, Tex.: Word, 1993.

Oakman, Douglas E. "Rulers' Houses, Thieves, and Usurpers: The Beelzebul Pericope." *Foundations and Facts Forum* 4.3 (1988): 109–23.

Obeyesekere, Gananath. "Psychocultural Exegesis of a Case of Spirit Possession in Sri Lanka." Pages 235–94 in *Case Studies in Spirit Possession*. Edited by Vincent Crapanzano and Vivian Garrison. New York: Wiley, 1976.

Oesterreich, Traugott Konstantin. *Die Besessenheit*. Langensalza, Germany: Wendt and Klauwell, 1921.

———. "The Genesis and Extinction of Possession." Pages 111–41 in *Exorcism through the Ages*. Edited by St. Elmo Nauman. New York: Philosophical Library, 1974.

———. *Possession Demoniacal and Other among Primitive Races, in Antiquity, the Middle Ages, and Modern Times*. Translated by D. Ibberson. New Hyde Park, N.Y.: University Books, 1966.

Oliver, Douglas L. *Oceania: The Native Cultures of Australia and the Pacific Islands*. Vol. 1. Honolulu: University of Hawai'i Press, 1989.

Olry, Régis, and Michel Cyr. "How Neuroscience May Face Up to Anneliese Michel's Alleged Demoniac Possession: A Contribution to Neuropathy?" Paper presented at the Society for Neuroscience Conference, 2010.

Olupona, J. K. "New Religious Movements in Contemporary Nigeria." *Journal of Religious Thought* 46.1 (1989): 53–68.

Omenyo, Cephas N. "African Pentecostalism." Pages 132–51 in *The Cambridge Companion to Pentecostalism*. Edited by Cecil M. Robeck Jr. and Amos Yong. New York: Cambridge University Press, 2014.

Ong, Aihwa. "The Production of Possession: Spirits and the Multinational Corporation in Malaysia." *American Ethnologist* 15.1 (1988): 28–42.

———. *Spirits of Resistance and Capitalist Discipline: Factory Women in Malaysia*. Albany: State University of New York Press, 1987.

Onyinah, Opoku. "Akan Witchcraft and the Concept of Exorcism in the Church of Pentecost." PhD diss., University of Birmingham, 2002.

Oosthuizen, G. C., S. D. Edwards, W. H. Wessels, and I. Hexam, eds. *Afro-Christian Religion and Healing in Southern Africa*. Lewiston, N.Y.: Mellen, 1989.

Orchardson-Mazrui, Elizabeth C. "Jangamizi: Spirit and Sculpture." *African Language and Cultures* 6.2 (1993): 147–60.

Ozturk, Orhan M. "Folk-Treatment in Turkey." Pages 343–63 in *Magic, Faith, and Healing: Studies in Primitive Psychiatry Today*. Edited by Ari Kiev. New York: Free Press, 1964.

Pakaslahti, Antti. "Family-Centered Treatment of Mental Health Problems at the Balaji Temple in Rajasthan." *Orientalia* 84 (2014): 129–66.

Pannenberg, Wolfhart. "Redemptive Event and History." Pages 15–80 in *Basic Questions in Theology*. Translated by George H. Kehm. Vol. 1. Philadelphia: Fortress, 1970.

Parsons, Mikeal C. *Body and Character in Luke and Acts: The Subversion of Physiognomy in Early Christianity*. Grand Rapids: Baker, 2006.

Paul, Jean-Marie. *Strauss et son époque*. Paris: Les Belles Lettres, 1982.

de la Perrière, Bénédicte Brac, and Guillaume Rozenberg. "Burma." Pages 59–61 in *Spirit Possession around the World: Possession, Communion, and Demon Expulsion across Cultures*. Edited by Joseph Laycock. Santa Barbara, Calif.: ABC-CLIO, 2015.

de la Perrière, Bénédicte Brac, Guillaume Rozenburg, and Alicia Turner, eds. *Champions of Buddhism: Weikza Cults in Contemporary Burma*. Singapore: NUS Press, 2014.

Pesch, Rudolf. "The Markan Version of the Healing of the Gerasene Demoniac." *Ecumenical Review* 23.4 (1971): 349–76.

Peters, Larry G., and Douglass Price-Williams. "Toward an Experiential Analysis of Shamanism." *American Ethnologist* 7.3 (1980): 397–413.

Petitpierre, Robert. *Exorcising Devils*. London: Robert Hale, 1976.

Petzke, G. "Die historische Frage nach den Wundertaten Jesu." *NTS* 22.2 (1976): 180–204.

Petzoldt, Leander. "Besessenheit in Sage und Volksglauben." *Rheinisches Jahrbuch für Volkskunde* 15–16 (1964–1965): 76–94.

Pfeiffer, Wolfgang M. *Transkulturelle Psychiatrie: Ergebnisse und Probleme*. Stuttgart: Georg Thieme Verlag, 1971.

Phuong, Pham Quynh. *Hero and Deity: Tran Hung Dao and the Resurgence of Popular Religion in Japan*. Chiang Mai, Thailand: Mekong, 2009.

Pierce, Benton H., Jill D. Waring, Daniel L. Schacter, and Andrew E. Budson. "Effects of Distinctive Encoding on Source-Based False Recognition: Further Examination of Recall-to-Reject Processing in Aging and Alzheimer's Disease." *Cognitive and Behavioral Neurology* 21.3 (2008): 179–86.

Pilch, John J. "Insights and Models for Understanding the Healing Activity of the Historical Jesus." Pages 154–77 in *Society of Biblical Literature 1993 Seminar Papers*. SBLSP 32. Atlanta: Society of Biblical Literature, 1993.

———. "Sickness and Healing in Luke-Acts." Pages 181–210 in *The Social World of Luke-Acts: Models for Interpretation*. Edited by Jerome H. Neyrey. Peabody, Mass.: Hendrickson, 1991.

Pinault, David. *Notes from the Fortune-Telling Parrot: Islam and the Struggle for Religious Pluralism in Pakistan*. Oakville, Conn.: Equinox, 2008.

Placido, Barbara. "'It's All to Do with Words': An Analysis of Spirit Possession in the Venezuelan Cult of María Lionza." *Journal of the Royal Anthropological Institute* 7.2 (2001): 207–24.

Plummer, Alfred. *A Critical and Exegetical Commentary on the Gospel according to Luke*. ICC. New York: Scribner, 1896.

Pócs, Éva. "A Magyar halottlátó és a keresztény Európa." *Népi vallásosság a Kárpátmendencében* 2 (1996): 25–41.

———. "Possession Phenomena, Possession-Systems: Some East-Central European Examples." Pages 84–152 in *Communicating with the Spirits*. Edited by Éva Pócs and Gábor Klaniczay. Budapest: Central European University Press, 2005.

Pressel, Esther. "Negative Spirit Possession in Experienced Brazilian Umbanda Spirit Mediums." Pages 333–64 in *Case Studies in Spirit Possession*. Edited by Vincent Crapanzano and Vivian Garrison. New York: Wiley, 1977.

Prince, Derek. *They Shall Expel Demons: What You Need to Know about Demons—Your Invisible Enemy*. Grand Rapids: Chosen, 1998.

Prince, Raymond. "Indigenous Yoruba Psychiatry." Pages 84–120 in *Magic, Faith, and Healing: Studies in Primitive Psychiatry Today*. Edited by Ari Kiev. New York: Free Press, 1964.

Quack, Joachim Friedrich. "Demons: Ancient Near East: Egypt." Pages 531–34 in *Encyclopedia of the Bible and Its Reception*. Edited by Hans-Josef Klauck, Volker Leppin, Bernard McGinn, Choon-Leong Seow, Hermann Spieckermann, Barry Dov Walfish, and Eric J. Ziolkowski. Vol. 5. Berlin: De Gruyter, 2012.

Quasten, Johannes. *Patrology: The Ante-Nicene Literature of Irenaeus*. Vol. 2. Allen, Tex.: Christian Classics, 1995.

Ram, Kalpana. *Fertile Disorder: Spirit Possession and Its Provocation of the Modern*. Honolulu: University of Hawai'i Press, 2013.

Ramble, Charles. *The Navel of the Demoness: Tibetan Buddhism and Civil Religion in Highland Nepal*. Oxford: Oxford University Press, 2008.

Rasmussen, Susan J. *Spirit Possession and Personhood among the Kel Ewey Tuareg*. New York: Cambridge University Press, 1995.

Rawson, Beryl, ed. *Family in Ancient Rome*. New York: Cornell University Press, 1986.

Razali, S. M., U. A. Khan, and C. L. Hasanah. "Belief in Supernatural Causes of Mental Illness among Malay Patients: Impact on Treatment." *Acta Psychiatrica Scandinavica* 96.4 (1996): 229–33.

Reed, Annette Yoshiko. *Fallen Angels and the History of Judaism and Christianity: The Reception of Enochic Literature*. New York: Cambridge University Press, 2005.

Reed, Jonathan L. *Archaeology and the Galilean Jesus: A Re-examination of the Evidence*. Harrisburg, Pa.: Trinity Press International, 2002.

Reis, João José. *Domingos Sodré, um Sacerdote Africano: Escravidào, liberddade e candomblé na Bahia do século XIX*. São Paulo: Companhia das Letras, 2008.

Rider, Catherine. "Demons and Mental Disorder in Late Medieval Medicine." Pages 47–69 in *Mental (Dis)Order in Later Medieval Europe*. Edited by Sari Katajala-Peltomaa and Susanna Niiranen. Leiden: Brill, 2014.

Robertson Smith, William R. *Lectures on the Religion of the Semites*. New York: KTAV, 1969.

Rogerson, J. W. *Anthropology and the Old Testament*. Oxford: Basil Blackwell, 1978.

Rohrbaugh, Richard L., ed. *The Social Sciences and New Testament Interpretation*. Peabody, Mass.: Hendrickson, 1996.

Roloff, Jürgen. *Das Kerygma und der irdische Jesus: Historische Motive in den Jesus-Erzählungen der Evangelien*. Göttingen: Vandenhoeck & Ruprecht, 1970.

Rosen, George. *Madness in Society: Chapters in the Historical Sociology of Mental Illness*. Chicago: University of Chicago Press, 1968.

Rothenberg, Celia E. *Spirits of Palestine: Gender, Society, and Stories of the Jinn*. Oxford: Lexington, 2004.

Rothschild, Clare K. *Luke-Acts and the Rhetoric of History: An Investigation of Early Christian Historiography*. WUNT 175. Tübingen: Mohr Siebeck, 2004.

Rouget, Gilbert. *Music and Trance: A Theory of the Relations between Music and Possession*. Chicago: University of Chicago Press, 1985.

Rozenberg, Guillaume. *The Immortals: Faces of the Incredible in Buddhist Burma.* Translated by Ward Keller. Honolulu: University of Hawai'i Press, 2015.

Salleh, Mohammed Razali. "The Consultation of Traditional Healers by Malay Patients." *Medical Journal of Malaysia* 44.1 (1989): 3–13.

Salo, Matt T. "The Structure of Finnish Shamanic Therapy." PhD diss., University of New York at Binghamton, 1974.

Sanders, E. P. *The Historical Figure of Jesus.* London: Penguin, 1993.

Sanneh, Lamin. "Healing and Conversion in New Religious Movements in Africa." Pages 108–34 in *African Healing Strategies.* Edited by Brian M. du Toit and Ismail H. Abdalla. New York: Trado-medic, 1985.

Sapir, Edward. "Speech as Personality Trait." Pages 533–43 in *Selected Writings of Edward Sapir in Language, Culture and Personality.* Edited by David G. Mandelbaum. Berkeley: University of California Press, 1949. Original 1927.

Saunders, Lucie Wood. "Variants in Zar Experience in an Egyptian Village." Pages 177–91 in *Case Studies in Spirit Possession.* Edited by Vincent Crapanzano and Vivian Garrison. New York: Wiley, 1977.

Sax, Marieka. *An Ethnography of Feeding, Perception, and Place in the Peruvian Andes: Where Hungry Spirits Bring Illness and Wellbeing.* Lampeter, UK: Mellen, 2011.

Schacter, Daniel L. "Memory, Amnesia, and Frontal Lobe Dysfunction." Pages 1–43 in *Memory Distortion: How Minds, Brains, and Societies Reconstruct the Past.* Edited by Daniel L. Schacter. Cambridge, Mass.: Harvard University Press, 1995.

Schäffler, Yvonne. "Besessenheit in der Dominikanischen Republik im Frühstadium: 'Wilde' Besessenheit (*caballo lobo*) aus psychodynamischer und praxistheoretischer Perspetive." *Curare* 35.1–2 (2012): 72–84.

———. "El caballo que se volvió lobo: Análisis del fenómeno de 'posesión espontánea.'" Pages 133–64 in *Etnografías de América Latina.* Edited by Ocho Ensayos, Eveline Sigl, Yvonne Schäffler, and Ricardo Ávila. Guadalajara: Universidad de Gudalajara, 2013.

———. "Diagnose 'Wolfspferd,'" in "Spontanbesessenheiten in der Dominikanischen Republik als Anstoß für den Werdegang zum Heiler/zur Heilerin." *Anthropos* 104.2 (2009): 445–56.

———. *Vodú? Das ist Sache der anderen! Kreolische Medizin, Spiritualität und Identität im Südwesten der Dominikanischen Republik.* Wiener ethnomedizinische Reihe. Vienna: LIT-Verlag, 2009.

———. "'Wild' Spirit Possession in the Dominican Republic: From Expression of Distress to Cultural Expertise." Pages 221–37 in *Dominicanidad/ Dominicanity: Perspectivas de un concepto (trans-)nacional / Perspectives on a (Trans-)National Concept.* Edited by Christine Felbeck and Andre Klump. Frankfurt am Main: Peter Lang, 2015.

Schäffler, Yvonne, Etzel Cardeña, Sophie Reijman, and Daniela Haluza. "Traumatic Experience and Somatoform Dissociation among Spirit Possession

Practitioners in the Dominican Republic." *Culture, Medicine, and Psychiatry* 40 (2016): 74–99.

Schieffelin, Edward L. "Evil Spirit Sickness, the Christian Disease: The Innovation of a New Syndrome of Mental Derangement and Redemption in Papua New Guinea." *Culture, Medicine, and Psychiatry* 20.1 (1996): 1–39.

Schmidt, Bettina E. "Afro-Atlantic Religions." Pages 2–5 in *Spirit Possession around the World: Possession, Communion, and Demon Expulsion across Cultures.* Edited by Joseph Laycock. Santa Barbara, Calif.: ABC-CLIO, 2015.

———. *Spirits and Trance in Brazil: An Anthropology of Religious Experience.* New York: Bloomsbury, 2016.

Schmidt, K. E. "Folk Psychiatry in Sarawak." Pages 139–55 in *Magic, Faith, and Healing: Studies in Primitive Psychiatry Today.* Edited by Ari Kiev. New York: Free Press, 1964.

Schmidt, Karl Ludwig. *The Place of the Gospels in the General History of Literature.* Translated by Byron R. McCane. Columbia: University of South Carolina Press, 2002.

Schmitt, Rüdiger. "Demons: Hebrew Bible/Old Testament." Pages 536–39 in *Encyclopedia of the Bible and Its Reception.* Edited by Hans-Josef Klauck, Volker Leppin, Bernard McGinn, Choon-Leong Seow, Hermann Spieckermann, Barry Dov Walfish, and Eric J. Ziolkowski. Vol. 5. Berlin: De Gruyter, 2012.

Schürmann, Heinz. *Das Lukasevangelium, Erster Teil: Kommentar zu Kap. 1,1–9,50.* Herders theologischer Kommentar zum Neuen Testament 3. Freiburg: Herder, 1969.

Schweizer, Eduard. *The Good News according to Luke.* Translated by David E. Green. Atlanta: John Knox, 1984.

Schwemer, Daniel. "Demons: Ancient Near East: Mesopotamia, Syria and Anatolia." Pages 534–36 in *Encyclopedia of the Bible and Its Reception.* Edited by Hans-Josef Klauck, Volker Leppin, Bernard McGinn, Choon-Leong Seow, Hermann Spieckermann, Barry Dov Walfish, and Eric J. Ziolkowski. Vol. 5. Berlin: De Gruyter, 2012.

Shaara, Lila, and Andrew Strathern. "Preliminary Analysis of the Relationship between Altered States of Consciousness, Healing, and Social Structure." *American Anthropologist* 94.1 (1992): 145–60.

Shorter, Aylward. "Spirit Possession and Christian Healing in Tanzania." *African Affairs* 79.314 (1980): 45–53.

Sidky, Homayun. "The State Oracle of Tibet, Spirit Possession, and Shamanism." *Numen* 58.1 (2011): 71–99.

Siikala, Anna-Leena. "The Siberian Shaman's Technique of Ecstasy." Pages 103–21 in *Religious Ecstasy: Based on Papers Read at the Symposium on Religious Ecstasy Held at Åbo, Finland, on the 26th–28th of August 1981.* Edited by Nils G. Holm. Stockholm: Almqvist and Wiksell, 1982.

Simon, Pierre J., and Ida Simon-Barouh. *Hâu Bóng: Un Culte Viêtnamien de Possession Transplanté en France.* Paris: Mouton, 1973.

Simons, Jon S., Andy C. H. Lee, Kim S. Graham, Mieke Verfaellie, Wilma Koutstaal, John R. Hodges, Daniel L. Schacter, and Andrew E. Budson. "Failing to Get the Gist: Reduced False Recognition of Semantic Associates in Semantic Dementia." *Neuropsychology* 19.3 (2005): 353–61.

Smith, Frederick M. "The Current State of Possession Studies in Cross-Disciplinary Project." *Religious Studies Review* 27.3 (2001): 203–13.

———. "Possession, Embodiment, and Ritual in Mental Health Care in India." *Journal of Ritual Studies* 24.2 (2010): 21–35.

———. *The Self Possessed: Deity and Spirit Possession in South Asian Literature and Civilization*. New York: Columbia University Press, 2006.

Somer, Eli, and Meir Saadon. "Stambali Dissociative Possession and Trance in a Tunisian Healing Dance." *Transcultural Psychiatry* 37.4 (2000): 580–600.

Somfai-Kara, Dávid. "Living Epic Traditions among Inner Asian Nomads." Pages 179–91 in *Rediscovery of Shamanic Heritage*. Edited by Mihály Hoppál and Gábor Kósa. Bibliotheca Shamanistica 11. Budapest: Akadémiai Kiadó, 2003.

Sorensen, Eric. *Possession and Exorcism in the New Testament and Early Christianity*. Tübingen: Mohr Siebeck, 2002.

Spencer, F. Scott. *Acts*. Sheffield: Sheffield Academic, 1997.

Spiro, Melford E. *Burmese Supernaturalism*. New Brunswick, N.J.: Transaction, 1996.

Sterling, Gregory E. "Jesus as Exorcist: An Analysis of Matthew 17:14–20; Mark 9:14–29; Luke 9:37–43a." *CBQ* 55.3 (1993): 467–93.

Stirrat, R. L. "Demonic Possession in Roman Catholic Sri Lanka." *Journal of Anthropological Research* 33.2 (1977): 133–57.

Stocking, George W. *Victorian Anthropology*. New York: Free Press, 1987.

Stol, Marten. "Psychosomatic Suffering in Ancient Mesopotamia." Pages 57–68 in *Mesopotamian Magic: Textual, Historical, and Interpretative Perspectives*. Edited by Tzvi Abusch and Karel van der Toorn. Groningen: Styx, 1999.

Stoller, Paul. *Fusion of the Worlds: An Ethnography of Possession among the Songhay of Niger*. Chicago: University of Chicago Press, 1989.

———. "Horrific Comedy: Cultural Resistance and the Hauka Movement in Niger." *Ethos* 12.2 (1984): 165–88.

Strauss, David Friedrich. *Charakteristiken und Kritiken: Eine Sammlung zerstreuter Aufsätze aus den Gebieten der Theologie, Anthropologie und Aesthetik*. Leipzig: Wigand, 1839.

———. *The Life of Jesus Critically Examined: Translated from the 4th German Edition*. Translated by George Eliot. New York: MacMillan, 1892.

———. "Zur Wissenschaft der Nachtseite der Natur." Pages 301–90 in *Charakteristiken und Kritiken: Eine Sammlung zerstreuter Aufsätze aus den Gebieten der Theologie, Anthropologie und Aesthetik*. Leipzig: Wigand, 1839.

Summers, Ray. *Commentary on Luke*. Waco, Tex.: Word, 1973.

Sundberg, Carl. "Revealed Medicine as an Expression of an African Christian Lived Spirituality." Pages 335–54 in *Faith in African Lived Christianity:*

Bridging Anthropological and Theological Perspectives. Edited by Karen Lauterbach and Mika Vähäkangas. Leiden: Brill, 2020.

Swantz, Marja-Liisa. "Dynamics of the Spirit Possession Phenomenon in Eastern Tanzania." *Scripta Instituti Donneriani Aboensis* 9 (1976): 90–101.

Sweet, James H. *Domingos Álvares, African Healing, and the Intellectual History of the Atlantic World*. Chapel Hill: University of North Carolina Press, 2011.

———. *Recreating Africa: Culture, Kinship, and Religion in the African-Portuguese World, 1441–1770*. Chapel Hill: University of North Carolina Press, 2003.

Tannehill, Robert C. *The Narrative Unity of Luke-Acts: A Literary Interpretation*. Minneapolis: Augsburg, 1994.

Tate, Henare Arekatera. "A Māori Perspective on Spirit Possession." Pages 1–21 in *Spirit Possession, Theology, and Identity: A Pacific Exploration*. Edited by Elaine M. Wainwright with Philip Culbertson and Susan Smith. Hindmarsh, Australia: ATF Press, 2010.

Taysom, Stephen. "'Satan Mourns Naked upon the Earth': Locating Mormon Possession and Exorcism Rituals in the American Religious Landscape, 1830–1977." *Religion and American Culture* 27.1 (2017): 57–94.

Tekle-Haimanot, Redda, Mekonnen Abebe, Lars Forsgren, Ayele Gebre-Mariam, Jan Heijbel, Gösta Holmgren, and Jan Ekstedt. "Attitudes of Rural People in Central Ethiopia towards Epilepsy." *Social Science and Medicine* 32.2 (1991): 203–9.

ter Haar, Barend J. "China." Pages 76–83 in *Spirit Possession around the World: Possession, Communion, and Demon Expulsion across Cultures*. Edited by Joseph Laycock. Santa Barbara, Calif.: ABC-CLIO, 2015.

ter Haar, Gerrie, and Stephen Ellis. "Spirit Possession and Healing in Modern Zambia: An Analysis of Letters to Archbishop Milingo." *African Affairs* 87.347 (1988): 185–206.

Theissen, Gerd. *The Miracle Stories of the Early Christian Tradition*. Translated by Francis McDonah. Philadelphia: Fortress, 1983.

———. "The Political Dimension of Jesus' Activities." Pages 225–50 in *The Social Setting of Jesus and the Gospels*. Edited by Wolfgang Stegemann, Bruce J. Malina, and Gerd Theissen. Minneapolis: Fortress, 2002.

———. *The Social Setting of Pauline Christianity*. Philadelphia: Fortress, 1982.

Theissen, Gerd, and Annette Mertz. *The Historical Jesus: A Comprehensive Guide*. Minneapolis: Fortress, 1998.

Tibbs, Clint. "Mediumistic Divine Possession among Early Christians: A Response to Craig S. Keener's 'Spirit Possession as a Cross-cultural Experience.'" *BBR* 26.2 (2016): 17–38.

Togerson, Heidi. "The Healing of the Bent Woman: A Narrative Interpretation of Luke 13:10–17." *CurTM* 32.3 (2005): 179–80.

Tolbert, Mary Ann. *Sowing the Gospel: Mark's World in Literary-Historical Perspective*. Minneapolis: Fortress, 1989.

Torrey, Charles, trans. *The Lives of the Prophets: Greek Text and Translation.* Atlanta: Society of Biblical Literature, 1946.

Trapp, M. B., trans. *Maximus of Tyre: The Philosophical Orations.* Oxford: Clarendon, 1997.

Troeltsch, Ernst. "Historiography." Pages 716–23 in *Encyclopedia of Religion and Ethics.* Edited by James Hastings. New York: Scribner's Sons, 1914.

Trübswasser, Gerhild, Sandra David, and Sasha Marley. "Algo anda mal: El bla o wakni en el Río Coco: Occasional Paper." IMTRADEC. Puerto Cabezas, Nicaragua: URACCAN, 2005.

Turner, Edith. "The Anthropology of Experience: The Way to Teach Religion and Healing." Pages 193–205 in *Teaching Religion and Healing.* Edited by Linda L. Barnes and Inés Talamantez. Oxford: Oxford University Press, 2006.

———. *Experiencing Ritual: A New Interpretation of African Healing.* Philadelphia: University of Pennsylvania Press, 1992.

———. "The Reality of Spirits." *Re-vision* 15.1 (1992): 28–32.

———. "A Visible Spirit Form in Zambia." Pages 149–72 in *Readings in Indigenous Religions.* Edited by Graham Harvey. New York: Continuum, 2002.

Turner, Victor. *The Forest of Symbols: Aspects of Ndembu Ritual.* Ithaca, N.Y.: Cornell University Press, 1967.

———. "A Ndembu Doctor in Practice." Pages 230–63 in *Magic, Faith, and Healing: Studies in Primitive Psychiatry Today.* Edited by Ari Kiev. New York: Free Press, 1964.

Twelftree, Graham H. *In the Name of Jesus: Exorcism among Early Christians.* Grand Rapids: Baker, 2007.

———. *Jesus the Exorcist: A Contribution to the Study of the Historical Jesus.* Eugene, Ore.: Wipf and Stock, 2011.

Tylor, Edward Burnett. *Primitive Culture: Researches into the Development of Mythology, Philosophy, Religion, Language, Art and Custom.* London: John Murray, 1903.

Unger, Merrill F. *What Demons Can Do to Saints.* Chicago: Moody, 1991.

van Binsbergen, Wim M. J. *Religious Change in Zambia: Exploratory Studies.* Boston: Kegan Paul International, 1981.

Van Ruiten, Jacques. "Angels and Demons in the Book of *Jubilees.*" Pages 585–609 in *Angels: The Concept of Celestial Beings—Origins, Development and Reception.* Edited by Friedrich V. Reiterer, Tobias Nicklas, and Karin Schöpflin. New York: De Gruyter, 2007.

Vargas, M. Carolina Escobar. "Demons in Lapidaries? The Evidence of the Madrid MS Escorial, h.I.15." Pages 256–70 in *Demons and Illness from Antiquity to the Early-Modern Period.* Edited by Siam Bhayro and Catherine Rider. Leiden: Brill, 2017.

Vecchiato, Norbert L. "Health, Culture, and Socialism in Ethiopia." PhD diss., University of California, Los Angeles, 1985.

———. "Illness, Therapy, and Change in Ethiopian Possession Cults." *Africa* 63.2 (1993): 176–96.

Versteeg, Peter. "Deliverance and Exorcism in Anthropological Perspective." Pages 120–38 in *Exorcism and Deliverance: Multi-disciplinary Studies*. Edited by William K. Kay and Robin Parry. Milton Keynes, UK: Paternoster, 2011.

Votaw, Clyde Weber. "The Gospels and Contemporary Biographies." *AmJT* 19.1 (1915): 45–73; 19.2 (1915): 217–49.

Von Glahn, Richard. *The Sinister Way: The Divine and the Demonic in Chinese Religious Culture*. Berkeley: University of California Press, 2004.

von Harnack, Adolf. *The Expansion of Christianity in the First Three Centuries*. Vol. 1. New York: Arno, 1972.

Wagner, Roy. *The Invention of Culture*. Englewood Cliffs, N.J.: Prentice Hall International, 1975.

Wainwright, Elaine M., ed., with Philip Culbertson and Susan Smith. *Spirit Possession, Theology, and Identity: A Pacific Exploration*. Hindmarsh, Australia: ATF Press, 2010.

———. "Introduction." Pages v–x in *Spirit Possession, Theology, and Identity: A Pacific Exploration*. Edited by Elaine M. Wainwright with Philip Culbertson and Susan Smith. Hindmarsh, SA: ATF Press, 2010.

Wallis, Ian G. *The Galilean Wonderworker: Reassessing Jesus' Reputation for Healing and Exorcism*. Eugene, Ore.: Cascade, 2020.

Wallis, Robert J. "Witchcraft and Magic in the Age of Anthropology." Pages 225–52 in *The Oxford Illustrated History of Witchcraft and Magic*. Edited by Owen Davies. New York: Oxford University Press, 2017.

Walton, John H., and J. Harvey Walton. *Demons and Spirits in Biblical Theology: Reading the Biblical Text in Its Cultural and Literary Context*. Eugene, Ore.: Cascade, 2019.

Wang, Xing. "Rethinking the 'Magic State' in China: Political Imagination and Magical Practice in Rural Beijing." *Asian Ethnology* 77.1–2 (2018): 331–51.

Ward, Colleen A., ed. *Altered States of Consciousness and Mental Health: A Cross cultural Perspective*. Newbury Park, Calif.: Sage, 1989.

Weatherhead, Stephen, and Anna Daiches. "Muslim Views on Health and Psychotherapy." *Psychology and Psychotherapy* 83.1 (2010): 75–89.

Wedel, Johan. "Bridging the Gap between Western and Indigenous Medicine in Eastern Nicaragua." *Anthropological Notebooks* 15.1 (2009): 49–60.

———. "Involuntary Mass Spirit Possession among the Miskitu." *Anthropology and Medicine* 19.3 (2012): 303–14.

Weiss, Johannes. *Das älteste Evangelium*. Göttingen: Vandenhoeck & Ruprecht, 1903.

Weissenrieder, Annette. *Images of Illness in the Gospel of Luke*. WUNT II/164. Tübingen: Mohr Siebeck, 2003.

Whisson, Michael G. "Some Aspects of Functional Disorders." Pages 283–304 in *Magic, Faith, and Healing: Studies in Primitive Psychiatry Today*. Edited by Ari Kiev. New York: Free Press, 1964.

Wilkins, Michael J. *Matthew*. NIV Application Commentary. Grand Rapids: Zondervan, 2004.

Wilson, Peter J. "Status Ambiguity and Spirit Possession." *Man* 2.3 (1967): 366–78.

Wink, Walter. *Unmasking the Powers: The Invisible Forces That Determine Human Existence*. Vol. 2 of *The Powers*. Philadelphia: Fortress, 1986.

———. "Write What You See: An Odyssey." *The Fourth R* 7.3 (1994): 3–9.

Winkelman, Michael James. "Shamans and Other 'Macro-Religious' Healers: A Cross-cultural Study of Their Origins, Nature and Social Transformation." *Ethnos* 18.3 (1990): 308–52.

Winzeler, Robert L. *The Peoples of Southeast Asia Today: Ethnography, Ethnology, and Change in a Complex Region*. Lanham, Md.: Altamira, 2011.

———. "Shaman, Priest and Spirit Medium: Religious Specialists, Tradition and Innovation in Borneo." Pages xi–xxxiii in *The Seen and the Unseen: Shamanism, Mediumship and Possession in Borneo*. Borneo Research Council Monograph Series 2. Edited by Robert L. Winzeler. Williamsburg, Va.: Borneo Research Council, 1993.

Witherington, Ben, III. *The Acts of the Apostles: A Socio-rhetorical Commentary*. Grand Rapids: Eerdmans, 1998.

———. "The Gobeckli Tepe Temple and the Origins of Religion: Are Humans Inherently Religious?" Paper presented at Bible and Archaeology Fest XIV, 2011.

———. *The Gospel of Mark: A Socio-rhetorical Commentary*. Grand Rapids: Eerdmans, 2001.

Witmer, Amanda. *Jesus, the Galilean Exorcist: His Exorcisms in Social and Political Context*. LNTS 459. London: T&T Clark, 2012.

Wood, Connor. "Zar." Pages 379–81 in *Spirit Possession around the World: Possession, Communion, and Demon Expulsion across Cultures*. Edited by Joseph Laycock. Santa Barbara, Calif.: ABC-CLIO, 2015.

Worobec, Christine D. *Possessed: Women, Witches and Demons in Imperial Russia*. DeKalb: Northern Illinois University Press, 2001.

Wright, Barbara S. "Dance Is the Cure: The Arts as Metaphor for Healing in Kelantanese Malay Spirit Exorcisms." *Dance Research Journal* 12.2 (1980): 3–10.

Young, Allan. "Why Amhara Get *kureynya*: Sickness and Possession in an Ethiopian *Zar* Cult." *American Ethnologist* 2.3 (1975): 567–84.

Young, Francis. *A History of Anglican Exorcism: Deliverance and Demonology in Church Ritual*. London: I. B. Tauris, 2018.

———. *A History of Exorcism in Catholic Christianity*. Cambridge: Palgrave, 2016.

Zempleni, Andras. "From Symptom to Sacrifice: The Story of Khady Fall." Pages 87–139 in *Case Studies in Spirit Possession*. Edited by Vincent Crapanzano and Vivian Garrison. New York: Wiley, 1977.

Author Index

Scripture Index